Shaping Femininity

Shaping Femininity

Foundation Garments, the Body and Women in Early Modern England

Sarah A. Bendall

BLOOMSBURY VISUAL ARTS
LONDON · NEW YORK · OXFORD · NEW DELHI · SYDNEY

BLOOMSBURY VISUAL ARTS
Bloomsbury Publishing Plc
50 Bedford Square, London, WC1B 3DP, UK
1385 Broadway, New York, NY 10018, USA
29 Earlsfort Terrace, Dublin 2, Ireland

BLOOMSBURY, BLOOMSBURY VISUAL ARTS and the Diana logo are trademarks
of Bloomsbury Publishing Plc

First published in Great Britain 2022

A catalogue record for this book is available from the British Library.

Library of Congress Cataloging-in-Publication Data
Names: Bendall, Sarah A., author.
Title: Shaping femininity : foundation garments, the body and women in early modern England / Sarah A Bendall.
Description: London ; New York : Bloomsbury Visual Arts, 2021. | Includes bibliographical references and index.
Identifiers: LCCN 2021005655 (print) | LCCN 2021005656 (ebook) | ISBN 9781350164109 (paperback) |
ISBN 9781350164116 (hardback) | ISBN 9781350164123 (pdf) | ISBN 9781350164130 (epub)
Subjects: LCSH: Foundation garments–England–History. | Human body–Social aspects–England–History. |
Women--Physiology--Philosophy. | Femininity (Philosophy)
Classification: LCC TT677 .B46 2021 (print) | LCC TT677 (ebook) | DDC 391/.20942—dc23
LC record available at https://lccn.loc.gov/2021005655
LC ebook record available at https://lccn.loc.gov/2021005656

ISBN: HB: 978-1-3501-6411-6
         PB: 978-1-3501-6410-9
         ePDF: 978-1-3501-6412-3
         eBook: 978-1-3501-6413-0

Typeset by RefineCatch Limited, Bungay, Suffolk
Printed and bound in India

To find out more about our authors and books visit www.bloomsbury.com
and sign up for our newsletters.

Contents

Acknowledgements

This book is the result of many years of research, writing and pricking my fingers with sewing needles. My first thanks must go to those who supported me both during and after my PhD and have also provided sound advice about how to turn that research into this book. I thank Susan Broomhall, Nicholas Eckstein, Andrew Fitzmaurice, John Gagné, Laura Gowing, Erin Griffey, Maria Hayward, Chris Hilliard, Beverly Lemire, Michael McDonnell, Peter McNeil, Penny Russell, Julie Ann Smith and Evelyn Welch.

My ideas have been challenged, refined and enriched through conversations with Chelsea Barnett, Sarah Birt, Samantha Bullat, Sophie Cope, Hilary Davidson, Einar Docker, James Dunk, Serena Dyer, Catriona Fisk, Charlotte Fletcher, Emmet Gillespie, Emma Gleadhill, Amanda Herbert, Rohan Howitt, Minerva Inwald, Emily Ireson, Rachel Kennedy, Brittany King, Emma Kluge, Georgia Lawrence-Doyle, Jennifer MacFarland, Dolly Mackinnon, Giulia Mari, Lauren Marks, Una McIlvenna, Alanna McKnight, Angela McShane, Lauren Morris, Rebecca Morrison, Harry Newman, Anna Parker, Michael Pearce, Hollie Pich, Rebecca Pinchin, Jenny Spinks, Hannah Spracklan-Holl, Miranda Fay Thomas, Danielle Thyer, Rebecca Unsworth, Ben Vine, Mark de Vitis, Natalie Rachel Walker, Lindie Ward, Marama Whyte and Charles Zika, as well as countless others on Twitter who have helped with palaeography or references over the years.

This project would not have been possible without generous funding from the Australian Postgraduate Research Support Scheme, the University of Sydney Doctoral Research Travel Grant, John Frazer Travelling Scholarship, Department of History Grants in Aid and a Pasold Research Fund Project Grant. Research for this book was also supported by visiting fellowships at the Bodleian Libraries, University of Oxford and the Folger Shakespeare Library in Washington, DC, as well as a McKenzie Postdoctoral Research Fellowship at the University of Melbourne. Funding for the many colour images featured in this book was generously provided by a Pasold Research Fund Publication Grant and a University of Melbourne Universal Grant.

A huge thank you must also go to the staff at the Bodleian Libraries, Folger Shakespeare Library, Museum of London, Victoria and Albert Museum's Clothworkers' Centre and the National Archives in Kew. Special thanks to Vanessa Jones at Leeds Museums and Galleries, Frances Lennard at the

Textile Conservation Centre, Sally Wright at the Sittingbourne Heritage Museum, Hilary Goode and Rebecca Ellison at Claydon House National Trust, Penny Fussell at the Drapers Company London, Hannah Dunmow at the Clothworkers' Company London, Christine Reynolds at Westminster Abbey, Donna Curtain and Connor Gaudet at Pilgrim Society and Pilgrim Hall Museum, Irene Julier at the Louvre Paris and Ruth Domínguez Viñas at the Museo Etnográfico de Castilla y León.

My reconstruction experiments could not have been possible without my friends and models, Gaby Debreceny, Isabelle King, Rachel Kennedy and Emily Knowles, who let me dress them up on more than one occasion, and Georgia Blackie who took many of the photographs featured in this book. Special thanks must also go to Catriona Fisk for lending me her expertise in mounting garments on a pregnant form, and to Catherine D'Angelo who let me turn her garage into a makeshift photography studio.

I owe much gratitude to the editorial and production teams at Bloomsbury, especially Frances Arnold who was enthusiastic about this book from the start. Some of the content in this book has previously been published in *Gender & History* and *Renaissance Studies* (John Wiley & Sons Ltd) and *Fashion Theory* (Taylor & Francis Group). I am grateful to the journal editors and publishers for permission to use revised material from these articles.

Finally, I must thank my family and friends for their constant support over the years, whether it be sleeping in their spare rooms while overseas on my various archival trips or listening to me go on endlessly about strange historical clothing. To Robert D'Angelo, I am grateful for your unwavering support in the final stages of writing this book, even during the stress of a pandemic and an interstate move. To my parents, Bob and Cathy, and my other close family, thank you for encouraging my love for history from a young age and for supporting this farm girl's determination to pursue such interests at university.

Finally, this book is dedicated to my late grandmother, Joan Hoy, who I very much wish was still here with us to see it and my reconstructions.

Notes to the reader

On terminology: original terminology has been retained to refer to objects of dress and textiles, unless otherwise specified. Significantly, the early modern term 'bodies' has been used to refer to those garments that we now call 'stays' or 'corsets', as this was the language used by contemporaries until the closing decades of the seventeenth century. A glossary of dress, textile and sewing terminology is provided.

On spelling, punctuation and translation: all English spelling has been modernized, except when referring to foundation garments. In these instances, original spelling has been retained to show the wide variety of ways that these garments could appear in historical sources. Original punctuation, grammar and word order have all been retained; however, most abbreviations and contractions have been extended. English translations have been given in the body of the text; original quotations are given in the endnotes. All translations are my own unless otherwise noted.

On currency and dates: the prices of English goods are written in pounds (£), shillings (s.) and pence (d.). There were 12 d. in a shilling and 20 s. in a pound during the early modern period. Throughout the book these currencies are abbreviated into £ s. d. Dates have been converted from the Julian Old-Style calendar and given in the modern Gregorian calendar (with the new year starting on 1 January).

On numbers and measurements: Roman numerals have been written in Arabic numerals when quoting from an original manuscript or printed source. Measurements are given in both the imperial and metric systems. I have placed imperial measurements such as yards, inches and feet first, as these were the units of measurement in use during the early modern period. Approximate abbreviated modern metric measurements (metre = m, and centimetre = cm) are provided after in parentheses.

List of abbreviations

AN	Archives nationales, Paris
BL	The British Library, London
BLO	Bodleian Libraries, University of Oxford
CUL	Cambridge University Library, Cambridge
DCA	Drapers' Company Archive, London
EBBA	English Broadside Ballad Archive (Online)
ECCO	Eighteenth Century Collections Online
EEBO	Early English Books Online
ERO	Essex Record Office, Chelmsford
FSL	Folger Shakespeare Library, Washington, DC
LMA	London Metropolitan Archives
NRO	Norfolk Record Office, Norwich
NRS	National Records of Scotland, Edinburgh
OBP	The Proceedings of the Old Bailey (Online)
OHC	Oxford Historical Centre, Oxford
ROLLCO	Records of London's Livery Companies Online
SHC	Surrey History Centre, Woking
TNA	The National Archives, Kew

Introduction
Investigating the structured female body

In 1597 news reports circulated detailing the possession of the Starkey household of Cleworth in Lancashire. In these reports, fourteen-year-old Margaret Hurdman, a ward of Nicholas Starkey, was described as uttering the following in a trance that her contemporaries believed to have been caused by demonic possession:

> Thus, my lad, I will have a fine smock of silk. It will be finer than thine. I will have a petticoat of silk . . . it will have a *french bodie*, not of whalebone, for that is not stiff enough, but of horn, for that will hold it out; it shall come low before, to keep in my belly: my lad, I will have a *french fardingale*, It shall be finer than thine; I will have it low before and high behind, & broad on either side, that I may lay my arms on it . . . My lad, I will have a *busk of Whalebone*, it shall be tied with two silk points, and I will have a drawn wrought stomacher embroidered with gold, & a girdle of gold finer than thine.[1]

Whatever the underlying cause, it seems that even during the stupors to which she was prone the desire to have the fashionable body of the time shaped by foundation garments such as bodies, busks and farthingales, was still very much at the fore of Margaret's mind. This book explores the preoccupation that both women and men had with achieving or denouncing the feminine bodily ideal that was shaped from foundation garments stiffened with whalebone, wood, metal and cloth in early modern England.

It is generally accepted that the sixteenth century was the first real sculptural age of fashion in Europe, when both men and women's clothing was intentionally distorted, and ideas of form, size and structure were artfully explored and taken to the extreme.[2] The sixteenth-century reshaping of the European silhouette saw both men and women adopt wide starched ruffs and collars, ballooning sleeves, stiffened or bombast upper garments and puffy lower garments (see Fig. 0.1). Such movement towards structure in dress has been attributed to the powerful influence of the Spanish Habsburg

Fig. 0.1 *Abraham de Bruyn, 'Clothing of Noble English Men and Women', from* Omnium pene Europae, Asiae, Aphricae atque Americae Gentium Habitus, *c. 1540–87, engraving with gouache colouring, Los Angeles County Museum of Art.*

dynasty that spread throughout Europe, as well as artistic movements such as mannerism, that focused on artificial forms.[3] Yet, even before the sixteenth century, a gradual stiffening and shaping of European dress had been occurring for many centuries through the refinement of tailoring methods that allowed for a tighter fit to clothing, as well as technical innovations that permitted fabrics to be stiffened through starching or paste on linen.[4] However, this shift in fashionable dress during the sixteenth and seventeenth centuries was the first time that the silhouette of the human body had been so totally and so drastically altered and reconstructed by a combination of structured garments.

It was during the sixteenth century that solid materials such as wood, whalebone and wire began to be recorded frequently in English wardrobes. The basic fashionable silhouette for English women during the sixteenth and seventeenth centuries was achieved using two main foundation garments:

bodies and farthingales. Bodies (also called bodices) were torso-covering garments designed to hold the female body in a conical shape, specifically by compressing the stomach and flattening or raising the breasts.[5] By the seventeenth century they were boned and often contained an interchangeable element called a busk which consisted of a long piece of wood, metal, whalebone or horn that was placed into a stitched channel between layers of fabric at the front of the garment. Some readers may be more familiar with the term *stays* to describe these early modern foundation garments. However, this word was not used by contemporaries to refer to boned torso-shaping garments until the final quarter of the seventeenth century.[6] Farthingales were skirt shaping undergarments that enlarged the lower half of the female body. They ranged from simple padded rolls (colloquially termed bum-rolls) to large cage-like structures that covered the body from waist to ankles. It was this structured female silhouette, first seen in sixteenth-century fashionable European dress, that led to the widespread use of stays and hoop petticoats in the eighteenth century and then to the corsets and crinolines of the nineteenth and twentieth centuries.

Later eighteenth- and nineteenth-century foundation garments have received significant scholarly attention, particularly from museums who have utilized their collections of extant apparel to display these changing fashions.[7] Although foundation garments have shaped the female form for nearly 500 years, less attention has been paid to their sixteenth- and seventeenth-century predecessors and to their relationship with ideals of femininity.[8] In larger histories of Western female-shaping garments, the foundation garments of the sixteenth and seventeenth centuries are usually briefly summarized before moving onto later centuries.[9] In the case of farthingales, to date there have been no large-scale studies of these garments published in monograph form.[10] However, studies have considered farthingales within the wider themes of early modern dress.[11] More recently, publications by Lynn Sorge-English, the School of Historical Dress and the Bayerisches Nationalmuseum have addressed the design and construction of early modern foundation garments, particularly eighteenth-century stays, in wider European contexts.[12] However, the fact that bodies are still referred to as stays in almost all these publications, even though this word was not used in English before 1680, is telling of the need for a further contextualization of sixteenth- and seventeenth-century foundation garments and their meanings for women.

This book primarily focuses on England between the years 1550 and 1700. This date range not only charts the fashionable rise and fall of bodies and farthingales, but also places them within the context of the great social, cultural and political upheavals that characterized English society during these centuries. From the splendour of the Tudor and Stuart courts, to the heyday of the early modern theatre, as well as the proliferation of popular literary forms such as broadside ballads in this period, literature, music and the visual arts flourished. This was also a time of often extreme political and religious unrest. The years following the English Reformation saw the rise in Puritanism and the reigns of the early Stuart kings, followed by the Wars of the Three Kingdoms (also known as the English Civil Wars) and the execution of Charles I in 1649. Political instability and social unrest continued under Oliver Cromwell's interregnum government and during the restoration of the monarchy in the 1660s under Charles II until the Glorious Revolution of 1688.

Importantly, this 150-year period saw significant economic change in England. By the second half of the seventeenth century, preindustrial growth in North-West Europe quickened the economy, leading to irreversible changes in traditional social categories.[13] By the end of the century, economic power had begun to shift away from the court and landed gentry towards urban commercial centres. Subsequently, communities in these economic centres saw an increase in their education, wealth and power due to their economic involvement in what has now come to be described as early capitalism.[14] The increased economic growth, wealth and consumption practices of these affluent, educated non-elites also challenged the traditional social and cultural meanings of consumer goods, including textiles and items of clothing.[15] For these reasons this period is defined by 'sartorial confusion and overlap' and it is this contextual backdrop that creates a rich tapestry on which to explore not only sartorial change, but the reasons for, and reactions to, that change.[16]

There is no widely accepted notion of how to define pre-industrial society in terms of social hierarchies and, as a result, it can be incredibly difficult to discuss social status in this period.[17] Although early modern authors often liked to classify England into various stratas based on power, wealth and privilege, social status was by no means a rigid construct or hierarchy. Ideas of wealth, power and social standing meant different things to different people – there was no particularly neat sliding social scale by which to classify men and women. As such, I have followed the general language of 'sorts' – elite, middling and common – used by historians of early modern England to discuss the social status of women who consumed and wore foundation garments during this century.[18] These status categories will be outlined in more detail in the relevant chapters. My focus on the dissemination of these garments and their meanings through various sorts of women in English society also means that this book is not just a study of fashion, that is, popular or desirable styles that were novel and always changing. Rather, it is a study of dress and dress practices. I am interested in what women wore, how they sourced their clothing and why they used their clothing, both new and old, in certain ways to express or negotiate their identities that were tied to social, cultural, economic and political factors.

Gender and the dressed body

The conceptual foundations for this study were set in the early twentieth century by scholars such as the German sociologist Norbert Elias who first proposed that the medieval to early modern period saw the development of a 'civilising process' – the growth of a self-conscious way of thinking about bodily manners, behaviour and appearance. Elias explored the ways that discourses in conduct manuals and literature led to 'very specific change[s] in the feelings of shame and delicacy' regarding the body, thus moulding thoughts and behaviour through sociogenic change.[19] Elias's work and periodization have been consistently debated and contested since the publication of *The Civilising Process* (1939).[20] However, his placing of ideas of socialization, personality formation and bodily discipline into an historical and sociological context has paved the way for other fascinating studies into the changing nature of social norms, particularly in relation to the body and appearance, during this period.

Scholars such as Georges Vigarello have built on this to argue that garments such as smocks and shirts became a person's 'second skin' due to hygiene practices that advised against full immersion bathing and instead relied on these undergarments to absorb sweat and other body excretions.[21] As a result, the cleanliness of smocks not only denoted the cleanliness of their owner, but their association with the skin underneath meant that over time nakedness became synonymous with wearing smocks. This led Vigarello to conclude that during the early modern period it was as if 'the existence of the body was delegated to the objects which covered and encased it'.[22] Literary scholars such as Will Fisher have also explored how dress accessories like codpieces helped to materialize ideas of gender in late fifteenth- and early sixteenth-century England. Fisher has argued that in literary descriptions of codpieces and male genitals, both carried 'equal weight', and in many texts men did not have penises but they did have codpieces.[23] The codpiece was therefore conflated with male genitals and helped to 'remake the male body, and by extension, the ideologies of gender' at the time.[24]

Humans are, to an extent, the social creation of their clothes, and perceptions of bodies and, in turn, identities are filtered through and articulated by clothing.[25] If clothing can 'make "the body" into [a] "person"', then it can also influence notions of gender, as the body was the primary site where gender differences were discussed, debated and policed during the early modern period.[26] In early modern England, clothing was often used to control bodies within society. The most obvious way this was attempted was through sumptuary legislation that sought to visually regulate and delineate social status. Another difference that was regulated was gender. The idea that dress should reflect a gender prescribed by biological sex was reinforced in popular religion during this period by theologians such as John Calvin, who explained in his *Sermons on Deuteronomy* (1556) that 'God intended to show us that every bodies attiring of themselves out to be such, as there may be a difference between men and women'.[27] It was also an idea reiterated in the popular press by writers such as the English pamphleteer Phillip Stubbes, who wrote in 1583:

> Our Apparel was given us as a sign distinctive to discern betwixt sex and sex, & therefore one to wear the Apparel of another sex, is to participate with the same, and to adulterate the verity of his own kind.[28]

Men and women were visually separated and understood by their attire which was ordained by God, so items of clothing were deemed to be either masculine or feminine.

By gender I refer to the socially and culturally constructed roles, attributes and behaviours that are enforced onto sexed bodies, or more specifically characteristics that are intended to reflect physical sex difference.[29] These characteristics are not static. At any given time, notions of gender can be contradictory, unstable and ambiguous due to their ever-changing nature.[30] Gender norms are even more prone to difference and change over time – what counts as masculine or feminine depends on the meanings given to these terms in a particular time and place, and these meanings are never fixed.[31] Aspects of dress that were considered masculine in Western society during the early modern period, such as lace, ribbon and accessories, may be considered particularly effeminate in modern society, where excessive ornamentation is now often associated with feminine dress.[32]

Any discussion of clothing and gender must also draw attention to the performative qualities of both. As gender norms are products of culture and never stable, they are manipulable ideas and ultimately, at times, a performance staged for specific audiences through a 'repeated stylization of the body' in time.[33] Being feminine or masculine is not the inherent result of natural biological impulses determined by sex difference at birth. Rather, gestures, acts, discourses and visual representations of what it means to be masculine or feminine are enforced by culture onto the sexed body, and then performed by those who identify or are identified with the corresponding gender. Examining dress and dressing practices therefore allows us to uncover what gender ideals and norms existed in a particular time and place, how these were formulated in relation to bodies, and subsequently how these ideas were performed and expressed by groups and individuals through their dress.

Making, consumption and meaning: examining women's lives through material culture

The inevitable challenge for anyone researching the history of women during the sixteenth and seventeenth centuries is the lack of self-representation of women within surviving material. Most sources that survive from both these centuries were either written or recorded by men – very few sources were written by or contain the unfiltered voices of women. Of those voices that have endured, most are representative of only a small minority of women of the elite. In order to gain access to the worlds and experiences of women during this period one must often learn to reapproach sources about women that were created by men, which inevitably involves quite a lot of reading between the lines. One way to overcome some of the hurdles presented by more traditional historical sources is to examine the material record; that is, the objects that women left behind or those traces of them.

Several studies have found ways to access early modern women's experiences and agency by using material culture as the lens through which to examine their lives. Notable studies include those that have focused on dress items such as tie-on pockets, jewellery, fashion dolls and albums of fabric samples.[34] Like the recently published book *The Pocket: A Hidden History of Women's Lives* (2019) by Barbara Burman and Ariane Fennetaux, this study utilizes specific types of objects as the lens through which to examine history. More broadly, over the last two decades scholars from the fields of art history and history have researched a range of clothing and accessories in order to understand not only the complexities of early modern material culture, but also to show how these material objects impacted the subject, the society and the culture of the time.[35] Following in these footsteps, this book also examines the trajectory of a select group of objects, foundation garments, as they passed through time in order to explore how the uses of and reactions to such material things can reveal information about historical change, particularly in relation to the lives of women. Using these garments as both sources and the thematic lens through which to examine women's history uncovers previously lost voices and experiences of women in early modern England.

The starting point for any history of material culture is making and consumption. I have examined both these aspects in relation to early modern foundation garments in order to explore how makers, retailers and consumer habits shaped the dressed female body in early modern England. The history of dress, the history of women and the history of how these two things interconnect also demands that any study of foundation garments must investigate what these garments meant for all sorts of women in England. As Merry Wiesner-Hanks has noted, the history of gender must interrogate how experiences differed depending on social class and geographic location, be it urban or rural.[36] Although records relating to women of the elite are inevitably more numerous and easier to find, I deliberately set out to conduct a study that would uncover as much information about the consumption habits and experiences of as many different women as possible. This includes women from a range of social positions, both urban and rural. The result, as this book will show, is that there is irrefutable evidence that by the mid-seventeenth century, foundation garments could be consumed by women from almost all social sorts. This supports the findings of other studies that argue for the rise of modern consumer culture in North-West Europe in the seventeenth century, rather than the eighteenth century as is usually asserted.

Yet foundation garments were not objects plucked out of thin air by women. Changing economic climates and consumption habits during the seventeenth century also led to an increased diversification and growth in the textile marketplace of early modern England, where, as Beverly Lemire has noted, 'the making of various commodities' was increasingly done by 'differently organised workforces'.[37] Indeed, the story of bodies and farthingales shows this development, as there were vast networks of makers and sellers who supplied these garments in early modern England, in bespoke, ready-made or second-hand forms. Using previously untapped archival sources, two specialist trades that arose as the result of rising demand for foundation garments and the increased diversification in garment production are also given special attention here: farthingale-making and body-making. As Clare Haru Crowston has argued, cloth artisans helped to 'produce, reproduce, and ultimately change the gender ideologies of their society'.[38] So the skills and knowledge of these makers, alongside the material literacy of their female and male customers, are explored to show that both maker and buyer worked together to shape the dressed female body in early modern England, and thus shape also ideals of femininity.

Closely tied to histories of consumption is the meaning of dress once on the body. It is not enough just to look at what women consumed and how this affected local and global economies. We also need to examine why women consumed what they did. Why did women want to buy and wear foundation garments, and what did they mean to them? What do reactions to the wearing of garments by various groups in the community tell us about women? Core to the argument of this book – that foundation garments shaped femininity in early modern Europe – is the understanding that social and cultural norms shape the meanings of objects, and objects in turn shape social and cultural norms. Karen Harvey has argued that 'objects are not merely cultural receptacles that acquire meaning', but rather through 'their materiality – their shape, function, decoration, and so on – they have a role to play in shaping and creating experiences, identities and relationships' within society and culture.[39]

Interaction between humans and objects in specific times and places creates cultural meaning. This is because people depend on objects, and the existence of any object is dependent on human need and use, which creates an entangled cycle of dependence and dependency.[40] In other words, humans instil objects with meanings through their uses of them. These objects then operate with their own agency by reinforcing or producing meaning through their role as recognizable social and cultural agents.[41] Foundation garments were originally objects created and used by the aristocratic elites of Europe and so imbued with very specific ideas of elite femininity such as bodily grace and magnificence (see Fig. 0.2). However, as other social groups began to consume and use these objects, initially to gain social capital through the ideals of elite femininity that these garments signified, the meanings of these objects slowly began to change.

As Leah R. Clark has noted, 'objects are absorbent and sticky things; with each transaction, something of the social sticks to them'.[42] Indeed, the use of objects by different individuals and social groups over time, in this case different social groups of women, imbued foundation garments with other types of meanings such as modesty, meanings which were then reinforced onto other individual female bodies when worn. As summarized by Ulinka Rublack, the matter and form of material objects, as well as their uses, contributed 'to shaping the period's sentiments, ideas and practices, rather than just representing existing values and aesthetic ideals'.[43] This was especially true of dress objects, as they 'constituted a sense of the body and a way of life'.[44]

By taking an interdisciplinary object-focused approach that examines a wide range of women, this book uncovers the multitude of everyday experiences and attitudes towards how women should look and act, what their role within society should be and how they should be regulated. This in turn highlights contrasting cultural and social expectations of women. As such, this book accepts that there was no one true *femininity* – that is gestures, acts, discourses and visual representations that are linked to the sexed female body – in early modern England.[45] Rather, there could be multiple *femininities* at any one time, depending on the dominant social discourses of the particular social group being examined.[46]

Fig. 0.2 *Crispijn van de Passe after Isaac Oliver,* Portrait of Elizabeth I, Queen of England, *c. 1603–20, engraving, Rijksmuseum, Amsterdam.*

I use the term 'femininity' to refer to all these collective ideas, rather than to one singular monolithic idea of how women should be. As Derek Neal has explained in his work on medieval masculinity, where he also uses the term masculinity to refer to the plural, when we use terms like genders, masculinities and femininities, 'we have lost sight of gender as a system of signification that people make' and have made '"genders" into reified categories to which people belong'.[47] After all, not all femininities are created equal. Like any system of signification, some were normative, while others were transgressive, and usually there was at least one manifestation that was idealized as the most desirable. From shaping the artificial court woman, to signifying the ambitions of the upwardly mobile London servant girl and, finally, reflecting the straight-laced sensibilities of a middling status wife, what all these femininities had in common was that they were defined, challenged and redefined by the use or lack of foundation garments that shaped the dressed body in early modern England.

Experimental history and the embodied turn

In her 2003 book, *Dressing the Elite: Clothes in Early Modern England*, Susan Vincent offered an accurate summation of the challenges that face historians of early modern dress, noting that evidence for apparel is 'everywhere, and nowhere', with commentary about clothing 'dispersed widely throughout a range of records whose main subject is almost always something other than dress'.[48] There is not a single archive or type of source that the historian can consult. As a result, I have examined a wide range of sources in addition to surviving garments to construct what Chandra Mukerji has called 'patterns of materialism', that is to build an accurate picture of a past material world that is otherwise lost.[49] These range from intimate sources such as letters and diaries to more mundane records such as household papers, guild records and probate documents. While the primary focus of this study remains England, sources from neighbouring countries with similar fashions, such as Scotland, France and the Dutch Republic, have also been consulted to help elicit meaning and contextualize the themes present within English sources.

To supplement these records of everyday consumption and to provide a better understanding of what foundation garments meant when placed on the body, I have also examined popular forms of literature and entertainment such as conduct manuals, satires, treatises, plays, broadside ballads, news pamphlets and religious literature which were widely circulated and consumed by the masses. While historians should be careful about taking what these types of sources say at face value, as many often presented polemical and sometimes outrageous diatribes on fashionable dress during this century, these sources can convey cultural sensitivities about objects that tailoring bills and probate inventories cannot.[50] Written sources that described or criticized foundation garments can help us to understand the ways in which dress and notions of femininity were publicly debated during this period, as well as the ways that objects and their meanings circulated within early modern culture.

Artworks are also helpful to examine dress and its meanings. Of course, artistic representations of dress were not always straightforward. In seventeenth-century England, the minimalistic clothing styles visible in the portraits by Anthony Van Dyck and the *en déshabillé* styles in those of Peter Lely are not representative of what was worn by their sitters in daily life, and as these conventions of portraiture became increasingly popular during the century, fewer portraits with detailed and accurate depictions of everyday dress were produced. In portraiture, details of dress could also be fabricated or omitted depending on what the sitter wished to portray about themselves. On the other hand, comparisons between portraits and surviving garments reveal that dress could be, and often was, faithfully represented in art during the early modern period.[51] There are also other ways of understanding dress during the seventeenth century in England that do not rely on portraits. Etchings, engravings, fashion prints and watercolours of everyday life feature frequently in this book, particularly those by the Bohemian artist Wenceslaus Hollar. As Aileen Ribeiro has argued, his works were usually a 'faithful record of what he saw' during his time in England, and he meticulously recorded the dress and accessories of a variety of women.[52] By the second half of the seventeenth century, styles of dress in England and the Dutch Republic tended to be quite similar and so this book also uses the work of many Dutch masters, particularly genre scenes of daily life, which are also incredibly detailed in their depiction of material things.

Although my research utilizes this wide range of documentation, there are limitations to using traditional historical sources when telling this history of foundation garments and the female body.[53] Written sources like wardrobe warrants and probate inventories can tell the historian the economics of clothing production and consumption; however, they do not outline patterns or methods of construction or experiences of wearing. Other texts such as popular literature and personal correspondence provide us with information about how these items functioned socially but still leave the historian to pursue the relationship between ideas and everyday embodiment. While the life of a garment (and that of the person who wore it) may still be visible through sweat marks or wear and tear, many questions remain unanswered. Historical sources for the bodily experiences of women, especially in relation to dress, are often scarce and many written texts from the early modern period that concern women's dress were also the work of men, who did not wear these garments daily and so did not necessarily possess first-hand knowledge about the experiences of wearing them. Many of the myths started by these writings continue to be perpetuated, but without the physical or historical proof to interrogate whether these are fact or fiction, they are hard to overcome. Therefore, in order to overcome these limitations, we must look for other ways of accessing these experiences.

In their edited collection *Ways of Making and Knowing* (2014), Harold J. Cook, Pamela H. Smith and Amy R. W. Meyers observed that knowing has long trumped making in the history of science and art.[54] To put this another way, *technical rationality*, being theoretical and scientifically based, has long been favoured over *reflective rationality*, the latter being practical, arts-based and usually involving hands-on experimentation, trial and error and observation. When it comes to history, historians have tended to view the knowledge gained from textual descriptions and visual sources as akin to technical rationality, offering something closer to evidential certainty than the process of experimentally remaking historical things. The latter, which effectively amounts to a process of reflective rationality, 'raises and answers many questions that cannot be quantified through normal research methods.'[55] This is because making equips the historian with a tacit knowledge: that is, a type of knowledge and understanding of material things or methods that cannot be fully articulated in writings or spoken words until it is realized through actions and experience. Tapping into this non-textual world of embodied tacit knowledge therefore requires scholars to put their own hands to work and to engage with experimental methods of historical research.

In order to investigate the embodied experiences of artisans who made foundation garments and those experiences of women who wore them, this study utilizes four reconstructed pairs of bodies and two reconstructed farthingales that were made using historical materials and techniques. All the findings from these reconstruction experiments, including their limitations, are recorded in the book through reflections on the making experience, and observations and photographs of models wearing and moving in these reconstructed garments. The primary aim of this experiment is to elicit further meaning from the more traditional sources that I have drawn on, particularly in regard to gendered experiences, or to answer questions that cannot be satisfactorily answered by the fragmented surviving historical record, such as those relating to craftspeople and making. In this way, these reconstructions form a foundational part of the knowledge presented by this study. These experiments and their findings are used throughout this book to demonstrate that experimental methodologies equip the historian with a tacit knowledge of material things or methods that is just as valid as other types of traditional sources used in historical research.

Experimental methodologies have been prevalent for many years in disciplines such as archaeology, where experiments are regularly undertaken to replicate archaeological artefacts, technologies or processes. This is often done to test hypotheses or conclusions reached through traditional research, to gather data systematically or to simply learn more about an object.[56] In history, experimental practice-based research has been embraced by museum curators, conservators and historians of material culture and science who are showing that there is a lost vantage that can only be gained from deriving meaning through the making process. In the specific discipline of dress history, remaking historical clothing has been a valid and valuable research methodology for many years. Such emphasis on making began with publications such as Norah Waugh's *The Cut of Women's Clothes 1600–1930* (1968) and the *Patterns of Fashion* series (1964–2018) by Janet Arnold, as these scholars examined surviving garments and recorded detailed information about the cut, measurements, construction methods and fabrics used.[57] The more recent publication of the *Seventeenth-Century Women's and Men's Dress Patterns* series (2011–16) by Susan North and Jenny Tiramani has reinforced this point.[58] These series attest to the growing interest in, and appreciation of, historical reconstruction, which in turn allow us to, as Hilary Davidson has argued, 'engage with the many material and cognitive absences' that 'our understanding of the clothed past is predicated upon'.[59] The increased use of experimental methodologies in history, to which this book contributes, has recently been labelled the 'making turn' or 'embodied turn', as it is inherently concerned with tacit body knowledge and bodily experiences in relation to the making and use of material things.[60]

The six reconstructions featured in this book were sewn by me using two methodological approaches (see Fig. 0.3).[61] The first making approach focused on reproducing four surviving seventeenth-century bodies to their exact patterns and dimensions. The second was more experimental and exploited archival records, visual sources and knowledge of seventeenth-century sewing techniques to reconstruct two styles of French farthingale, of which no examples have survived. Reconstructions of the effigy bodies (see Figs. 1.13 and 5.7), the Sittingbourne Bodies (see Figs. 3.4

Fig. 0.3 *Image of reconstruction process. The author is binding the reconstruction of the Sittingbourne Bodies with strips of leather.*

and 3.8) and the Verney maternity bodies (see Figs. 6.9 and 6.10) were made from my own observations and patterns of the original garments taken by Arnold and the School of Historical Dress, and subsequently published in the *Patterns of Fashion* book series.[62] The Filmer bodies (see Figs. 1.20 and 5.8) were reconstructed using my own pattern drafted from observations and photographs of the garment. All these bodies were reconstructed to the exact size and dimensions of the original pieces.

The second making approach that I used, which involved constructing two French farthingales for which we have no surviving examples, was much more experimental and many methodological factors had to be considered. As Tiramani has noted of her reconstruction of an outfit based on an image of the Augsburg accountant Matthäus Schwarz dating from 1520 to 1561, commissioned by Rublack as part of her research on *The First Book of Fashion*, a reconstruction of an ephemeral garment or outfit can never be 'a precise copy' because such a reconstruction is always an 'act of interpretation'.[63] This is because in addition to using period-accurate materials, patterns and construction methods must be gleaned from other surviving examples and educated guesswork. The basic process I undertook involved designing a pattern using information from visual and archival sources, identifying period materials and, finally, constructing the garment using appropriate historical techniques. My approach to reconstructing these farthingales is outlined in more detail in Chapter 4.[64]

There are no widely accepted methodologies, protocols or principles that dictate how historians of dress should go about experimental history or interpret and document their findings. Terminology is also debated.[65] I refer to my bodies and farthingales as 'reconstructions' rather than 'replicas'. This is because a maker in the twenty-first century can never fully replicate an early modern garment, even if we are using a pattern taken from an original. While all my reconstructions, except for the Verney maternity bodies, were completely hand sewn using techniques and stitches visible in the originals, the uniformity, neatness and strength of my stitching is not comparable to those of early modern tailors, body-makers or farthingale-makers.[66]Although my stitching did noticeably improve as my fingers became used to the touch of a needle going through linen or silk, those who sewed by hand, day in and day out for most of their lives, honed such embodied knowledge over the course of many years that such precise needlework became second nature.

'Informed compromises' between modern and historical resources also had to be made.[67] All my reconstructions were made from natural fibre fabrics that were available during the early modern period: silk taffeta, linen, leather and silk or linen thread. However, differences in modern manufacturing and loom widths, and between historical and modern weaving techniques, make it impossible to precisely replicate the types of historical fabrics used in the original garments without employing a specialized mill to carry out the process.[68] The silks and linens used in my project were therefore modern mass-produced fabrics that are similar enough to stand in the place of their historical counterparts. I have also chosen not to replicate the fabrics used in each garment precisely. The effigy bodies from 1603 are made from fustian, a linen–wool–cotton mixed fibre fabric that is not widely available anymore, so my reconstruction of this garment has been made from silk taffeta, as this fabric is mentioned in relation to similar bodies in the wardrobe accounts of Elizabeth I and Anne of Denmark. Whalebone, or baleen, is also no longer available due to the protected status of baleen whale populations. Instead I used a modern lightweight plastic boning from Germany that is made from spun polyester, which mimics the properties of baleen such as its strength and flexibility.

Finally, there are also limitations to investigating embodied experiences of wearing. The sixteenth- and seventeenth-century body is, as Laura Gowing has noted, 'almost unrecognisable to modern eyes', as the 'experience of lifelong labour, famine, disease, childbirth and menopause left permanent visible marks'.[69] Historical notions of comfort and other sensory experiences also vary widely; it would also be anachronistic to place these garments on a modern body unburdened by years of wearing restrictive clothing to assess historical ideas of comfort or to accurately recapture bodily experiences from the past. In this regard, it may well be impossible to ever fully recover past embodied experiences. However, this does not mean that experimental history cannot attempt to provide an account of the possibilities of the early modern female experience. As the reconstructions used in this book were made using the same measurements of the original garments, fittings with different models to find one who had the correct body shape and measurements also provided insights into the body of the original owner and how this might affect wear. My use of reconstructions in this book does not involve interviewing models and asking how they felt in these garments. Rather, it is observational: I assess the visible physical limitations that these garments place on the modern female body and then apply those observations to my historical research (see Fig. 0.4).

By seeking to combine experimental history methodologies with those of gender history, my reconstructions are not relegated to a stand-alone chapter; rather, they are integrated throughout the book and used as evidence to interrogate female experience in the same way that written, visual and extant material sources are used. The information gained from placing my own reconstructions on female models has been used alongside insights obtained from reconstruction experiments conducted by other scholars to move beyond the often-polemical sources relating to women and their dress during the sixteenth and seventeenth centuries. While notions of comfort and other sensory experiences have varied widely over place and time, and perception of bodily experiences are subject to social and cultural norms, using reconstructions of foundation garments to test movement, restriction and wear allows us to move closer towards bridging the divide between discourse and experience. Experiments using reconstructions enable us to account for the diverse ways that women could have experienced their dressed bodies, experiences that would otherwise be lost to us if we relied solely on the fragmented historical record.

Fig. 0.4 *Back view of the author's reconstruction of the bodies and stomacher of Elizabeth Filmer, c. 1640–60.*

Chapter outline

This book reorients the periodization of the female body to encompass the lively and sophisticated discourses over feminine attire in English early modernity. The era of female foundation garments – with all their attendant discourses – began in the sixteenth century, and the debates over corsets and crinolines that peaked in the Victorian era had developed over the course of several centuries. Although these garments evolved in size, shape and style over time, what remained consistent was the close association of foundation garments with the female body.

Chapter 1 begins by giving an overview of historical silhouettes, tracing the emergence of foundation garments in English wardrobes during the sixteenth and seventeenth centuries. It contextualizes these garments within early modern clothing practices and demonstrates how they were materially, visually and linguistically conflated with the physical female body in popular imagination. Chapter 2 examines the crucial role that foundation garments played in court culture, where they fashioned women according to ideas of elite femininity such as wealth, power and grace, but increasingly came under scrutiny by those who sought to assert their own vision of femininity that focused on the natural female body. Chapter 3 examines the sartorial habits and consumption practices of the non-elite sorts in England to show that a much wider range of women than has been previously thought consumed foundation garments between 1560 and 1650, and that they did so to make very specific statements about their social status.

Chapter 4 explores how and where women's foundational garb was commissioned, made and sold in early modern England. It examines the tailoring, body-making and farthingale-making trades, and considers how the material literacy and technical skills of both consumer and maker shaped the dressed female body. Chapters 5 and 6 analyse the role that foundation garments played in the everyday and sexual lives of all women in sixteenth and seventeenth-century England and examine the ways that traditional social structures sought to regulate and control these practices. Finally, Chapter 7 demonstrates how widespread consumption practices of the late seventeenth century radically altered the meanings and uses of foundation garments by women in England, underpinning later eighteenth-century notions of idealized femininity that were based on politeness and sensibility, ideals that would come to define the female body for centuries to come.

The history of foundation garments is a history of the female body and of female embodiment, and the two were inseparable during the early modern period. Examining changes in production and consumption, and the uses of, and attitudes towards, foundation garments allows us to observe changing early modern ideas about women, and thus to understand the changing nature of gender norms. Ultimately this book argues that foundation garments of the sixteenth and seventeenth centuries did not just reflect changing social and cultural ideas about how women should be. Rather, through the consumption and use of bodies and farthingales, women and men actively shaped notions of femininity in early modern England, and thus many enduring Western ideas of femininity

1

The foundations of the body
Foundation garments and the early modern female silhouette

It was in the late fifteenth century when the now tired proverb 'clothes make the man' was first recorded in English, referring to the way that people are judged according to their dress. At the start of the sixteenth century, the Dutch humanist Desiderius Erasmus also famously noted that clothing is 'the body's body, and from this too one may infer the state of a man's character.'[1] Although these sayings were uttered decades apart, what they have in common is an understanding of the ways that dress and the body are intimately connected, and how in the minds of many early modern people they were often inseparable. This chapter will consider how foundation garments came to make the early modern English woman, creating a new female form out of materials other than flesh.

Historical dress and dressing norms can seem foreign to modern readers. 'If the past is a foreign country,' Susan Vincent has observed, 'then it certainly dresses in alien ways.'[2] Just as solid additions to clothing began to form the foundation of the female figure in England during the sixteenth and seventeenth centuries, this chapter will form the foundation of this book by shedding light on early modern dress norms. Charting fashionable changes in dress in England from the late medieval period to the late Stuart period, it will uncover the emergence of foundation garments from underneath the many layers of clothing worn by English women. As this chapter focuses on fashionable change during these centuries, it primarily draws on sources relating to the social elites who dictated many of these styles. However, due to the fragmentary nature of early modern evidence, I also draw on other European examples, primarily from Spain, France and the Low Countries, to create a more accurate picture of fashionable change during these centuries.

In addition to providing an overview of historical silhouettes, fashions and terminology, this chapter also explores how English sources from the early modern period materially, visually and linguistically conflated foundation garments with the parts of the body that they clothed or concealed.

As Laura Gowing and Patricia Simons have argued, early modern bodies existed 'in a different conceptual world'.[3] Mental, emotional and physical experiences were entwined and metaphors had real influence on the ways that gendered bodies were understood, and these metaphors about bodies played roles in everyday life through 'practice, spectacle, object and sign'.[4] Establishing the ways that the social female body was imagined from the objects that covered it, this chapter takes as its foci the latter two aspects – object and sign. Whalebone hips replaced real hips of human bone, boned bodies were seen to correct the physical faults of real female torsos, and foundation garments were often used to construct the recognizable feminine silhouette on boy actors on the theatre stage. Consequently, in early modern England, foundation garments became constitutive of not just fashion but of the female body itself as they irrevocably shaped how it was understood and perceived. Acknowledging these popular metaphors for foundation garments and female bodies allows us to understand how different ideals of femininity were mediated by these objects. Subsequent chapters will further explore these ideals through the three lenses of spectacle, embodiment and actual lived experience.

Women's structural fashions before the mid-sixteenth century

The basic elements of early modern English dress were established in the Tudor courts of Henry VII and Henry VIII, where fashionable styles evolved from dress and tailoring developments of the preceding late medieval period. Men and women's styles of the early medieval period were characterized by simplicity, with garments often made from simple T-shaped patterns with flowing lines of draped fabric that followed the natural contours of the body or loosely concealed it. Beginning in the fourteenth century, innovations in tailoring such as curved seams, buttons and tight sleeves saw the cut and construction of men and women's dress become more complex.[5] For women, *surcoats* or *bliauts* were worn over the top of *cottes*, sleeved garments that were laced at the front, and chemises or smocks made of plain linen. Bliauts were also laced at the sides to create shape to the figure.[6] These garments were not stiffened but they did give a level of support to the breasts and define the shape of the body.[7]

For many years the garments described above were believed to be the extent of medieval women's underdress. That was until 2008 when excavations at Lengberg Castle in East Tyrol, Austria, uncovered approximately 2,700 individual textile fragments that were carbon dated to the mid-fifteenth century.[8] Among these textiles were many types of female undergarments, including what modern observers would term a corselet – a modern bra-like garment with additional fabric that extended to the navel, which was then fastened at the side with laces.[9] The garment gave support to the breasts and it is also possible that it had an attached skirt, making it similar to what the English called a cotte.[10] The very design of this undergarment indicates that during the fifteenth century the female body had already undergone some form of body shaping. Most probably these garments were used to create a sleek and slender looking torso, removing unsightly bulges where gowns would have hugged the figure.

By 1450 a soft and wide silhouette characterized by the *houppelande*, a voluminous gown that could have a wide V-neck that revealed the contrasting kirtle underneath, was preferred.[11] These gowns were widely worn and were often girdled or belted just below the breasts, sometimes with contrasting fabrics, and laced at the back, as is visible in an illuminated manuscript bearing the arms of Margaret of York and Edward VII (see Fig. 1.1). The soft silhouette of the female torso during the late medieval period was contrasted with highly sculptural headdresses that were popular among elite women. Two common styles during the fifteenth century were the *escoffion* and the *hennin*. The escoffion was a headdress made from padding or rolled fabric stiffened with starch, that resembled two horns over which were draped veils of sheer silk or gauze. The hennin was a cone-shaped cap worn at the back of the head to which a long shear veil of varying lengths was attached.[12] Playing with form and structure, these headdresses foreshadowed later developments in structural fashions that pushed these aesthetics to the extreme in the sixteenth century.

In the last quarter of the fifteenth century, after Henry Tudor defeated King Richard III at the Battle of Bosworth and became King Henry VII of England, English women's dress was characterized by a combination of both tightness and looseness. The general silhouette retained many features of

Fig. 1.1 *'Court of Love', in* Poems; Art D'amour; Les Demandes d'Amour; Le Livre Dit Grace Entiere sur le Fait du Gouvernement d'un Prince, *third quarter of the fifteenth century before 1483, British Library, London.*

Fig. 1.2 *'Castle of Love' in* Poems; Art D'amour; Les Demandes d'Amour; Le Livre Dit Grace Entiere sur le Fait du Gouvernement d'un Prince, *third quarter of the fifteenth century before 1483, British Library, London.*

medieval dress that emphasized the shapes of breasts and belly.[13] However, gowns also began to show features of later Tudor styles such as bodices with a square neckline (see Fig. 1.2). In these early Tudor courts, the most basic layer of clothing for women was a smock, a voluminous T-shaped undergarment made from linen or silk. On top of this was worn the cotte (now known as a kirtle), and gowns had fitted bodices and trained skirts.[14] Separate interchangeable elements, such as foreparts, sleeves and partlets, were also common.

The vocabulary of fashion during the medieval and early modern period was regional and flexible. Contemporary writings assumed knowledge and so there were a variety of names for one item, or conversely, one term could be used to indicate a variety of different garments.[15] Given these variations, it may well be impossible to date when particular garments first entered into English literature or records. *Bodies* in clothing can be traced to the start of the sixteenth century when this term simply referred to the torso-covering part of any garment. One of the earliest references to bodies comes from a Richmond wardrobe warrant pertaining to Mary Tudor, sister of King Henry VIII, dated 28 November 1510: 'Item for furring upper bodies' and 'To Robert Johnson for making the upper bodies'.[16]

In this context, upper bodies referred to the bodice of the gowns made for the princess rather than a separate structured undergarment. The rigid bodices of gowns worn by ladies in the court of Henry VIII were achieved by paste on linen or cardboard inserts that stiffened the material of the bodice.[17] However, these fitted bodices often still showed the contours of the female body underneath. This is best visualized in Hans Holbein the Younger's preliminary study of Thomas More and this family dating to 1527 (see Fig. 1.3). In the lower right-hand corner of the sketch, More's wife and two of his daughters sit or kneel on the floor with books in their laps. The clothing that they are depicted as wearing is characteristic of the period. The necklines of their bodices are wide and square, and the soft contours of their breasts and stomachs are also visible below their gowns.

Notably absent in this informal portrait of the More family is any form of skirt stiffening or farthingale. The oldest foundation garment of this study, the Spanish farthingale, was named so because its origins are found in fifteenth-century Spain, where it was called the *verdugado*.[18] The Spanish style of the fifteenth century was not a separate underskirt; rather, it comprised the outer skirt of the gown and was stiffened with hoops that began just below the waistline and descended to the feet. Such hoops

Fig. 1.3 *Hans Holbein the Younger,* Study for the Family Portrait of Thomas More, *1527, pen and brush in black ink, Kunstmuseum, Basel.*

were often bound in a contrasting fabric, creating ornamental decoration as is visible in Pedro García de Benabarre's painting *Herod's Banquet* (see Fig. 1.4). This style was first worn in England by the Spanish wife of King Henry VIII, Catherine of Aragon, and her Spanish ladies at the beginning of the sixteenth century. English sources recorded that upon her arrival she wore 'beneath her waist certain round hoops, bearing out their gowns from their bodies after their country manner'.[19] However, as the More family portrait demonstrates, this was not a fashion that quickly caught on in England, and Catherine only wore this foundation garment periodically during her time as queen of England.[20]

Although Catherine did not immediately popularize the farthingale in England, over time this Spanish fashion did come to be worn more regularly by Tudor court women. The earliest surviving archival reference to this garment in Tudor royal wardrobes comes from records that describe purchases for Princess Elizabeth in 1545: 'Crimson Satin of Bruge for one farthingale'.[21] The following year, Princess Mary also received 'a vardingalle of crimson Satin' in July 1546.[22] By the 1540s, this

Fig. 1.4 *Pedro García de Benabarre,* Herod's Banquet, *c. 1470, painting, Museu Nacional D'Art De Catalunya, Barcelona.*

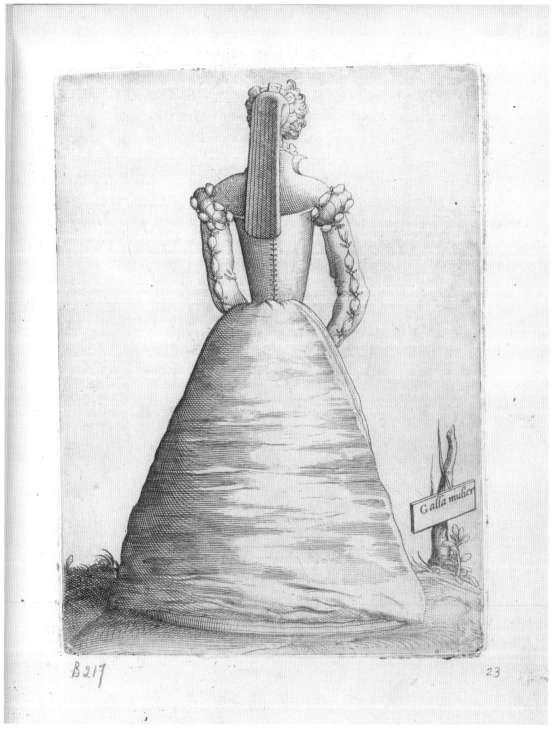

Fig. 1.5 *Enea Vico, 'French Woman', from* Diversarum Gentium Nostrae Aetatis Habitus, c. *1558, engraving, Rijksmuseum, Amsterdam.*

cone-shaped garment was worn as an underskirt in England, just as it was in France (see Fig. 1.5), and so these garments were likely hooped skirts that were made to be worn underneath gowns.

Contemporary English sources referred to the farthingale in a variety of ways, the common spelling variations being vardingale, verdingall and fardingale; but Randle Cotgrave's 1611 French–English dictionary later noted that this style was 'A vardingale of the old fashion; or a Spanish vardingale', indicating that the term Spanish farthingale was also used at the time.[23] The general shape and style of this garment changed very little in England and it likely resembled the doll-sized Spanish linen *verdugado* stiffened with bents and wire that was discovered on a vestal effigy in Spain (see Fig. 1.6). Although this Spanish example is made from yellow linen, the Spanish farthingales worn by Tudor women were often brightly coloured and made from a variety of fabrics.[24] They could also contain colourful, interchangeable foreparts of silk, that were visible through the front opening of the outer gown as seen in a portrait of King Henry VIII's final wife, Katherine Parr (see Fig. 1.7).

Fig. 1.6 *Spanish Farthingale on a wooden vestal effigy, c. sixteenth or seventeenth century, Spanish, Colección Museo Etnográfico de Castilla y León Zamora. This is the only known surviving example of any farthingale and is made from linen, esparto grass and wire.*

Fig. 1.7 *Attributed to Master John,* Katherine Parr, c. *1545, oil on panel, The National Portrait Gallery, London.*

The structuring of the European silhouette during the sixteenth century is generally attributed to the influence of the Habsburg dynasty in Spain, whose military campaigns in Italy, Bohemia and the Spanish Netherlands spread their influence throughout the continent.[25] Indeed, rivalries amongst Renaissance princes, notably Charles V, King of Spain and Emperor of the Holy Roman Empire, King Francis I of France and King Henry VIII of England, encouraged the spread of Renaissance humanism, art and culture throughout Europe, and this competitiveness further opened the Tudor court to new fashion influences from places like Italy and Spain.[26] The slow uptake of Spanish fashions by the Tudor court, as evidenced by the Spanish farthingale, may account for why references to bodies that were separate from gowns did not appear frequently in archival records until the reign of Mary I in the mid-1550s.[27] This is when the queen began to order garments, such as 'one pair of bodies of crimson satin'.[28] The increased references to bodies in Mary's accounts during this decade are likely the result of further Spanish influence through her marriage to Phillip II in 1554, as the Habsburg monarchy's modes of dress were known for their geometric *corpiños* (bodies) made from black or crimson satin that appear to have been undergarments.[29] Such bodies were also common in Florence, as Elenora of Toledo and her daughters owned several unstiffened bodies of velvet that were stand-alone garments without accompanying skirts.[30] Although Queen Mary I was increasingly influenced by the southern fashions of her husband and mother's natal lands, there is no evidence to prove that bodies were stiffened with anything other than heavy fabrics during her reign.[31] However, separate garments, that were referred to as either bodies or pairs of bodies, had emerged.

The sculptural body: the Elizabethan and Jacobean silhouette

By the mid-sixteenth century the fashionable silhouette exemplified by women at the Tudor courts combined many different elements. The basic and universal undergarment was still the smock. On top of this, kirtles and petticoats were worn, and the now very fashionable Spanish farthingale increasingly completed this ensemble of undergarments. Outerwear for elite women consisted of sleeved gowns of various types, usually named after the region from which they originated – Flanders, Spanish, French, Italian, Venetian or Polish – as well as loose gowns that provided an extra layer of warmth. For those further down the social scale, everyday wear commonly consisted of a petticoat with an attached bodice that was often worn with a waistcoat. Accessories like shoes, coifs, ruffs, partlets and detachable sleeves completed the outfit.

The fashionable feminine silhouette of the mid-sixteenth century created by the Spanish farthingale was soon rivalled by other newcomers during the reign of Elizabeth I. A second type of farthingale appeared in the 1570s. Called the French farthingale, or French farthingale rolls, this style passed to the Elizabethan court via the French – although it may have originated in Flanders, as the English used the term French farthingale rolls, and the Spanish referred to these hip rolls as Flemish rolls.[32] Such exchanges in fashion were common and the introduction of this style to England may have been the result of French diplomatic gifting. On 17 March 1577 the English ambassador to Paris, Amyas Paulet, sent a new type of farthingale to Queen Elizabeth I, writing that it was 'such as is now used by the French Queen and the Queen of Navarre'.[33] Janet Arnold has surmised that this new style was probably a Spanish farthingale which was extended at the hips by a French farthingale roll, giving the skirts a bell-shaped appearance.[34] Tailoring records seem to confirm this as they mention both 'vardinggale[s]' and 'French verdeinggale Rolles' in the same bills. A 'vardinggale' likely denoted the earlier Spanish style, while 'french verdeinggale rolles' referred to the new roll that sat around the waist.[35]

By the 1580s these rolls were commonly worn alone, and the silhouette that they created is visible in a French painting from the Valois court (see Fig. 2.12). In this painting female courtiers wear large rolls around their waist and hips from which the skirts of their gowns softly drape. An Elizabethan warrant from April 1581 to the Queen's farthingale-maker Robert Sibthorpe requested 'a roll of orange tawny & watchet damask Stuffed with cotton wool whale bone & bent'.[36] A later satirical Flemish engraving, *The Vanity of Women* (1600), shows such a silhouette to be the result of this garment – as two women are depicted being outfitted with these large rolls in a tailor's shop (see Fig. 1.8). No French farthingale rolls have survived but as these sources suggest, they consisted of a series of stiffened round casings of bents or whalebone that formed the tube of the roll into which stuffing would have been added to give it shape. The resulting garment resembled a modern lifebuoy that tied around the waist.

It was not long before another style of French farthingale emerged in the portraits of Elizabethan courtiers during the 1590s. Establishing an exact terminology for this last style of farthingale is complicated and perhaps futile – there were likely many styles or variations of farthingales that came and went and left no definitive mark in the historical record.[37] What is clear is that this was a variation of the previous French style that sat around the waist, which is why I have chosen to refer to it using the modern term French wheel farthingale. The descriptor wheel comes from the shape of this new

Fig. 1.8 *Attributed to Maerten de Vos,* The Vanity of Women: Masks and Bustles, c. *1600, engraving, Metropolitan Museum of Art, New York.*

Fig. 1.9 *Daniel Rabel,* Entrée des Esperlucattes; *six figures, c. 1626, drawing and watercolour, Musée du Louvre département des Arts graphiques, Paris.*

style of farthingale, which consisted of several hoops made from bent or whalebone that graduated outwards from the level of the waistline in a wheel shape, and was, as the young Margaret Hurdman had claimed in 1597, 'broad on either side, that I may lay my arms on it'.[38] The watercolour *Entrée des Esperlucattes* (1626) by French artist Daniel Rabel, which portrays a scene from *The Royal Ballet of the Dowager of Bilbao's Grand Bal* held by Louis XIII in February 1626, confirms this (see Fig. 1.9).[39] The scene depicts three masked ballet dancers performing in large, round stiffened structures with visible casings for stiffening around their waist. This trio is overseen by two other fully clothed dancers who appear to be wearing the same hooped structure underneath their skirts.

The angular silhouette created by this garment on the lower half of the female body is best visualized in two artworks from this period. The first is a portrait of Mary Kytson, Lady Darcy of Chiche (later Lady Rivers), dating from 1590. The portrait depicts Kytson wearing a black loose gown, with a bodice of white sleeves and stomacher, and a red skirt embroidered with hops and carnations (see Fig. 1.10). The second is an engraving of King James I of England and his wife Anne of Denmark (see Fig. 2.4). In both images, the lower half of the body is shaped by a flat wheel-like structure worn around the waist, creating a sharp edge, or shelf, from which the skirts drape. While French rolls were rounded and formed a gentle

MARY
COVNTES. RIVERS.

Fig. 1.10 *British School,* Portrait of Mary Kytson, Lady Darcy of Chiche, later Lady Rivers, c. *1590, oil on Canvas, Tate Gallery, London.*

curve as the skirts fell over the hips, this wheel style of farthingale clearly plateaued around the hips and the skirts dramatically fell from the edges. The pinning of skirt flounces to the top of the farthingale in a variety of different ways could also have made this distinction appear more dramatic.

By the late sixteenth century these new skirt-shaping fashions not only shaped the silhouettes of the English elite, but they were increasingly conflated with the real female body underneath. Art historian Anne Hollander has explored the ways in which the human figure in early modern art was rendered in such a way that it retained the imprint of fashionable shape, indicating that ideals about the human body and gender are fundamentally constituted by clothing. According to Hollander, the Spanish farthingale left an 'imprint' on the painted female nude in sixteenth century art, with more focus placed on the belly, thighs and stance to imitate the silhouette given by the farthingale.[40] Farthingales also came to define and create women's bodies in mid-sixteenth century English literature, with passages on woman's hips or bums referring to stiffened material, rather than flesh. In an Epigram from 1550, Robert Crowley described a woman with 'A bum like a barrel, / with hoops at the skirt, /

Her shoes of such stuff / that may touch no dirt.'[41] Here, rather than noting that the woman wore a farthingale with hoops in the skirt, Crowley likened her 'bum' to a barrel. This visual construction of the body of the woman in the reader's mind demonstrates how clothing such as the Spanish farthingale had notionally replaced the real female buttocks in some elite literary texts only a few short years after it became fashionable court attire. In this context, 'bum' no longer referred to an anatomical part of the female body, but the new sixteenth-century female body that the garment had constructed.

Literary works also took advantage of the properties of the new French styles of farthingales that sat around the hips. In a 1599 satire by Thomas Middleton he used a linguistic slip to comment on the excesses of women and their vain apparel: 'Amongst gallant dames, and then she wipes her lips, / Placing both hands upon her whalebone hips, / Puffed up with a round-circling farthingale.'[42] According to this author, women no longer possessed hips of flesh that they could place their hands on, but instead they now had 'whalebone hips' made from French farthingales. Over the channel in France, the metonym *hausse-cul* was also used to describe these new garments. This colloquialism highlighted how the garment reshaped the female body as it quite literally meant 'raised bum'.[43]

Similarly, the metonymic properties of the sixteenth- and seventeenth-century term 'bodies' also helped to materialize the female body during the Elizabethan period, as women now replaced their natural bodies with new and better straight bodies. The most common references to bodies during the mid to late sixteenth century were in relation to sleeved or sleeveless bodies, as well as kirtle bodies and petticoat bodies (fitted bodices attached to skirts).[44] However, a 1562 warrant for the robes of Elizabeth I also recorded a 'French gown with a strait Bodie of Buckram the sleeves drawn out with white sarcenet, of our great wardrobe'.[45] In this context, 'strait Bodie' referred to the bodice of the gown that was stiffened with buckram, a heavy coarse fabric that could be further stiffened with paste, starch or even pad stitching, creating a straight torso.[46] The increased focus on stiffening the bodies of petticoats, kirtles and gowns is also observable in other wardrobe warrants of Elizabeth I, particularly after 1580. An entry from 1582 requested an 'Item for making of a pair of bodies of black satin the sleeves embroidered with venice gold and silver covered with black sipers [cypress] the bodies lined with canvas stiffened with buckram of our great Garderobe'.[47] This warrant specifically recorded that strong fabrics such as canvas and buckram were being used to stiffen the bodies, as opposed to earlier references that specify that bodies were simply to be lined with these fabrics. This is indicative of a conscious turn during this period towards using these garments to materially shape the female body.

During the 1580s, busks also began to appear regularly in the wardrobe accounts of Elizabeth I, with fourteen busks ordered in the year 1581 alone.[48] The busk was an independent, interchangeable part of bodies, and consisted of a long piece of wood, metal, whalebone or horn (see Fig. 1.11). According to a definition given by Randle Holme in *The Academy of Armory and Blazon* (1688), the busk existed to keep the posture erect, to 'keep it [the bodies and subsequently a woman's torso]

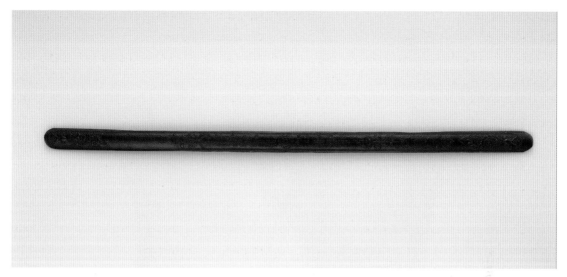

Fig. 1.11 *Busk made from baleen, c. 1660, French, Metropolitan Museum of Art, New York.*

straight and in compass' so that the 'Breast nor Belly shall not swell too much out'.[49] In the clothing of Elizabeth I, these accessories were originally placed in between bodies and smocks or tacked inside the bodices of gowns, as velvet and taffeta cases for busks are listed in Elizabeth's wardrobe warrants from April 1583.[50] Alternatively, these accessories could also be placed into a stitched channel in the centre front of the bodies and secured into place at the bottom by a small piece of ribbon called the *busk-point*. Such a channel with eyelets for the busk-point is observable on the oldest surviving pair of bodies that belonged to the Countess Palatine Dorothea Sabina of Pfalz-Neuburg, who was buried in Lauingen (now in Bavaria) in 1598 (see Fig. 1.12).

The focus on straightening the body and flattening the belly is apparent in this sixteenth-century German example. Most of the stiffening has been placed in the front of the garment in the form of a busk that was made from wood or horn and boning channels that likely contained bents, which would have pushed down any unsightly bulges at the front of the torso. The basic geometric shape of the garment not only resembles the design of men's doublets during this century (see Fig. 2.12), but the general shape implies that the female body was meant to conform to the garment itself, creating a cylindrical shaped torso. Interestingly though, unlike later examples, the bust of the Pfalz-Neuburg bodies has been left unboned, allowing for some roundedness to be retained.[51] Anne Hollander has noted that the torsos of nudes depicted in art from this period are also cylindrical in shape, with only the hint of breasts, just as they would be if they were wearing this garment.[52] David Kunzle has also noted that in sixteenth-century France the busk had become common enough to discursively 'take over' women, as some sources by this period described women as 'this charming busked-one' – the word 'busquée' here replacing the word 'woman'.[53]

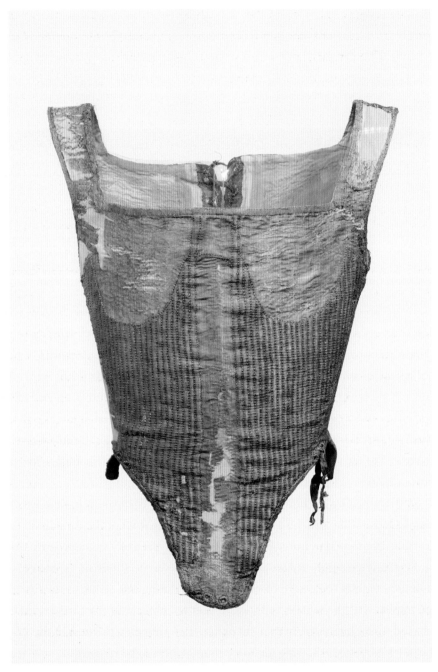

Fig. 1.12 *Bodies worn by Countess Palatine Dorothea Sabina of Pfalz-Neuburg, German, c. 1598, Bayerisches Nationalmuseum, Munich. The bodies were found amongst Dorothea's burial clothes when her tomb in Lauingen was exhumed. They are made from watered silk, backstitched in silk thread, and were boned with bents or baleen (now disintegrated). Eyelet holes where the busk would have fastened into the garment with a busk-point are still visible at the bottom centre.*

In 1688, Randle Holme explained that the centre-front of bodies that contained busks reached to the lady's 'Honor'.[54] In other words, the bottom of the busk containing the busk-point, as demonstrated by the Pfalz-Neuburg bodies, sat over a woman's sexual organs where chastity determined her honour. Just as the genital associations of codpieces in sixteenth-century men's clothing were exploited and used to stress the virility and masculinity of the wearer, as *cod* colloquially meant scrotum, the associations between busk-points and female genitals were exploited throughout the seventeenth century using playful euphemisms and double entendres.[55] The play *The Malcontent* (1603) took advantage of the position of the busk-point in a scene when the Maquerelle (a madam) warns her ladies 'look to your busk-points, if not chastely, yet charily: be sure the door be bolted'.[56] In this passage, busk-points metaphorically denoted female sexual organs and these girls were warned to keep their doors shut and not give them away to lovers as keepsakes, or in other words, to not give their bodies and sexual organs away so freely. This view of the busk-point that conflated it with the sexual organs that it covered was also indicated in two more works from the period. Barnabe Rich's *Faults, Faults, and nothing else but Faults* (1606) used the busk to refer to a woman's groin: 'he must play with her little Puppy, he must adore the point of her Busk'.[57] An anonymous work from 1600 also jested, 'A wit, as nimble as a Seamstress needle, or a girls finger at her Busk point.' To which was replied 'Your jest goes too low sir.'[58] These double entendres clarified the genital associations of the busk-point and show the ways that they were conflated with the female sexual organs and the female body.

It was not until 1590 that the first true foundation garment that modern observers would call a corset – that is, a sleeveless garment stiffened with solid additions – appeared in England.[59] A royal wardrobe warrant from that year listed a garment made for the queen that was described as a 'pair of french bodies of carnation Taffeta Lined with fustian stitched all over with whales bone of our great wardrobe'.[60] The bodies described in this entry may have looked similar to a pair of front-lacing pink bodies with visible channels for whalebone worn by Elizabeth Vernon, Countess of Southampton, in a portrait from 1600 (see Fig. 2.10). During the closing decade of Elizabeth's reign, tailors working in the royal wardrobe also began to use whalebone in the queen's petticoat bodies, as a 1592 wardrobe warrant described 'petticoat bodies of orange colour Taffeta stitched with silk lace all over and bound with lace lined with Fustian and whales bone of our great wardrobe'.[61] These new boned foundation garments stiffened with baleen were referred to as *whalebone bodies,* or *French bodies*, indicating that this new style came to England via the French.[62] A court case from rural Dorchester in 1608, in which Matthew Chubbe was accused of defaming a tailor, John Condytt, contained as evidence poems written by Chubbe, one of which included the line, 'I name not french bodies that whale bone are Made.'[63] By the Jacobean era then it appears that the implications of the term French bodies was well known throughout England, and not just by the royal court in London.[64]

Due to this increase in the use of whalebone in clothing by the turn of the seventeenth century, the linguistic slippage between real bones and boned clothing, real bodies and bodies of bone and cloth,

Fig. 1.13 *'Straight bodies', from the Effigy of Queen Elizabeth I, c. 1603, English, Westminster Abbey, London. The bodies are made of fustian, baleen, linen thread and leather.*

became commonplace. One would not break her ribs with laughter, but rather she could 'crack my Whalebones, break my Buske, to think what laughter may arise from this' as a comedy from this period exclaimed.[65] Yet bodies of whalebone and real bodies were not just conflated in popular imagination. The earliest surviving English bodies belong to the effigy of Queen Elizabeth I in Westminster Abbey (see Fig. 1.13). Funerary records dating to 1603 show that these 'straight bodies' were specially constructed for 'the Image [effigy] representing her late Majesty'.[66] It appears that this garment was made in haste for the queen's funeral as the bodies in Elizabeth's wardrobe accounts were always finished with materials such as silk satins and silk taffetas, not basic fustian cloth as this pair is. However, the size, design and construction were most likely based on bodies that the tailor William Jones had previously made for the queen. Importantly, this 'pair of straight bodies' was used to help create the torso of the dead queen on her effigy, to stand in literally and metaphorically for the deceased monarch's real body at her final resting place in Westminster Abbey.

By the Elizabethan and Jacobean eras, bodies and farthingales had come to define the socially recognizable female body so much so that they became visual prompts for femininity on the stage.

Fig. 1.14 Twelfth Night *by William Shakespeare, a Shakespeare's Globe, London, production, directed by Tim Carroll, 2012. Standing over Stephen Fry (Malvolio), male actor Mark Rylance (Olivia) is dressed in typical late Elizabethan fashions, with a pair of bodies and a Spanish farthingale creating a female silhouette.*

During this period, women were barred from performing on stage in England, so in lieu of female actresses, young boys dressed as women took female roles in the playhouse. Bodies and busks transformed the torso into a uniformed conical shape underneath the bodice of the gown, while the farthingale created exaggerated hips and backside underneath the skirts, both reshaping the silhouette of the body underneath outer clothing. This created a socially recognizable female body on top of a male sexed body on the Elizabethan stage. As Robert I. Lublin has argued, 'the stage relied upon and forwarded an essentialist view' of sex and gender.[67] Therefore since all actors at the time were male, the theatrical stage productions relied on these foundation garments to essentially make the woman, or at least her silhouette. A boy actor dressed in the height of Elizabethan or Jacobean fashions that included female foundation garments would be indistinguishable from a fully-grown woman, as is visible in this modern staging of William Shakespeare's *Twelfth Night* at Shakespeare's Globe Theatre in London (see Fig. 1.14). Thus, bodies and farthingales were, and still are for modern productions of Shakespearean plays, powerful visual symbols of femininity on the stage and in popular imagination.

The softer body: the superficial relaxation of the Caroline silhouette

Unlike the preceding Elizabethan and Jacobean eras, the early Stuart period was characterized by a perceived turn to voluminous softness in dress rather than rigidity. Waistlines rose and the small, slender figure that had been so desired years earlier seemed to disappear. Smocks remained the basic linen undergarments that were changed and laundered regularly, and kirtles had disappeared in English wardrobe records, replaced by the petticoat. The petticoat was worn by all women regardless of social status as both an outer garment or as an undergarment beneath a gown, and when worn with a waistcoat made from the same fabric the outfit was known as a suit.[68] Gowns consisted of two separate parts, the bodice and skirt, made from matching fabrics as is visible in a portrait of Elizabeth Cavendish, Countess of Devon (see Fig. 1.15).

As with Elizabethan and Jacobean fashions, during the Stuart era fashions for men and women continued to mirror each other closely in shape and style. During this period bodices and doublets resembled each other in cut and silhouette, as a French doublet with a slashed chest and sleeves in the collection of the Metropolitan Museum of Art in New York shows (see Fig. 1.16). These new styles of male and female dress that characterized the reign of King Charles I give the appearance of comfort, yet visual sources can be deceiving. Although wide stiff ruffs had become falling collars, and structured gowns were now softer with swaths of fabric that gave the illusion of roundness, it would be wrong to believe that women's bodies were now less structured by foundation garments than they had been in the previous period. Women still wore padded rolls and bodies continued to be stiffened with whalebone or busks.

The large styles of farthingales discussed in the previous section remained fashionable in English circles until the mid-1620s. However, they may have fallen out of favour with some English courtiers

ELIZABETH. COMITISSA DEVONIÆ.

Fig. 1.15 *Pierre Lombart, after Anthony van Dyck,* Elizabeth, Countess of Devon, c. *1630s, engraving, National Gallery of Victoria, Melbourne.*

Fig. 1.16 *Slashed silk doublet, early 1620s, French, Metropolitan Museum of Art, New York.*

Fig. 1.17 *Wenceslaus Hollar, 'Lady with fan and mirror', from* Ornatus Muliebris, *1639, etching, Rijksmuseum, Amsterdam.*

earlier as the twenty-seven-year-old Anne Clifford noted in her diary in November of 1617 that 'All the time I was at Court I wore my Green Damask Gown embroidered without a Farthingale.'[69] Instead, smaller rolls, referred to as either bum-rolls or farthingale rolls, were worn. These undergarments concentrated fullness around the bum and hips and shortened the torso, creating the fashionable female body shape of the 1630s. As outlined in an English–French language book that described a scene of a gentlewoman being dressed, these rolls likely sat on top of the petticoat but underneath the outer gown.[70]

The royal household bills of Queen Henrietta Maria contain many rolls that were made by a farthingale-maker. These 'small rowlls' could be made from buckram or silks like satin and taffeta, and came in a variety of colours, such as blue, black, green, crimson and carnation.[71] It is probable that these rolls were stuffed with cotton wool like those in the accounts of Elizabeth I, or, as records from the French court of Lorraine describe, they may also have been padded with horsehair.[72] Engravings from the artist Wenceslaus Hollar are valuable in understanding how the silhouette of the female body was constructed by these fashionable undergarments during the 1630s and 1640s. The high-waisted styles of the 1630s, as depicted in a series of prints by Hollar in his work *Ornatus Muliebris Anglicanus* (1640), largely concealed the rolls that were being worn underneath (see Fig. 1.17). However, within three or four years, waistlines descended and padding around the hips and backside in Hollar's prints was once again pronounced, as is visible in an etching of a gentlewoman from 1643 (see Fig. 1.18). Her backside is noticeably enlarged and rounded, much more so than a mere layering of skirts would be able to achieve. Throughout the 1630s these small rolls were probably made from tubes of fabric stuffed with wool; however, bum-rolls in a household bill for Henrietta Maria covering the months of October 1638 to March 1639 also record wire being used in a roll 'of a new fashion'.[73]

John Bulwer referred to rolls that sat around the bum and hips in his 1653 treatise, *Anthropometamorphosis*, which focused on fashions around the world that altered the natural body. In the treatise, Bulwer wrote that when Sir Peter Wyche was an English ambassador to the Ottoman court between the years 1627 and 1641,

> . . . the Sultaness desired one day to see his [Wyche's] Lady, whom she had heard much of; whereupon my Lady Wych (accompanied with her waiting-women, all neatly dressed in their great Verdingals, which was the Court Fashion then) attended her Highness. The Sultaness entertained her respectfully, but withal wondering at her great and spacious Hips, she asked her whether all English women were so made and shaped about those parts: To which my Lady Wych answered, that they were made as other women were, withal showing the fallacy of her apparel in the device of the Verdingall, until which demonstration was made, the Sultaness verily believed it had been her natural and real shape.[74]

Fig. 1.18 *Wenceslaus Hollar,* Noble Gentlewoman of England or Mulier Nobilis aut Generosa Anglica, *1643, etching, Rijksmuseum, Amsterdam.*

It appears that what most interested Bulwer was the way in which these bum-rolls had seemingly consumed the natural female body replacing it with the 'fallacy' of apparel, so that the Sultaness, who was unfamiliar with Western European fashions, mistook Lady Wyche's 'great and spacious hips' created by the farthingale as 'her natural and real shape'. More importantly, however, this passage testifies to the fact that even by the mid-seventeenth century, almost a century after the first farthingales appeared in wardrobe accounts, the English imagination was still very much intrigued by the ways that the female body could be created by structured clothing such as the farthingale or bum-roll.

Bodies stiffened with whalebone also continued to shape the female silhouette during the reign of Charles I. In January 1625, Dame Honor Procter of Cowling in Yorkshire outlined in her will that 'a pair of French bodies of taffeta' were to be given to her daughter, and Queen Henrietta Maria's wardrobe accounts during the 1630s show that she ordered many types of bodies.[75] An examination of a bill from the queen's tailor, George Gelin, dating from April to June 1631 reveals all the forms that bodies could manifest in during this period. In April 1631 the queen had an embroidered white satin

Fig. 1.19 *Bodice of silk satin, c. 1630–9, English, Victoria and Albert Museum, London.*

gown made and the bodies of the gown contained sleeves and a stomacher.[76] This bodice likely resembled a surviving ivory silk bodice in the Victoria and Albert Museum's collection that was typical of fashions during the 1630s (see Fig. 1.19). The bodice has a sturdy foundation layer of canvas and buckram that has been covered with an outer ivory silk fabric that has been decoratively slashed. The boning inside is focused vertically at the front and sides and horizontally at the back, and the voluminous skirts indicate that it was worn over a roll. Missing from this surviving example is the stiffened stomacher that would have been pinned into the front of the bodice, as is demonstrated in the portrait of Elizabeth Cavendish (see Fig. 1.15).

In May of this same bill, the queen also had pink rose-coloured petticoat bodies made that were stitched with whalebone (the term 'stitched' indicating that the stitching for the boning channels was visible).[77] She likely wore this garment underneath several waistcoats and gowns that were also ordered at this time. Finally, in this same bill the queen received four satin pairs of bodies: two yellow, one green and one blue. All these garments were 'stitch[ed] with whalebones', were sleeveless and were decorated with silver lace.[78] These garments likely resembled a pair of bodies dated 1630–60 attributed to Elizabeth Filmer of Little Charlton Manor in Kent (see Fig. 1.20).[79] The Filmer bodies are made from crimson silk satin and stiffened with whalebone and the straps sit off the shoulder in order to accommodate the wide necklines of fashionable outer dress during this period.

Like the bodies given to Henrietta Maria, this garment is also trimmed with a silver-gilt braided lace. Unlike the earlier effigy bodies, the Filmer bodies also have a separate fully boned stomacher that lies beneath the front lacing. Many of the queen's garments contained stomachers, as they were both fashionable and allowed for adjustments to fit. Just as bodies and bum-rolls were named after the anatomical part of the female body they covered, the stomacher was a triangular piece of the garment that sat over the woman's bust and stomach (see Fig. 1.21). At various times during the sixteenth and seventeenth centuries, stomachers also began to be used as separate accessories made from embroidered fabric and pinned to the front of the bodies. The location of this object on the female body not only gave the garment its name, but it also reimagined what it meant when someone referred to their stomach – were they referring to clothing or real flesh?

There has been a tendency for scholarship to anachronistically comment on the ways that bodies and busks hardened and masculinized the female form, making women look like men.[80] In reality, these ideas were much more nuanced and contemporaries rarely associated stiffening in clothing with masculinity. Pairs of bodies were so closely associated with the physical female body that around 1660 the Reverend John Ward, who was a physician and natural historian, noted in his diary that he saw,

> An hermaphrodite at a place 4 miles of Worchester: his testicles large and his penis out of measure big yet unfit for generation as my Landlord said he did believe. I and Mr. Trap saw him. He goes dressed upward as a woman in a kind of waistcoat and bodies; but breeches on.[81]

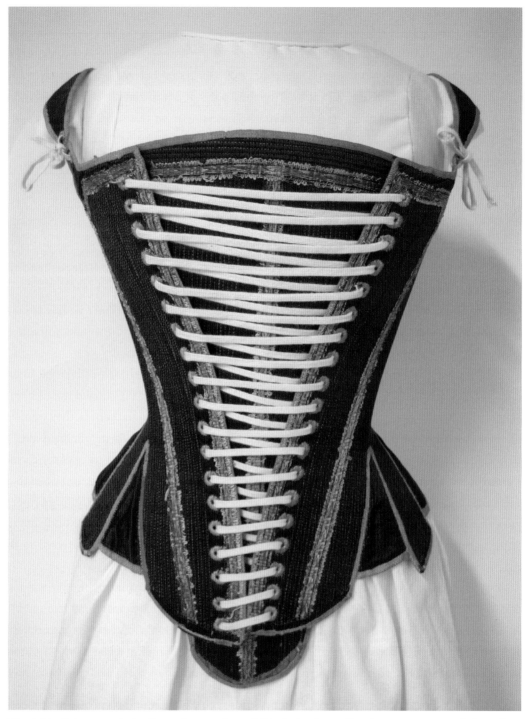

Fig. 1.20 *Crimson satin bodies and stomacher of Elizabeth Filmer (front), c. 1640–60, English, Gallery of Costume, Platt Hall, Manchester City Galleries. The bodies are made of silk satin, twill-weave linen, baleen, silk thread, silk grosgrain ribbon and gilt braid.*

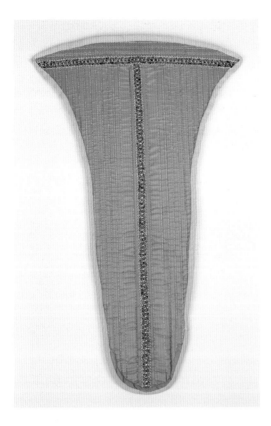

Fig. 1.21 *Author's reconstruction of the stomacher from the Filmer bodies.*

In this description Ward labels the individual he saw as a 'hermaphrodite' due to the combination of what they wore. Breeches, as this source makes clear, were a symbol of masculinity while 'bodies' were a metaphor for the female body, and so, by wearing both the person appeared to be a mix of both sexes. The fact that Ward described but ignored the physical bodily signs of sex (penis and testicles), and instead focused on the body that was understood through dress, demonstrates that bodies were thoroughly understood as feminine during this period.

In fact, it was believed that women needed these garments due to the imperfect nature of their bodies. This was expressed in a seventeenth-century analogy from a jestbook in which Sir Nicholas Le Strange mused,

> When man and woman were first made, they had each of them a lace given to lace their bodies together, the man had just enough to lace himself home, so he left his tag hanging down; the womans proved somewhat too short, and seeing she must leave of her body open, in a rage she broke off her Tag, and threw it away.[82]

Gowing has commented that in this source Le Strange attributed the competence of men to the fact that they have a 'tag' (a colloquial term for penis), whereas 'women's rage at being short-changed' left her with no penis and an opening instead.[83] However, to push the analogy further, Le Strange was also commenting on why women needed garments such as bodies that were laced in the first place: to correct their imperfect form.

Popular culture also made a connection between the ways that women's inferiority was manifested materially in their clothing. Ben Jonson's play *Eastward Hoe* (1605) made a similar statement to Le Strange's regarding the weakness of women's bodies when he has a tailor in the work proclaim,

> Fine and stiffly I faith . . . here was a fault in your body, but I have supplied the defect, with the effect of my steel instrument which, though it have but one eye, can see to rectify the imperfection of the proportion.[84]

Jonson intentionally plays with the ambiguous nature of the line 'fault in your body', allowing it to be read at least three ways. Firstly 'fault' refers to the female genitalia indicating that the bodies are female. Another reading is that the bodies that the tailor had produced for his client were faulty and thus he needed to 'rectify the imperfection of the proportion'. The third interpretation is that the client's body, being female, was faulty and therefore its 'imperfection of proportion' needed to be rectified with a pair of bodies. Women therefore required stiffened clothing like bodies to correct their physical inadequacies.

The laced and hardened female form therefore did not make women masculine in the sense that it made them into men. After all, bodies still defined the waist, allowed for breasts and were increasingly viewed as fundamental objects of female dress, as this book will explore. To return to Le Strange's analogy then, while men had enough lace to pull themselves together and thus produce a perfect body, women through their own fault did not. Hence, women were continually searching for more lace to produce the perfect body, which is why they turned to artificial means such as laced bodies and bodices to achieve it.

Ambiguous bodies: underwear, outerwear and the Restoration silhouette

Fashions in England during the second half of the seventeenth century continued to mirror the general silhouette of those of the French and the Dutch. For everyday wear, the lines of the 1650s generally followed the preceding decade with wide necklines and full sleeves that were cartridge pleated. The wardrobes of most women still consisted of a combination of smocks, petticoats, waistcoats and gowns, and bodies stiffened with whalebone were still retained along with smaller bum-rolls (see Fig. 1.22).[85] Rolls remained in fashion throughout the century as Randle Holmes described 'Bearers, Rowls, fardingales' in 1688 as 'things made purposely to put under the skirts of Gowns at their setting on at the Bodies; which raise up the skirt at that place to what breadth the wearer pleaseth'.[86]

Beginning in the 1650s, formal court gowns became long waisted and form hugging once again, and stiffening was placed in the bodice of the gown itself. Bodices from the 1660s that have survived

Fig. 1.22 *Pieter de Hooch,* Figures in a Courtyard behind a House, *c. 1663–65, oil on canvas, Rijksmuseum, Amsterdam. The woman standing over the table wears a brown waistcoat possibly over a pair of bodies, the woman sitting in front left wears a boned bodice and skirt, and the maid in the background wears a blue petticoat with a pair of yellow bodies over her smock.*

Fig. 1.23 *Green Silk Bodice (front), c. 1660s, English, Museum of London.*

in English collections all share very similar design features: a low round neckline that exposed the shoulders, short or elbow length sleeves that were cartridge pleated low into the back of the bodice, heavy vertical boning and a long pointed centre front (see Fig. 1.23). Nearly all these bodices contain a channel at the centre front into which the busk was inserted from the bottom and fastened into place by a busk-point tied to a small hook.

Bodices like the green silk example from the Museum of London in Fig. 1.23 were clearly elaborate outerwear made for formal occasions. However, it is useful to consider that, like tie-on pockets that were detached and could be worn underneath clothing or on top of it, many styles of bodies during the early modern period defy strict modern definitions of under or outer dress.[87] Early modern clothing was much more fluid in its uses, especially for those down the social scale who had limited wardrobes and for whom garments needed to fulfil multiple functions. Petticoats are a useful example of this. These skirts could have attached upper bodies and were, alongside the smock, the most basic item of dress for women in England throughout the period studied in this book. Women often wore multiple petticoats at any one time depending on the season, and these garments were not always underskirts. Women may have worn a petticoat with an attached pair of bodies and a waistcoat on top

Fig. 1.24 *Bodies of pink watered silk trimmed with pink silk taffeta ribbons and detachable sleeves, c. 1650–80, Dutch or English, Victoria and Albert Museum, London. The bodies are lined with linen and boned with baleen. The Victoria and Albert Museum notes that these bodies may be of Dutch origin as they resemble bodies with detachable sleeves worn in Dutch genre art. However, English women likely wore similar garments during this period as these pink bodies resemble a well provenanced English garment from the Verney family of Claydon House (see Fig. 6.9).*

as everyday wear, while a gown may have been placed over the top of the petticoat for more formal occasions.

Many of the bodies discussed so far in this chapter likely functioned as both underwear and outerwear during the seventeenth century. This ambiguity accounts for the frequent slippages between the terms *bodies* and *bodices* in early modern sources.[88] Bodies with ornamental trims like the crimson satin garment that belonged to Elizabeth Filmer were clearly made to be seen and likely worn as both a bodice and as a foundation garment under a waistcoat. Many bodies from this century also feature detachable sleeves that allowed them to easily become outer garments. A pair of bodies made of watered pink silk that date from 1650 to 1680 demonstrate this (see Fig. 1.24). These bodies feature a pair of sleeves that attach to the shoulders of the garment with silk ribbons that threaded through worked loops on the outer binding (see Fig. 1.25). When worn with sleeves and a matching outer petticoat, it is likely that this garment formed the bodice of a gown. However, when the sleeves were removed it could also be worn as an undergarment underneath a waistcoat or in a more informal ensemble. This style was popular in both England and on the continent, as women wearing bodies with detachable sleeves are also visible in various Dutch artworks from the period (see Fig. 1.26).

Fig. 1.25 *Sleeve detail of bodies of pink watered silk trimmed with pink silk taffeta ribbons and detachable sleeves, c. 1650–80, Dutch or English, Victoria and Albert Museum, London. The sleeves are attached by ribbon threaded through worked loops on the outer silk grosgrain binding.*

Fig. 1.26 *Gabriel Metsu,* The Intruder, *c. 1660, oil on panel, National Gallery of Art, Washington, DC. The ribbons that attach the sleeves are clearly visible.*

Like petticoats and bodies, smocks were garments that often held an ambiguous status as under- or outerwear at this time. During the early modern period, linen as a porous fabric replaced the role of skin in bathing practices, as it was believed to absorb dangerous matter from outside and inside the body that could then be laundered.[89] Instead of washing their physical skin, one would simply remove and clean their 'second skin' – their smock.[90] This not only had implications for cleanliness but also for the way that early moderns viewed the body. In Europe, smocks were indicative of the smooth, often white skin underneath, and consequently of nakedness.[91] Outer garments often played with these implications. Doublets and sleeves were regularly slashed to give excitable glimpses of the white smock or shirt underneath (see Fig. 1.16). By the 1670s, court styles in both England and France placed the bellowing sleeves of smocks trimmed with lace or ribbon on full display. The playful nod to undress hinted at by these sleeves was further emphasized by the elaborately embroidered bodies that they were worn with during this decade, as depicted in Jacob Ferdinand Voet's *Portrait of a Lady* (see Fig. 1.27).[92] These sorts of bodies contained short sleeves that could be either attached

Fig. 1.27 *Jacob Ferdinand Voet, Portrait of a Woman, c. 1670s, painting, Petit Palais, musée des Beaux-Arts de la Ville de Paris.*

or removed, thus making them elaborate outerwear that could be worn as a supportive under layer as well.

The ambiguity of bodies as under- and outerwear continued until the end of the seventeenth century, even after the rise in popularity of the fashionable loose-fitting mantua gown in the late 1670s. The mantua consisted of two lengths of fabric joined in a T-shape that were then draped or pleated to create an unstiffened bodice with attached overskirts. These skirts were looped up over the hips into a bustle with a train and then worn over a contrasting petticoat, resembling those skirts of the 1670s.[93] The silhouette created by this new gown is visible in a French fashion print from the late 1680s (see Fig. 1.28). The woman in the centre of the image wears a claret-coloured mantua gown. The loose bodice is pinned to the yellow bodies or stays underneath, and the skirts of the mantua are bustled over a contrasting blue petticoat. The little girl to the left wears an older-style gown with a boned bodice and contrasting petticoat. The mantua served as a model for later eighteenth-century fashions that would follow a similar design – a petticoat

Fig. 1.28 The Statue of Jupiter, c. 1688–90, etching, Rijksmuseum, Amsterdam. The adult women wear the new fashions of the 1680s including mantua gowns and fontange headdresses.

skirt worn with an over-gown that was pinned to the stays at the front – exemplified by the *robe à la française*.

While the mantua gown established the fashionable silhouette of the eighteenth century it did not herald in the invention of *stays* as a separate boned undergarment.[94] As this chapter has shown, boned torso-shaping garments existed simultaneously as under and outer garments for the entirety of the seventeenth century; just because this stiffening was incorporated into the bodices of fashionable gowns of the 1660s and 1670s does not mean that other stiffened bodies did not exist and were not worn underneath other garments of everyday wear. This narrative of fashionable dress and change also highlights another issue in the study of late seventeenth-century women's dress: the tendency to ignore other dressing practices that did not include the mantua gown. While the mantua was indeed very fashionable and did revolutionize women's dress, it was not the only outfit worn by women in the final decades of the seventeenth century.

The wardrobe accounts of Queen Catherine of Braganza during the 1680s are useful in demonstrating the variety of garments still worn by women during this decade. While her accounts did contain the new fashionable mantua gown, they also contained 'under petticoats', petticoats, waistcoats (some of which were stiffened with whalebone), gowns, morning gowns and cloaks.[95] Catherine's wardrobe accounts are interesting as this is the first time that bodies appear to be designated as either under or outerwear in the seventeenth century. The queen continued to receive 'under boddeys' from her tailor Peter Lombard that were likely made to be worn with petticoats underneath her waistcoats and mantuas. These bodies are strictly defined as different from those pairs of 'gown boddeys' which are also listed in her accounts, which referred to the bodices of other styles of gowns that were not mantuas.[96] This change in terminology towards designating bodies are either under or outerwear may be because the mantua, while not creating a new type of stiffened underwear, necessitated a new use for bodies.

In 1688, Randle Holme described the mantua as 'a kind of loose coat without any stays in it'.[97] In this instance 'stays' referred to stiffening usually found in the gown itself, but during the 1680s this term was also increasingly used to refer to the bodies worn underneath the mantua as well (this transition in terminology is discussed in detail in Chapter 7). The draped bodice was pinned to the bodies/stays, leaving the front of this foundation garment exposed. The front of bodies and stays therefore began to be covered in pieces of decorative fabric that concealed the boning channels at the front or were covered with trims such as lace. The use of decorative foreparts on foundation garments is demonstrated by a pair of blue wool and silk bodies/stays dated 1670–90 at the Museum of London (see Fig. 1.29). Unlike earlier bodies of the seventeenth century, this style is back lacing and the front panel is made from brocade decorated with metallic braid, indicating that the garment was made to be worn with a new mantua gown which exposed the front of the garment. While this garment was likely referred to at the time as an *under boddey* or stays, it was not meant to be totally unseen. In this sense, by the end of the

Fig. 1.29 *Bodies or Stays of Wool, Silk and Linen, c. 1670–80, English, Museum of London. The bodies are made of striped blue worsted wool, blue silk brocade, green silk ribbon, gilt braid, silk thread and baleen.*

seventeenth century bodies were, as they always had been, both simultaneously under and outer garments and they continued to structure the fashionable silhouette of the eighteenth century as *stays*.

Conclusion

During the early modern period, clothes made the man and foundation garments came to make the woman. To explore the ways that foundation garments helped to shape different ideas of femininity in sixteenth- and seventeenth-century England, one must first understand not only the changing styles of the garments themselves, but also how they were associated with the physical female body of flesh. The evolution of the female silhouette from 1450 to 1700 was not a simple linear process. The stiffened and exaggerated Elizabethan silhouette was soon replaced by a softer, albeit still somewhat structured, silhouette of the Caroline and Restoration courts. Cycles of dress that incorporated voluminous softness were contrasted by structure and rigidity before being replaced again. What was different was that foundation garments – farthingales, bodies, busks and rolls – began to structure fashions during the sixteenth century in England and were retained as both under and outerwear during these two centuries. A history of foundation garments in sixteenth- and seventeenth-century England is therefore inextricably linked to the history of the female body.

Although the styles, size and function of these foundation garments varied over time, what stayed the same was the way in which bodies and farthingales were materially, visually and linguistically conflated with the parts of the physical female body that they covered. The use of metonyms that described anatomical parts of the human body and the garments themselves, such as bodies, bum-rolls and even stomachers, meant that these garments were fundamentally connected to the real body of flesh in all aspects of everyday culture. Garments, whose names did not have metonymic properties, such as farthingales and busks, were connected to the physical female body in other ways: busk-points were conflated with the female sexual organs over which they sat, while the use of whalebone in farthingales was again exploited with women replacing their real hips and buttocks with whaleboned hips. Understanding early modern clothing and recognizing the connections made between real bodies and garments of whalebone, wood, metal and cloth allows us to further examine how ideals of femininity were mediated by foundation garments during this period, which the rest of this book will do.

2

The artificial body

Courtiers, gentlewomen and disputed visions of femininity, 1560–1650

Elizabethan court fashions of the late sixteenth century were both ostentatious and fantastical, transformative and artificial, and, more importantly, imbued with significant meanings that were tied to aristocratic cultural aesthetics of the early modern period. During this century new innovations in colour, texture and cutting techniques were utilized by the aristocrats of Europe to manipulate the meanings attached to clothing and to bolster their own power and prestige.[1] It is unsurprising then that foundation garments were products of these social elites who spent lavishly on clothing to maintain their social status, and so dictated fashionable trends. In England, this top level of society typically held political and social power through birth, marriage or royal appointment. They were usually titled or landed and consisted of the monarchy, the aristocracy, the nobility and those top members of the gentry. They accounted for only 2–5 per cent of the population but owned over 50 per cent of the land in England.[2] Although holding a title and political power did not always equate with wealth, for the most part elites had power that was based on privilege and was largely separate from monetary benchmarks.[3] As foundation garments were borne out of those European courts frequented by these elites, bodies and farthingales were initially intended to visually manifest qualities associated with this small section of early modern society.

This chapter examines how elite court aesthetics of the sixteenth century reshaped the female body. Innovations in fashionable dress gave birth to bodies and farthingales and these garments symbolized very specific ideas of elite femininity related to wealth, power and grace. However, during the first half of the seventeenth century these elite styles were increasingly challenged by moralizing writers and dramatists, all of whom attacked not only court culture in general, but also the vanity and artificiality of the women who symbolized those courts. In doing so, these writers established a dichotomy between visions of femininity, largely defined by artificial body-altering garments such as bodies and farthingales, and other visions that focused on the pious, natural female body untouched by form-altering fashions. These debates reveal tensions between court femininity and non-court femininity, and show how male moralists sought to control how women should look and behave during the turbulent political and religious tensions of pre-civil war England.

Shaping the aristocratic body

Early modern royal courts were theatrical spaces with complex rules of courtesy and precedence. Kings and queens used dress to impart a sense of wealth and magnificence associated with monarchy, and courtiers dressed to impress their monarch as they competed for honours and favour.[4] In this environment courtiers were always on display and so they were consciously aware of their role and how their actions were viewed by others.[5] The performativity of court life meant that all actions and gazes were interpretive. Courtiers were constantly aware of being watched, and thus all actions demanded considerable forethought: how can I make this look good, or good on me? Performance was complemented by the watchers who reacted to and scrutinized those actions: is she doing that because I am watching her? In the culture of the court, every day life was therefore a calculated performance where all actions became subject to scrutiny by those seeing and those being seen.[6]

Farthingales were perfectly suited to court life and to performative display. These garments expressed the wealth and status of the wearer by increasing the size of her lower half and the amount of fabric required for the outer gowns. In early modern England, cloth was expensive due to the use of natural fibres such as silk, wool and flax, as well as the time-consuming nature of hand spinning, weaving and finishing. The nature of how the fabric was woven and sold, such as by the yard, ell or piece in England, also affected the cost.[7] Woollen fabrics such as kersey and broadcloth were usually sold in ¾ to 1¾ of a yard (68.5 to160 cm) widths, while already costly silks were made even more expensive by the practice of being woven and sold in smaller 20- or 22-inch (approx. 51 to 56 cm) widths.[8] This meant that more yards of silk fabrics than wool fabrics were required to make a garment, even if the exact same garment was being made, as silk fabric widths were narrower.

Fabrics that were commonly used to make elite dress were silks of all kinds – satin, velvet, taffeta and damask – and sometimes even cloth of silver and gold for those of the most noble rank, meaning that the materials for a gown could be incredibly expensive. When Thomasine Petre, a young lady from the rising gentry, entered the household of a marchioness in 1557, an array of fine garments were made for her to reflect this advancement in her social station. Two of these garments were a russet damask gown and an accompanying Spanish farthingale of russet fustian. The gown required a staggering 11 yards (10 m) of damask fabric at 10s. 4d. a yard to be made. This was Thomasine's most elaborate and expensive gown to date, and possibly the first that was made to be worn alongside the newly fashionable farthingale, as it appears to have been a new style in her wardrobe.[9] Considering that the average labourer's daily wage was approximately 4d. in the mid-sixteenth century, the 11 yards of damask (totalling £5 13s. 8d.) used in Thomasine's dress would have cost a commoner nearly a year of wages.[10]

In addition to fine silks, Elizabethan and Jacobean court gowns were also made from elaborately embroidered fabrics that at times contained threads of gold and silver, as well as precious gemstones and pearls.[11] In this sense, farthingales were also structures used to display ornate textiles such as the forepart worn by Katherine Parr in her portrait of 1545 (see Fig. 1.7). This expensive display is also visible in a 1606 portrait of Princess Elizabeth Stuart, the daughter of King James I and his wife Anne of Denmark, who wears a gown that has been intricately embroidered with popular Jacobean floral and insect motifs over a French wheel farthingale (see Fig. 2.1). This gown would have required many yards of expensive embroidered fabric to make, as the princess also wears her skirts with fashionable flouncing, a decorative detail created by pinning extra fabric at the top of the skirt on to the edge of the wheel farthingale. A gown that required such large amounts of expensive fabrics and trimmings automatically made a woman more noticeable in elite socio-economic spheres. This appears to have been the case in the summer of 1548 when Ann Cavendish, the daughter of Sir William Cavendish and the step-daughter of courtier Bess of Hardwick, received 'a vertyngall'.[12] Besides being one of the earliest references to a farthingale outside the royal family, such a purchase for nine-year-old Ann was indicative of her place in the social order. Not only was Ann expected to compete sartorially with other aristocratic girls, but the need for her to be seen in aristocratic spaces as a representative of the Cavendish family, and for future marriage prospects, was of vital concern.

Unlike Thomasine Petre, whose farthingale was made from a cheaper fustian fabric to offset the costs amassed by the accompanying gown, no expense was spared for those members of the court who belonged to the royal family. Spanish farthingales often required just as much fabric to make as gowns. A 1560 wardrobe warrant for Elizabeth I requested 5 yards (4.5 m) of purple taffeta for the farthingale and another farthingale from 1569 used a staggering 'eleven yards quarter [10.3 m] of blue satin'.[13] For royal women, the same types of expensive fabrics used in their outer gowns were also used to make their farthingales. A 1608 inventory of the wardrobe of Anne of Denmark listed thirty-six farthingales of silk satin, taffeta and damask that belonged to the queen. These came in a variety of colours including those that were commonly used in her outer garments such as crimson, carnation and white, as well as blue and 'popinjay green'.[14] Almost all the small rolls or farthingales found in bills from Queen Henrietta Maria's household between the years 1629 to 1639 were made from silk taffeta, with 'sky blue' and carnation being the most popular colours requested for the queen.[15] The ability to consume the fine materials needed to make not only the outer gown, but also the farthingale underneath, therefore allowed for the conspicuous display of wealth and consumption, something which a member of the rising gentry like Thomasine Petre with her fustian farthingale could only aspire to.

Fig. 2.1 *Robert Peake the Elder,* Princess Elizabeth, Later Queen of Bohemia, *c. 1606, oil on canvas, Metropolitan Museum of Art, New York.*

Such displays were indicative of the high social position that women of the court enjoyed. In 1633, long after large Elizabethan and Jacobean farthingales had ceased to be worn, John Bulwer recalled that during those times 'women did take pleasure to wear great and stately Verdingales', directly linking the farthingale with the idea of being stately, or grand and physically imposing.[16] This was a quality that poet and attorney William Warner commented on in 1586 when he stated that women who wore 'Fardingales' were 'so bombe-thin, yet she cross like seems four square', meaning they had a large and solid appearance.[17] As well as projecting power, it has also been suggested that large farthingales made female monarchs and courtiers somewhat unapproachable and created a physical barrier to protect these women from crowds.[18] Being allowed to access the close physical space of a monarch was a privilege. This was clearly demonstrated by Bernardino de Mendoza, a Spanish ambassador at the English court, who wrote to King Phillip II of Spain in January 1579 describing a meeting with Queen Elizabeth I. In the correspondence he remarked that while he was seated by her side, he had pressed matters relating to Franco-Scottish political affairs, in which both Spain and England took a keen interest, and the queen 'even raised her farthingale in order that I might get closer to her and speak without being overheard'.[19] Including such a detail about the queen's farthingale in this official correspondence was clearly done to show Phillip that Mendoza had gained the English queen's trust and esteem. Women who wore these undergarments did not just display power through their wealth, but the correspondence between the personal body and the body politic of women such as Elizabeth I meant that the use of this garment could also signal who had access to her favour.[20]

Connections between farthingales and power are best visualized by portraits of Queen Elizabeth I. The *Ditchley Portrait* by Marcus Gheeraerts the Younger (1592) demonstrates Elizabeth's political authority and adequacy as a ruler (see Fig. 2.2). In the portrait, the queen's skirts are enlarged by a French wheel farthingale, which was the height of court fashion at the time, and span from one side of the country to the other. Such a depiction visually reinforces her embodiment of England and role as mother of its people in a way that would have been unattainable if she was dressed as a man or in a gown with smaller skirts. The stance represented in this portrait, with broad shoulders created by wired sleeves and with arms resting squarely on her farthingale, is also reminiscent of her father, Henry VIII. However, instead of Henry's broad shoulders and hands on hips that presented masculine power in his portraits, the stance created by the farthingale represented a form of feminine power in portraits of Elizabeth. Clearly this was something that women of the period wished to emulate, as the previously mentioned Margaret Hurdman, who had been possessed in 1597, noted in her stupor that she wished her farthingale to be wide so she could rest her arms on either side of it, copying those elite stances presented in the portraits of Elizabeth I and her courtiers.

Likewise, the *Armada Portrait* by George Gower (1588), which celebrated the English defeat of the Spanish Armada, depicts the queen dressed in a large French farthingale, a ruff and wired sleeves (see Fig. 2.3). Her dressed body envelops the foreground of the painting and her hand rests on a small globe,

Fig. 2.2 *Marcus Gheeraerts the Younger, Queen Elizabeth I ('The Ditchley Portrait'), c. 1592, oil on canvas, National Portrait Gallery, London.*

the defeated Spanish Armada depicted in the background. In this portrait, the queen's dressed body makes a bold statement about the power of England and its ruling elite over the invading Spanish forces. The rejection of any Spanish influence on dress in this portrait in favour of exaggerated Anglo-French fashions was a deliberate political manoeuvre on behalf of Elizabeth and the artist. Anglo-Spanish relations, which had always been hostile during Elizabeth's reign, began to sour in the late 1570s, eventually leading to the expulsion of the Spanish ambassador Mendoza in 1584 and the Armada of 1588.[21] It is no coincidence then that the Spanish fashions that had dominated Elizabeth's wardrobe in the early years of her reign began to disappear from her accounts during this time. April 1575 was the last time that a 'Spanish Gown' was ordered for the queen and in April 1580 her warrants instructed her tailor, Walter Fyshe, to make a French gown by reusing fabrics and sleeves from an older Spanish gown.[22] As Chapter 1 demonstrated, it was also around this time that French farthingales began to feature prominently in portraits of the queen. While Spanish leather, silk and lace continued to be used during the rest of her reign, it appears that by 1590 Elizabeth had made a conscious decision to discard recognizably Spanish

Fig. 2.3 *George Gower, The Armada Portrait, c. 1588, oil on panel, Woburn Abbey, Bedfordshire, UK.*

styles in favour of French ones. Rejecting Spanish influence in her own wardrobe, and wearing styles influenced by Spain's other enemy in this portrait, therefore served to add further insult to injury.

French farthingales became so emblematic of Elizabethan fashions that various scholars have suggested that they were considered old-fashioned and backward-looking garments by the Jacobean era.[23] Yet large farthingales did persist among those courtiers who set the fashionable trends in the Jacobean court such as Anne of Denmark (see Fig. 2.4) and her daughter Elizabeth. While Anne certainly may have initially used these garments alongside others left in the royal wardrobe by Elizabeth to stress the continuity between their reigns, her continual wearing of the wheel farthingale throughout her reign in England was more indicative of her following of continental fashion trends, as demonstrated by portraits of the French queen Marie de' Medici (see Fig. 2.5) and numerous prints of wealthy Dutch townspeople (see Fig. 2.6).[24] Farthingales therefore continued to play an integral role in reinforcing notions of aristocratic bodily behaviour at the Jacobean court.

Fig. 2.4 *Johannes Wierix,* Double portrait of James I of England and Anne of Denmark, c. *1601–5, engraving, Rijksmuseum, Amsterdam.*

Fig. 2.5 *Frans Pourbus the Younger,* Marie de' Medici, Queen of France, c. *1606–7, oil on canvas, Bilbao Fine Arts Museum.*

Fig. 2.6 *Jan van de Velde (II),* Fashionable Dressed Couple, c. *1610–20, etching, Rijksmuseum, Amsterdam.*

While farthingales commanded attention due to their size, bodies were worn by European courtiers in more subtle displays of power and authority. Courtiers were expected to conform to certain ideals regarding comportment and behaviour as the aristocratic body was a civilized body, one that was not the product of nature but shaped by political, social and cultural forces.[25] Royal courts during the sixteenth century, influenced both directly and indirectly by Baldassare Castiglione's *The Book of the Courtier* (1528), emphasized what Castiglione termed *sprezzatura,* or acting and speaking elegantly without revealing effort or thought.[26] This did not just encompass the ability to disguise what one really desired, felt, thought and intended, behind a mask of apparent reticence and nonchalance, but it also focused heavily on the body and on dress, particularly on self-presentation. One of the most important elements of *sprezzatura* was the idea of grace. All social levels during this period believed that there was a connection between outward appearances and inward qualities. For courtiers, these outward appearances were dictated by bodily grace.[27] In order for a courtier to create the desired social impression there had to be grace in all their actions, including bodily deportment and movement.[28] If one lacked the grace inherent to their station in life, they must pretend to have it. In doing so they had to conceal the trouble that they had gone to, so as to give the impression of gracefulness, in effect, conducting themselves with *sprezzatura.*

Bodily grace was overwhelmingly concerned with what Georges Vigarello has termed the 'upward training of the body', or rules of bodily deportment that focused on having and maintaining an upright posture.[29] From at least the Middle Ages, bad posture had been attributed to deformity and lack of proper deportment. However, during the sixteenth century there was a marked increase in writings that insisted upon a strict control over aristocratic posture, as to slouch showed arrogance. Sixteenth-century Italian treatises also stressed geometric and measured descriptions of the ideal (mainly male) body that was 'wonderfully desirous of beauty, proportion and decorum'. In order to achieve this body it was recommended that men should 'avoid as much as possible that [clothing], which is heavy, shapeless and deformed'.[30] The unstraightened body therefore lacked grace, one of the most desirable traits of a courtier, and diminished the rank and power of the elite, running the risk of associating them with deformity, laziness and an imperfect character.

Elite ideals therefore dictated that male and female bodies should be erect and physically restrained to project the proud virtues of the state and its ruling classes.[31] It is little wonder then that during the sixteenth century garments that quite literally embodied these ideas appeared in both men and

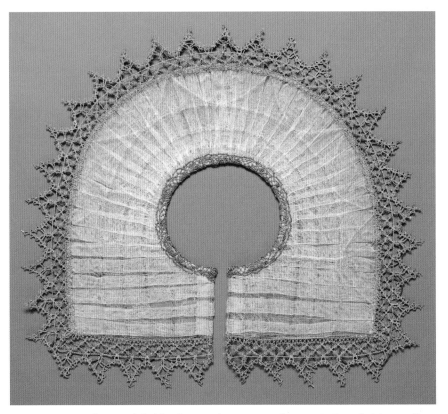

Fig. 2.7 *Wire Rebato with bobbin lace, early seventeenth century, French, Metropolitan Museum of Art, New York.*

women's wardrobes. Some were accessories worn by both genders, such as starched ruffs and standing collars that were supported by stiffened structures called *piccadills*, *underpropers* or *rebatos* (see Fig. 2.7). These accessories created a halo around the head as they were made from bright white, sometimes translucent, linen or silk that was often trimmed with expensive bobbin lace. Such neckwear forced wearers to keep their head held high as they slightly impeded normal neck and head movement, which could result in a rather haughty aristocratic appearance. Farthingale sleeves such as those worn by the queen in her *Armada Portrait* were also a common Elizabethan court fashion. These voluminous sleeves were shaped by the addition of whalebone and bents, and some early moderns joked that they resembled wings.[32] The sleeves of men's doublets could also be sewn with a bend at the elbow.[33] In both instances, these sleeves restricted movement and forced the wearer to adopt a graceful but imposing stance.

For women, gracefully wearing a farthingale required the wearer to walk in a more sedate way and to daintily rest her arms on the top of the farthingale to stabilize it, something that is depicted in most portraits from the period.[34] However, the primary garments that achieved these elite bodily ideas of femininity dictated by grace were bodies and busks. Upright or straight female bodies that were created by these foundation garments were constantly referenced during this period in relation to feminine beauty ideals. Elizabeth I was often praised for having this pleasing body shape by observers such as John Hayward, who wrote that the Queen 'was slender and straight'.[35] In 1625 an English–French grammar book, which contained scenarios from everyday life, stated, 'But what do you say of the lady. There is nothing in her but very hand some, she hath a very good face a straight body, she is richly clothed.'[36] Thomas Middleton's Jacobean play *Women Beware Women* (1657) also emphasized the desirability of a straight body in a potential wife from the elite. In the play a rich young heir named Ward and his servant Sordido discuss the qualities of an aristocratic wife, claiming that wives 'should be pretty, straight and slender'.[37] This passage also suggested that straight bodies signalled that a woman did not have congenital birth defects, which were clearly undesirable to prospective grooms and their families. Finally, Margaret Cavendish wrote in her *Sociable Letters* (1664) that there were 'Fashions of Grandeur, which are more for Grace, and Becoming, than for Ease, or Use' and this included gowns with long trains, high-heeled shoes and 'Straight Bodies'.[38] This affirms that ideas about straight bodies and grace continued to be held by elites throughout the seventeenth century and that foundation garments were created to achieve and maintain these ideals (see Fig. 2.8).

Vigarello's research has shown that males were also expected to conform to similar ideals, as men and boys were encouraged to effortlessly hold themselves upright to show grace.[39] Sartorially, this was achieved using doublets and jerkins. Like bodies, these garments were tight fitting around the torso and they were often bombast and sometimes even stiffened with whalebone. Several early seventeenth-century doublets in the Victoria and Albert Museum contain triangular belly-pieces made from pad stitched canvas, cork, or bents that kept in the belly, and one or two strips of whalebone placed either side

Fig. 2.8 *Wenceslaus Hollar,* Lady of the Court of England, *1643, etching, Rijksmuseum, Amsterdam. The upright graceful posture created by boned bodies is displayed in this etching of an English court lady.*

of the centre front opening to straighten the front of the garment (see Fig. 5.25).[40] The resulting effect was a geometric or triangular shaped torso that pulled back the shoulders and pushed the chest forward, forcing the wearer to maintain an upright posture in much the same way as bodies did for women.

The desired aristocratic posture created by the doublet is clearly visualized in a portrait of Prince Henry Frederick during a hunt by Robert Peak the Elder from 1603 (see Fig. 2.9). The young prince stands boldly sheathing his sword, his legs spread in typical regal fashion while his torso is upright, straight and controlled. The graceful figure cut by the prince is very similar to that of his sister (see Fig. 2.1), something that Henry Fitzgeffry's satirical poem *Satires and Satirical Epigrams* (1614) made clear when he referred to a man's doublet as containing 'Whalebone-bodies, for the better grace'.[41] Here Fitzgeffry pokes fun at elite men's fashions being similar to women's whalebone bodies, but exposes the fact that the aristocratic male body also conformed in many ways to the same expectations of bodily grace.

Although all members of the elite held these ideas about slender bodies, beauty and grace, not all women's foundation garments were the same. Tailoring and wardrobe records show that there

Fig. 2.9 *Robert Peake the Elder,* Henry Frederick, Prince of Wales, with Sir John Harington, in the Hunting Field, *1603, oil on canvas, Metropolitan Museum of Art, New York.*

were many variations in the types of fabrics used in the bodies of women of the elite. As with farthingales, the bodies of England's queens were usually made from luxurious fabrics. The wardrobe warrants of Elizabeth I and Henrietta Maria discussed in the previous chapter show that the bodies of both queens were regularly made from fabrics like silk satin, silk taffeta and silk velvet, and after 1590 stiffened with whalebone. The 1608 wardrobe inventory of Anne of Denmark also confirms that even those bodies that were described as 'made up plain' were made from materials like ash-coloured taffeta and yellow sarcenet.[42] An exception are purchases made by the Dowager Queen Catherine of Braganza for pairs of bodies of paduasoy stiffened with packthread in 1685.[43] Packthread produced garments that were much lighter and less stiff than those of whalebone, and as Catherine was now in her late forties, widowed and no longer had to sartorially assert her position as queen consort, it appears that she now preferred this more relaxed fit. The bodies of royal women were therefore usually made from luxurious fabrics and stiffened with whalebone to maintain a constant appearance of magnificence.

What about other elite women though? Some elite women clearly did own fashionable bodies made from expensive fabrics and used these garments to proclaim their beauty and social position. A year after the appearance of French bodies in the wardrobe warrants of Elizabeth I, the family members of Sir Nathaniel Bacon, son of Sir Nicholas Bacon and brother of Francis Bacon, were also provided with French bodies by their Norfolk tailors.[44] Although Bacon was a member of the Norfolk gentry who was more interested in being a county magnate than a courtier, it is evident that not only were his wife and children at the cutting edge of fashion, and that their provincial tailors were well equipped to provide these garments, but they were clearly concerned with maintaining the same aristocratic ideals of grace as those who frequented the courts.

One of the earliest visual depictions of a pair of bodies in England comes from a portrait of Elizabeth Wriothesley (née Vernon), Countess of Southampton, who, in a state of undress, is depicted brushing her long hair with a comb at her toilette in her bedchamber (see Fig. 2.10). Elizabeth was a lady-in-waiting to Elizabeth I who had married Henry Wriothesley, third Earl of Southampton, without permission, subsequently falling from the queen's favour in 1598. In the portrait, underneath an embroidered waistcoat, Elizabeth wears a pair of front-lacing bodies made of pink silk and with visible boning channels, which likely resembled the carnation-coloured pair of French bodies ordered by Elizabeth I in 1590. The bodies are pointed to the embroidered petticoat skirt through eyelet holes in both garments, as small pink points are visible under the sheer pink skirts of the bodies. The silk French bodies, combined with the ruff, intricately embroidered petticoat skirt and waistcoat, as well as the jewellery on her table and the ermine-lined robe or cushion on her bed, all display her grace, wealth and high social status.

Other elite women had to consider the use of expensive fabrics in their foundation garments more carefully though. The 1618 wardrobe inventories of Lady Jane Stanhope demonstrate this.[45] At the

Fig. 2.10 Elizabeth Vernon, Countess of Southampton, *c. 1600, oil on panel, Buccleuch Collection, Boughton House, Northamptonshire.*

time of her death, Jane's wardrobe contained taffeta waistcoats, silver tinsel and velvet doublets and bodies with sleeves (bodices) of cloth of silver – all statement outer garments that were made to be seen. However, the same entry also records a 'pair of Canvas boddis Covered with fustian' and 'a pair of striped Canvas bodies' – foundation garments made from durable cheaper fabrics like canvas and fustian – as well as 'buckram Rowles'.[46] Like the fustian farthingale that belonged to Thomasine Petre, these bodies and rolls were made to shape the silhouette but not to be seen, and so they were constructed out of plainer fabrics. Thus, it was not just queens or high-ranking courtiers who used foundation garments to conform to ideas of uprightness and grace, but many other elite women also strove to fashion their appearances with foundation garments of varying degrees of luxury.

The desire of non-courtly gentlewomen to wear bodies stiffened with whalebone is perhaps unsurprising if we consider that these garments also aided other early modern visions of femininity concerned with beauty such as slender bodies, narrow waists and small busts.[47] From the sixteenth to the eighteenth centuries the ideal dressed court woman had a flat stomach and slender tapering torso.

Due to the conical shape and design of bodies, tight lacing was not achievable, although a small reduction of waist size was possible. Instead, waists appeared reduced due to the flat conical shape that bodies gave the torso and the use of the farthingale.[48] In 1577 the Venetian ambassador at the French court, Jerome Lippomano, remarked that:

> French women have extremely slender waists: they like to swell out their gowns from the waist downwards by gathers of fabric and farthingales and other artifices … Over the chemise they wear a bodice they call 'corps piqué' which makes their shape more delicate and more slender.[49]

The combination of 'corps piqué' (bodies with visible stitched boning channels) and a large farthingale created an optical illusion that visually created a smaller waist, as the tailor in the play *Eastward Ho* explains to his client that her farthingale 'twill. . . make your waist so small'.[50]

As Tudor and Elizabethan portraiture reveals, for much of the sixteenth century small busts were also desirable. This was not necessarily a sixteenth-century phenomenon. For much of the preceding fourteenth and fifteenth centuries in England small pert breasts were linked to beauty standards that idealized the youthful, virginal and chaste body unmarred by wantonness or reproduction.[51] Beauty treatments that claimed to give users this desirable breast size and texture were regularly promoted in treatises and recipe books, and those modern-looking linen bras found at Lengberg Castle indicate that some breast support was common.[52] Kim Phillips has argued that these bras are suggestive of the fact that large breasts were perceived to be unattractive and disgraceful, so women used these garments to restrain them.[53] By the sixteenth century, when new ways of shaping the female body were adopted, these new foundation garments therefore gave early moderns even more ways to achieve the ideal of small breasts.

In sixteenth-century Italy it appears that breasts were often compressed to achieve the ideal upper body.[54] Holbein's portraits of women in the court of King Henry VIII also show that even the largest bust was rendered slight and barely defined.[55] Experimentation by costume interpreters at Hampton Court Palace has shown that stiffening the bodies of the kirtle was vital to suppressing large busts in order to achieve this Holbein look of the 1540s.[56] Clothing of the Elizabethan era such as the surviving bodies on the effigy of the queen were also designed in such a way as to push down the bust (see Fig. 1.13). Unlike bodies of later decades, the placement of boning in the bodies is not angled over the bust. So rather than accommodating, or even pushing the breasts upwards, the boning in this garment flattens the chest area. This intentional design feature was clearly observable in my own reconstruction experiment using this garment (see Fig. 2.11). Even by the mid-seventeenth century when bodies enhanced the bust, as seen on my models (see Fig. 3.8), high firm breasts were associated with fashion, health and youth.[57] Bodies were therefore vital to elite ideals of early modern beauty that dictated that women should be slender and straight with small busts.

Fig. 2.11 *Author's reconstruction of the Elizabeth I effigy bodies and French wheel farthingale. The style of the Elizabethan bodies flattens the breasts, and the centre-front of the garment sits over the farthingale creating a fashionable tilt.*

Finally, foundation garments also served a very practical purpose for women in court-related performances. The farthingale was a practical garment in dance, as it helped to keep a woman's skirts away from her legs where she could otherwise easily become tangled and trip.[58] During the Elizabethan and Jacobean age, one of the most popular court dances was the *Volta*, which had come to England from France. At first the dance was considered rather risqué due to moves which involved sections of kicks and a lift where the male partner raised the woman up by her waist or back in a moving turn, as is depicted in a ball scene at the Valois court (see Fig. 2.12).[59] In his dancing manual *Orchésographie* (1589), Thoinot Arbeau described this move:

When you want to turn, let free the left hand of the demoiselle, & cast your left arm on her back, taking and pressing her with your left hand by the waist above her right hip, and at the same time cast your right hand underneath her busk to help her to jump when pushing her before you with your left thigh.[60]

Just as Arbeau describes, in modern reconstructions of the Volta the dance partner places their right hand underneath the bottom of the bodice where the busk is located and using this rigid front as leverage, they lift their partner up into the air while their other hand supports the small of the back.[61] The rigidity of bodies therefore provided a dance partner with something to hold onto during this turning movement and it would also have been much more comfortable for the woman.

An elite woman's femininity was therefore a performance that was staged visually through her clothed body. To achieve this idealized female form, fashionable courtly ladies devised ways to create it artificially. The most vital or even constitutive elements of this elite vision of femininity were

Fig. 2.12 Ball at the Valois Court, c. *1580, oil on canvas, musée des Beaux-Arts, Rennes. The couple in the centre of this painting dance the Volta. The male dance partner's hand is placed on the bottom of the woman's bodice in order to lift her up using her busk.*

farthingales and bodies, foundation garments that were developed in the courts of Europe. These garments reshaped the female silhouette, creating a uniform fashionable ideal that conformed to the elite cultural aesthetics of the period, where women displayed their wealth and status through large farthingales, and showed their good breeding and inner grace, as well as beauty, through an upright bodily deportment and slender torso.

Critiques of fashion and the artificial body

While courtiers conformed to court aesthetics through artificiality in dress, early seventeenth-century writers were more concerned with the ability to see through appearances. In the eyes of many moralists, clothing was not intended for flamboyant show. Instead 'habit' should be 'used as an Ornament of Decency; without the least border or Edging of Vanity'.[62] Decency was achieved by wearing clothing that was considered, as the frontispiece of Richard Brathwaite's *The English Gentlewoman* (1631) stated, 'comely not gaudy'.[63] In other words, it was achieved by avoiding clothing such as bodies and farthingales that were conceived for ostentatious display in the courts. During the seventeenth century, Anglicans and Puritans alike shared the same attitude and general worldview when it came to many issues, including adornment.[64] The dislike of ornamentation and flamboyance was widespread in early modern England and can be traced back to Reformation aesthetics of non-adornment, as well as ideas about the temptations of luxury, that pervaded the beliefs of all English Protestants at the time.

One of the main charges against women who wore elaborate clothing and used cosmetics during this period was vanity. Moralists considered vanity a predominantly feminine vice and during the early modern period vanity was associated with narcissism and self-idolatry, as well as the sin of pride. Popular literature from the beginning of the seventeenth century, such as cheap illustrated ballads that were sold on the street or stuck to tavern walls, often poked fun at the vanity of women and their seemingly unquenchable thirst for the newest and best fashions, no matter the cost. Bodies and farthingales visually structured elite female fashions and so these garments were mentioned in many popular writings. One broadside ballad titled *The Lamentation of a New Married Man* stated, 'A new Gown she must have: / A dainty fine Rebato / About her neck so brave: / French bodies, with a Farthingale / She never sins to crave'.[65] The groom of this ballad laments his marriage because, among other things, his new bride seems determined to spend all his money on the latest fashions, such as French bodies and farthingales, with no regard for his wishes or his pockets. An earlier domestic tract stated that 'The duties of the husband is to get money and provision: and of the Wives, not vainly to spend it'.[66] If they did, wives disobeyed both their husbands and the gender norms set down for married women by God. Like the wife in this ballad, women who consumed these items were commonly portrayed in literature as being flippant and vain when it came to their appearances.

Puritan satirist Stephen Gosson's *Pleasant Quips for Upstart Newfangled Gentlewomen* (1595), which was dedicated to speaking out against 'the pride of vainglorious Women' and 'the Fantastical Foreign Toys, daily used in Women's apparel', is an example of the nasty overtones that more satirical texts could take.[67] From smocks to busks and even ruffs, no item of women's dress escaped the wrath of Gosson:

> If barrelled bums were full of Ale,
> they might well serve Tom Tapsters turn:
> But yielding nought but filth and stale,
> no loss it were if they did burn.
> Their liquors doth so smell and stink,
> That no man can it use for drink.[68]

Here Gosson linked farthingales to the wooden barrels that held alcohol. However, instead of serving a useful function like a barrel, he concluded that they were nothing but filth, linking these foundation garments to the idea of futility and corruption. In Gosson's mind the farthingale was pointless and the women who wore them were also useless, as they were too consumed by their own vanity.

One source that summarizes moralizing attitudes towards the farthingale on both sides of the English Channel is the Flemish engraving from 1600, *The Vanity of Women*, attributed to Maerten de Vos (see Fig. 1.8). The engraving depicts two fashionable women being made ready in a shop of 'vanity, & pride & other such tricks'. The woman on the right is having a French farthingale roll fastened around her waist and signs with writing in both French and Dutch hang on the walls. One sign above the seamstress in the background of the scene reads, 'Come beautiful women with skinny buttocks: / Quickly we shall make them round and merry.'[69] This sign criticizes not only the vanity of women who wished to conform to the aesthetic ideal of beauty that the farthingale created, but also points out that the farthingale could recreate the body from that intended by nature – by turning skinny women into voluptuous ones. The engraving also depicts the women being outfitted with masks and a sign reads, 'Adorn me with the ugly and dirty mask: / Because ugliness is in my main beauty.'[70] Full-faced masks, or vizards, were used to shade the faces of elite women from the sun, as their pale skin reflected their position in life. However, masks were often criticized for allowing women to deceive those around them or for making women look like monsters.[71] This engraving serves to reiterate the common assertion that dress should reflect inward decency and morality, rather than be used for deception or ostentatious show.

Bodies were similarly criticized for vanity. In France, Michel de Montaigne wrote that fashionable women became 'slender in the waist' in order to 'have a straight spagnolised body, what pinching, what girdling, what cringing, will they not endure … that their very skin and quick flesh is eaten and consumed to the bones; whereby they sometimes work their own death'.[72] Montaigne portrayed the bodices of gowns as a type of early modern torture device, stating that women who vainly desired to obtain a 'straight spagnolised body' with a slender waist laced themselves tightly, often to the detriment of their own health. In the 1613 English edition of Montaigne's work, translator John Florio made explicit what caused such damage: bodies that contained 'iron-plates, with whalebones, and other such trash'.[73] By purchasing items such as masks, farthingales and bodies to conceal physical flaws, women automatically signified their inner ugliness in their vain attempts to use them for beauty.

Historians have noted that early modern criticisms of fashion were usually directed equally at both men and women.[74] Elite men of the courts were also targeted for their excesses in apparel, usually their large breeches and slashed doubles. However, subtle differences did exist. Many of the critiques levelled at women had their origins in religious ideas that stressed the inferiority and deviousness of women. Men who occupied themselves with fashion were usually perceived as foolish and at risk of spiritual malaise, or simply told that, as the more rational sex, they should know better.[75] Women, on the other hand, as daughters of Eve who had caused mankind's fall from Eden and subsequent acknowledgement of nakedness, were seen to belong to a tradition of temptation that threatened the stability of social order. Clothing was an invention of the sin that women had caused, and women who were lured by rich clothing were demonstrating their inferiority to men and the weak nature of their sex. Women's clothing was also much more likely to be discussed in terms of vanity because it was technically superfluous, as most women could not hold positions of power. Men's clothing, on the other hand, indicated a real social position, profession or rank and so was treated with more respect if used appropriately.[76] Women's clothing was therefore more likely to be discussed in relation to notions of the moral inferiority of the female sex.

Pride was a moral weakness commonly associated with women who were biblically and culturally expected to be meek and submissive. The expensive and extravagant nature of farthingales led to these undergarments receiving harsh criticism in relation to pride. As early as 1552, these foundation garments were publicly condemned in sermons such as one delivered by Bishop Hugh Latimer on St Stephen's Day in Grimsthorp. In this Protestant address he considered the birth of Christ and Mary's obedience to God. He criticized the women of Bethlehem who had 'farthingales and such fine gear' but who would not go to comfort Mary in the stable. He contrasted these selfish women of 'fine raiment' to the selfless and humble Mary who 'had not much fine gear' and 'had never a farthingale, for she used no such superfluities as our fine damsels do nowadays'. To Latimer, farthingales were 'nothing else but an instrument of pride' and he instructed that 'every Godly woman should set them aside'.[77]

The belief that farthingales made women unchristianly selfish was still held some fifty years later when M. Thomas Carew delivered a sermon in 1603 in which he stated that 'The want of religion in many women is seen in their apparel, their hearts being as hollow as their verdugales, their minds being as light as their feathers'.[78] The previously mentioned possession of thirteen-year-old Margaret Hurdman was believed to have been caused by the spirit of pride, which taught her 'all the tricks of pride' and caused her to express 'by words and gestures' her desire for the fashionable attire of 'proud' women.[79] Similarly, a 1609 broadside detailing the story of a monstrous birth in France made the connection between farthingales and pride. The broadside detailed how the pregnant wife of a 'poor labouring man' asked her wealthy and fashionable sister for help but was rebuffed and called a beggar. After the incident she gave birth to 'three Monsters', babies who all had deformities that resembled the fashionable attire of her rich sister. Strikingly, one of these deformities was a 'fleshly Vardingale about the middle', which was shown to resemble a French wheel farthingale in the woodcut featured in the broadside (see Fig. 2.13). Such deformities that resembled fashionable attire were God's punishment for having a proud and unnatural sister whose preoccupation with fashion and status overtook her Christian duty of charity.[80] Foundation garments were therefore popular targets for moralists and religious leaders as they were indicative of vanity and prodigality which widely corrupted the land 'with intolerable pride'.[81]

Bodies and farthingales also came under scrutiny because they reshaped the female silhouette from that intended by nature: women who wore them were deforming God's vision by altering their naturally perfect state.[82] The most damning publication against bodies was Bulwer's previously mentioned treatise *Anthropometamorphosis* (1653), which argued against clothing and ornamentation from all over the world that altered the body from the natural form that God had created. In his book, Bulwer devoted a whole chapter to 'Dangerous Fashions, and desperate Affectations about the Breast and Waist' and critiqued trends that idealized straightness and smallness, stating that young virgins:

> ... are led blindfold by Custom to a fashion pernicious beyond imagination; who thinking a slender waste a great beauty, strive all that they possibly can by straight-lacing themselves to attain unto a wand-like smallness of waste, never thinking themselves fine enough.[83]

Like Montaigne before him, Bulwer also wondered why women would voluntarily subject themselves to something that he associated with prison, as he berated women for using the 'deadly artifice' of bodies to narrow the breasts and 'shut up their Waists in a Whale-bone prison' (see Fig. 2.14).[84]

Although Bulwer's critique is couched in the language of health, his further assertion that forming and shaping oneself according to one's own will was also blasphemous indicates that he did not care so much for the health of the body but rather the health of the soul.[85] Such criticisms also reflected a pushback against what was perceived as women expressing too much agency over their own bodies. Similar debates over nature and artifice were also had in relation to cosmetics, as women were thought

Fig. 2.13 *'Title Page' of* A True Relation of the birth of three Monsters in the City of Namen in Flanders *(1608), Folger Shakespeare Library, Washington, DC.*

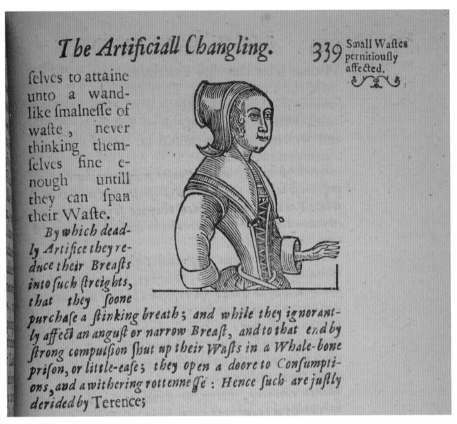

The Artificiall Changling.   339 Small Wastes pernitiously affected.

selves to attaine unto a wand-like smalnesse of waste, never thinking them-selves fine e-nough untill they can span their Waste.

By which dead-ly Artifice they re-duce their Breasts into such streights, that they soone purchase a stinking breath; and while they ignorant-ly affect an angust or narrow Breast, and to that end by strong compulsion shut up their Wasts in a Whale-bone prison, or little-ease; they open a doore to Consumpti-ons, and a withering rottennesse : Hence such are justly derided by Terence;

Fig. 2.14 *'Small Waists perniciously affected', in John Bulwer,* Anthropometamorphosis *(1653), Wellcome Library, London.*

to paint their faces to conceal physical flaws or increase their beauty. Frances E. Dolan has argued that many of these debates surrounding cosmetics reveal tensions between female agency and larger social forces that sought to control their representation. Cosmetics gave women licence to be creators or manipulators of their own bodies in defiance of God and male authority. While men were also criticized for doing the same, such power in the hands of women was viewed more negatively.[86] Those women who engaged in cosmetics and fanciful fashions were not just subjecting their bodies to torture but actively defying God, who had created them in his vision, and so they would be judged in heaven by their Creator.

Farthingales were also criticized for shaping women's bodies in a way that deviated from God's creation. The text at the bottom of the Flemish engraving *The Vanity of Women* (see Fig. 1.8) linked farthingales with sinfulness and the devil, as it warned women that garments of vanity and pride 'which do adorn stinking flesh' would ensure that women would 'go with the devils to the flames of hell'.[87] The tailor and seamstress who are making masks and farthingales are portrayed as helpers of the devil, as they possess horns, strangely shaped tongues and animal-like faces, portrayals not dissimilar to depictions of the devil or his servants during this period. Similar links were commonly made between farthingales and the devil in early modern England. In 1552, Bishop Hugh Latimer preached that farthingales were cunning inventions of the devil.[88] Later, in the play *Mad World, My Masters* (1605) by Calvinist playwright Thomas Middleton, the adulterous sinner Penitent is confronted with a Succubus that tries to seduce him by taking the form of his mistress. He successfully resists the Succubus and this demonic being is described as wearing 'The Farthingale above the Navel, all; As if the fashion were his own invention.'[89]

Such extreme reactions to artificiality in dress are probably best captured by dramatist Ben Jonson who stated, 'Nothing is fashionable, till it be deformed.'[90] To many, these fashions did not enhance the aristocratic body, but rather, they deformed it. Discussions of clothing that changed the shape of the body often underlay early modern fears about the origins of deformity, which they believed lead to monstrosity.[91] In the eyes of such moralists, these fashions acted to dehumanize rather than fashion an individual as they were reduced into a 'monster, machine or body'.[92] One broadside ballad from 1620, titled *Jone is a good as my Lady*, implied that clothes not only made women's bodies monstrous, but also that they made them subhuman. The ballad describes women in the town as wearing 'painted clothes the body shapes', making them look like 'fantastic Apes'.[93] Mass-produced woodcuts printed alongside the ballad give an idea as to what clothes it is referring to, as they depict women wearing ruffs, straight bodies, ballooning sleeves and different types of farthingales. According to the ballad these garments made women ugly like apes.

Another mid-century broadside ballad titled, *The Fantastic Age: OR, The Anatomy of Englands Vanity*, called on many tropes from the period, claiming that both men and women had 'grown strange and Phebe-like they often change'. The writer of the ballad criticized men for embracing fashionable dress as they should know better, while women were accused of nagging their husbands, fathers and friends to buy them fashionable goods, making them vain, proud and devoid of 'all thoughts of piety'. Importantly, each verse of the ballad concludes with the lines, 'O monsters, / Neutral monsters, / leave these apish toys.'[94] Once again, woodcuts show that the types of clothing targeted by this ballad are those that changed the body, such as large ruffs, whalebone sleeves, foundation garments and bombast doublets.

Ape metaphors were persistently used in popular literature by moralizing writers not just because they dehumanized their subjects but also because they decried those who uncritically followed or imitated others, which symbolized a lack of control and judgement, making humans more reminiscent of apes than men.[95] The constant reiteration that body-altering fashions like bodies and farthingales were 'apish toys' and that the women who wore them were 'fantastic apes' didn't just paint fashionable women as monsters or unthinking monkeys, but the comparisons between followers of fashion and apes emphasized human folly.[96] Following fashionable dress that deformed God's creation therefore made men weak and foolish and magnified the female vices of vanity and pride.

Anti-court sentiments and disputed visions of femininity

During the sixteenth century, court authors like Castiglione had directly connected outward appearances to good breeding and a refined character that was civilized and polished by culture, and these ideas had come to define aristocratic display across Europe by the end of that century. In England, such ideas passed from the Tudor courts to the Stuart courts and women continued to use garments such as bodies and farthingales to adhere to aristocratic notions of bodily behaviour. However, during the seventeenth century the voices of moralists became increasingly hostile to aristocratic styles, arguing that dress should mirror a woman's inner soul and humility, reflecting the increasing Puritan overtones of the century.[97] Writers, who were overwhelmingly male and from the lower gentry and middling sorts, pursued these objectives by focusing not just on the vanity and pride of women in relation to fashion as previously discussed, but also by stressing a dichotomy between nature and artifice. Specifically, moralists linked the natural with those pious, submissive and humble female bodies untouched by cosmetics or extravagant dress, while notions of artificiality were linked to monstrous aristocratic female bodies shaped by the form-altering fashions of a morally dubious royal court. Although some commentators entertained ideas of artificiality, most moralists agreed with the sentiments voiced by Phillip Stubbes in *The Anatomy of Abuses*, where the author stated that 'when they have all these goodly robes upon them, women seem to be the smallest part of themselves, not natural women, but artificial Women, not Women of flesh, & blood, but rather puppets.'[98]

Attempts to regulate fashion had long been an objective of moralists, particularly those from religious or monastic communities. However, several historians have noted that moralizing attitudes towards dress were particularly strong in the first half of the seventeenth century in England. Such views not only suggest the beginnings of a struggle for sartorial supremacy between the different levels of society, but these attitudes may also have contributed to the political and cultural climate of the century in which anti-royalist and anti-court sentiments thrived.[99] Indeed, those debates over fashionable dress that have been examined so far in this chapter were part of larger disputes of the period that increasingly utilized the tropes of antithesis and mirroring. Contrasting good with evil, man with woman, king with tyrant, and the country with the court, were all common ways that early modern people attempted to understand their world. For seventeenth-century writers who were increasingly influenced by Puritan and anti-royalist thoughts, discerning truth from falsehood and vice from virtue became ever more important. The deepest fear of this period, voiced by many of the authors already discussed, was that outside appearances were artificial and did not reflect the inner moral qualities of a person.[100] This made sixteenth-century court culture, which had championed ideas such as sprezzatura and self-fashioning, the very antithesis of wider seventeenth-century political and cultural thought. Visually, clothing was the most obvious personal display of court culture; bodies and farthingales were the most recognizable garments that constituted the courtly female form. Foundation garments that reshaped the female body therefore received vehement critiques as they were indicative of the artificiality and vanity of court women, pursued at the expense of their humanity, their inner civility and of their souls.[101]

In addition to using critiques of court fashions to contrast natural and artificial female bodies, and thus pious, humble women against vain, proud women, early modern writers also pitted visions of the English body against the foreign body. England's obsession with continental fashions and lack of distinct national dress was a theme reiterated during the sixteenth and seventeenth centuries. In 1542 an engraving in Andrew Borde's *The First Book of the Introduction of Knowledge* mockingly depicted a naked Englishmen who was bewildered by the various foreign dress options available to him.[102] Two decades later, William Harrison remarked that 'the fantastical folly of [the English] nation' was that 'nothing is more constant in England than inconstancy of attire'.[103] The previously mentioned ballad, *The Fantastic Age*, also quipped that 'English man or woman now / I'll make excuse for neither, / Composed are I know not how, / of many shreds together: / Italian, Spaniard, French, and Dutch, / of each of these they have a touch.'[104] Such notions about the mixture of continental influences in English dress were exacerbated by the fact that foreign royal brides often introduced new court fashions to England. As discussed in the previous chapter, Catherine of Aragon is credited with introducing the Spanish farthingale to England at the start of the sixteenth century, which she wore intermittently during her time as queen.

While Catherine made a conscious effort to adopt the styles of her new court, the French bride of King Charles I, Henrietta Maria, did not. When Henrietta Maria came to England in 1625, the new English queen seemed determined not to forget her French sartorial roots. Alongside a retinue that included her ladies, servants and Catholic priests, she insisted on bringing with her two French tailors, George Gelin and Jacques Bardou, and a French farthingale-maker named John Huguitt.[105] Although portraits of the queen painted during the 1630s portray her in typically English dress (see Fig. 2.15), Erin Griffey has argued that there was a notable disjunction between these formal portraits and the French garments that the queen ordered and wore, with the contents of her actual wardrobe more closely resembling the fashions of her natal land.[106] Indeed, the farthingale-maker Huguitt and his English successor John Ager made 'Smale Rowles' for the queen that resembled those 'bourlets' made in the French court for Henrietta's sister-in-law, the French Queen Anne of Austria.[107] The queen's royal wardrobe records show that she used all her garments, including these small rolls, to maintain a sense of French identity at the Stuart court – even if her portraits depicted her in English styles to appease the growing body of royal critics.

Anti-court writings that viewed extravagant dress as symptomatic of the moral weakness of the court animated the discourses of the early seventeenth century as England saw an increasing divide between the court and the rest of society.[108] Conduct literature began to address men and women of

Fig. 2.15 *Anthony van Dyck*, Queen Henrietta Maria with Sir Jeffrey Hudson, *1633, oil on canvas, National Gallery of Art, Washington, DC.*

the lower gentry and middling sorts, warning them against lavish spending and corruption like that of the courts, and authors such as Brathwaite began to question 'how a wise state should employ so much time in inventing variety of disguises to disfigure their shape'.[109] Bodies and farthingales were all fashions adopted from the courts of continental Europe, so reproaches of foundation garments should also be understood as criticisms of what it meant to be or to look English. On the one hand, there was the idea that was wedded to continental fashions and politics, where foreign and sometimes Catholic brides, such as Henrietta Maria, brought with them their clothing, artisans, customs, and courtiers. While another notion was concerned with the values of pure country simplicity that seemed to bespeak the true civil English ideology. Debates about court fashions such as foundation garments therefore surpassed simplistic notions of feminine weakness and vanity; they became part of national discussions in the decades leading up to the English Civil Wars about what it was to be English and where the monarchy and royal courts sat within these visions of England.

Conclusion

Foundation garments provoked debates over beauty or vanity and kindled wider disputes over nature and artifice, which in turn highlighted contrasting early modern ideals of bodily performance, spectatorship and control. In the English courts, bodies and farthingales created an ideal courtly female body that complied with aristocratic notions of wealth, refinement, grace and a sound moral character defined by good breeding and self-control. In the eyes of ever more vocal moralists, however, these garments signified the exact opposite – vanity, monstrousness and lack of religious piety. More importantly though, the intense criticism of these garments on the grounds of vanity, pride and monstrosity during the first half of the seventeenth century reveal that moralists, predominantly male, were attempting to assert a regime of embodied femininity, which focused on humble dress, religious piety and modesty that did not deform the natural female body created by God. These critics not only tried to assert sartorial supremacy on the female silhouette in early seventeenth-century England, but their campaign belonged to wider social, political and religious upheaval of the period leading up to the English Civil Wars that criticized the court and courtiers. However, as we will find in the next chapter, the meanings of foundation garments for women transcended the moralizing voices of critics and women did not always conform to the visions of femininity that were dictated by men.

3

The socially mobile body
Consumption of foundation garments by middling and common women, 1560–1650

Faith sir, our Country girls are a kin to your London Courtiers, every month sick of a new fashion, the horning busk and silken bride laces are in good request with the Parsons wife, your huge poking stick, and french periwig, with Chamber-maids, and waiting-gentlewomen, now your Puritans poker is not so huge, but somewhat longer, a long slender poking stick is the all in all with your Suffolk Puritan, your silk band, half farthingales, and changeable Fore-parts are common, not a wench of thirteen but wears a changeable forepart.[1]

As outlined in the introduction to this book, attempting to stratify early modern England's population into neat classes or sorts is a rather complicated endeavour. However, there was a very clear group with elite status who held political and social power through birth, marriage or royal appointment and it was this group who developed and first wore foundation garments in the royal courts of Europe. Yet as Thomas Heywood made clear in his play *If You Know Not Me, You Know Nobody* (1606), by the end of the reign of Elizabeth I the commodities most desired by English country girls were those worn by London's courtiers, including busks and farthingales.[2] As explored in Chapter 2, by the start of the seventeenth century the writings of many male moralists in England juxtaposed the ostentatious dress of the corrupted courtier with the humble dress of the non-court woman, revealing how debates about the use of foundation garments were framed by power struggles between differing visions of femininity. Yet the ideas preached by moralists about how women from different social backgrounds should look did not always translate so neatly into reality.

Many studies of sixteenth- and seventeenth-century dress focus primarily on the English elites as, understandably, much surviving evidence relates to them. Focusing on such a small social group though can skew our understanding of certain dress objects and inadvertently dismiss the realities of who was really wearing what. This has led many to assume that non-elite English women during these centuries did not own or wear foundation garments.[3] It is increasingly obvious though that this was not the case, as several historians have begun to focus on the dress of the lower sorts.[4] They argue that although the elites of society generally had better access to the latest fashionable innovations, those below this status were actually quite receptive to fashionable change and tried to incorporate many fashionable garments into their wardrobes, whether it be in original or modified form, in what could be considered appropriation rather than simply emulation.[5] While much of this new research focuses on the Italian and German experience, these general observations are also applicable to sixteenth- and seventeenth-century England, where those of the middling and common sorts were known to aspire to sartorial display through colour, fabric choice, trimmings and accessories.[6]

By *middling sorts* I refer to those of the lower gentry, yeomen, merchants, craftspeople and educated professionals in towns and cities such as lawyers and clerks.[7] Although social mobility was constant and recognized, these people made up between 30 and 50 per cent of the population in early modern England.[8] Whilst this category is broadly defined – standards of living varied significantly between people of the same profession and definitions of what constituted *middling* varied between county, between town and city, and even between individual circumstances – these groups were usually termed the 'better sorts' by contemporaries.[9] *Common sorts* refers to those people who ranked below these better sorts and who were, at the time, referred to as 'the poorer, meaner, vulgar, baser' sorts.[10] These were people with little wealth and no title, such as those tradespeople with low incomes, the working poor such as labourers and lowly domestic servants, poor country folk, as well as vagrants. Although these *sorts* are by no means rigid constructs, they are useful to think about ways that both dress and gender were negotiated in relation to social status during the sixteenth and seventeenth centuries.

This chapter explores how foundation garments contributed to the process of social emulation and distinction in England among the middling and common sorts between the years 1590 and 1650. It shows that a much wider range of women than has been previously addressed consumed foundation garments in England during this period. This consumption was accelerated by an expanding second-hand clothing trade and ready-made clothing market, as well as increased access to raw materials such as baleen. Foundation garments were used by non-elite women to make visual statements about advancements in social status, which was based on wealth and moveable property rather than birthright or inherited land. However, emulating the same fashionable silhouette as their social superiors sometimes led to an unease over how foundation garments could blur the social hierarchies of women's bodies. As a result, these women often trod a fine line between using these garments to display social mobility and being ridiculed by those both above and below for doing so. Just as bodies, busks and farthingales were used by the courtiers of England to shape elite displays of femininity, foundation garments helped shape and define often ambiguous social hierarchies and notions of femininity for middling and common sorts women in late sixteenth- and early seventeenth-century England too.

Evidence of consumption of foundation garments by the middling and common sorts

Unlike women of the nobility whose records were more readily preserved and are easily accessible, it is much harder to get a grasp on the lives of women of the middling and common sorts before the mid-seventeenth century. One way that the material lives of these women has been uncovered in recent years is through the examination of probate wills and inventories. These were legal documents that were made upon the death of a person and outlined not only inheritance and debts, but also all the items in that person's possession. In England, inventories were required by law from at least 1520 and were completed by appraisers who were usually people who had knowledge of the correct value of household items.[11] While these documents can tell us much about the material goods owned by men and women during the early modern period, they can also pose challenges.

In order for a will or inventory to be made, one had to have enough money or moveable property worth recording, so the poorest of society are not represented.[12] The majority of women's probate inventories relate to either spinsters and widows, as married women's property belonged to their husbands, although married women's wills are common.[13] As inventories only list the possessions owned by a woman days after her death, they do not contain any information on when or how items were acquired. Items may also have been removed by the deceased's family or friends between the date of death and the date of the inventory, so there is no way of knowing how complete a probate inventory is.[14] In the case of London, many wills and inventories are damaged and very few have survived from the period 1583–1640. By the late seventeenth century, clothing was also less likely to have been itemized and individually accounted for as nearly all late-century inventories surveyed in this study listed the value of the clothing simply under *wearing apparel*, rather than valuing individual items as was more common in the first half of the century. Yet despite their flaws, probate records are an invaluable resource to the historian as they allow for a general understanding of who was consuming what during this period.

The first references to farthingales owned by middling sorts women are found in probate records drawn up less than two decades after this garment was first recorded in English royal wardrobe accounts. On 28 July 1559 a probate inventory taken for 'Margaret Pyd of Southampton, widow, late deceased' listed among her possessions 'a verdigalle', as well as other luxurious gowns of 'welted velvet faced with damask' and kirtles 'of a tawny silk chamlet ... guarded with velvet'.[15] This farthingale was valued at 3s. 4d., which was only one shilling less than the previously mentioned farthingale that was bought for the aristocrat Ann Cavendish in 1548, indicating that it must have been well constructed from fine fabrics.[16] Margaret also possessed a considerable amount of fine Holland linens, guns, silverware, gold jewellery and even curtains made of calico, a textile which was imported via Southampton from India during this period.[17] It is likely that Margaret was part of a wealthy merchant family as an earlier debt court case from 1554 listed a John Pyd of Southampton, who was a merchant, as the defendant.[18] That same year, the probate will of the widow Cicely Bolton from Thames Ditton, a village near Hampton Court Palace in Surrey, bequeathed to her friend a velvet hat, a half kirtle, black satin sleeves and a farthingale.[19] Like Margaret, Cicely was also a relatively wealthy urban woman and possibly the widow of a clerk associated with the palace or a mercantile group. These probates are evidence of the power and wealth of those who belonged to the merchant class that developed in England during the sixteenth century. It was these urban groups that had both the money and inclination to keep up with the sartorial habits of their social superiors, which, for women, included the use of foundation garments.

Middling and common women also owned bodies in the closing decade of the sixteenth century, although it is unlikely that they were separate undergarments stiffened with whalebone. Accounts for poor relief in Ipswich in Suffolk show that bodies, usually attached to petticoats, were worn by the elderly, orphaned, sick and poor in late Elizabethan England. An entry from Christ's Hospital, Ipswich, noted that in 1596 it 'paid for 2 yards 3 quarters of canvas for 3 upper bodies for 3 of the great wenches' petticoats'.[20] Rather than bents or whalebone, the upper bodies of common women's petticoats were likely stiffened with materials such as buckram, cords, quilted fabrics, or as this example shows, canvas.[21] Tailor Samantha Bullat has made several pairs of canvas petticoat upper-bodies for historical interpreters at the Jamestown–Yorktown Foundation in Williamsburg, Virginia (see Fig. 3.1). Provided that they are fitted correctly, she says that these bodies are both comfortable and supportive, and the interlining layer of linen canvas and wool flannel prevents too much creasing after doing daily activities that include bending. While these petticoat bodies are relatively stiff, Bullat has observed that they do tend to soften over time and need replacing to maintain a structured silhouette.[22]

As canvas and buckram bodies soften over time, it appears that non-elite women as well as courtiers began to look elsewhere to achieve the straight-bodied look that became so desirable at the end of the sixteenth century. One of the first references to non-elite women wearing solid materials such as wood in their bodies comes from a rather obscure description by Thomas Platter, a Swiss man who visited England in 1599. In the records of his travels he noted that:

Fig. 3.1 *Reconstruction of Elizabethan petticoat with upper bodies by Samantha Bullat. The petticoat skirt is made from wool baize and the upper bodies are made from herringbone linen with a quilted linen canvas and wool flannel interlining.*

English burgher [urban middling sorts] women usually wear high hats covered with velvet or silk for headgear, with cutaway kirtle when they go out, in the old-fashioned style. Instead of whalebone they wear a broad circular piece of wood over the breast to keep the body straighter and more erect.[23]

What exactly the circular piece of wood worn over the breast was, and where it sat in relation to the layers of clothing, is hard to determine from this source. It could have been something like a busk, or, it may have been what the Spanish called a *tablón/tablilla* and the Florentines a *la doppia*. These were large wide boards made from cardboard or wood that women placed down the front of their bodices to smooth out the front of their gowns and to keep the torsos upright.[24] As this fashion was common in Spain and parts of Italy in the middle of the sixteenth century, it is possible that its influence had also reached England by the end of that century too. Regardless of what exactly this circular piece of wood was, it is evidence that during the 1590s middling English women were attempting to fashion and straighten their bodies like court women.

The turn of the seventeenth century saw a marked increase in the consumption of bodies, including those stiffened with materials such as whalebone, by middling and common sorts of women. In 1603, Tomison Johnson, the widow of a wealthy London haberdasher who had remarried the English separatist Francis Johnson, was criticized by members of her Amsterdam-exiled Presbyterian congregation for 'the wearing of a long busk' and bodies of 'whalebones' that were 'tied to the petticoat with points'.[25] A decade later the maidservant Ellen Stone who died in London's King's Hospital in 1615 is reported to have had possessions which included a gown, a petticoat, bands, ruffs and 'a new pair of bodies'.[26] The use of foundation garments by middling and common women was not just confined to major metropolitan centres such as London though. The 1617 probate inventory of Anne Lloyd, the widow of a barber surgeon from Stratford-upon-Avon, contained the latest fashions including ruffs, gowns, stomachers and 'one pair of whall bon bodyes'.[27] In Oxford, the 1621 probate inventory of Elenor Ell who was a maidservant in Banbury recorded 'a pair of old bodies' and her will specified that these were to be given to her friend Margery Cundercott who was also a maidservant.[28] Bristol resident Katherine Ware, a single woman who possessed many items of clothing including gowns and kirtles, was recorded as possessing a 'pair of bodisses' in her 1625 probate inventory.[29] Finally, the spinster Frances Jodrell of Stockport was also recorded in 1631 as owning 'an Apron and two pair of french bodies' priced at 3s. 6d.[30]

As Thomas Heywood's play made clear in the excerpt given at the beginning of this chapter, country women also desired the fashionable silhouette of London's courtiers, and probate sources indicate that some were successful in achieving these sartorial aims. The 1611 probate inventory of Jane Gooden of Tymperley in Lancashire, the widow of a yeoman farmer, contained 'one pair of French bodies', 'French' here indicating that they were stiffened with whalebone.[31] In 1615 an expensive pair of whalebone bodies valued at 3s. 4d. were procured for Elizabeth Wright, the daughter of a husbandman in St Nicholas-at-Wade in Kent.[32] Lastly, in 1626, Susan Smyth, the daughter of a yeoman of Sussex, was given a pair of 'whale boane bodyes' for best wear and another pair of bodies for workwear.[33] Husbandman and yeoman farmers saw an increase in their wealth during this period due to rising grain prices driven by increased population.[34] This increase in wealth seems to have enabled country women to purchase items such as French bodies, which only two decades earlier had been the latest fashions in the Elizabethan courts, even if they were reserved for special occasions rather than everyday wear.

Farthingales appear to have been less common outside major metropolitan areas, as were farthingale-makers, who are discussed in the next chapter. However, this does not mean that provincial women did not aspire to the silhouettes that these garments created. Interestingly, a widow in Essex in 1581 is recorded as having a 'red petticoat welted about beneath', with welts being extra bands of fabric

Fig. 3.2 *Wenceslaus Hollar, 'The Kitchen Maid', from* Ornatus Muluebris Anglicanus *or* The Several Habits of English Women, *1640, etching, Rijksmuseum, Amsterdam.*

that were added to the hem of a skirt usually made from cotton, kersey or thick woollen fabrics.[35] This would not have rigidly held out the skirts as those hoops of bent or whalebone in Spanish farthingales did, but it would have achieved a similar shape. Other tailoring methods such as pleating the skirts with padding or buckram could also have been employed in order to achieve a more structured look.[36]

No mention of bum-rolls is made in probate accounts from this period. However, their absence in these records does not mean that they were not worn. Engravings by Wenceslaus Hollar show that they were conventional attire among common women by the 1640s. One etching, titled 'The Kitchen Maid' (1640), depicts a humble kitchen maid holding a basket and wearing a coif, a waistcoat with a neckerchief, a petticoat and pattens on her shoes (see Fig. 3.2). The second etching, titled 'Country Woman' (1643), shows a country woman holding a basket. She wears neat attire: a broad-brimmed hat, a waistcoat with a neckerchief, a petticoat and an apron (see Fig. 3.3). Both women are depicted in profile with similar clothing and, interestingly, the upper parts of both their skirts appear to be artificially enlarged, indicating that both were wearing a roll underneath. The absence of bum-rolls in probate records then is likely explained by the fact that these foundation garments were probably inexpensive and easy to make and repair at home.[37]

The most definitive proof of the use of foundation garments by middling and common sorts of women in the first half the seventeenth century is a surviving pair of bodies found in the Sittingbourne cache (see Fig. 3.4). The cache refers to a group of garments that were found within the walls and under the floors of a seventeenth-century public house that sat on the main road between London and Dover in the town of Sittingbourne, Kent. Although this public house had seen extensive renovations before it was demolished, researchers uncovered a seventeenth-century pair of breeches, a coif, shoes, gloves and the fragments of a doublet, as well as a pair of bodies dated 1630–50.[38] How and why these garments were concealed remains a mystery. However, Dinah Eastop has noted that garments found in concealed caches were often old, had been heavily worn and sometimes even purposely damaged before being hidden.[39] The bodies found in this cache were well made from two layers of herringbone-weave linen, are bound with leather and they lace at the front over a stomacher, although only the lower fragment of this separate piece has survived (see Fig. 3.5). Sustained rodent damage throughout the years of their concealment shows that the Sittingbourne bodies are also stiffened with whalebone, not bents (see Fig. 3.6).

The most fascinating aspect of this surviving garment lies not in its construction, but rather in its repairs. Although stylistically these bodies are believed to date to the 1630s–1650s, they are heavily worn and were continually mended. This indicates that they were probably worn for years or even decades after their creation, possibly by many women of differing sizes, before being disposed of in the public house in Sittingbourne. The outside of the bodies contains various leather patches that have been added to reinforce or cover up holes in the garment, and the whip stitching in the side seams has become loose and more visible due to years of continued wear and strain. Extra strips of leather have

Country:woman

W: Hollar fi 1643

Mulier Anglica habitans in Pago .

Fig. 3.3 *Wenceslaus Hollar, 'Country Woman', from* Mulier Anglica habitans in Pago *or* English village woman, *1643, etching, Rijksmuseum, Amsterdam.*

been added underneath the arms, possibly to stop the boning from poking through the top and into the armpits after continued wear. The inside of the bodies also has evidence of patching and repair and, at some point, waist tape in the form of a strip of fabric was added (see Fig. 3.11). Waist tape is commonly found in later Victorian and Edwardian corsets and was used to ease stress along the seams at the waistline in order to increase the durability and wear of the garment. This may also account for its use in the Sittingbourne bodies, as many of the eyelet holes, particularly those at the waistline, have ripped due to the strain of continued tight lacing and movement around the waist (see Fig. 3.7).

The bodies follow the general silhouette of fashions of the mid-seventeenth century and my own reconstruction demonstrates how this garment would have looked when new (see Fig. 3.8).[40] As I have previously shown, a woman who lived or worked in a public house certainly could have owned pairs of bodies during this period. Like the possible owner of the Sittingbourne bodies, Ellen Bicke, a spinster from Cropedy in Oxfordshire living in a tavern upon her death in 1627, left her 'best pair of bodyes' to her sister in her will.[41] Other women of similar status also owned whalebone bodies by the

Fig. 3.4 *Sittingbourne Bodies (outside), c. 1630–50, English, Plough Finds Collection, Sittingbourne Heritage Museum. The bodies are made from herringbone linen, baleen, linen thread and leather.*

Fig. 3.5 *Fragment of the bottom of a stomacher belonging to the Sittingbourne Bodies, c. 1630–50, English, Plough Finds Collection, Sittingbourne Heritage Museum. The stomacher is also made from linen and has been bound in leather; boning channels are still visible.*

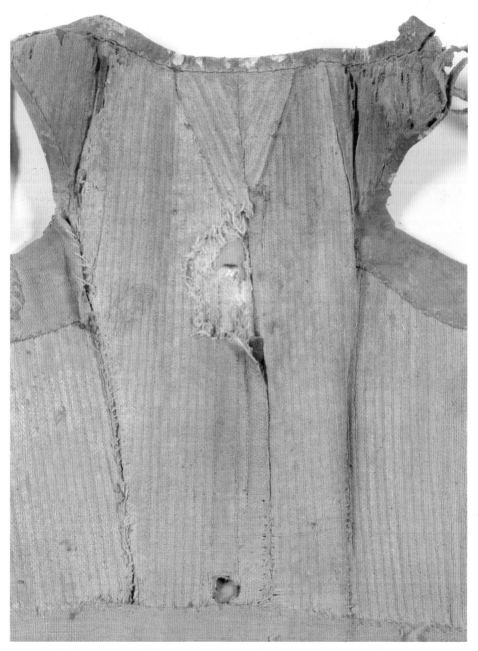

Fig. 3.6 *Back section of the Sittingbourne Bodies, c. 1630–50, English, Plough Finds Collection, Sittingbourne Heritage Museum. Holes in the garment reveal the dark strips of baleen that have been used to stiffen the bodies. Evidence of seam strain is also visible.*

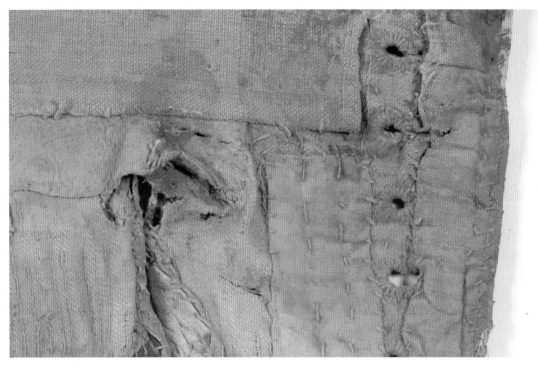

Fig. 3.7 *Detail of centre front of the Sittingbourne Bodies, c. 1630–50, English, Plough Finds Collection, Sittingbourne Heritage Museum. The strain on the eyelet holes is visible and several are ripped.*

1630s, as probate records examined so far in this chapter have shown. Most interestingly, however, my reconstruction demonstrates that the shoulder straps of the Sittingbourne bodies are designed to sit horizontally across the upper back and on the edge of the shoulders (see Fig. 3.9). These off-the-shoulder straps limit arm movement as my model could not lift her arms up above her head (see Fig. 3.10). This restrictive design feature suggests that these bodies were intended for a woman of leisure who did not need to do any sort of manual labour, as these straps are designed to control bodily movement in order to portray a sense of grace and refinement. However, how garments were supposed to be worn and how they were actually worn in everyday life are two different things.

This garment gives a glimpse into the daily embodied experiences of the last woman who wore it, as its condition suggests that she may not have used the shoulder straps. Eyelet holes where the straps would have laced to the front of the garment near the armpits are missing, possibly covered up by additional leather binding that was added at some point (see Fig. 3.11). On one side of the garment there is a small loop of leather and this may have been used to fasten one of the shoulder straps. When the shoulders straps of my reconstruction were unlaced, my model had a full range of arm movement. This may explain why the straps were not used by the last wearer, as she likely took part in daily tasks that required manual labour. The last eyelet on the right side of the garment (when viewed from the inside) has also been

Fig. 3.8 *Author's reconstruction of the Sittingbourne Bodies. The bodies are made from two layers of twill linen and the conjectured stomacher is made from a lighter plain weave linen. Both are bound in lambs leather, boned with plastic imitation baleen and hand sewn with linen thread. Worn over a linen smock.*

Fig. 3.9 *Back of the Sittingbourne Bodies reconstruction. The bodies are worn over a linen smock, woollen petticoat and bum-roll. The off-the-shoulder straps are typical of mid-seventeenth century fashions.*

Fig. 3.10 *Model lifting her arms as high as she can in the Sittingbourne Bodies reconstruction. She wears the bodies with a linen smock, a woollen petticoat and a bum-roll.*

Fig. 3.11 *Sittingbourne Bodies (inside), c. 1630–50, English, Plough Finds Collection, Sittingbourne Heritage Museum. Waist tape is visible, as are several linen and leather patches. Extra leather has also been added under the arms.*

patched over, meaning that it was not used. All of this shows that the last owner may not have worn these bodies fully laced or with the arm straps attached, indicating that she adapted the garment to suit her own use and comfort. The question of how a woman who frequented this tavern came to possess an originally luxurious garment, wear and then continually repair it is therefore intriguing and points to both a long lifecycle and to multiple ownerships, both typical of early modern clothing.

Affordability and modes of consumption

In 1604, James I repealed England's sumptuary legislation and the state could no longer seek to control what people did and did not wear.[42] Sumptuary laws were originally intended to protect the consumption rights of England's elites, as their inherited and titled status gave them the privilege to wear certain fashions that those without such a birthright, no matter how wealthy, could not. Although sumptuary legislation had existed in England since the fifteenth century, these regulations were primarily concerned with male dress.[43] In fact, it was not until 1574, when Queen Elizabeth I released her Statutes of Apparel, that female dress was specifically targeted. Yet even in these statues there are no references to bodies, busks or farthingales. Instead, the statutes were more concerned with outlining what colour and types of fabrics, such as cloth of gold, silver tissue, crimson velvet or fur, could be used in the clothing of women of different ranks.[44] So there were no legal restrictions that prevented women of the non-elite from wearing stiffened foundation garments. Yet even if there had been, contemporaries frequently noted the difficulty of enforcing sumptuary legislation. In 1552, Bishop Hugh Latimer preached that 'There be laws made and certain statutes, how everyone in his estate shall be apparelled but God knoweth the statutes are not put in execution.'[45] Thirty years later, Phillip Stubbes's *Anatomy of Abuses* (1583) remarked that in England:

> Nowhere is such a confused mingle-mangle of apparel and such preposterous excess thereof, as anyone is permitted to flaunt it out in what apparel he lusteth himself, or can get by with any kind of meanness, so that it is very hard to know who is noble, who is worshipful, who is gentleman, who is not.[46]

Historical studies have confirmed Latimer's and Stubbes's observations, noting that many simply ignored these laws and that there were few recorded prosecutions.[47] Rather than sumptuary legislation then, social and economic pressures were more likely to dictate what women could and could not wear.

Due to these lax sumptuary laws in England it was common for high status garments to be part of servile dress or for old clothing to be gifted to servants by their mistress when they were no longer desired, and so the Sittingbourne bodies could have come into the possession of their tavern dwelling owner that way.[48] Certainly, this habit is alluded to in the play *Ralph Roister Doister* (1567) when two maids to the rich widowed Dame Christian Custance discuss the gossip of the streets and abroad: 'And we shall go in our French hoods every day / . . . / In our trick [handsome] ferdegews [farthingales] and biliments of gold; / Brave in our suits of change, seven double fold.'[49] Mistresses like Dame Custance who wished for the clothing of their servants to reflect the status of the household often encouraged them to be finely dressed and so may have given their female servants foundation garments.[50] As previously shown, women also regularly bequeathed clothing items to friends and family after their deaths. It was also common for middling sorts of women to give charitable gifts of clothing to the deserving poor, which could then be worn, bartered or sold onto the second-hand market for cash, so it is possible that foundation garments were passed on through these female networks too.[51] Garments could also be temporarily lent or gifted between family members. An entry in the accounts book of Joyce Jeffreys, a lower gentry spinster and moneylender from Hereford, noted in March 1639 that she gave her niece Eliza Acton a 'pair of fine whalbon bodies' that were valued at 4s. 8d. and that Eliza wore these bodies 'when she went to Worcester'.[52]

The Sittingbourne bodies could also have been purchased on the thriving seventeenth-century second-hand clothes market. Clothing did not just visually symbolize wealth; it was also literal stored wealth. Clothing goods were often the main possessions that women owned. Take for example the spinster Elizabeth Dixon who died in Oxfordshire 1622. Of all the worldly goods listed in her probate inventory, fifteen out of seventeen items were clothing goods. These included hats, coifs, aprons, petticoats, waistcoats, 'a pair of bodies' and a gown, all of which were valued as part of her estate.[53] Just as fabrics were expensive and often reused to make other garments, clothing could also be sold on by those who no longer needed it or by those who needed quick cash. There was an extensive second-hand clothes trade in medieval and early modern England, much of which was centred in London where many dealers could hold respected positions such as mayor. Smaller second-hand clothes markets and dealers were present in provincial towns too.[54] During this time, almost everyone had the opportunity to pawn their clothing and even those at the highest end of the social spectrum participated.[55]

The establishment of the London Season in the sixteenth century, a time in spring when the English nobility descended on London for the sitting of Parliament, has been credited with creating the modern fashion cycle, as these elites needed to constantly distinguish themselves from the common masses through their dress.[56] Old clothes were therefore sold off to upholders or fripperers, who were recognized sellers of second-hand clothing, or to more unregulated merchants such as street sellers and hawkers, to make room for newer fashions in the wardrobes of elites.[57] One common place where these clothes ended up, either gifted or pawned, was the playhouse.[58] Not only did London's theatres require sumptuous clothing for their actors who played the parts of elites, but theatre audiences were also criticized by contemporary commentators for ignoring sumptuary legislation and coming to the playhouse 'in their holidays apparel, and so set forth, so trimmed, so adorned, so decked, so perfumed, as if they made the place the market of wantonness'.[59] In fact, there is even evidence of theatre companies, as well as the regulatory Office of the Revels, renting out their elaborate costumes (which were used in Court Masques and balls) to 'the meanest sort of men' in London.[60]

But how affordable were foundation garments, even those bought through the second-hand clothes market, for middling and common women? Court records reveal that typical wages for maidservants in London at the start of the seventeenth century were between 30 and 40 shillings per year, and this decreased the further away from the capital one worked, with the annual income for a maidservant in Norfolk being around 20s. in 1613.[61] The average cost of a newly tailored pair of bodies in the Norfolk tailor Peckover's accounts from 1590 to 1592 was approximately 7s., and farthingales cost between 2s. 8d. and 4s. 4d., meaning that a new a pair of bodies would have cost a London maid a fifth of her yearly wage, and a Norfolk maid a third, and farthingales less than that again. Bodies also varied significantly in price depending on what they were made of, such as silk French bodies compared to canvas bodies, and where they were made and by whom. Joyce Jeffreys recorded many payments for bum-rolls, busks and whalebone bodies between the years 1638 and 1648 and these varied widely in price. The pair of whalebone bodies that she gave to her niece Eliza in March 1639 cost 4s. 8d., while later that year in September Joyce paid nearly three times the price at 11s. for a 'paier of whalbon bodies from London'.[62] The reason for this may be that these bodies were made in London by specialized body-makers, rather than provincial tailors, and so they demanded a higher fee for their skills. These bodies sourced from London may also have been made with better quality fabrics such as imported silks. The use of whalebone in these bodies could not account for their price disparity as both contained the material, and over the course of the sixteenth and seventeenth centuries whalebone became more readily available.

In England, imports of *whale-fin*, the name given to whalebone (baleen) when sold in its raw form, during the sixteenth and seventeenth centuries came from the Newfoundland and Arctic whale fisheries. Although the Muscovy Company of England was granted a twenty-year monopoly to kill and import whale products in 1577, whaling was not a major business venture for the English until the start of the seventeenth century – the same time that foundation garments made from whalebone began to appear in a variety of English wardrobes.[63] Before this, much of the whalebone used in dress in England was imported through merchants from the Basque region of Spain and France, which was famous for its fishermen. A letter dated 12 December 1607 petitioned the Lord Mayor of London and the Lords of the Council to not impose a duty on 'whalebone-fins' that were 'used [in] the trade of making Vardingales, Boddyes, and Sleeves for Women in and about the City' and supplied by those merchants trading to 'Biskey', meaning the Bay of Biscay in the Basque region of Spain.[64] Four years later, in 1611, the company was granted a charter to whale around Spitsbergen (now in northern Norway) and made their first kill that same year.[65] In 1614, King James I issued a proclamation 'concerning the bringing in of Whale-fins into his Majesties Dominions' that stated that from thenceforth the Muscovy Company, who had 'procured Biscainers, skilful in striking the Whale, [to] teach and Instruct the English Nation … of the benefit of the Whale-fishing', had the sole rights to import whale-fin into the English kingdom and dominions.[66] However, it seems that this proclamation did not have the desired effect as in 1619 another proclamation was released that acknowledged that the previous order had taken 'not that good effect' and sought to reassert the position of the Muscovy Company as the sole traders of whale-fin in England.[67] This was reiterated by James I's son and successor, King Charles I, in 1636, highlighting that the demand for these goods was fuelling illegal imports from other nations more successfully involved in the whaling industry, such as the Dutch.[68] The demand for such a raw material, fuelled by the fashionable tastes of elites and non-elites alike, made whalebone a relatively affordable material as it was both legally and illegally imported into England in increasingly large quantities by the start of the seventeenth century.

What about women who could not afford to have a new pair of bodies made bespoke? Valuations in probate records also offer a glimpse into the affordability of foundation garments once they were on sold onto the second-hand clothes market. While a new pair of French bodies at the start of the seventeenth century could have cost around 7s., a second-hand pair may have been only a quarter of that price. Jane Gooden's French bodies were valued at only 2s. in her probate inventory.[69] A second-hand pair was therefore much more affordable for a non-elite woman who desired a fashionable silhouette but for a fraction of the cost. Ready-made garments were also more affordable than their bespoke counterparts. A ready-made market had certainly existed since the sixteenth century in England, and during the seventeenth century it exploded, with tailoring guilds consistently attempting to curb its spread as it threatened their livelihoods.[70] Early retailers of ready-made garments were often tailors, merchants, woollen drapers and linen drapers, who already had pre-existing shops and clients.[71] One such seller was the linen draper John Uttinge of Great Yarmouth in Norfolk, whose probate inventory listed '6 pair of bodyes' valued at 2s. each in his shop in 1627.[72] These were obviously ready-made garments priced at a point that was certainly within the range of affordability for non-elite women. Body-sellers also began to appear in London during the 1630s and it appears that these tradespeople specialized in selling ready-made garments (these tradespeople are discussed in more detail in Chapter 4).

Finally, women may have come across their foundation garments during this period through theft. Clothing goods did not just represent stored wealth, but were also incredibly portable and easy to sell in early modern England.[73] Unsurprisingly, in the seventeenth century the theft of clothing and household linens could account for anywhere between 14 and 27 per cent of theft cases across different parts of England.[74] It appears that bodies were a popular garment to steal. The Essex Assize records show that in 1601 the labourer Thomas Dixon of Moulsham in Chelmsford stole a petticoat and a pair of 'boddyes' from the widow Joan Browne; and later in 1635, Richard Read, a weaver from Colchester, was also indicted for stealing 'five pair of bodies' worth 10s.[75] As both Thomas and Richard were men, this loot was likely intended to be sold onto the second-hand clothes market. Women were also frequently accused of stealing bodies. On 12 May 1611, Martha Bowers of Birch in Essex was also indicted for stealing 'One pair of bodies' worth 18d.[76] Records from London's Old Bailey courts also contain numerous references to bodies and stays being stolen, demonstrating that at the end of the century the desire for these goods still led to theft. In 1687, Mary Biglin and Elenor Bayly were tried and later acquitted for allegedly stealing 'one pair of Bodice and other things, from Jane Thacker' in Shoreditch.[77] In 1692, Hannah Mayle was accused of stealing 'a pair of Bodice' along with other things from the widow Margaret Young of Whitechapel and then pawning them in East-Smithfield. Mayle claimed that Young had lent her the goods, but this excuse was not enough to avoid the sentence of whipping that she received.[78] Many women below the level of the elite therefore had ready access to foundation garments in a variety of forms, be it bespoke, ready-made, second-hand or stolen.

Foundation garments and upward social mobility

Why did the city and country girls of England desire the structural silhouettes of London's courtiers so much that they would risk penalties such as death if found guilty of theft? Although many contemporary authors attributed these desires to women's innate vanity and weakness, relating fashion to an 'Epidemical disease, first infecting the Court, then the City, [and] after the Country', foundation garments not only signified grace, power and wealth but, more importantly, the social status that came with that.[79] A desire for social mobility (or at least stability) was shared by most people during this period, and one way that men and women could reflect the status they had or wished to achieve was through their sartorial choices.[80] Indeed, for a country such as England, which by the seventeenth century lacked sumptuary legislation and traditional folk costume and where status categories were often ambiguous and highly dependent on context, clothing and other material goods became important but easily manipulable markers of status.

Indeed, Alexandra Shepard's study of social order as expressed in English court records has revealed that for those of the middling and common sorts, social status was largely based on movable property, as these 'people rated their net moveable wealth and thereby their relative social position with reference to monetary benchmarks'.[81] She notes that witnesses consistently drew attention to the importance of goods and chattels, including clothing, in establishing social rank.[82] For members of the non-elite sorts who did not have the birthright to claim high social status or political power, it was monetary wealth that defined where one sat, or was perceived to sit, in the social hierarchy. This is important, as the ability to purchase certain goods and then wear them was a very visual indicator of one's monetary wealth and thus social status.

This was an observation made by foreign visitors. The previously mentioned Swiss traveller Thomas Platter wrote in 1599 that 'the women-folk of England . . . have far more liberty than in other lands, and know just how to make good use of it, for they often stroll out or drive by coach in very gorgeous clothes', revealing that fashionably dressed women from all social sorts must have been common on the streets.[83] Margaret Spufford and Susan Mee's examination of probate records from 1570 to 1700 has also found that those who had moveable wealth worth over £125, such as yeoman and urban artisans, displayed distinctive elements of fashionability in their dress, and owned items that the authors note were 'not to be expected'.[84] Being fashionable, even if not at the cutting edge, was therefore an important way of claiming status in society, as well as pursuing (or at least proclaiming) one's own ambitions. However, this desire for upwardly mobile attire not only fuelled an extensive second-hand clothes trade and an emerging ready-made clothing sector, but the increased availability of these goods amongst women of the non-elite also fuelled anxieties about social mobility during the sixteenth and seventeenth centuries.

Of particular concern was the ability to discern paid labourers, such as maidservants, from their mistresses who were superior in both wealth and status. Despite attempts to reintroduce bills of apparel after the repeal of sumptuary legislation at the start of the seventeenth century, attempts by the state to control dress continued to falter, and so others with professional and commercial power took it upon themselves to try to regulate clothing choices.[85] In 1611 an 'Act for Reformation of Apparel to be worn by Apprentices and maid-servants, within the City of London' was proclaimed by Sir William Craven, the Lord Mayor of London, and 'his right Worshipful Brethren the Aldermen of the same City' (see Fig. 3.12). The act sought to control both male and female dress. Male apprentices were reprimanded for wearing silk doublets and breeches, as well as piccadilly collars; however, they were not accused of being proud or foolish in their excessive dress. Female servants on the other hand were decried for the 'many and great inconveniences and disorders which daily grow, by the inordinate pride of Maid-servants and Women-servants, in their excesses of Apparel and folly in variety of new fashions'. It was stated that 'no maid-servant and women-servants' within the city of London should, among other things,

> Wear any Gown, Kirtle, Waistcoat, or Petticoat, old or New, of any kind of Silk stuff, or stuff mingled with silk, nor any other stuff exceeding the price of two shillings five pence the yard … Nor any Silke Lace or Guard upon her Gown, Kirtle, Waistcoat or Petticoat, or any other garment, Save only a cape of Velvet. Nor any fardingale at all, either little or great, nor any bodie or Sleeves, of Wire, Whale-bones, or With any other stiffening, saving Canvas, or Buckram only.

If maidservants were found guilty of violating these rules they were fined 3s. 4d. for the first offence and eight pence for the second.[86] Yet as previously discussed, probate records show that many maids still wore these garments and years later John Evelyn in *A Character of England* (1659) also complained that it was hard 'to distinguish the Lady from the Chamber-Maid; Servants being suffered in this brave Country, to go clad like their Mistresses', indicating that this proclamation was largely ignored.[87]

During the seventeenth century the analogy between household and state, both with a male figurehead such as the king or father, was commonly invoked. Within the household there existed three hierarchies: husband and wife, employer and servant and parent and child.[88] From sermons to conduct literature it was preached that this order must be maintained if chaos in the household, and likewise the state, was to be avoided. Thus, upholding these power relationships within the household was crucial. Yet, as these sources show, if the bodies of both mistress and maidservant were shaped by the same foundation garments of 'wire, whalebone, or with any other stiffing', how was one to tell who had the authority over whom?

Conflicts of interest often arose for employers who not only took pride in having well-dressed servants who helped to confirm their high social status, but at the same time wanted to maintain the correct social order that was visually dictated by dress.[89] Such anxieties frequently appear in court records during the period, as maids working in elite households who were handed down items from their mistresses or who invested their wages in good clothes could be mistaken for women of higher

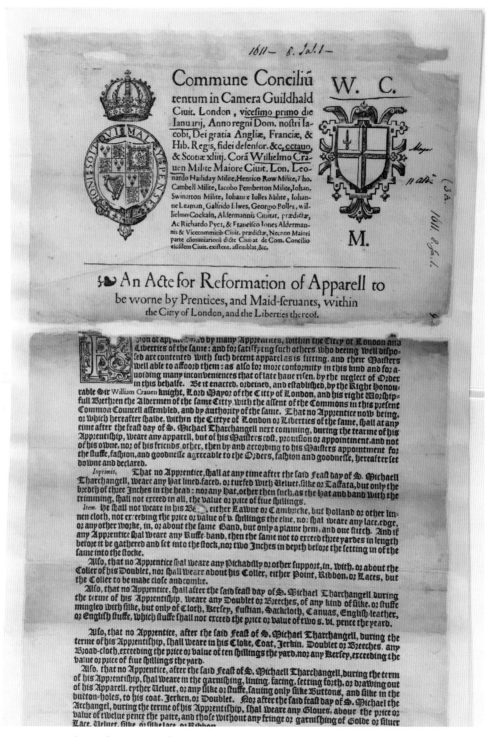

Fig. 3.12 Act for Reformation of Apparel to be worn by Prentices and maid-servants, within the City of London (detail), c. *1611, London Metropolitan Archives.*

status.[90] Often maidservants had a good reason for doing so, as appearance and dress was seen as a crucial part of obtaining a good marriage match, particularly in London where maidservants flocked.[91] Although maidservants expected clothing from their mistresses and sought to wear fashionable attire to attract husbands on the marriage market in cities such as London, their desire to obtain the same fashionable silhouette as their mistresses also led to an unease over the ways in which foundation garments could blur the social hierarchies of women's bodies within the household, leading to proclamations such as the one in 1611 being issued.

This unease reflects responses to social mobility in early modern English society more generally, where social status was often defined more by a defensive response to threats of downward social mobility, rather than by ideas of belonging or by social exclusivity.[92] Eleanor Hubbard has also noted that defamation cases brought to court by women in London reveal that they had a 'clear idea of where they stood in local estimation' and that they strove to protect themselves from lowering attacks.[93] Unsurprisingly then, foundation garments were also caught up in social anxieties concerning non-elite women and status. This is demonstrated through the character of Chloe in Ben Jonson's 1602 satirical play, *Poetaster*. Chloe, who was 'gentlewoman born' but married below her station, exclaims of her social decline, 'Nor you, nor your house were so much as spoken of, before I debased myself, from my Hood and my Fartingall, to these Bumrowles, and your Whale-bone Bodies.'[94] Although the wardrobe records from both Elizabeth I and Anne of Demark show that rolls were still owned and worn by queens during this period, it appears that they were not the cutting edge of fashionable attire. Randle Cotgrave's *A Dictionary of the French and English Tongues* (1611) later confirmed this as he noted that the 'French Vardingale' or '*hausse-cul*' was 'the kind of roll used by such women, as wear (or are to wear) no rolls.'[95] So smaller bum-rolls were commonly worn by women who were not supposed to wear farthingales, likely referring to those of the non-elite sorts. Chloe had therefore swapped her French wheel farthingale for the less fashionable French farthingale roll, indicating her fall from the fashionable court and the loss of her elite feminine identity.

The reference to 'whale-bone bodice[s]' as being a low-status garment is more ambiguous, as bodies stiffened with whalebone were at the cutting edge of fashion at the turn of the seventeenth century. What this source could perhaps be suggesting is that status dictated the different ways that bodies were worn by different sorts of women. As noted in Chapter 1, in the seventeenth century there was no firm distinction between under- and outerwear when it came to items of women's dress such as petticoats and bodies, as these garments were commonly worn as both. However, visual sources suggest that in the first half of the seventeenth century the elite usually wore bodies underneath fashionable gowns or as undress inside, while the bodies of non-elite women were more likely to be visible in public. This is depicted in a Dutch artwork of a maid wearing a pink laced pair of bodies with visible boning channels (see Fig. 3.13), over a smock, a skirt and an apron. The female servant standing behind her preparing meats is likely also wearing the same ensemble but with an additional waistcoat over the top. A later French artwork dated to 1630 also

Fig. 3.13 *Attributed to Pieter Cornelisz van Rijck,* Kitchen Scene with the Parable of the Rich Man and Poor Lazarus, c. *1620–20, oil on canvas, Rijksmuseum, Amsterdam.*

depicts a vendor who is wearing her boned front-lacing bodies as outerwear (see Fig. 3.14). The only garments she wears over her bodies are a partlet which covers her chest for modesty, a black apron and what could be detachable sleeves. The foundation garments of her wealthy customer are not visible under the fashionable gown that she wears. It is possible that the last owner of the Sittingbourne bodies looked like this street seller when fully dressed. When my reconstruction of these bodies was paired with a linen smock, bum-roll, wool petticoat, linen partlet and apron, my model closely resembled the street seller depicted in this artwork (see Fig. 3.15).

Samuel Pepys remarked in his diary on 1 May 1667 that he went to Westminster and on the way he 'saw pretty Nelly standing at her lodgings' door in Drury-lane in her smock sleeves and bodice, looking upon one: she seemed a mighty pretty creature.'[96] Nell Gwyn was a low-born actress of the Restoration stage who would the following year become the mistress of King Charles II. In the context of this entry it appears that wearing bodies and even a smock as outerwear was a type of casual everyday dress for lower sorts of women as depicted in the earlier French artwork. The use of bodies as both under- and

Fig. 3.14 *Louise Moillon,* Market Scene with a Pick-pocket, *c. 1630s–40s, oil on canvas, Private Collection.*

Fig. 3.15 *Author's reconstruction of possible mid-seventeenth-century outfit worn with the Sittingbourne Bodies. The model wears a linen smock and coif, a bum-roll and woollen petticoat, a pair of whalebone bodies and a linen partlet and apron. An additional waistcoat could have been worn for extra warmth.*

outerwear by non-elite women could explain Chloe's bitter remarks, as she had gone from wearing these garments exclusively as underwear to outwear as well. As mentioned in Chapter 1, this distinction might also explain the ambiguity of the terms *bodies* (which usually denoted an undergarment) and *bodice* (which often denoted an outer garment), and why these two terms were so interchangeable during this period. It appears then that it was not enough to simply own these garments; the ability to wear them a certain way also reflected a woman's status too.

During the sixteenth century there was a transition towards novel modes of consumption whereby people placed, as Shepard has argued, more importance on 'the status-bearing function of goods rather than on their value as repositories of wealth and the means of exchange'.[97] Such excessive consumption is visible in artworks from the period such as Wenceslaus Hollar's etching of the Mayor of London's wife who is depicted in all the latest fashions – hat, ruff, partlet, rosette, boned bodice, fur trimmings, gloves and feather fan – that were clearly intended to show off her status as the wife of a wealthy citizen (see Fig. 3.16). Many Jacobean city comedies of the period commented on this turn towards novel consumerism of dress at the start of the seventeenth century and identified farthingales as notable examples. Thomas

Fig. 3.16 *Wenceslaus Hollar,* The Mayor of London's Wife, *1649, etching, Rijksmuseum, Amsterdam.*

Dekker's play *The Shoemaker's Holiday* (1600) reveals how social mobility was reflected by the consumption of farthingales, as when her already wealthy shoemaker husband is made a Sheriff, the character Margery Eyre exclaims, 'Art thou acquainted with never a fardingale-maker, nor a French-hood maker? I must enlarge my bum, ha ha.'[98] Around the turn of the seventeenth century it was not uncommon for a skilled and successful artisan in London to earn an average weekly wage of 6s., which was nearly ten times the yearly wage of a maidservant in the capital, meaning that the wives of wealthy London artisans would certainly have been able to afford these bespoke garments.[99]

Fashionable styles of French farthingales at this time were also likely to be cheaper to make as they required less fabric. While Elizabeth I's Spanish farthingales could incorporate up to five yards of fabric, my own reconstruction experiments (discussed in detail in the next chapter) show that the French styles required significantly less yardage. My French farthingale roll took under 1½ yards (1.4 m) of modern 44-inch-wide (112 cm) silk taffeta, which is the equivalent of 3 yards (2.7 m) of 22-inch-wide (56 cm) silk in the sixteenth century. My French wheel farthingale also required just over a yard (91 cm) of modern silk taffeta (the equivalent to 2 yards of historical silk) and the same again in linen. Wealthy urban tradespeople and merchants therefore appear to have placed more value in the status bearing function of French farthingales rather than their stored value, which was often determined by the type and amounts of fabric used.

Yet the bold sartorial statements that farthingales made about social status did not come without some anxiety on the woman's behalf, as a letter written by Anne Williamson reveals. Anne was the wife of Nicholas Williamson who was an educated servant, possibly a clerk, to the Earl of Shrewsbury in Sawley, Derbyshire. In this letter from Anne to her husband, dated 9 December 1590, after briefly commenting on her continued stay at 'Bolde' she wrote, 'I pray you send to the tailor to make me a pair of verdingale Sleeves, & a french verdingale, and let it not be too big but of a reasonable size, for if there had been any to have been gotten here I would not have troubled you with it.'[100] This letter reveals that women like Anne used farthingales to assert their status based on their husband's connections to the elite and that their husbands often took an active role in enabling their consumption. However, Anne's letter also seems to imply that she *needed* to wear one, so much so that when she could not find one in the countryside, she wrote to her husband about it. The concern she voices in the letter over the size of the farthingale is also most likely connected with status – either Anne did not want to dress above her status by wearing one too big, or due to the fact that no one else had farthingales where she was lodging, she did not feel the need to wear her biggest and best in order to show her social position.

The ability to source one's farthingale bespoke from a tailor or farthingale-maker must also have made a clear statement about a woman's social status, as she did not need to rely on second-hand or ready-made clothes but could get them from the same source as her social superiors. Clearly then to enlarge one's bum, especially via a farthingale-maker, was a sign of a woman's rise through the social orders of Elizabethan and Jacobean England. The same was also true in France, as two sources from this period describe wealthy urban bourgeois women wearing farthingales. However, these sources also voice alarm over the ability of these garments to level the hierarchy of silhouettes, as Étienne Médicis, a merchant of Puy, noted that bourgeois women often 'exceed their status' by wearing 'aristocratic farthingales'.[101] The author of *Discours Nouveau Sur la Mode* (1613) also mused, 'what are great ladies to do if the bourgeoisies now appear with small ones, too?', poking fun at the apprehension caused by these garments in relation to social status.[102]

Although Anne Williamson's concern over the size of her farthingale could have been because she did not want to dress above her social status, it is also a possibility that Anne did not want to be the target of scorn. As many studies have noted, fashion was (and arguably still is) coded. Being in or out of fashion required one to gain access to ever changing rules that were often guarded by those elites who set the fashionable trends.[103] So while both men and women sought to gain and then maintain a level of fashionable appearance, such as a graceful torso and reasonably sized bum, many non-elite city women in fashionable dress did not know how to play the game. As a result, they were criticized as upstarts by authors of creative literature from the period who explored the changing social landscape of London where old social codes based on inherited privilege were increasingly challenged by the newly monied who could afford to buy luxury commodities.[104] This led to several city comedies that not only made fun of courtiers but also lampooned the dress of those who were perceived to be obnoxiously displaying their changed social status.

Characters such as Margery in *The Shoemaker's Holiday*, no doubt based on real early seventeenth-century city women, were therefore created by playwrights in order to mock women who were perceived as appropriating higher social status by using these garments, without actually earning that status or having the taste or refinement to carry it off. When Margery's husband Simon Eyre sees his wife in her new apparel he exclaims, 'Lady Madgy, thou has never covered thy Saracens head with this french flap, nor laden thy bum with this farthingale, tis trash, trumpery, vanity.'[105] Although a rise in social position required Margery and her husband to dress differently, as enlarging one's bum with a farthingale was a sign of social improvement, it also seems to have been associated with an immediate slide into moral disrepute. Margery's sartorial preoccupation soon renders her a 'comic stock figure of consumer wife' and she is dismissed by other characters in this play.[106] Non-elite women in late sixteenth- and early seventeenth-century England therefore often found it difficult to maintain a balance between confidently asserting their newfound status with foundation garments and avoiding being ridiculed for doing so.

Conclusion

As this chapter has shown, personal records such as probate documents confirm that foundation garments were consumed and worn by the middling and common sort of women in England much earlier than previously thought. These records show that merchant's wives and clerk's wives, as well as maidservants and country women, all strove to have a fashionable silhouette shaped by foundation garments and that they acquired these garments in either bespoke, ready-made, second-hand or stolen forms during the seventeenth century. Although moralists, preachers and guilds decried these fashions on both moral and practical grounds, in reality women still sought to wear these signifiers of movable property and wealth in order to manipulate their place in a world that was shaped by often strict social and gender norms.

Single maidservants wore foundation garments to be fashionable and possibly attract an upwardly mobile marriage match, while married women such as Anne Williamson and the fictional Margery Eyre used these garments to show their social positions obtained through their husband's newly acquired wealth or connections to the elite. Yet the desire of non-elite women to obtain the same fashionable silhouette as their social superiors also led to an unease over the ways in which foundation garments could blur the social hierarchies of women's bodies, where often maidservant and mistress were not discernible, and non-elite and elite women claimed the same sartorial form as each other. Foundation garments therefore helped to visually define often ambiguous social hierarchies and ideals of femininity for middling and common sorts of women in early modern England, but these women often trod a fine line between using these garments to display social mobility and being ridiculed by those both above and below them for doing so.

4

The body makers

Commissioning and making foundation garments in early modern England

In 1630 the famous common-born poet of Elizabethan and Jacobean London, John Taylor, wrote that 'those [artisans] that make the Verdingales and bodies' got the 'most they have, from idle witless nodies'.[1] As this book has explored so far, those women who wore fashionable garments such as bodies and farthingales were regularly proclaimed to be silly, weak and foolish monkeys that uncritically mimicked fashionable dress. Similar stereotypes were linked to men and their tailors too, with Samuel Butler's *A Huffing Courtier* (1667–9) stating that 'His Taylor is his Creator, and makes him of nothing.'[2] Across Europe the image of affluent men and women as monkeys or puppets controlled by their tailors was common during the sixteenth century.[3] However, such stereotypes ignore the complexities of the process of obtaining a tailor-made garment in early modern Europe, a process that required material knowledge on behalf of the consumer, and the tacit skills and ingenuity of the maker. This process was founded upon a relationship between craftsperson and client that relied on trust and communication. This relationship was so important that throughout the seventeenth century in England many tailors were regularly punished by their guilds for selling ready-made clothing, an act which undermined the bespoke nature of their work.[4]

This chapter explores the interactions between those who consumed foundation garments, from queens to country ladies, and the artisans who made their clothing. It traces the emergence of two previously unexplored trades that specialized in making foundation garments, body-making and farthingale-making, and the experiences of these artisans in early modern England. It examines the strategies that women employed to commission and buy their foundation garments and, by examining the construction of surviving garments and reflecting on my own experiences of making, charts the evolving skill and ingenuity of those who made bodies and farthingales. An exploration of the process of commissioning and making reveals that the design of early modern foundation garments required material literacy on behalf of the buyer, usually female, and considerable skill on behalf of the maker, in order to fashion the female form during the sixteenth and seventeenth centuries.

The body-making and farthingale-making trades

When bodies and farthingales first appeared in the wardrobes of English women in the sixteenth century, these foundation garments were made by tailors. However, as consumption increased in centres such as London, specialist trades were established to meet production demands. During the sixteenth and seventeenth centuries it is estimated that over a fifth of Londoners worked in clothing-related trades, and this figure increases to a third if leather trades are also included.[5] This made London a centre of innovation and consumption where cloth artisans like tailors, if skilled, versatile and adaptable to changing fashions, could thrive.[6] It is unsurprising then that the first evidence of farthingale- and body-makers in England comes from the capital. The earliest mention of specialist makers of foundation garments is in the wardrobe records of Elizabeth I. These records reveal that the queen had two farthingale-makers under her employ during her reign. The first was John Bate, who had taken over the production of farthingales from the tailor Walter Fyshe in 1567. By 1570, the Great Wardrobe had a second farthingale-maker called Robert Sibthorpe, who was regularly employed by the queen until her death.[7]

When James I ascended the English throne in 1603 the household records of his queen consort, Anne of Denmark, show that she employed a man called Robert Hughes as her farthingale-maker until her death in 1619.[8] It appears that Hughes had also supplied farthingales to Elizabeth I in the last decade of her reign as he was recorded in the Drapers' Company as being the 'Queens Vardingsall maker' in December 1593.[9] Hughes does not appear in any of the queen's wardrobe records but it is possible that he worked as a journeyman farthingale-maker for Robert Sibthorpe. In 1630 a man called John Ager began to supply farthingales to Henrietta Maria.[10] Apprenticeship records from the Drapers' Company reveal that Ager had served his apprenticeship under Robert Hughes and so probably obtained these commissions through this connection.[11] The wardrobe accounts of Elizabeth I, Anne of Denmark, Henrietta Maria and Catherine of Braganza all show that their master tailors (William Jones, James Duncan, George Gelin and Peter Lombard) supplied pairs of bodies to these queens during their reigns. Many of these were part of gowns, while some were separate undergarments.

Although tailors continued to make bodies for the royal household, outside the court body-making was quickly established as a specialized trade at the turn of the seventeenth century.[12] As Barnabe Rich exclaimed in 1614, members of this new trade were said to be swarming about all parts of London, and the sudden emergence of body-makers in the records of London's Livery Companies between the years 1590 and 1615 attests to this.[13] The Livery Companies of London, which originated from medieval guilds and fraternities that oversaw the training and practice of their respective crafts, enforced quality control and created representative bodies for different trades to protect their interests in the city. By the seventeenth century there were dozens of companies in London and the twelve largest Livery Companies had considerable political power, as their Liverymen played a key part in electing the city's sheriffs, mayors and Members of Parliament for the City of London. Breaking from traditions still held elsewhere in England, by the early seventeenth century the custom of London allowed anyone who had served an apprenticeship to practice any trade irrespective of their Livery Company.[14]

It is impossible to know exactly how many farthingale-makers and body-makers there were in London during the seventeenth century, but examining the records of two of the largest companies – the Drapers' and the Clothworkers' – reveals valuable information about these specialized artisans and their trades. Between the years 1590 and 1700 there were at least fifty-four active freeman farthingale- and body-makers or sellers in the Drapers' and the Clothworkers' companies.[15] While this number appears rather small, there were likely many more of these artisans in the Merchant Taylors Company, who represented the largest number of tailors in the city.[16] Others may also have worked outside the jurisdiction of the Livery Companies beyond the walls of the city, as members of these trades were also concentrated in places such as Middlesex, Southwark and Spitalfields.

During the seventeenth century, farthingale-makers and body-makers in the Drapers' and Clothworker's Companies lived and worked in two of London's premier shopping destinations: Cheapside and the Strand (see Fig. 4.1). Some 13 per cent worked outside the city in the Strand where fashionable shopping arcades such as the New Exchange had been established at the start of the seventeenth century. By 1630 all sorts of luxury goods were sold at the New Exchange and it quickly became a place where fashionable Londoners mingled, as it was also a hub for court women who frequented the principal residence of Queen Henrietta Maria, Demark (Somerset) House.

While the Strand was a new fashionable shopping hub, 41 per cent of farthingale- and body-makers in the Drapers' and Clothworkers' companies lived and worked within the city walls around Bow Lane and Cheapside. Cheapside was the ceremonial and commercial centre of the City of London and it served as a main thoroughfare that connected the court and city.[17] Its tall buildings were occupied by merchants and dealers who attracted many visitors from both London and abroad, and thousands of people walked by every day to shop or socialize.[18] The makers and sellers of foundation garments who lived and worked in this area were therefore well placed to attract a variety of customers, and their shop fronts likely resembled those depicted in the 1638 etching of the procession of Marie de' Medici along Cheapside (see Fig. 4.2). While some artisans had shop fronts that faced outwards onto Cheapside, others plied their trade in lanes and alleys behind this busy thoroughfare in properties that contained mazes of workshops, storerooms, warehouses, vaults and cellars.[19] These properties were primarily located in Bow Lane, which ran north to south between Cheapside and Watling Street and derived its name from the church built in its south-west corner, St Mary-le-Bow (see Fig. 4.1).

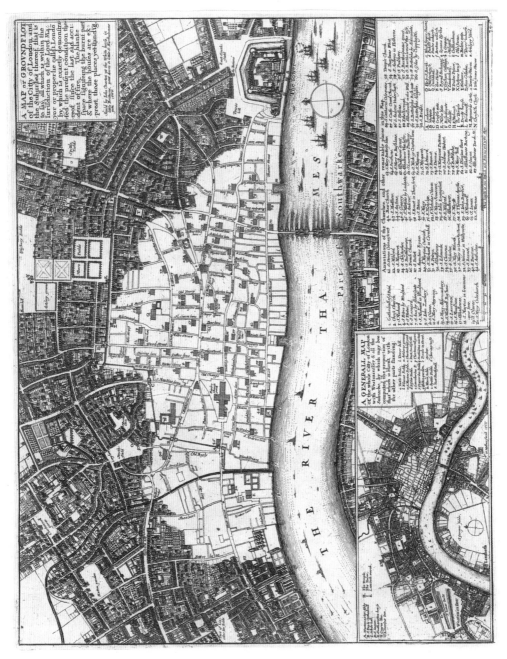

Fig. 4.1 *Wenceslaus Hollar, John Overton, A Map of the City of London and the Suburbs showing the part of the city that was destroyed during the great fire of 12–15 September 1666, c. 1666, etching, Rijksmuseum, Amsterdam. Bow church (number 42 on the Map) is located on the corner of Cheapside and Bow Lane. Temple, the Strand and Somerset House were untouched by the Great Fire and are located in the bottom left-hand corner of the map (marked by I).*

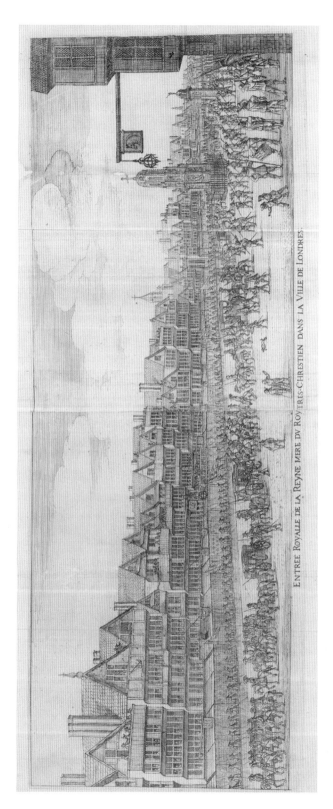

ENTRÉE ROYALLE DE LA REYNE MÈRE DV ROY TRÈS-CHRESTIEN DANS LA VILLE DE LONDRES.

Fig. 4.2 *George Thomason, Octavian Pullen, Jean Raworth, Arrival of Marie de' Medici in London, c. 1639, etching, 2.91 x 7.75 cm, Rijksmuseum, Amsterdam. The view is from the west looking onto buildings on the north side of Cheapside. To the right behind Cheapside Cross, which is in the centre of the image, is a fountain that was known as The Standard. The Cheapside shop frontage owned by body-maker and seller Theophilus Riley was located on the south side of the thoroughfare and looked out onto this fountain and to the buildings shown on the opposite side of the road.*

Between the years 1638 and 1647, Francis Ager (brother of the queen's farthingale-maker John Ager) rented and worked in a messuage (a dwelling with adjacent buildings) owned by the Goldsmiths' Company on the north-east corner of Bow Lane and Watling Street. He appears to have held two tenements in the property, one in the rear called the *Pellican* and another at the front known as the *Black Swan*.[20] Between each residence was a paved yard, a cellar and a warehouse that was divided into two parts. The *Black Swan* contained a first floor with a kitchen and a second floor with two chambers and two garrets. On the ground floor, over a cellar, was a large shop divided into a front and rear that faced out into Bow Lane.[21] It is here that Francis and his apprentices would have sat or stood to create pairs of bodies and farthingales. Such a scene may have resembled that depicted in Quiringh Gerritsz van Brekelenkam's *The Tailor's Workshop*, which shows Dutch tailors sewing near a window for light, with shears, a bodkin and chalk sitting beside them on the shop board (see Fig. 4.3).

As this painting suggests, most garment-making trades required only a few small portable tools to carry out their craft. These included shears, pressing irons, parchment for making patterns, a measuring stick, compass, chalk, needles, thimbles and bodkins.[22] Another important object was the shop board,

Fig. 4.3 *Quiringh Gerritsz van Brekelenkam,* The Tailor's Workshop, *c. 1661, oil on panel, Rijksmuseum, Amsterdam.*

a table on which these artisans sat cross-legged while they stitched, using their bodies to bend and shape the garment into place as they sewed.[23] Such a piece of workshop furniture is visible in another Dutch engraving from 1635 that depicts two tailors sitting cross-legged on a shop board in the background, while another cuts cloth on a solid cutting table in the foreground using shears and a measuring stick (see Fig. 4.4). Under the tables are baskets where scraps of fabric called cabbage were kept, and above them hang finished garments or those in need of repair.[24]

Many body-makers (or bodice-makers, as they were also known) appear to have always had large quantities of whalebone on hand, as it was the most popular choice of stiffening for these garments in England. The 1668 probate inventory of John Chock, a 'Bodicemaker', contained a list of 'Goods in the shop' such as 'Bodice made and unmade' as well as cloth, thread, leather and whalebone.[25] Another probate inventory from that same year belonging to Edmund Fleare, a 'Bodyes Maker' from Lincoln, also listed tools and materials such as 'a silver bodkin', ticking and silk, thread, as well as 'seventeen dozen of Whale bone'.[26] Whalebone, or more accurately, baleen, was one of many stiffening agents used to make clothing during this period. Other common materials included bents, pasteboard, wool,

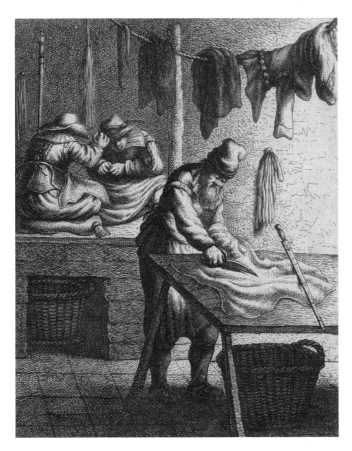

Fig. 4.4 *Jan Georg van Vliet,* Tailors, *1635, etching, Rijksmuseum, Amsterdam.*

horsehair and wire, and heavy fabrics such as buckram, canvas, fustian and kersey. Whalebone had an advantage over other materials as it was essentially the equivalent of modern-day plastic – lightweight, elastic and flexible. Importantly, it could be shaped using heat.[27] This made it the perfect stiffening agent for foundation garments.

During the seventeenth century the number of body-makers in England continued to grow until they were gradually replaced by stay-makers in the eighteenth century (discussed in Chapter 7). Farthingale-making on the other hand appeared to reach its peak in the 1610s – coinciding with the fashionable trend for large French farthingales in the Jacobean court, and the wider dissemination of these garments outside of court circles. Of those affiliated with the Drapers' and Clothworkers' companies after 1620, there was only one craftsman who claimed to be a farthingale-maker and there were four artisans who claimed at various times to be makers of both farthingales and bodies. John Ager was one of these members. Although he was commissioned to make 'Small Rowlls or vardingalls' for Henrietta Maria during the 1630s, he also was recorded as a body-maker during this period and so it appears that specializing solely in making this garment was no longer a viable option.[28]

This demise in the farthingale trade was likely due to the unfashionability of large styles of farthingales after the 1620s, as new fashionable tastes required smaller rolls that could be easily and quickly made by tailors, or perhaps by the wearer herself. Besides those members of the Drapers' company, I have found no other evidence of farthingale-makers in London after 1615 and there is no evidence for any farthingale-makers outside of London during this century.[29] While the demand for these garments, which shaped the silhouettes of London's courtiers and elites, offered many opportunities for farthingale-makers who lived in the capital between 1570 and 1620, it appears that this demand did not exist for those outside London. Such a specialization in making one item of fashionable dress, such as a farthingale, was therefore only possible in London due to its population size and its well-known reputation as the centre of textile industry in seventeenth-century England.

Commissioning and buying foundation garments: interactions between consumers and artisans

Shopping for clothing and other goods is an activity that occupies a large portion of everyday life. Increasingly historians are interested in the strategies that people employed to go shopping in the past, as well as where, when and how this process operated before the twentieth century. Several studies have explored shopping during the medieval and early modern period in England and Europe. These have highlighted that there was a wide market of goods available to consumers during this period, and that this activity was undertaken with enthusiasm by both men and women.[30] Whether it was buying garments brand new in bespoke or ready-made forms, or on the second-hand clothes market, through gifting or even inheriting, the ways that early modern people acquired their dress were wide and varied. So far, this book has touched on the acquisition of dress by those of the middling and common sorts through the channels of gifting and the second-hand clothing market. However, having a garment made bespoke was another activity that most people undertook at least once in their lifetime.

The process of obtaining bespoke dress in the early modern period involved a much more discerning eye and active engagement with making than modern shopping experiences. Knowledge of fashion was shared primarily through word of mouth or observation, and consumers had considerable input in dictating what the end product would look like.[31] The material knowledge utilized by early modern consumers when it came to acquiring material things has been termed *material literacy*. This term refers to the knowledge that consumers held in relation to artisanal skill, or in other words, the understanding of how something was made and why things were done in certain ways, even if the consumer did not possess the making skills themselves.[32] The time-consuming task of choosing fabrics, trims and designs show that early modern consumers had constant involvement in the making and customization of their clothing.[33] Browsing, shopping and interacting with makers was therefore central to building the material literacy skills that allowed early modern consumers to effectively patronize artisans such as farthingale-makers and body-makers.

Recent studies have explored this concept in relation to early modern consumers of male dress. They argue that men's relationship with their artificers functioned in a state of mutual dependency and benefit, as commissioning clothing helped to define the identities and status of both parties. These discerning male customers had considerable input in dictating their purchases, revealing the extensive material literacy that they had developed through their relationships with the makers of their clothing.[34] Yet few studies exist that examine the relationship between English women and their artificers, particularly those below the status of monarchs or consorts. Examining how women in sixteenth- and seventeenth-century England obtained their foundation garments allows us to understand how women exercised their material literacy. Although much of the evidence I provide here relates to women of the middling and elite sorts, recognizing how women, both urban and rural, could and did interact with their artificers is one step towards understanding how all women could go about consuming bespoke or ready-made foundation garments.

Queen Elizabeth I is one English woman whose relationship with her artificers is well understood. This is due, in part, to the extensive archival material that was left after her reign and to the pioneering work of Janet Arnold.[35] All of Elizabeth's artisans, including her tailors and farthingale-makers, plied their trades in the workrooms of the Great Wardrobe where their materials, tools and orders were supplied to them. The Great Wardrobe was a government department of the royal household and was responsible for goods such as furnishings and tapestries, as well as livery and the queen's clothing, which were handled by a sub-department called the Wardrobe of Robes. It was housed in a large building in Blackfriars near the River Thames that allowed for easy transportation of its goods. Books belonging to the wardrobe contain detailed descriptions of the work carried out, the materials and style of garments made, and the identity of the artisans who fashioned them. Warrants survive that bear Elizabeth's signature or were issued 'by the Queens commandment', and these manuscripts show that the queen was very active in commissioning her clothing.[36] The nature of ordering bespoke clothing also meant that the queen's tailors and farthingale-makers would have required close access to the royal body for fittings and alterations. Presumably on these occasions the queen interacted with and directly dictated her wishes regarding the unfinished garment to these artisans when they visited her in Whitehall, Richmond or Greenwich.[37]

While Elizabeth I's artificers worked in-house in the Great Wardrobe, queens consort such as Anne of Denmark and Henrietta Maria relied on external artisans. During his time in the employ of the royal household of Anne of Denmark, the farthingale-maker Robert Hughes worked in the Strand and then Bow Lane near Cheapside, areas that were well located to service the royal palaces and residences. John Ager, who made farthingales for Henrietta Maria, also lived and worked in Bow Lane.[38] The bills that Ager sent to Henrietta Maria's household still survive and contain clues as to how the queen commissioned her foundation garments. The bills typically began with the introduction 'John Ager her Majesties Vardingall maker prayeth allowance for diverse Small Rowlls or vardingalls delivered into her Majesties Rowlls [Robes] for her Majesties own wearing', and then listed items made for the queen with their price, which were adjusted and processed by clerks such as Hugh Aston (see Fig. 4.5). Over the course of the 1630s these bills were written in two different hands using italic script, one of which belonged to Ager. Many of the bills contain comments or readjustments from the clerks that worked in the queen's royal household, as well as the signature of her Mistress of the Robes, Susan Feilding, Countess of Denbigh.

Henrietta Maria strongly dictated her sartorial desires in person and through intermediaries, and her French tailor George Gelin made regular visits to the queen at Greenwich Palace.[39] While Ager may have been required to visit the queen for fittings on occasion, it is more likely that he liaised with her tailor so that the farthingales that he made would fit well with her outer garments. After making the queen's farthingales in his Bow Lane workshop, Ager likely delivered them to Somerset House where her extensive wardrobe was housed. After checking that the garments met the queen's expectations, all the bills were signed off by Denbigh and processed by the Queen's treasurer, Sir Richard Wynn. Ager was then required to acknowledge his receipt of payment and he signed off many of the bills himself.

Unlike bodies and farthingales, busks in these royal accounts were sourced from a variety of artisans. In April 1581, eight busks ordered for the wardrobe of Elizabeth I came from Thomas Greene, a carpenter and coffer-maker, meaning they were likely made from wood or metal.[40] Two years later, in April 1583, nineteen busks made of whalebone were sourced from the farthingale-maker Robert Sibthorpe.[41] By this time whalebone was a staple of the farthingale trade and Sibthorpe would have

Fig. 4.5 *Bill for small rolls and busks from John Ager, farthingale-maker, to Queen Henrietta Maria, Michaelmas 1637, The National Archives of the UK.*

had much of it at his disposal. The household accounts of Henrietta Maria reveal that in 1639 she ordered a dozen busks from her farthingale-maker John Ager too.[42] Later in the century, Catherine of Braganza's records show that her 'whalebone Busks' were bought from her tailor Peter Lombard.[43] Busks were therefore sourced from a variety of artisans who worked with those stiffened materials such as whalebone or metal.[44]

The bespoke nature of tailoring-related work meant that customers had to trust the reputation and skills of their makers and communicate their desires effectively, partly due to the high cost of fabrics.[45] While body- and farthingale-makers may have maintained a small quantity of stock such as whalebone, fabrics such as silk, woollens and trims were usually purchased by the customer from a mercer, draper, silk man or haberdasher, and then given to the tailor. The customer's active role in this process is demonstrated by an account book belonging to Bess of Hardwick, where she noted in her own handwriting that sometime between Michaelmas 1548 and 1550 she had 'paid for cloth to line my vertyngegale'.[46] Whether she had taken the cloth to the tailor herself or paid a messenger to deliver it with her instructions is unclear. Customers also had to be sure that they provided the correct amount of fabric. Later in 1585, Bess's half-sister Elizabeth Wingfield wrote to her about a gown that was to be made for Arbella Stuart, Bess's granddaughter. In the letter, Elizabeth wrote that she sent for a tailor who advised her that although they had five and a quarter yards (4.8 m) of green velvet, he needed at least seven yards (6.4 m) to make the gown.[47] Due to the high cost of fabrics, customers usually wished to buy no more than was required, and in this case it is clear that Wingfield underestimated how much would be needed. Such a miscalculation was probably not uncommon and is an example of the ways that the material literacy of the consumer could be lacking.

While most women would have patronized local tailors or seamstresses for much of their daily wear, women across England could and did obtain garments from London's specialized artisans. As Danae Tankard has shown, during the seventeenth century provincial men and women had three main options for securing fashionable goods from London: they could travel to the capital, communicate with suppliers via letter or get somebody to shop on their behalf.[48] All these options were utilized by women who purchased foundation garments. Although provincial women travelled less than their male counterparts, Martha Mayhew was one woman who was lucky enough to join her uncle, Giles Moore, a minor-gentry rector from Horsted-Keynes in Sussex, on two of his London shopping trips in 1669 and 1672. On these trips Martha bought items such as gowns, petticoats, bodies, masks and gloves. Some of these items were purchased by her uncle and other things like bodies Martha bought herself.[49] The fact that Martha purchased bodies for herself implies that she probably had these garments made bespoke by one of the many body-makers or tailors in the city who could fit her exact measurements and needs.

Alternatively, Martha and her uncle could have purchased her bodies from those who called themselves 'body-sellers'. There were many of these merchants around Cheapside and Bow Lane and those who called themselves sellers were more likely to occupy desirable retail fronts in Cheapside.[50] One prolific body-maker and seller was a man named Theophilus Riley, who occupied a large property known as the *Black Raven* with a shop that faced out onto Cheapside's busy thoroughfare.[51] Riley also rented another property on the corner of Bow Lane and Goose Lane. This place was a similar size to the *Black Raven* and contained living chambers where his own family dwelled, as well as cellars, warehouses and a shop.[52] Records from the Drapers' Company always listed Riley's place of residence as Cheapside when he was referred to as a 'body-seller'; however, those records that identified him as a 'body-maker' recorded his location as Bow Lane.[53] This suggest that most of Riley's stock, likely a combination of bespoke and ready-made, was made and stored in his Bow Lane shop and warehouse before being sold in his retail frontage on Cheapside.

Although the previously mentioned moneylender Joyce Jeffreys likely had the means and freedom to travel to London, it seems that she preferred to send detailed instructions to the capital by carriers. In September 1639, Jeffreys wrote in her accounts book that she had bought a 'pair of whalbon bodies from London' valued at 11s. In addition to the cost of the bodies their transportation required '2 elles [2 ½ yds or 1.14 m] of canvas to lap them in' and a 'carriage of [for] them from London', which cost her an additional 4s. 6d.[54] These bodies were nearly three times the price of others found in her accounts, and so must have been a special piece made bespoke from luxurious materials. Presumably the tailor or body-maker who made this garment had been patronized before and so had Joyce's measurements on record, or she had sent them with her commission. Not all cloth artisans had access to the homes of their customers but many would have had an intimate knowledge of their clients' body shapes and changes due to sustained interaction over time.[55] Indeed, for foundation garments that sat close to the body often underneath layers of outer clothing, this personal knowledge of the customer's form was vital. The intimacy that artisans such as body-makers had with their clients was highlighted by eighteenth-century satirical prints that emphasized the erotic overtones of stay-makers who fitted these garments on their undressed female clients (see Fig. 4.6).[56] Although ridiculed in print, this type of access to the female body by male craftspeople was generally accepted; after all, if one was to pay for a bespoke garment then it needed to be fitted correctly.

Yet there is evidence that women were involved in this intimate process too. Women had always been involved in textile and garment production during the early modern period, whether it was mending, knitting, lacemaking, spinning or helping their husbands in the shop.[57] While men did dominate the body-making trade during the seventeenth century, there is evidence of female body-makers. Two women, Anne Simpkins and Elizabeth Cooke, were body-makers in the Drapers' and Clothworkers' Companies during the late seventeenth century, and both appear to have been widows who were carrying on the trade of their husbands, which included taking on and training apprentices.[58] Yet it is possible that some women may have made bodies much earlier than this too. In 1631, Rape

Fig. 4.6 *Pierre Thomas Le Clerc, Dupin, 'Tailor tests a pair of stays of the latest fashions', in* Gallerie des Modes, *1778, engraving, Rijksmuseum, Amsterdam.*

Oxley, a journeyman tailor, was fined ten shillings by the Oxford tailors Guild because his wife was found to have 'made petticoats', which at this time could have included whaleboned petticoat-bodies, and 'sold them in the market'.[59] Presumably Oxley's wife had learned the trade from her husband and it appears that she had successfully made and sold many of these garments before being fined. Sarah Birt has also found at least four female apprentices that were bound to 'bodice-makers' in the Merchant Taylors' Company between the years 1658 and 1688, including Bridget Webb who was apprenticed to a 'bodicemaker' named Edward Corne in Clerkenwell in 1658.[60]

Wives and female servants also oversaw the running of retail frontages and dealt with female customers, while masters, apprentices and journeyman worked elsewhere in the shop to make these garments. The 1696 will of 'bodice-maker' Richard Hall from Middlesex thanked a Mary Bethell 'for her good service' and dictated that she 'shall continue in my house till she shall dispose and sell my bodyes and afterwards shall continue in the Eastern part or side of my shop if she shall think fit'.[61] Mary appears to have been a either household servant or even an apprentice who had always assisted Hall in his shop, and he clearly wished her to continue to serve his clients after his death.

The final way that women could obtain foundation garments from London's specialist makers was to send male acquaintances to make purchases for them when they visited the capital on business. This process necessitated many steps and competencies and, above all, required trust in the material literacy of their proxy shopper.[62] In such instances, artisans probably relied on measurements previously obtained in-person or through old garments to gain a second-hand knowledge of their customer's bodies.

This is demonstrated by a letter from James Gresham to his mother Judith Morley in Chichester in 1641. In the letter, Gresham informed her that:

> Your waistcoat I carried to the tailors as soon as I received it, where I saw him lay your old pattern on it & it proved the very same size, not withstanding he will make it according to that pattern you sent, I have told him all the faults & he hath faithfully promised to be very careful in the amendment which I wish may be to your liking ... he says likewise that he cannot take off the skirt [of the waistcoat] to make it to wear like a gown, unless he had the petticoat to sew to the body all which you may make one of your tailors there doe for you: if he should send you a rowle he says your petticoat would be too short to wear with it.[63]

The waistcoat in this exchange was one that the tailor had previously made for Judith from a pattern either provided by his client or taken previously when she had visited London. When the waistcoat proved too small it was sent back to London to be checked against the 'first pattern', which proved to be the same size, leading the tailor to conclude that Judith must have grown bigger. By comparing this new garment against this old pattern, Judith's tailor was able to obtain a knowledge of her changed body measurements, and assured James that he would be able to make a new amended waistcoat that would fit her. The new waistcoat was not mentioned again once delivered and so it appears that Judith was pleased with the outcome.[64]

These letters between mother and son also show that during the seventeenth century outer garments had to be tailored around female figures constructed from whalebone and padding, as James relayed the tailor's advice that a roll would make her petticoat too short. In this instance, Judith's bum-roll sat underneath her petticoat and the enlarged hips and bum created by this foundation garment had to be considered when customizing the length of the skirts.[65] The need for outer garments to be tailored around foundation garments is demonstrated by the display of an embroidered Jacobean waistcoat at the Metropolitan Museum of Art in New York. When the garment is displayed without a farthingale roll underneath, the bottom skirts of the waistcoat appear oddly proportioned and too big for the mannequin, and the back of the garment does not sit smoothly (see Fig. 4.7). However, when the waistcoat is placed over a suitably sized roll, the proportions and size of the skirts of the waistcoat sit correctly and give a desirable shape (see Fig. 4.8). The skirts of another waistcoat at the Victoria and Albert Museum also show evidence of alterations done to decrease their circumference when larger styles of farthingale fell out of fashion.[66] Makers and consumers therefore had to effectively communicate and consider how outer garments would correctly fit and sit on the female body shaped by foundation garments.

Letters such as those from Gresham to his mother also demonstrate that male family members willingly carried out the wishes of their female relatives and expressed their instructions on their behalf. In a letter from London to his brother in Norfolk in 1593, Philip Gawdy explained that he was

Fig. 4.7 *Embroidered linen Waistcoat (view 1)*, c. 1616, English, Metropolitan Museum of Art, New York. When worn without a roll the skirts of the waistcoat do not sit correctly.

Fig. 4.8 *Embroidered linen Waistcoat (view 2)*, c. 1616, English, Metropolitan Museum of Art, New York. When worn over a roll the garment sits correctly on the body.

sending many new fashions from London such as a hat to his brother, and to his sister-in-law 'all such things as she requested' which included 'a fuardingal of the best fashion'.[67] Even if a woman could not express her desires explicitly to one of these artisans, many had male relatives eager to do it on their behalf, meaning that they also must have had a complex material knowledge of women's garments. While women's ability to shop and commission garments was more circumscribed than their male counterparts who regularly visited key shopping locations such as London on business and who often controlled the family finances, these examples show that they did have frequent input into the process of commissioning their own dress.[68]

Making and observation: the evolution in design and tacit skills of body-makers

While the commissioning of clothing honed the material literacy of consumers, it was long formal apprenticeships that allowed those who made clothing to learn the 'Craft & mystery' of tailoring and its related trades.[69] In the Drapers' and Clothworkers' Companies alone, approximately 194 men and women entered or completed apprenticeships associated with farthingale- and body-making between 1590 and 1695, and on average these apprenticeships took seven to eight years to complete. Despite this, we know very little about the methods and skills of these craftspeople and of tailors, as they were not recorded in written form. This was done deliberately to ensure that knowledge was kept within the trade to maintain its retail monopoly.[70] However, another reason for the lack of documentary evidence is that the knowledge and experiences of early modern craftspeople was largely tacit, meaning knowledge that was learnt and taught by modelling, imitating and observing master artisans.[71] Traces of this lost tacit knowledge are visible in surviving garments and can be teased out by learning to *read* such evidence. The remainder of this chapter utilizes surviving objects, and my own experience of making, to explore the evolution of the construction of foundation garments and to describe the skills and ingenuity of their makers.

The basic process of putting together a pair of bodies changed very little during the sixteenth and seventeenth centuries. The first step for a body-maker or tailor was to obtain their client's measurements, either in person or from other garments, and to note these on a strip of parchment. The most important measurements to take for bodies or stays were likely from the top of the back and underarm to the hip, the centre front, and then the bust and waist.[72] From these measurements a pattern would be drafted. There are many ways that artisans could have come to the final pattern for a pair of bodies. One method was to copy pre-existing apparel and another was to use a pattern book. Although several European pattern books from this period have survived, these reveal very little about how garments were constructed after the fabric had been cut. Such knowledge was a learned skill that passed from master to apprentice, or exchanged by word of mouth between craftspeople.[73] It appears that fashion knowledge spread fast among customers and makers in England, as only a year after the appearance of French bodies in the wardrobe accounts of Elizabeth I, Norfolk tailors were also making these garments for the Bacon family of Sitffkey. Besides these designs that circulated between craftspeople, innovative artisans also drafted their own bespoke patterns. By the eighteenth century the ability to draw a pattern from scratch separated the best stay-makers from those who were mediocre, and this technical skill enabled the sort of experimentation that created new fashions.[74]

Once a pattern was drafted it was cut on cheap material (to make a *toile*) and adjustments were made during a fitting. Thrifty artisans often used pieces from the left-over toile to interline the garment.[75] Once the pattern pieces were cut and pressed, boning channels would then have been sewn. The lines for these channels were first evenly marked out, usually with ink, and then backstitched over.[76] Some bodies could have over 200 boning channels, and my own experience of body-making proved that backstitching all of these channels was by far the most time-consuming part of constructing each garment.[77] This laborious task was commonly outsourced to women who were employed to do piecework in places such as London, as in 1619 the middle-aged widow Elizabeth Jordayne claimed that 'she getteth her living by stitching of bodies for the shops and otherwise by her needle'.[78] Hiring women to do the most time-consuming part of this process was still common over a century later, as the diary of stay-maker Richard Viney reveals that he also hired women to stitch the boning channels for his stays.[79] It is also possible that some body-makers may have had panels with pre-stitched channels in stock that were simply cut to measure and then assembled for customers who required a quick turnaround time.[80]

After these channels were completed, boning made from whalebone, which had been shaved down to a desired thickness, was inserted. Whalebone was by far the most common material used in the bodies belonging to English women; however, other materials could also be used. The bodies made for the Bacon women of Norfolk were stiffened with whalebone and bents, and those supplied to Catherine of Braganza were made with packthread.[81] After these channels were complete and the boning was inserted and secured, the tabs (or skirts as they were called at the time) would be cut, the panels of the bodies would be sewn together using a whipstitch, and the eyelet holes would be added. Once the fit was checked and corrected, the raw edges would be bound with leather or ribbon, and then finishing touches such as trims would be added.[82]

Sometimes garments were sent back for alterations due to inaccuracies on the part of the body-maker. In a scene from Thomas D'Urfey's play *The Campaigners* (1698) the character Angellica complains, 'No not like them [stays], they pinch me here upon the breast, pucker here on the Shoulder, and the whalebone hurts me.' This, the play makes clear, was due to an incorrect fitting by her 'blockhead' tailor.[83] Such adjustments usually involved taking the garment apart to fix the issue and then putting it back together again. Other alterations may have been needed due to general wear and tear over time or to refresh an old garment. In 1664 a tailoring bill addressed to a Mrs Suthwell from the Clayton family of Marden and Bletchingly in Surrey noted the cost of 'new boning' for the bodies of a green petticoat.[84] A 1694 bill in the household accounts of the Hussey family of Doddington Hall in Lincolnshire also requested payment for 'a pair of stays taken in pieces & made up again', covered and 'fitted before'.[85]

A pair of bodies of gold-brown floral silk brocade dating from the period 1665–80 in Leeds Museums and Galleries demonstrate that alterations were also done to accommodate a growing body (see Fig. 4.9). These bodies are what Randle Holme called 'open before' or front lacing, and they sit off the shoulders as other examples from this period also do.[86] Two side panels made from a contrasting silk fabric of pale pink and burgundy, with a different lining fabric and stitching in a lighter yellow thread, have been added underneath the armpits. These were certainly later additions that were done by someone who was not as skilled as the original body-maker or tailor, as the stitching in the boning channels, side seams and binding is not as neat as the original (see Fig. 4.10). The placement of these additional panels suggests that they were done to resize the garment for a growing body or for a differently sized owner, as adding this allowance enlarged the garment evenly along the waist, rib and bust lines.

While these basic processes remained the same, over the course of the seventeenth century the design of bodies and the skills of their makers evolved. Bodies from the first half of this century all share similar design characteristics: up to four panels made from two layers of fabric, with straight boning

Fig. 4.9 *Bodies and Stomacher, c. 1665–80, English, Leeds Museums and Galleries, West Yorkshire, United Kingdom. The bodies are made from gold-brown silk with floral motifs, possibly of Chinese origin, and lined with linen. They are sewn with yellow silk thread, boned with baleen and bound with yellow silk grosgrain ribbon. Additional panels made from a different silk have been added at the sides.*

Fig. 4.10 *Bodies and Stomacher, c. 1665–80, English, Leeds Museums and Galleries, West Yorkshire, United Kingdom. Detail of the additional panel that has been added to enlarge the garment.*

and front lacing. The bodies from the effigy of Elizabeth I dating to 1603 are made from two layers of twill weave fustian cloth bound by green leather, and they consist of three separate parts: two front panels and a back panel with straps that come over the shoulders to attach to the front (see Fig. 4.11). The bodies are fully boned with vertically placed baleen and contain eyelet holes near the skirts for the attachment of a farthingale or petticoat.[87] The Sittingbourne bodies that date to over thirty years later differ very little in their basic construction (see Fig. 3.4). They are comprised of three panels and lace at the front over a stomacher. Each panel is made from two layers of a strong herringbone linen fabric and boned with vertical strips of baleen. Unlike the 1603 effigy bodies, the edges of the Sittingbourne bodies were double bound; first with a strip of thick dark leather and then with a narrower strip of lighter coloured leather (see Fig. 4.12). My own reconstruction experiments demonstrated that double binding the bottom edges was necessary if intending to wear this garment for any length of time, as it prevents the boning from poking out and digging into the skin when worn. This demonstrates that over time the construction of these garments evolved to correspond to their increased daily use.[88]

The mid-century Filmer bodies are extremely similar in design to the Sittingbourne bodies (see Fig. 3.4). The garment consists of four separate parts: two front panels and two back panels, with vertically placed baleen strips, and a stomacher. They are also double bound, this time with a strip of the same silk satin used on the garment and then with blue silk grosgrain ribbon (see Fig. 4.13). No eyelet holes near the skirts are present, reflecting changes in fashion during this century – as the rolls of the 1640s and 1650s were not attached to the bodies as earlier farthingales were. In all three garments, the boning channels have been stitched vertically except on the centre front where they curve over the bust. This would have given the female torso a conical or cylindrical shape when laced. The simplicity of the design of early pairs of bodies is indicative of the fact that tailors made and followed the basic design principles for both men and women's clothing. Fashionable women's bodies and bodices and men's doublets and jerkins all formed a conical shape that was achieved by using three or four panels that tapered at the waist with skirts that then spread over the hips.

After the mid-seventeenth century, however, the design of bodies became much more complex. Evidence of this is visible in the watered pink silk bodies that date between 1650 and 1680 at the Victoria and Albert Museum in London.[89] These bodies are made up of ten different panels, not including the stomacher. Boning was no longer vertical but increasingly sat at an angle too, giving the garment a more curvaceous shape (see Fig. 4.14).[90] Similarly, an Ivory Silk Bodice from the 1660s in the collection of the Victoria and Albert Museum is also comprised of ten panels, with multiple layers of lining and interlining (for a similar bodice, see Fig. 1.23).[91] These examples show a profound design change in the construction of bodies during the seventeenth century and innovations in the technical skills of their makers. This is possibly due to an increase in the expertise of body-makers who specialized solely in the making of these garments, as well as increasing demand that led to further design improvements (this increase in consumption is discussed in Chapter 7).

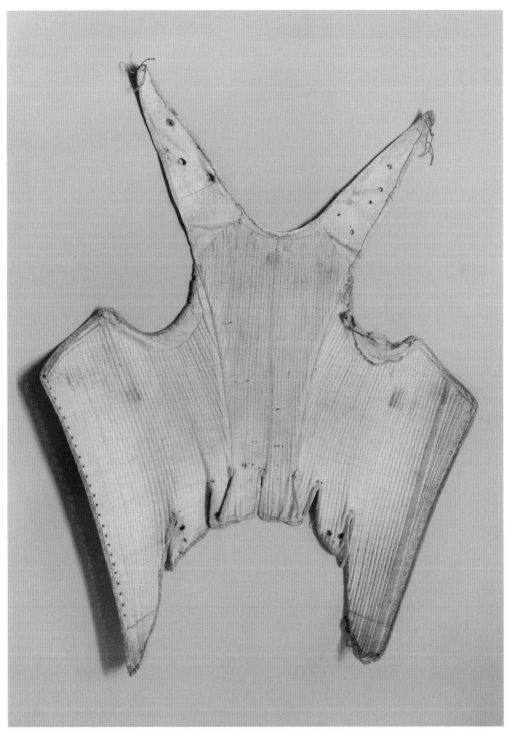

Fig. 4.11 *Bodies from the Effigy of Queen Elizabeth I (inside), c. 1603, English, Westminster Abbey, London. The whip stitching on the size seams is visible and one underarm sweat guard is still attached.*

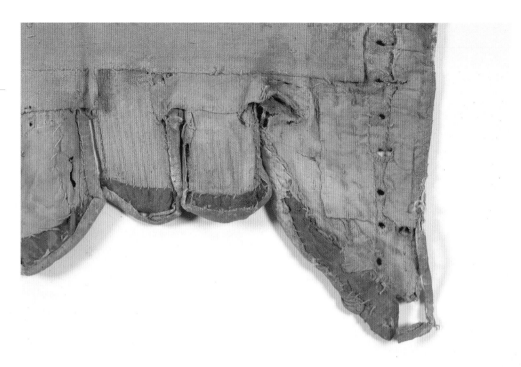

Fig. 4.12 *Double bound skirts and waist tape of the Sittingbourne Bodies, c. 1630–50, English, Plough Finds Collection, Sittingbourne Heritage Museum.*

Fig. 4.13 *Detail of binding and trims on the crimson satin bodies and stomacher of Elizabeth Filmer, c. 1640–60, English, Gallery of Costume, Platt Hall, Manchester City Galleries.*

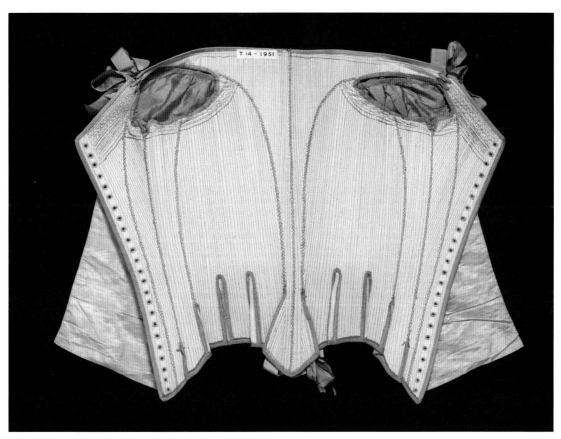

Fig. 4.14 *Inside of bodies of pink watered silk trimmed with pink silk taffeta ribbons and detachable sleeves (inside), c. 1660–80, Dutch or English, Victoria and Albert Museum, London.*

By the end of the seventeenth century these garments were typically constructed of eight or more panels, as demonstrated by a body-maker or stay-maker's trade card from 1692 (see Fig. 4.15). More pattern pieces required more time to correctly size the garment to the customer's body, and boning placed at an angle required varying lengths of baleen to be cut and prepared, which was much more time- and labour-intensive. My own experience of reconstructing the Verney bodies from Claydon House demonstrated this (see Fig. 4.16). These bodies, which are similar in style to the watered pink silk bodies, took over twice as long to make compared to earlier styles, such as the Sittingbourne example, due to the complexity of their design. While the overall shape of the female body still resembled an inverted triangle, later seventeenth-century bodies, with their multiple layers of fabric, curved seams and angled boning, were therefore much more complicated to make.

Final design changes made to English bodies in the late seventeenth century were the addition of an outer fashion layer of fabric and back lacing, two elements that Randle Holme referred to in 1688 as 'smooth covered' and 'open behind'.[92] Such design changes are indicative of changing fashions of the late

Fig. 4.15 *Draft trade card for 'HSH', a maker or seller of bodies or stays, 1692, paper, The British Museum, London.*

Fig. 4.16 *Author's reconstruction of the Verney maternity bodies from Claydon House, Buckinghamshire (see Fig. 6.9), c. 1665–75.*

seventeenth century, notably the rise of the draped mantua gown in the 1680s which exposed the front of this garment (see Fig. 1.28). The previously mentioned pair of blue bodies (or stays as they were increasingly called) dating from 1670–90 in the collection of the Museum of London demonstrates this shift. These bodies are made from four layers of fabric: two interlining layers of linen or canvas containing the boning, an inner lining of linen and outer fabrics of blue striped wool and silk brocade. The stays are back lacing and have sixteen thin skirts that spread over the hips (see Fig. 4.17). Smooth-covered bodies and stays were convenient, as the outer fabrics on these garments could be changed to suit a new outfit or to refresh an aging garment. During the 1690s there are several references to stays receiving 'new coverings' or to new foreparts being added to stays.[93] This was done without having to take apart and remake the whole garment again, which was significantly cheaper than having a new pair made.

Another smooth-covered example from this period belonged to the Mayflower passenger Mary Chilton Winslow. This early North American example was recorded in her 1679 probate inventory as a 'pair [of] body's' and likely date to that decade.[94] The garment consists of ten panels with an interlining of linen that holds the boning, likely baleen (see Fig. 4.18). This surviving example offers a glimpse of the workmanship put into such a garment, as the original outer layer of yellow silk has disintegrated. Each panel has been whip stitched together and the seams felled on the right side. Lines of horizontal stitching cover the boning channels, and this is evidence of the body-maker or tailor stitching through the baleen or bents in order to secure them in place. Such a technique was also used on earlier garments. However, as the stitching on this garment was covered by the outer silk fabric, there are many more rows of stitching securing this boning into the garment. The boning channels in the side

Fig. 4.17 *Bodies of Wool, Silk and Linen (back view), c. 1670–80, English, Museum of London.*

Fig. 4.18 *Pair of Bodies that belonged to Mary Chilton Winslow (front), c. 1670s, North American, Pilgrim Hall Museum, Plymouth, Massachusetts. The bodies are made from two layers of linen and were originally covered in yellow silk satin. Stiffened with baleen or bents. Mary was the wife of a Boston merchant.*

Fig. 4.19 *Pair of Bodies of Mary Chilton Winslow (back), c. 1670s, North American, Pilgrim Hall Museum, Plymouth, Massachusetts.*

and back panels are vertically placed (see Fig. 4.19), but the centre-front panels contain diagonal boning to shape and accommodate the bust.

Like the blue bodies from the Museum of London, the Winslow bodies also have long thin skirts that spread over the hips. Binding these thin skirts in the same manner as previous styles of bodies was finicky and time consuming, something that I learned while binding the skirts of the Verney maternity bodies. However, this design feature did serve a purpose as these skirts create a more curvaceous shape as they spread out of over the hips or bum-roll. All these changing design features show that body-makers and tailors evolved and adapted their designs to their clients' desires and wardrobes, and to fit with changing outer fashions during the seventeenth century.

Making and experimentation: recovering the artisanal knowledge of farthingale-makers

While there are many surviving examples of early modern bodies that we can draw on to understand their manufacture, appreciating how the design of farthingales and the skills of their makers evolved over time is much harder to determine. A sixteenth-century pattern for a Spanish farthingale in Juan de Alcega's *Tailors Pattern Book* (1580) does exist, however, this manual contains only garment patterns and cutting instructions (see Fig. 4.20). In the past, then, historians had to make informed guesses about how these garments were constructed. Arnold used this manual by Alcega to reconstruct a Spanish farthingale. She concluded that hoops were added to the garment by creating tucks in the fabric of the skirt for the stiffening to be inserted into.[95] This was the standard interpretation of how to construct a Spanish farthingale until a doll-sized Spanish *verdugado* was discovered in a church in Spain in the late twentieth century. It appears that this garment was adapted from a full-sized farthingale and cut down to fit a Catholic vestal effigy. The effigy farthingale is made of yellow linen and shows evidence of a fabric-piecing technique recommended by Alcega's pattern. It contains twelve hoops and a hem of seven ropes made from esparto grass and wire that have been bound in strips of linen and then sewn onto the outside of the skirt. It is also possible that it was further stiffened with rabbit skin glue (see Fig. 4.21).[96]

The discovery of this effigy farthingale not only confirms how such garments were constructed but also helps us to understand how farthingales were made in England. In April 1576, Robert Sibthorpe made and altered several Spanish farthingales of silk taffeta and satin. The wardrobe warrants noted that in order to do so he required silk for the garments and bent for stiffening. Also listed were several yards of 'fine broad ribbon employed upon the said verthingalls', 'one piece' each of cotton, baize and

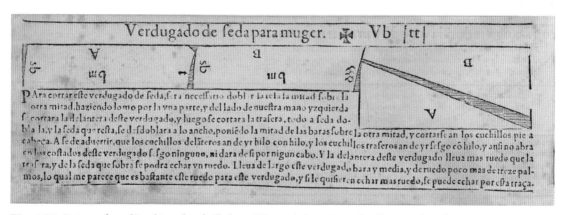

Fig. 4.20 *Pattern for a 'Farthingale of silk for a Woman', from Juan de Alcega,* Libro de geometria, practica y traça *(1580), Biblioteca Nacional de España.*

Fig. 4.21 *Detail of hoops of Spanish farthingale, c. sixteenth or seventeenth century, Colección Museo Etnográfico de Castilla y León Zamora.*

buckram cloth, 'two bundells of browne paper', wooden ell measuring sticks and '4 white brushes'.[97] Using Alcega's manual and the Spanish effigy farthingale to inform our reading of this source, it appears that the wooden ell sticks and brown paper were used for pattern making the farthingale skirt. After this had been constructed, the fabric was possibly further stiffened by applying a paste such as rabbit skin glue using the 'white brushes'. Lengths of bent were then bound in baize, cotton or buckram and formed into hoops that were wrapped in the 'broad ribbon' and sewn to the outside of the skirt.

The royal wardrobe warrants of Elizabeth I also contain many references to farthingales being altered by replacing their hoops. In 1570, the farthingale-maker John Bate was recorded as 'translating', in this context meaning altering, a farthingale of 'crimson and white tufted taffeta with new bent Rope'.[98] As the surviving example from Spain demonstrates, this process likely involved removing the old ropes of bent that had become soft and limp and replacing them with new ones. Such an alteration would have been much easier to do if the hoops were covered in fabric and then attached to the outside of the skirt, rather than if they were incorporated into the garment itself.

Prior to 1580 the queen's farthingales had contained hoops made from ropes of bents or ropes of kersey fabric stiffened with buckram.[99] However, after 1580 whalebone was always used in conjunction with these older materials to structure the various types of farthingales made for the queen. The properties of whalebone – lightweight, flexible and durable – made it a superior alternative to the materials that had been used prior to this. Whalebone was used in the farthingales of other female monarchs much earlier than those of Elizabeth I. During the 1560s, wardrobe accounts for Mary Queen of Scots, whose wardrobe was very much reflective of French fashions of the time, mentioned hoops of whalebone.[100] Later in the 1570s, Margaret of Valois, Queen of Navarre, also had farthingales of damask with whalebone made by her farthingale-maker Nicholas Regnault.[101] It is possible then that this technique had been learned from the French who had clearly been making their farthingales with whalebone since at least the middle of the sixteenth century.

While the effigy informs our understanding of how Spanish farthingales were made, information regarding the construction of French farthingales is much harder to obtain. As Chapter 1 outlined, in England there appears to have been two main types of French farthingale – one that consisted of a large roll and another that resembled a wheel-like structure. In order to better understand how these design features might work, during my research for this book I set about reconstructing both styles of French farthingales. This was a rather experimental process that drew on surviving archival evidence, visual images and understandings of other contemporary garments. As such, it involved identifying the key features of these garments, as outlined in Chapter 1, as well as utilizing knowledge of seventeenth-century sewing techniques and the construction of other contemporary garments, to make French farthingales that reflect my interpretation of the historical record.[102]

My completed French farthingale roll is comprised of semicircular top and bottom pieces made from two layers of blue silk taffeta. Each piece was sewn with ten backstitched boning channels and stiffened with imitation baleen, before being sewn together using a whip stitch to form a tube. After adding wool stuffing, I gathered up each piece at the end and sewed them together with grosgrain ribbon ties (see Fig. 4.22). The completed roll resembles the shape of the roll hanging in the top right-hand corner of *The Vanity of Women* engraving (see Fig. 1.8). My French wheel farthingale imitates the 1626 French watercolour *Entrée des Esperlucattes* by Daniel Rabel (see Fig. 1.9). It consists of two semicircular pieces of black silk taffeta and two bottom pieces of grey linen. These were backstitched together with white silk thread to form four boning channels. The outside edges of the garment are bound with grosgrain ribbon, mirroring the technique used to bind the raw edges of bodies during this period (see Fig. 4.23).

Notably, my design for the wheel farthingale is set apart from other reconstructions as it incorporated a farthingale roll, made of red silk taffeta and stuffed with lambswool, into the garment itself.[103] This was done as the French watercolour *Entrée des Esperlucattes* depicts a red section of padding that appears to sit around the waistline, implying that a roll was part of the garment. A tailoring bill from the Bacon family of Norfolk in 1591 also requested payment for '3 pair of french vardinggales with roules'.[104] The phrase 'with roules' seems to indicate that the French wheel farthingale and French farthingale rolls were two separate parts that could be worn together, or incorporated into the one garment, which is what I chose to do (see Fig. 4.24). My reconstruction further mimics Rabel's watercolour as it is designed to fit with a reconstructed pair of bodies, as the V-shaped placement of the red padding accommodates the centre-point of this torso-shaping garment.

Fig. 4.22 *Author's reconstruction of French farthingale roll, c. 1600. The farthingale is made from silk taffeta, silk thread, imitation baleen and lambswool. It is based on the design shown in the c. 1600 Flemish engraving* The Vanity of Women *(see Fig. 1.8).*

Fig. 4.23 *Author's reconstruction of French wheel farthingale. The farthingale is made from silk taffeta, linen, silk thread, imitation baleen and wool. It is based on those garments worn on the figures in the c. 1626* Entrée des Esperlucattes *(see Fig. 1.9). The model wears it with a smock and a reconstruction of the effigy bodies.*

Fig. 4.24 *Author's reconstruction of French wheel farthingale. View from the back shows the red roll that has been incorporated into the design.*

Since my experiment allowed me to test assumptions about farthingale design, it produced knowledge about the making process that I would never have gained from surviving written and visual sources. During the reconstruction process, it became clear that the modern synthetic whalebone I used was unable to support the circumference of the wheel farthingale and the additional weight of added skirts. To rectify this, I added wire to the circular boning channels. Wire is not mentioned in Elizabeth I's wardrobe accounts, as bents appear to have added extra support to the baleen. However, wire does appear later in the records of Queen Henrietta Maria, and it was also used in the Spanish effigy farthingale. Other patterns for French wheel farthingales have recommended using two long steel bones sewn to the underside of their farthingale perpendicular to the hooped boning, in order to provide support.[105] Although struts were certainly a possible addition, there is no evidence of steel being used in the historical record. Instead, it is possible that thicker, and thus stronger, pieces of baleen were cut and inserted into the garment or that wire was also used in this way. These observations raised significant questions about how these structures were engineered and how large they could realistically could have been (a question that is explored in the next chapter).

My experience of making both farthingales and bodies also demonstrated that similar skills were needed to construct all foundation garments. All required the sewing of boning channels, the cutting of baleen and the use of other stiffened materials. The techniques I used to construct my farthingales were heavily influenced by the techniques I had learned while reconstructing those pairs of bodies that are discussed throughout this book. This crossover of skillsets is supported by the historical archive. As previously mentioned, records of the London Drapers' Company reveal that some members switched between body-making, farthingale-making and tailoring during their careers, or, more probably, specialized in all of them. Take for example the Ager brothers, John and Francis. John Ager was the farthingale-maker who supplied farthingale rolls to the household of Henrietta Maria, and Francis Ager was a body-maker in Bow Lane. Both had been apprenticed under Robert Hughes, who had supplied farthingales to the households of Elizabeth I and Anne of Denmark. Over the course of three decades the Ager brothers appear in various records as both farthingale-makers and body-makers.[106] All these examples, as well as my own experiments, demonstrate that the construction of these garments shared the same basic principles of tailoring and that those who were trained in these crafts could, if necessary, make all types of foundation garments as tailors in the countryside did.

The real ingenuity of early modern tailors and farthingale-makers was revealed once my reconstructions were placed on the actual female body (see Fig. 4.25). Although my French farthingale roll may appear to sit oddly on the body, creating a short, out-of-proportion torso, the clothed silhouette of my model did mirror those of the period (see Fig. 4.26; see Fig. 6.8 for comparison). The short torsos that these rolls created also explain why bodices from the era, such as an English bodice

Fig. 4.25 *Model is wearing the French farthingale roll over a smock, crimson petticoat and pair of bodies.*

dating to 1600 in the collection of the Kyoto Costume Institute, are short-waisted in the sides and back with long centre-fronts that extend to the groin.[107] As indicated in archival and visual sources, incorporating a roll into the French wheel farthingale not only helped to stabilize the garment when on the body, but the padding distributed the weight of the skirts evenly around the hips. Far from being a heavy or cumbersome garment, my reconstructed wheel farthingale is quite lightweight and flexible.

When my model was dressed in both the wheel farthingale and a pair of bodies, it also became apparent that these two garments were designed to work together, as I observed that the rigid centre-front of the effigy bodies that sits over the farthingale helps to anchor it under the weight of the skirts (see Fig. 4.23). This appears to have been a common way to have worn bodies and farthingales, as visual sources often depict the front of long stiffened bodices pushing the front of the hoop down, creating a fashionable tilt, as seen in a watercolour from the Folger Shakespeare Library (see Fig. 4.27). Just as Judith Morley's tailor considered the size of her bum-roll when making her petticoat, body-

Fig. 4.26 *Model wears a French farthingale roll underneath a doublet bodice and skirt. The short-waisted silhouette created by the roll mimics the silhouette of a Dutch woman in Fig. 6.8.*

Fig. 4.27 *Unknown Italian artist,* Royal, military and court costumes of the time of James I *(detail),* c. *early seventeenth century, drawing and watercolour, Folger Shakespeare Library Washington, DC. The wheel farthingale is worn in a way that creates a fashionable tilt.*

makers and farthingale-makers also had to consider how bodies and farthingales would fit together when worn on the female body.

Conclusion

Obtaining foundation garments in early modern England was a multifaceted process that required material literacy on behalf of the consumer and the tacit skills and ingenuity of the maker. Over the course of the seventeenth century, two new craft trades – farthingale-making and body-making – arose to fashion the silhouettes of England's women. While these trades did not monopolize the making of these garments, their service to the royal households and their presence in the fashionable shopping districts of London such as the Strand and Cheapside indicates that they were well known and patronized. Far from being silly clueless monkeys that unquestioningly aped fashion, women were calculated consumers of foundation garments who used their material literacy to commission them. Archival sources show that both queens and country women dictated their wishes to those craftspeople who made their bodies and farthingales, either directly in person or indirectly through letters or proxy-shoppers. These women therefore had considerable input into the final design of their bodies and farthingales.

Finally, tracing the evolution in construction of bodies over the course of the seventeenth century also charts the evolution in skills of body-makers. Over the course of the century these garments became more complex and sophisticated as they moved away from their similarities to male dress and reacted to changes in outer fashions, such as the introduction of the mantua gown. Experimenting with the process of reconstructing farthingales also revealed the shared materials, skills and methods of these artisans, reflecting archival records that show how some craftspeople regularly switched between farthingale-making and body-making. These experiments also raise questions about the lost skills and tacit knowledge of these crafts. The fashion for bodies and farthingales was therefore influenced by both consumers and makers whose material literacy and making skills mutually worked to shape the appearances of early modern women.

5

The everyday body
Assumptions, tropes and the lived experience

By the mid-seventeenth century the silhouettes of women from all social sorts were shaped to varying degrees by foundation garments in England, from the queen and her courtiers, to farmers' wives and household servants. When considering the wide range of women who consumed these garments, questions of size and restrictiveness arise: how tight and uncomfortable were bodies? How big and cumbersome were farthingales? Most importantly, how did women live their vastly different everyday lives while wearing these garments of whalebone, wood, metal and cloth? Answering any of these questions with certainty is difficult, as few female voices survive that describe what it was like to wear these garments and much literature about them was polemical and written by men. Scholars and the general public have also perpetuated myths about these garments, using emotive language such as 'tyrannical costume' to describe them, placing subjective modern assessments onto both historical garments and bodies.[1] Exaggerated myths that stem from eighteenth-century satirical prints or outrageous nineteenth-century newspaper reports, which describe women fainting and even dying from lacing their corsets too tightly, are still commonly perpetuated and also applied to bodies of the sixteenth and seventeenth centuries. Perceptions of the farthingale are no better, as they are blamed for impeding mobility, causing women to trip and expose themselves, and have even inspired modern cartoons of women struggling to fit through doorways.

When trying to uncover the embodied experiences of women who wore bodies and farthingales during the early modern period we must examine the practical realities of these garments: their utilitarian function in dress and everyday life, as well as the sliding scale of physical effects that they had (or could have) on the female body, depending on how they were worn or how often. By using a variety of sources this chapter constructs a picture of the everyday lived experience for women in sixteenth- and seventeenth-century England. While foundation garments did shape the everyday lives of women during the sixteenth and seventeenth centuries – defining gendered milestones in childhood, contributing to the management of disease, shaping the physical movement of everyday life, as well as influencing the ways that women navigated spaces – much of what we know about these garments, from contemporary writings to popular myths, is exaggerated and simply plays into common tropes about women and their bodies, such as their weakness and sinfulness, during the early modern period. This chapter seeks to uncover the variety of everyday lived experiences of women who wore foundation garments and to dispel highly gendered and historically subjective myths about them.

The life cycle, disease and deformity

In April 1617 Anne Clifford noted in her diary that 'The 28th was the first time the Child put on a pair of Whalebone Bodice.'[2] The child described was Anne's daughter, Lady Margaret Sackville, who was just two years and nine months old at the time. Margaret and many other girls like her were placed in foundation garments from a young age during the seventeenth century. A 1641 portrait of William II, Prince of Orange, and his bride, the nine-year-old Princess Mary Stuart, demonstrates how elite young girls were dressed in whalebone bodies like fully grown women, as the rigidity of the bodice is evident on the young princess (see Fig. 5.1). Later in the century, Reverend Thomas Larkham also

Fig. 5.1 *Anthony van Dyck,* William II, Prince of Orange, and his Bride, Mary Stuart, *1641, oil on canvas, Rijksmuseum, Amsterdam.*

recorded in his diary that he paid for 'a pair of bodies' for his young granddaughter Jane Miller in 1662.[3] Dressing children as miniature adults in the early modern period was not unusual and, in many cases, marked an important stage in the life cycle that signified a coming-of-age recognition of the child's gender. It is well known that until the late nineteenth century young boys wore gowns or dresses until they reached six to eight years of age, or possibly earlier, when they had full control of their bowels, and then underwent the rite of passage of breeching.[4] Similarly, Susan Vincent has proposed that Clifford's description of her daughter being placed in bodies 'was crucial to the performance of gender' as the *bodying* of little girls seems to have performed the same function as breeching in boys.[5]

This idea is supported by visual sources. A portrait of Barbara Sidney, Countess of Leicester, with her six children by Marcus Gheeraerts the Younger, from 1596, depicts her children of different ages in various states of gendered dress (see Fig. 5.2). In the portrait the heavily pregnant Barbara is surrounded by her two young daughters in the bottom left, her two sons – the infant on the left and

Fig. 5.2 *Marcus Gheeraerts the Younger,* Barbara Gamage, Lady Sidney, later Countess of Leicester, with two sons and four daughters, *c. 1596, oil on canvas, Penshurst Place.*

the unbreeched son on the right – and her two eldest daughters to the far right, both of whom are dressed as adult women would have been. While both her sons wear what could be interpreted as genderless clothing as they are not old enough to be breeched, her four daughters all possess the same long and slender torsos created by bodies and busks. Interestingly, the two eldest daughters also both appear to be wearing farthingales, indicating that this garment may also have played a part in gender and age milestones during childhood. While not enough evidence has survived to confidently assert that bodies or farthingales played similar roles in female childhood to that of breeches in boys, it is certain that bodies were a common part of childhood, used for both utilitarian and aesthetic purposes during the seventeenth century in England.

Foundation garments were regularly used to address orthopaedic problems in both male and female children. In 1651 *A Treatise of the Rickets being a Disease Common to Children*, translated from an original French edition, stated that to 'straighten the trunk of the Body [of children], or to keep it straight, they use to make Breastplates of Whalebone put into two woollen Cloths and Sewed together', indicating that some sort of medical brace similar to bodies was used in the treatment of rickets.[6] In May 1676, Madame de Sévigné also advised in a letter to her daughter that she should put 'little bodies on him [her grandson], a bit hard, that hold his waist' so that he would grow in proportion.[7] The bodies of children were believed to be moister and therefore more malleable than those of adults, making them more susceptible to disease.[8] Therefore, in order to 'to strengthen the body', Franciscus de le Boe wrote in his book *Of Childrens Diseases* (1682) that many children wore 'Bodice with Whalebone', indicating that by the late seventeenth century the therapeutic uses of these garments in orthopaedic disease was well known.[9]

Extant bodies made from metal demonstrate that these garments were used to treat orthopaedic problems in adults too. Early modern examples found in English, French and Italian collections are all believed to have been used to treat issues such as spinal deformities (see Fig. 5.3).[10] French surgeon Ambroise Paré remarked in the late sixteenth century that 'breast-plates of iron, full of holes all over' were worn to 'amend the crookedness of the Body' in many, 'especially young maids or girls' (see Fig. 5.4).[11] Indeed, there is no evidence from this period to suggest that these types of metal bodies were ever fashionable or widely worn, either in England or Europe. Many surviving bodies of metal in European collections have also been discovered to be fakes that were made to satisfy the curiosities of nineteenth-century collectors. Although the Florentine wardrobe inventories of Eleonora of Toledo, the wife of Cosimo I de' Medici, show that she owned two bodies of steel made by an armourer that were then covered in blue taffeta by her tailor, these are an anomaly in her wardrobe accounts, indicating that they were not items of fashionable dress.[12] Rather, for Eleonora and many others in Europe, these garments may have been worn in everyday life for therapeutic purposes, aiding the treatment of orthopaedic disease in much the same way as modern back braces aid scoliosis sufferers.

Although these garments did play a role in the treatment of disease, the introduction of heavily boned bodies and bodices into the wardrobes of healthy girls during the late sixteenth century

Fig. 5.3 *Bodies made from steel and decorated with pierced scrollwork, French, c. 1640, The Wallace Collection, London. The bodies are closed and fastened by two hinges.*

prompted many debates over the medical effects of these garments on young growing bodies. Critics like John Bulwer blamed the 'folly' of mothers and nurses as they 'too straitly lace the Breasts and sides of Girls' with the desire to 'make them slender' and 'have their young Daughters bodies so small in the middle as may be possible'. Instead of creating a beautiful body shape for their daughters, Bulwer argued that mothers actually ran the risk of deforming torsos by 'pluck[ing] and draw[ing] their bones awry', making them 'crooked'.[13] However, these moralizing treatises were simply repeating previous complaints, almost word for word, as earlier sixteenth-century works by Ambroise Paré spoke of the 'folly of mothers, who while they covet to have their young daughters bodies so small in the middle as may be possible, pluck and draw their bones awry and make them crooked'.[14] Although Paré advocated for the orthopaedic use of bodies, he also linked 'the tightening of the corps [bodies] of girls in their youth' to the prevalence of adult women who were 'hunchbacked' when they removed them.[15]

Such criticisms of foundation garments likely grew out of other debates during this period that decried the ills of swaddling, a common technique practised throughout Europe in order to soothe babies and to ensure that they grew correctly. Such debates contended that swaddling too tightly

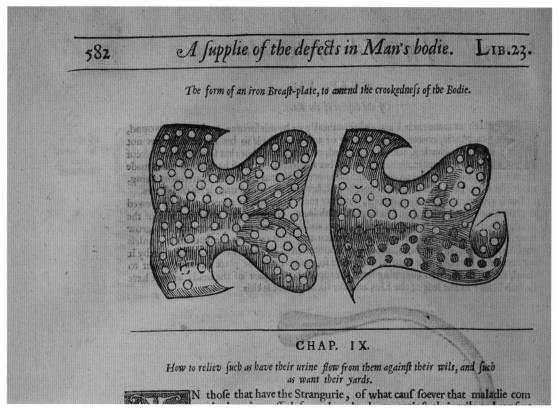

Fig. 5.4 *'The form of an iron Breast-plate, to amend the crookedness of the Body', in Ambroise Paré,* The workes of that famous chirurgion Ambrose Parey *(London, 1649), Wellcome Library, London.*

caused orthopaedic problems in children, and some argued that mothers and nurses attempted to mould their babies into a desirable shape in the process.[16] As explored in Chapter 2, many debates about foundation garments during this period were concerned with ideas surrounding nature and artifice, and more importantly deformity. Were children's bodies created perfectly or did they need assistance? Reflecting many of the moralizing voices that focused on women and their dress, by the mid to late seventeenth century, writers believed that when it came to children's bodies, nature should be left to take its course. This was made explicit by John Locke in his *Thoughts concerning education* (1693): 'Let Nature have scope to fashion the Body as she thinks best; she works of her self a great deal better, and exacter, than we can direct her . . . I have seen so many Instances of Children receiving great harm from *straitlacing*.'[17]

Later seventeenth-century conduct literature such as the *Gentlewomans Companion* (1673), attributed to Hannah Woolley, echoed earlier concerns, stating that the 'Mothers and Nurses' of young girls and gentlewomen desired a 'small Waist thinking that the most exquisite proportion'. To attain this, they strait-laced and girdled their 'tender bodies' so that they would be 'as slender in the middle as the Strand-May-pole is tall in its height'. As a result of this practice, the *Gentlewomans Companion* argued that women's bodies were reduced

> . . . into such pinching-extremities, that it engenders a stinking breath; and by cloistering you up in a Steel or Whalebone-prison, they open a door to Consumptions, with many other dangerous inconveniences, as crookedness: for Mothers striving to have their *daughters bodies small in the middle, do pluck and draw their bones awry*; for the ligatures of the back being very tender at that age, and soft and moist, with all the Muscles, do easily slip aside. Thus Nurses, while they too *straitly do lace the breasts and sides of children on purpose to make them slender*, do occasion the breast-bone to cast itself aside, whereby one shoulder doth become bigger and fuller than the other.[18]

Not only did this conduct manual use the exact same language as both Paré and Bulwer, but it is now believed that it was penned by a male employee of the publisher Dorman Newman.[19] Rather than being a work based on the experiences of the real female author Hannah Woolley, it was instead an amalgamation of several previous works compiled by a male author that continued this trope of the folly and vanity of mothers and nurses.

But did bodies really pluck and draw the bones awry? In her examination of English and French female skeletons from the eighteenth and nineteenth centuries, anthropologist Rebecca Gibson has noted that 'all exhibited rib and spinous process deformation consistent with long-term pressure on growing ribs and vertebrae' and that these were inconsistent with disease such as rickets or congenital deformity. Specifically, these changes deformed the ribcage downward and laterally, which produced a distinct, angled appearance to the female torso.[20] These downward deformities to the ribs are characteristic of compression, most probably from stays and corsets. Katherine Marie Klingerman has undertaken a similar study examining eighteenth- and nineteenth-century female skeletons from Christ Church cemetery in Spitalfields, London, paying specific attention to differences in the shape and style between stays and corsets over this 200-year period. While deformities in the ribs were noted in many of the eighteenth-century skeletons, these skeletons were much less likely to have deformities to the pelvis like those from the nineteenth century.[21] This is because the conical design of stays, and their predecessor bodies, meant that pressure was primarily placed on the ribs, and not on the waist, hips or lower back, as was the case with the hourglass-shaped corsets of the nineteenth century that could cause muscle atrophy in the back and abdominal muscles.[22] Although eighteenth-century stays, which were similar in shape and design to earlier bodies, appear to have slightly deformed the ribs and spine, this did not impact female lifespan as many of the skeletons examined by Gibson 'lived longer than the average age for their times'.[23]

Placing women in bodies and stays from a young age could inhibit the normal growth of the ribs and cause slight deformities. However, this was not enough to cause scoliosis, premature death or other great medical harms described by authors in the sixteenth and seventeenth centuries. Instead, the continued repetition of Paré's sixteenth-century story of deformities by moralizing authors throughout the seventeenth century in England was fear-mongering that can be attributed to common early modern anxieties surrounding ideas of monstrosity and deformity. In the sixteenth and seventeenth centuries, discussions of deformity were overwhelmingly underlined by social, religious, political and moral concerns.

In early modern England these cultural concerns surrounding deformity and disability have primarily been explored by historians in relation to *monstrous births*, where births involving congenital abnormalities were met with fear, repulsion and dismay and interpreted as omens or punishment from God for sin, predominantly the sins of those women involved with the birth.[24] In some of these births the congenital deformity resembled fashionable apparel, such as the case of a 'Childe with Ruffes borne' from Surrey in 1566, whose deformity supposedly resembled a fashionable ruff around the neck. Such births were widely condemned as the deforming result of women's pride and fashion excess.[25] Criticism of bodies causing deformities in children can be interpreted in much the same way as these monstrous births: children were punished with deformity and disease as a result of the follies of mothers and nurses who tight-laced them from a young age in the vain pursuit of beauty and perfection. These moralizing myths were then perpetuated throughout the early modern period and beyond as reality.

Women also continued to wear these garments throughout their lifetime into old age. What exactly constituted old age in early modern England was far from straightforward, although according to contemporaries it was generally believed to be after the age of forty-nine.[26] The life cycle for women was not marked using the same metrics as men, nor was it counted using the same metrics of age as we do in modern times. The three cycles of female life generally followed the rule of maid, wife and widow, but a woman could be a young widow or an old single woman (spinster). A life event that occurred regardless of marital status was menopause, usually around age fifty, and this was generally considered to be a woman's entry into old age as this bodily occurrence brought with it irreversible physical changes associated with aging.[27] Early modern literature was often critical of both men and women who indulged in fashion when they were past their youth.[28] However, what is clear is that post-menopausal women did wear foundation garments in early modern England and they do not appear to have been heavily criticized for it.

Many of the women I have mentioned in this book so far were old by early modern definitions. The first, and most well-known, was Elizabeth I, whose French bodies were first made during her sixties. Although her status as queen meant that even in old age Elizabeth was expected to dress magnificently, other women of the aristocracy also wore foundation garments well into old age. Lady Jane Stanhope was seventy-one years old when she died, leaving several bodies and farthingales of the latest fashion in her 1618 inventory (as mentioned in Chapter 2). As discussed in Chapter 4, by the mid-seventeenth century provincial women like Judith Morley and Joyce Jeffreys the latter of whom would have been in her mid-fifties to late sixties, were also consuming foundation garments. Jeffreys may even have found garments such as bodies and busks useful in old age. By 1645 it appears that she had mobility issues, as that year she bought a 'fir wood staff'.[29] Limited mobility and menopause likely contributed to changes in her stance, which may account for the multiple busks that Jeffreys purchased for herself during the 1640s, as these would have helped to improve her posture.[30] For the most part we can only speculate how elderly women used foundation garments and if any of these were to counter or relieve the effects of aging. What is clear, though, is that these women still cared about their appearance and wished to maintain a fashionable (and increasingly commonplace) body that was supported and shaped by foundation garments.

Bodies: movement and everyday life

Anthropological studies show that bodies and stays did not deform the ribs or pelvis in ways that caused severe disease or death. However, there are few surviving female voices from the period that tell us about what sort of challenges (if any) these garments posed for the practicalities of everyday life. Although bodies were originally a high-status garment imbued with elite social meanings, they were also functional garments of early modern dress. As Ninya Mikhaila and Jane Malcolm-Davies have explained, the use of darts, which help eliminate wrinkles in modern garments that hug the natural curves of the body, was basically unknown during the early modern period. So a structured foundation was required to keep the torso looking smooth and composed.[31] At a time when women often wore many layers of heavy skirts and gowns, bodies also provided a solid base that anchored these layers to the body. Playwright John Marston made this point explicit in his play *The Malcontent* when the character of the fool, Pasarello, states that 'What a natural fool is he that would be a pair of bodies to a woman's petticoat, to be trussed and pointed to them.'[32] The pair of bodies found on the funeral effigy of Elizabeth I perfectly demonstrate the utilitarian function of bodies in female dress. These bodies have two eyelet holes above the split, separating each tab that anchored (or pointed) the petticoats to the torso, and there are a total of six tabs designed to sit under both styles of French farthingale to distribute the weight of the outer garments (see Fig. 5.5).[33] In this sense, bodies were actually beneficial to women who were required to wear the elaborate and heavy styles of dress dictated by the courts of Europe.

Uncovering the other practicalities of foundation garments, however, requires a much more detailed observation of the effects of dress when worn. As part of Jules Prown's method for analysing objects, he instructs that after the researcher describes, measures and weighs the object, they should put themselves in the picture during the second stage of deduction, to 'engage in a sensory experience

Fig. 5.5 *Bodies from the Effigy of Queen Elizabeth I (back), c. 1603, English, Westminster Abbey, London. The eyelet holes where the petticoat or farthingale would have been pointed or attached to the bodies is visible above the skirts (tabs).*

of the object', and contemplate what it was like to use or wear it.[34] For some garments it is indeed possible to imagine what restrictions they may have posed for the body. Highly boned court bodices from the 1660s must have limited the movement of the arms and forced the wearer to maintain an upright composure, as the sleeves are set low at the back, which would pull the arms and shoulders backward (see Fig. 5.6). Yet for other garments these observations about restrictiveness are not easily made. For obvious reasons, it is not viable to wear 400-year-old garments to investigate their effects on the body. In terms of measuring notions of comfort, it would be anachronistic to place these garments on a modern body to see how *we* would feel wearing them, as historical notions of comfort and other sensory experiences vary widely. Focusing solely on recapturing bodily experiences would also disregard the mental comfort that early moderns sought in their clothing.[35] With all this said, however, well-researched reconstructions using historically accurate methods can expand our knowledge and help to examine primary sources that discuss or depict wearing and movement.

In 2004, Hilary Davidson reconstructed a pair of Spanish bodies dating to the late sixteenth century from Juan de Alcega's tailoring manual using the Castilian measurement system and period-correct

Fig. 5.6 *Green Silk Bodice (back), c. 1660s, English, Museum of London.*

materials and sewing techniques. She noted that the bents she used to stiffen the bodies were 'light and flexible' and gave similar structure and stiffness to the garment as modern spring steel boning. When four women of varying body shapes and heights tried on the garment it consistently created the same coned shape to the body that was independent of the natural shape underneath. More importantly, Davidson found that although the garment did impose an artificial shape on the body it also allowed a wide range of movement.[36] Many historical interpreters have also noted that over time, if used frequently, bodies and stays made from both whalebone and bents soften and mould to the shape of the wearer. As previously mentioned, heat makes whalebone (baleen) malleable and this was one of the most desirable aspects of this material. If heat makes baleen soft, then over time a woman's body heat would also have made this garment pliable and mould to the wearer's own body.

As the study by Klingerman found, the style of foundation garments shaped the historical impression left on a woman's skeleton and so we must acknowledge that these garments would also have influenced a woman's daily movements. Unlike corsets of the nineteenth century, Davidson found that the Spanish bodies she recreated left the natural waistline relatively free and instead placed more restriction on the ribcage, meaning that the look of a reduced waistline is actually a visual trick.[37] My own reconstructions of the Elizabeth I's effigy bodies (see Fig. 5.7) and the Dame Filmer's bodies (see Fig. 5.8) also showed this. Placing these reconstructions on models allowed their effects on the female body to be observed. Trying my reconstruction of the effigy bodies on two models of slightly different sizes made little difference to the basic uniformed conical shape it gave to the torso, even though the garment did fit one model better than the other.[38] Unlike nineteenth-century hourglass-shaped corsets, lacing the bodies as tight as one of my models could endure only reduced her waist measurements by a small 1½ inches (3.8 cm), with much of the restriction placed on the ribs and not the waist. For everyday comfortable wear, then, it is unlikely that a pair of properly fitted bodies significantly reduced body measurements.

Experimentation with nineteenth-century corsets has shown that restriction to the ribcage through moderate lacing or chest binding reduces the wearer's total lung capacity, sometimes by 6–10 per cent, as these garments impede the movement of the diaphragm.[39] This reduction in lung capacity forces the wearer to adopt shallow upper-diaphragmatic breathing, which pregnant women and obese

Fig. 5.7 *Author's reconstruction of the straight bodies from the 1603 effigy of Elizabeth I. The bodies are made from two layers of pink silk taffeta, boned with plastic imitation baleen, bound with grosgrain ribbon and sewn with silk and linen thread.*

Fig. 5.8 *Author's reconstruction of the bodies and stomacher of Elizabeth Filmer, c. 1640–60. The bodies are made from one layer of yellow silk taffeta and one layer of linen, are boned with imitation baleen, bound with grosgrain ribbon and sewn with silk thread. The garment is decorated with metallic braid and the stomacher contains a wooden busk.*

individuals also experience.[40] Sixteenth- and seventeenth-century bodies would therefore have had some influence on the breathing abilities of the women who wore them. Yet women were still able to undertake activities such as dance, and, as Renaissance dance re-enactors have noted, they simply had to learn to adjust their breathing accordingly.[41]

These garments could also affect other aspects of daily life, especially if they were not fitted correctly. As noted in Chapter 4, the length of the torso was just as important as the width when measuring and patterning a pair of bodies or stays, and constructing a garment that was appropriate to the length of the torso was vital to maintaining comfort. This was demonstrated when I placed my reconstruction of Elizabeth I's effigy bodies on models of various heights and torso lengths. It became apparent that the original garment, which was made for the queen's wooden effigy but likely constructed from an earlier garment pattern, was made for a woman who was tall and long waisted.[42] When the effigy bodies were worn by a short model the underarms dug into the armpits, the shoulder straps were far too big and the back of the garment jutted up past shoulder height. These issues, however, were not apparent when the garment was worn by a taller model with a longer torso, thus seeming to corroborate contemporary reports of the queen being tall and slender.[43]

When models of differing heights sat down in this Elizabethan style of bodies, a noticeably rigid posture was produced, as the long centre-front of the bodies digs into the groin, forcing the wearer to maintain an upright posture to alleviate this pressure (see Fig. 5.9). While this outcome was less apparent on the taller model with a longer torso, this effect is also visible in portraits from the seventeenth century. One such artwork depicts Mary Stuart wearing a bodice with a long centre-front likely containing a busk that pushes down into the groin, forcing her to maintain an upright posture, indicating that in some cases this effect was clearly desired (see Fig. 5.10). Such an effect would also have encouraged a woman to sit open-legged, as Mary is depicted as doing, which supports the assertion made by Ruth M. Green that sitting with knees apart to make a 'broad lap' was the common and proper way to sit at this time.[44]

The effigy bodies did not contain a busk like later examples. So, when my model was instructed to sit and lean forward, my reconstruction of this garment bent and curved with the torso (see Fig. 5.11). Although busks were intended to keep the body straight, some surviving busks appear to curve outwards, which would have made the process of sitting easier (see Fig. 7.7). Several wooden busks from the seventeenth century are outwardly curved and do not contain stress fractures from wear.[45] Instead, it is likely that some long busks were intentionally created to be slightly bowed, either through carving or steaming, to accommodate the movement of the body and make sitting more comfortable for the wearer.

My reconstruction of the mid-seventeenth-century Filmer bodies yielded different results in restrictiveness again when placed on models. Although the stomacher of my reconstruction contains a wooden busk, it is not as long as the centre-front of the effigy bodies and so the peak did not dig

Fig. 5.9 *Model sitting in the effigy bodies reconstruction.*

Fig. 5.10 *Caspar Netscher,* Portrait of Mary Stuart *(later Mary II of England), c. 1683, oil on canvas, Rijksmuseum, Amsterdam.*

Fig. 5.11 *Model sitting and leaning forward in the effigy bodies reconstruction.*

deeply into my model's groin when sitting (see Fig. 5.12). As with the Sittingbourne bodies discussed in Chapter 3, the shoulder straps curve horizontally around the edge of the shoulders, as was fashionable during the mid-seventeenth century (see Fig. 5.13). As a result, my models found it difficult to raise their arms above shoulder height (see Fig. 5.14). While early modern garments, including doublets, could restrict arm mobility more than modern clothing due to the placement of the armholes, this style was much more restrictive than both Davidson's Spanish bodice and my effigy bodies. While some aspects of the garment were restrictive, others were designed for comfort. The inclusion of stomachers in mid-seventeenth-century styles such as the Filmer and Sittingbourne bodies was practical; these pieces allowed for the fit of the garment to be altered as the actual female body grew and changed through times of moderate weight gain and loss, without having to be taken apart and altered, or a new garment made.[46] Due to the use of a stomacher, my reconstruction of the Filmer bodies was able to be easily worn by four different models of varying bust and waist sizes.

Most extant seventeenth-century bodies in English collections are front lacing, meaning that women could dress themselves into these foundation garments without the help of a maid. The genius

Fig. 5.12 *Model sitting in Filmer bodies reconstruction.*

of using laces to construct a garment was that the wearer also had complete control over how tight or loose she wanted her bodies to be. Davidson's reconstruction experiment showed that even with back lacing it would have been perfectly possible for a woman with dexterity to lace a pair of sixteenth-century bodies by herself.[47] Women could therefore easily adjust the tightness of the garment throughout the day. The ability to easily access lacing would have been particularly helpful for breastfeeding mothers, as Dutch genre artworks regularly present mothers unlacing the tops of their bodies and pulling their breasts out over the top (see Fig. 5.15). This was a common way that early modern mothers nursed their babies, even during the eighteenth century when other stylistic changes were also made to stays to further aid this process.[48] Another Dutch genre painting also depicts a mother sitting next to her baby's cradle lacing up her bodies, seemingly after feeding the infant (see Fig. 5.16).

Women therefore had a large amount of control over how tight their bodies were laced and when, so that it did not interfere with daily activities that involved laborious movement or breastfeeding (pregnancy garments are discussed in Chapter 6). Short-waisted bodies like those represented in Jan

Fig. 5.13 *Crimson satin bodies and stomacher of Elizabeth Filmer (back), c. 1640–60, English, Gallery of Costume, Platt Hall, Manchester City Galleries.*

Fig. 5.14 *Model raising arms as high as possible while wearing the Filmer bodies reconstruction.*

Fig. 5.15 *Cornelis Pietersz Bega,* Interior with Mother Nursing her Child, *c. 1654–8, oil on panel, Städel Museum, Frankfurt am Main.*

Fig. 5.16 *Pieter de Hooch,* The Mother, *c. 1663, oil on canvas, Gemäldegalerie, Berlin. The mother in this scene wears a smock with red bodies that are underneath an outer grey gown and waistcoat trimmed with fur. Hanging behind her is a matching red petticoat skirt.*

Steen's 1660 painting *The Lovesick Maiden* (see Fig. 5.17) may also have been useful. This painting depicts a sick woman who is wearing a pair of front-lacing pink bodies being attended by a physician. These bodies appear to only extend to the natural waistline and there is no long centre-front or busk as seen in other examples from this period. These would not have heavily impacted bodily movements such as sitting and bending, and centuries before the modern brassiere had been invented, these bodies would also have provided breast support for all women.

The fact that bodies restricted types of movement could lead one to assume that labouring women did not own or wear these garments.[49] Yet as Chapter 3 confirmed, domestic servants and even farmer's wives owned bodies stiffened with whalebone in the seventeenth century, so corseting by the non-elites was certainly not uncommon. However, it is unlikely that they wore these garments all the time. Sisters Anne and Elizabeth Cocke from Bilsington in Kent were provided with French bodies during the 1620s, but unlike other clothing given to them during this decade these garments were not designated as being for 'working days'.[50] So these bodies stiffened with whalebone were probably worn as better

Fig. 5.17 *Jan Steen,* The Lovesick Maiden, *c. 1660, oil on canvas, Metropolitan Museum of Art, New York.*

wear, while those bodies reserved for working days may have been made from stiff canvas or lightly boned.

Most surviving clothing from the early modern period is quite small, as garments of average and larger sizes were passed on and worn by others until rags, or taken apart and remade into something else. As a result, most of the pairs of bodies examined in this book have waist sizes from 20 to 23 inches (51–58.5 cm).[51] This survival bias means that these extant garments are not necessarily representative of the diverse range of body shapes during this period. However, larger body sizes were still expected to conform to the fashionable straight silhouette of the time and there is no evidence that voluptuous women did not want to wear these types of garments. A pair of stays from the late eighteenth century with a waist measurement of 43 inches (109.2 cm) does exist in the Philadelphia Museum of Art, showing that a diverse range of bodies also existed in the past, just as they do today.[52] Rather, it was the use of foundation garments that created these historical silhouettes by conforming bodies of all sizes to a desirable shape.

Experimentation by other researchers affirms what my reconstruction tests on petite bodies demonstrated: all types of bodies and stays did not reduce waist measurements significantly. Rather, it was the breasts that were compressed and reduced the most. Historical costumer and artist Lauren Marks has noted that seventeenth-century bodies do not necessarily reduce body measurements on curvy women; rather, they simply redistributed the belly fat, creating the illusion of a smaller smoother silhouette.[53] In an experiment involving wearing a reconstructed pair of back-lacing 1680s bodies, Marks was able to achieve the fashionable silhouette of the decade while her body measurements remained largely unchanged. The bodies only reduced her bust measurement by one inch and actually increased her waist measurement by one inch. However, the garment creates the illusion of a long, tapering V-shape torso and, importantly for curvy women, gives excellent support to the breasts and the back.[54]

Most extant foundation garments that have survived the wear and tear of the centuries are therefore smaller-sized high-status garments that mostly reflect fashionable, rather than everyday, dress. So, they should not to be taken as representative of all the types of foundation garments or body types that existed during the sixteenth and seventeenth centuries. A wealthier woman in the 1640s may have worn a style like the Filmer bodies with a fashionable off-the-shoulder gown on formal occasions; however, in daily life the same woman may have worn a pair of bodies that were less restrictive, with straps that went over the shoulders and without a busk. The range of experiences of wearing bodies in the seventeenth century was quite varied and not a monolithic experience of pain, restriction and repression. The use of bodies therefore spanned a wide spectrum of comfort and restrictiveness that was based on the design of the garment itself – the cut, the length and how much it was boned – and also on how a woman chose to wear it: loose or tight laced, with or without a stomacher, every day or only for formal occasions.

Farthingales: walking, sitting and everyday life

Experiences of wearing farthingales during this period were also varied. At a time when women often wore many layers of heavy skirts that gathered and swirled around the legs, interfering with their ability to walk, farthingales could be quite liberating as they were weight-bearing garments. Re-enactors of early modern dance have noted this, stating that their reconstructed farthingales hold the fabric of their gowns away from their feet, allowing them to perform complicated dance steps.[55] In summer it appears that farthingales also kept women cool, as the tailor Poldavy in the Jacobean play *Eastwood Ho!* (1605) tells the character Gertrude Touchstone that her new farthingale 'twill keep your thighs so cool', because it freed legs from swathes of heavy fabric.[56] A later epigram found in William Goddard's book *A Nest of Wasps* (1615) also employed this use of the farthingale for comic effect, stating that his 'Ladies womans tail so oft doth cry' because 'her vardingales' a door so wide' and so 'lets more wind in than it can abide'.[57] 'Tail' during the this period was a colloquial term for a woman's genitalia, and as women rarely wore undergarments such as drawers at the start of the seventeenth century, the large size of the farthingale could let too much cool air into the skirts causing discomfort.

Despite these liberating aspects of farthingales, other literary sources offer glimpses into the limitations placed on the body by this foundation garment. The steps one needed to take to walk in such structures are also described in *Eastwood Ho!* when the character Gertrude receives a new farthingale, she asks, 'How must I bear my hands? light? light?', possibly referring to the method of resting the hands lightly on top of the farthingale as many women from the period are depicted as doing. Her tailor Poldavy replies, 'now you are in the Lady-fashion, you must do all things light. Tread light, light. I and fall so: that's the court-Amble.'[58] Gertrude, the aspiring daughter of a wealthy goldsmith, clearly now had to walk in a manner that would prevent her farthingale from moving in an ungraceful way. Such adaptations to walking are also described in William Shakespeare's *Merry Wives of Windsor* (1602), when the character Falstaff tells Mistress Ford that 'Thou art a tyrant to say so: thou wouldst make an absolute Courtier, and the firm fixture of thy foot, would give an excellent motion to thy gate, in a semi-circled Farthingale.'[59] Yet caution needs to be applied to creative works and plays, as almost all of these were written by men and reflect their views of the farthingale, not necessarily lived experiences of them.

As with bodies, historical dress reconstructions have proved particularly useful in understanding the farthingale. In 2009, literary scholar Carol Chillington Rutter conducted a practical performance experiment using the period-accurate costumes of the Globe Theatre in London. Her aim was to explore how an elite woman whose clothing was tied and pinned together could be undressed on the Shakespearean stage in the time given by the written scene. To do this, both versions of *Othello*, Act 4, Scene 3, where Desdemona is undressed by her maid, were performed. Although the experiment failed to disrobe Desdemona in the time allotted by both folios of the play, many other interesting dress observations were made. Actor John Trenchard remarked that to walk in a farthingale, both Spanish and Wheel, the actors had to be taught a particular way to move, which he referred to as the 'Elizabethan glide', just like the 'court-amble' described in both *Eastward Ho* and *The Merry Wives of Windsor*. This involved pushing the pelvis forward to lift the dress so that it did not have to be held when walking.[60] Jackie Marshall-Ward has similarly noted in her experiments with dancing in a Spanish farthingale that a gentle 'undulating and swaying movement is recommended' and small steps required to avoid kicking the sides of the farthingale.[61] As noted in the previous chapter, my own reconstruction experiment found that French wheel farthingales were stabilized when worn with a pair of bodies. The front of the bodies presses down on the farthingale, stopping it from swaying precariously when walking and creating a fashionable tilt (see Fig. 2.11). Pinning the overskirt to the farthingale to create the fashionable flounces of the Elizabethan and Jacobean eras also helps to stabilize the garment as it trusses its outside edges to the body.

How women approached the everyday act of sitting also needs to be considered when discussing farthingales and movement. A sixteenth-century Italian source noted of the Spanish farthingale that it 'is not very comfortable for sitting, since you first must take a great deal of trouble in arranging it if you do not wish to make a spectacle of yourself'.[62] This was likely due to the hoops of the garment that enclosed the legs from the waist to the feet. When sitting these hoops did fold down on themselves if made correctly, although it appears that one also needed to position the skirt in order to do this effectively. A century later, the French noblewoman Madame D'Aulnoy also expressed her dismay at having to wear a similar *guardainfante* (see Fig. 5.26) at the Spanish court:

> This was the first time I dressed according to the Spanish mode ... I had on a farthingale of prodigious bigness, (for you must wear that in the Queen's presence) I knew not what to do with myself with this strange invention; there is no sitting down in it, and I believe if I were to wear it all my life, I should never be reconciled to it.[63]

One wonders why D'Aulnoy had not been instructed by her Spanish acquaintances on how to sit in this structure. Possibly it is because only a few select women of the court, such as the queen or other highly ranked courtiers, were usually permitted to sit, and so the dilemma of how to navigate that process in these garments was not usually a concern at formal events. Yet embodied experiences are also subjective, and this personal account was from a French woman who came from a country where such garments were no longer worn, so it must be read with caution. In contrast, an earlier image of a North African woman wearing a Spanish farthingale by the Dutch artist Jan Cornelisz Vermeyen presents her comfortably sitting in her home with a sewing pillow on her lap (see Fig. 5.18). This image was possibly taken from life, when Vermeyen accompanied Emperor Charles V on his Tunisian campaigns in 1535, and the print shows that the flexible bents of the woman's farthingale are clearly not hindering. Construction choices may have been made to allow women to sit more comfortably, as wire, which is used in the surviving Spanish vestal effigy farthingale, was not placed in the top three hoops of the skirt around the area of the buttocks and upper thighs.[64]

Alternatively, the design of French farthingales that sat on the body at the waistline made these garments somewhat easier to manage. Many women at the French court of Henri III are also depicted sitting on low lounging chairs or stools (see Fig. 5.19). Indeed, when models wearing my French farthingales reconstructions were instructed to sit down on a modern dining chair, both were also able to do so without any difficulty (see Fig. 5.20). Although they could not fully lean backwards onto the back rest of the chair, they were not perched uncomfortably on the front edge of the seat either. The French wheel farthingale, despite being wider than the French roll, did not pose any additional difficulty as it is flexible and sits at an angle, giving the wearer more room behind them on the chair than one would think (see Fig. 5.21). The silhouette of my model when sitting in a French wheel farthingale also mimics those of women found in artistic depictions from the period (see Fig. 5.22). Most importantly, the design of the chair allowed my models to sit with ease as it was constructed without arm rests, just as were new styles of décor that first appeared in France during the reign of François I (1515 –47), called *chaises à vertugadins* (farthingale

Fig. 5.18 *Jan Cornelisz Vermeyen*, Seated North African woman, *1545, etching, Rijksmuseum, Amsterdam.*

Fig. 5.19 *French School,* Ball at the Court of King Henri III of France, *formerly known as* Bal du duc d'Alençon, c. *second half of the sixteenth century, oil on panel, Musée du Louvre, Paris.*

Fig. 5.20 *Model sitting in author's reconstruction of a French farthingale roll worn underneath an outer skirt.*

Fig. 5.21 *Model sitting in chair wearing reconstructed French wheel farthingale worn under a flounced skirt.*

Fig. 5.22 *Gillis van Breen,* Uneven Love, c. *1609–18, engraving, Rijksmuseum, Amsterdam.*

chairs).[65] Whilst these garments could therefore pose some problems for sitting, new styles of furniture were simply invented to remedy the problems caused by this new court attire.

Gendered perceptions of size and space

Writers during the sixteenth and seventeenth centuries did not just comment on the ways that women now had to navigate walking and sitting in various types of farthingales, but the size of these garments and how best to accommodate the women who wore them was a commonly reiterated theme. John Heywood lampooned the size of farthingales, and the inconveniences that they caused in close urban environments, in an epigram from 1562 that jested,

Alas! poor fardingales must lie in the street:
To house them, no door in the city made meet,

Since at our narrow doors they in cannot win,
Send them to Oxford, at Broadgates to get in.[66]

The narrow doors of London could not accommodate the expansive width of the farthingale and so Heywood joked that women must leave their farthingales in the streets in order to gain entry or go to the broad gates of what is now Pembroke College in Oxford to enter. Here Heywood used the play on words of 'broad gates' in comparison to London's 'narrow doors' to make a point about the folly of women who wore farthingales in urban city spaces.

Just three years earlier a Venetian visitor to a feast given by Elizabeth I at Whitehall Palace in May 1559 also described,

The Queen having washed her hands, and being at table under her canopy, insisted on having M. de Mountmorency at her little table . . . At the large table all the rest of the French lords and gentlemen sat on one side, and on the other all the ladies, of whom there was no small number, and who required so much space on account of the [Spanish] farthingales they wore that there was not room for all; so part of the Privy Chamber ate on the ground on the rushes.[67]

Although women of the courts occupied large palace complexes and were expected to wear farthingales to conform to aristocratic notions of femininity, it appears that even in these aristocratic spaces some monarchs could feel displaced by the increasing size of their fashionable female courtiers and took measures to ban the farthingale from being worn, or at least, to limit its size. This was the reaction by the French King Charles IX in 1563 who proclaimed in a sumptuary law that farthingales were not to reach more than 1.8 metres in circumference.[68]

Fifty years later, in February 1613, the English esquire John Chamberlain described the wedding of English Princess Elizabeth Stuart to Frederick V of Palatine in a letter to Sir Dudley Carlton's wife Alice. In this letter he explained that during all the revelries at the Palace of Whitehall in London 'the [great] hall was so full that it was not possible to avoid it or make room' and many of the ladies who had gone to the upper galleries of the palace to see the newlyweds arrive by boat could not get in. This prompted James I to proclaim 'that no Lady or gentlewoman should be admitted to any of these sights with a verdingale, which was to gain the more room, and I hope may serve to make them quite left off in time'.[69] It would seem that the farthingales belonging to his female guests limited the amount of space that could be occupied in the rooms of Whitehall, inconveniencing not only themselves but their male counterparts such as the king. Finally, in a frequently quoted account by the Venetian ambassador Horatio Busino from 1617, he described Queen Anne of Denmark as wearing 'so expansive a farthingale that I do not exaggerate when I say it was four feet wide [1.3 metres] in the hips',[70] referring to a French wheel farthingale worn at court (see Fig. 5.23).[71]

Fig. 5.23 *Marcus Gheeraerts the Younger,* Portrait of Anne of Denmark, c. *1605–10, oil on canvas, Woburn Abbey, Bedfordshire.*

But how large were farthingales? Juan de Alcega's previously mentioned tailoring manual from the 1580s does give some indication of how big the Spanish style of farthingale would have been. In instructions given in the manual, Alcega noted that the farthingale created by his pattern was 'a bara and a half' (approximately 49½ inches or 125.7 cm) in height and the circumference around the bottom was thirteen hand spans. While this size was adequate enough for this type of farthingale, Alcega also instructed that if more fullness was required it could be added to the pattern.[72] So it is possible that some women requested that their farthingale-makers or tailors make their farthingales wider than this. Janet Arnold's reconstruction of the farthingale in Alcega's manual resulted in a garment that was roughly 3¼ yards (3 m) in circumference at the base of the skirt and 39 inches (1 m) in width.[73]

An interrogation of the materiality of ephemeral garments such as farthingales is crucial to any discussion of size and space. As discussed in the previous chapter, my own process of reconstructing two French farthingales was quite experimental, but it yielded information about the construction of these garments that otherwise would not be attainable. After experimenting with different sized patterns within the limitations dictated by early modern silk fabric widths, which were generally 20 to 22 inches (51 to 56 cm) wide, I concluded that my farthingale could be no wider than 38 inches (96.5 cm) or have a circumference of more than 119 inches (3 m) in order to comply with these historical fabric widths.[74] My reconstruction of a French farthingale roll measures approximately 19½ inches (50 cm) in width and 62 inches (1.6 m) in circumference, while my reconstruction of the French wheel farthingale measures 31 inches (79 cm) in width and 97½ inches (2.5 m) in circumference. As previously mentioned, during the construction process my French wheel farthingale had trouble supporting the weight of its own circumference and the weight of added skirts when stiffened only with modern plastic whalebone, so wire was added to rectify this problem. Yet wire was not commonly used in this type of garment, so this issue encountered in the experiment suggests that both artisanal knowledge on how to engineer these items has been lost and that other materials missing from the historical record were used, or that the sizes of farthingales was exaggerated in contemporary writing.

While artisanal knowledge about how to construct these garments has certainly been lost, visual evidence also points to the size of farthingales having been overstated. It was often remarked in contemporary sources that the use of bodies and farthingales together created an optical illusion, making the waist small and the farthingale appear to be much wider than it actually was, an observation borne out by this experiment (see Fig. 5.24).[75] My reconstruction of a French wheel farthingale is much smaller than Queen Anne of Denmark's reported three-foot (1.3 m) wide garment, and yet it looks quite large as it is worn with a pair of bodies which tapered and streamlined the torso. The size of my French wheel farthingale also visually complements the proportionate size of farthingales in artworks from the period. As the average height of a Tudor woman was 5 ft 2¼ inches (158 cm), it is highly improbable that a farthingale of the French wheel style could be nearly as wide as a woman was tall, something which clearly contradicts depictions of women in contemporary portraiture.[76] Overall, experimentation with patterns and sizes based on historical sources suggests that it would simply be too hard to support a farthingale of such a large diameter as the garment reported for Queen Anne, as it would not be able to sit on the body parallel to the ground without additional help.

One then must pose the question, why was the size of farthingales often so exaggerated? As has been previously discussed in Chapter 2, when farthingales were worn by elite women certain views regarding the gendering of space were likely to be held. Farthingales were not originally designed to be worn by women in small cramped houses or in the narrow city streets, but by women in large estates with large halls, entrances and gardens. They were designed to project the notion of immense space and the associated ideas of importance because, after all, the occupation of large amounts of space was the prerogative of the elite. Yet as Chapter 3 explored, by the start of the seventeenth century in England farthingales began to be adopted by enthusiastic social climbers such as Margery from *The Shoemaker's Holiday* (1600), as the size of one's backside constituted a very clear message about the

Fig. 5.24 *Model wearing reconstruction of effigy bodies with reconstructed French wheel farthingale, without skirt flouncing.*

height of one's newfound social position. Women also regularly received more criticism in relation to their dress than men, even if it reflected the social status of their families.

During the late sixteenth and early seventeenth centuries men's breeches also reached considerable sizes (see Fig. 5.25). When this sartorial trend first began it also came under scrutiny. However, commentary on men's hose and breeches focused considerably less on their moral implications and the space that they consumed and much more on their ostentatiousness and expense. One text from 1577 ridiculed men for paying so much attention to their breeches, stating that 'thereunto bestow most cost upon our arses, and much more than upon all the rest of our *bodies*'.[77] While in 1583, Phillip Stubbes lamented in his *Anatomy of Abuses* that in times past kings were content with hosen costing 10 s., while now 'it is a small matter to bestow twenty nobles, ten pound, twenty pound, forty pound, yea a hundred pound of one pair of Breeches'.[78]

In fact, one Elizabethan sumptuary law of 1562 protested at the 'monstrous and outrageous greatness of hose' that had 'crept a late into the realm to the great slander thereof, and the undoing of a number using the same, being driven for the maintenance thereof to seek unlawful ways as by their

Fig. 5.25 *Doublet and breeches of slashed silk,* c. *1618, English, Victoria and Albert Museum, London.*

own confession have brought them to destruction'.[79] The legislation outlined the maximum yardage of fabrics to be used in the production of these garments, and, more importantly, it stated that the main abuse of rules such as these was by men of the 'meaner sorts' who were 'least able with their livings to maintain the same'.[80] These statutes, couched in the language of paternalism, reveal not only fears about social status being, or, in this case, not being accurately reflected by dress, but also fears over the economic hardships that fashionable dress could bring on those without the means to afford it.[81] While men were also labelled as vain and attempts via sumptuary legislation were made to curb their size, condemnations of the size of men's hose and breeches were more about regulating social status through maintaining financial stability, rather than criticizing their consumption of space.

The exaggerated nature of the claims made by mostly male observers about the size of farthingales therefore reveals the fears that early moderns held regarding the gendered consumption of space, and their criticism points to the perception that women were consuming too much of it. Early modern women often crafted their own spaces that were perceived to be challenging patriarchal norms. Men worried that women were either in spaces where they were not supposed to be, or that even when women were in approved spaces, they could not oversee them effectively.[82]

During the early modern period, relations between the genders were dictated by the use of space and consequently gender ideas helped to play a part in the creation and reinforcement of spatial practices.[83] In particular, women were often aware that they embodied space with a sense that it was not their own, particularly in urban environments such as London where space was limited and contested.[84] Women who wore large farthingales did not do so because it reflected their own status, but rather the status granted to them by their husbands or male relatives. Even if farthingales were not as wide as contemporary sources exaggeratedly claimed, these undergarments did give the impression of a physically imposing figure, and even a modestly sized farthingale of any style increased the amount of space that a woman consumed. This acknowledgement of female spatial subjectivity and their consumption of space, combined with the fact that women's presence in certain urban spaces could be seen as disorderly, reveals why so many voices, particularly male voices, arose at the beginning of the seventeenth century in relation to the size of farthingales.[85] Not only did ordinary men have to share their cramped urban space with monstrously enlarged women of the aristocracy, but now they were forced to do the same with some women of lower social rank whose spatial claims were often larger than their gender and their social status.

Such criticisms aimed at farthingales were not exclusive to England. In seventeenth-century Spain, critics viewed the *guardainfante* as a weapon that women used to undermine male authority as they encroached on public space and supposedly caused public commotions (see Fig. 5.26).[86] To the late seventeenth-century French court of Louis XIV, the *guardainfante* that belonged to the king's Spanish bride, Maria Theresa, positioned the princess's body as outdated and therefore undesirable (see Fig. 6.16). Its size and shape also physically displaced her husband, as upon their departure for France she was 'put into her beautiful carriage where she took up the whole front because of her *gard' Infant* that she did not wish to remove. The King and Queen Mother were in the back.'[87]

Gender and space were also at the heart of many discussions of the eighteenth-century hooped petticoat (see Fig. 8.1). Satirists were quick to point out and exaggerate the size of hoop petticoats in both England and France, and many of these complaints were made by men who decried the inconveniences that women in large hoop petticoats caused them and expressed the fear that women were creating spaces that men could not share or control.[88] The increased attention given to the size of farthingales and the space they consumed at the start of the seventeenth century should be viewed as the establishment of a common trope that was employed by satirists and moralists throughout the rest of the early modern period in England. In doing so, these commentators aimed to regulate women in response to the perceived threat that their physical consumption of space was subverting the correct gendered use of space. This was made explicit in 1603, when M. Thomas Carew of Bildeston in Suffolk preached that the wearing of 'monstrous vardugales' by women 'requires more stuff, and takes up more

Fig. 5.26 *Diego Velázquez,* Portrait of Infanta Margarita Teresa of Spain in a blue dress, *1659, oil on canvas, Kunsthistorisches Museum, Vienna.*

room in meeting then some of them are worth and worthy of'.[89] In the eyes of Carew, women in farthingales were simply not important enough to consume the amount of space that they did.

Conclusion

While it is undeniable that foundation garments did physically shape the everyday experiences of women during these centuries, and thus, notions of femininity pertaining to mundane daily acts, it appears that their inconvenience, their impact on health and movement and the consumption of space is almost certainly greatly exaggerated. Although the criticisms of bodies causing deformities in both children and women do have some place in fact, anthropological examinations of skeletal remains confirm that their effects on health were certainly overstated. Moralizing stories about deformity and disease in relation to these foundation garments are informed more by cultural understandings of women's vain nature and their weak bodies rather than common occurrences in everyday life. An investigation into the physical realities of bodies throughout these centuries reveals that far from being a monolithic experience of pain and restriction, these garments spanned a wide spectrum of comfort and restrictiveness in the everyday lives of the women who wore them, allowing for a range of bodily activities and functions.

The same is also true for farthingales. Although they most certainly required women to alter the way they walked and sat, they could be liberating for women, freeing their legs and feet from heavy skirts and allowing them to perform complicated dance steps. The claims that these garments often reached sizes of nearly one and a half metres wide and that they displaced courtiers in large palace complexes is not supported by the reconstructed materiality of the garments themselves. Instead, sources that were critical of these garments reveal a growing unease about changing social and gender dynamics during this period, which blamed the farthingale for allowing women to consume more space and, in doing so, challenge the normative gendered use of space. Concerns surrounding foundation garments and their impact on health, bodily movement and gendered spatial norms should not be viewed as reflective of the embodied experience of all women during the sixteenth and seventeenth centuries. Rather, these concerns established common tropes based on social anxieties that were employed by satirists and moralists throughout the rest of the early modern period and beyond in England in order to criticize women and their dress.

6

The sexual body
Eroticism, reproduction and control

For many years historians have sought to understand the ways that intimate items of material culture have influenced sexuality and sexual practices. Foundation garments have been the focus of many of these studies, with most attention given to those of the nineteenth and twentieth centuries: corsets and crinolines.[1] Like these later foundation garments, early modern bodies and farthingales were indeed sexually alluring and drew the male attention to what lay underneath. However, these garments were also linked to early modern concerns about illegitimate pregnancy and abortion, as well as the concealment of physical deformities, overweight bodies and venereal disease. In fact, many women who wore bodies and farthingales during the sixteenth and seventeenth centuries became patriarchal pariahs – as these garments became symbols of female sexual indiscretion and of the female defiance of male authority.

This chapter explores the numerous and often conflicting ways that foundation garments shaped perceptions of femininity and female sexuality for all women in sixteenth- and seventeenth-century England. Bodies and farthingales participated in and influenced the often playful and bawdy sexual world of early modern England. In doing so, they also materialized wider cultural concerns about female sexuality. Foundation garments were thought to inhibit the ability of men, and at times women, to visually read and control the sexual bodies of women around them. Women wearing silhouette-shaping garments were therefore not just viewed as deforming God's creation and destabilizing the correct class order; they also threatened to undermine patriarchal authority and the very organization of society itself.

Foundation garments, eroticism and sexual desire

Bodies and bodices during the sixteenth and seventeenth centuries originally served a utilitarian function as these garments were designed to keep down the belly and streamline the torso into the desired dressed silhouette. Unlike nineteenth-century corsets, these garments were also worn as both under and outerwear, so seeing a woman in only her bodies during this century was not necessarily considered overtly sexual or immodest. However, as these garments became ubiquitous in everyday female dress, male authors increasingly commented on the ways that they could erotically push up and enhance the bust. Unlike those examples discussed in Chapter 2, it seems that some Elizabethan women used bodies to enhance their bosom. In his work *Christs Tears over Jerusalem* (1594), Thomas Nashe claimed that, 'Their breasts ... they embuske up on high, and their round Roseate buds immodestly lay forth, to show at their hands there is fruit to be hoped'.[2] By the mid-seventeenth century, bodies regularly enhanced the bust rather than compressed it. In 1654 Puritan Clergyman Thomas Hall also declared that boned bodies and bodices were 'a temptation to sin' as 'their necks and breasts are in great part left naked'.[3]

Visual evidence from the period implies that in some cases boned bodies and bodices did threaten to expose the breasts. A Jacobean engraving of Lady Frances Carr, Countess of Somerset portrays her with her bodice neckline so low that her breasts are nearly fully visible (see Fig. 6.1). Wenceslaus Hollar's etching *Summer* (1644) also depicts a woman wearing a boned bodice that is laced tightly over a boned

Fig. 6.1 *Simon de Passe,* Frances, Countess of Somerset, *c. 1615–22, engraving, Rijksmuseum, Amsterdam.*

stomacher which has pushed up her breasts in much the same way that modern push-up bras also do (see Fig. 6.2). This effect was also observed when my own reconstruction of the Sittingbourne bodies, which are contemporary to this etching, were placed on a model (see Fig. 3.8). The prevalence and acceptance of bare-breasted woodcuts in broadside ballads, even those of royalty, suggests that low décolletage was common and acceptable in certain early modern spaces like the court and Restoration stage.[4] Male writers such as John Dunton commented on the ability of bodies to enhance the bust as he wrote that women 'begin to commit their Body to a close Imprisonment, and pinch it in so narrow a compass, that the best part of it's plumpness is forced to rise toward the Neck, to emancipate it self from such hard Captivity . . . her fair Breasts, they are half imprisoned, and half free; and do their utmost endeavour to procure their absolute liberty'.[5] In this sense, these garments also pleased the male gaze, as Dunton's moralizing commentary also described breasts that heaved out of the tops of boned bodies as 'two fair Apples'.[6] So while he was concerned about women's modesty, he also seemed to enjoy the show.

Flamboyant display was only one aspect of these garments that made them erotic. The fact that foundation garments covered the real female body of flesh and were in turn often concealed underneath

Fig. 6.2 *Wenceslaus Hollar,* Summer, *from* The Four Seasons, *c. 1644, etching and engraving on paper, Clark Art Institute.*

outer garments also stimulated the inquisitiveness of the male viewer, leading to a desire to see more.[7] Indeed, glimpses of these garments or the knowledge that a woman was wearing them inspired erotic imaginings of male writers. In the comedy *The Fathers Own Son* (1660), the playwright John Fletcher alluded to the sexual pleasures that waited underneath the now old-fashioned farthingale. In the play, three characters – Tom, Hylas and Sam – discuss the recent conversations that they have had with gentlewomen whom they intimately desire. Tom accuses Sam of being a 'weasel face' who uses conversation as an excuse to go 'ferreting About the farthing-ale', which in this context implied that Sam was sneaky and naturally inquisitive, and like the ferrets used in the traditional hunting practices, good at burrowing into holes, or in this context, underneath a woman's enlarged skirts.[8]

Like tight-laced corsets of the nineteenth century, bodies and busks were also fetishized in early modern sexual culture. *Fetish* can refer to many things, from objects believed to have magical properties to anything that is believed to be irrationally worshipped. However, in the sexual sphere, fetishism often refers to non-genital parts of the body or articles of clothing and accessories onto which erotic feelings have been placed.[9] Both highbrow and lowbrow literary sources often attached significant sexual connotations to busks and bodies, and these allusions were embedded within the everyday sexual cultures of early modern England. While the busk-point was commonly associated with female genitalia, as discussed in Chapter 1, the most common image attached to the actual busk itself was a phallic one. This phallic imagery was demonstrated by Edward Phillips in his handbook *The Mysteries of Love & Eloquence* (1685), when he jokingly wrote:

> A Lady was commanded to put her busk in a Gentlemans codpiece. Another Lady was commanded to pull it out, which occasioned some sport, for she laying hold upon something else, after two or three pulls gave over, excusing her disobedience, by pretending that the busk was tacked to the Gentlemans belly.[10]

References to the busk, however, were not always so flippant. The narrator of *The Rape of the Lock* (1714) also described a Baron with an 'altar' built by love. On this altar 'lay the Sword-knot *Sylvia*'s Hands had sown, / With *Flavia*'s Busk that oft had rapped his own'.[11] His own busk was not an item of clothing but rather his erection against which Flavia's busk had often brushed during their love making. In both these examples, busks did not necessarily symbolize an anatomical part of the male body, although they certainly alluded to it. Rather, the busk as a phallic object that was worn on the female body became an erotic symbol of male desire and potency.

The fetishization of busks in this manner allowed for many playful material expressions of desire during the sixteenth and seventeenth centuries. Inscriptions found on surviving busks often *speak* not just on behalf of the lover, but on behalf of busks themselves, giving these inanimate objects voices of their own. A seventeenth-century French busk, engraved on one side with a cupid and on the other a man's portrait (see Fig. 6.3), declares: 'He enjoys sweet sighs, this lover / Who would very much like to

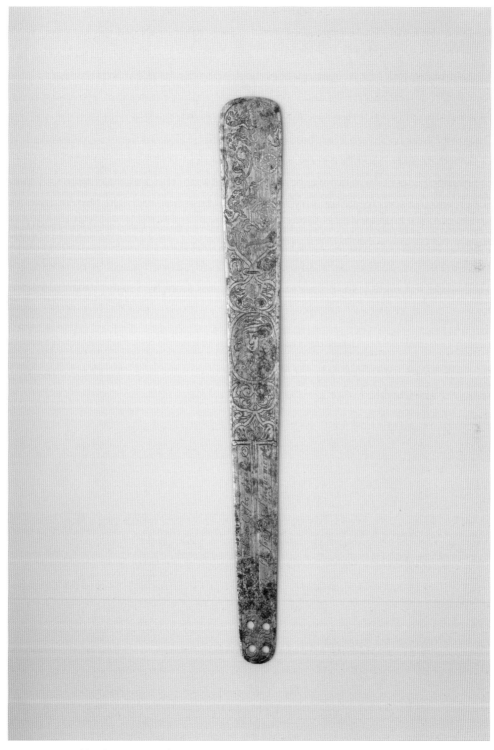

Fig. 6.3 *Metal busk, seventeenth century, French, Metropolitan Museum of Art, New York.*

take my place.'[12] This inscription shows the busk's anthropomorphized awareness of the prized place that it held on the female body. The earliest literary source that described this so-called 'busk envy' dates from 1598 and described a character who 'wished himself his Mistress buske' so that he 'might sweetly lie, and softly lusk / Between her pappes [breasts]' so that he might have 'an eye / At either end, that freely might descry / Both hills and dales'.[13] Romantic gifts or notes were often kept close to the heart in Renaissance Europe.[14] However, in this text it seems that the character Saturio wished himself a busk not to be near his lover's heart but so that he could be close to the two most sexually desired parts of the female body: her hills (breasts) and dale (groin).

Such an erotic fantasy, of a male lover becoming a busk so that he could be close to his lover's body, is visible on another seventeenth-century French metal busk that bears the portrait of a man (see Fig. 6.4). The busk belonged to Anne-Marie-Louise d'Orleans, Duchesse de Montpensier and the inscription on the object proclaims, 'How I envy you the happiness that is yours, resting softly on her ivory white breast. Let us divide between us, if you please, this glory. You will be there during the day and I shall be there at night.'[15] In this sense, a busk that was given by a man to a woman acted as an

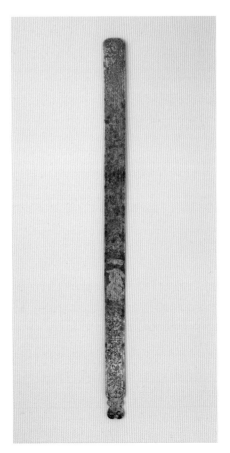

Fig. 6.4 *Metal busk, c. mid-seventeenth century, French, Metropolitan Museum of Art, New York. This busk belonged to Anne-Marie-Louise d'Orleans (1627–93), Duchesse de Montpensier and contains her arms. One side shows the portrait of a man and the other a portrait of a woman.*

extension of her male lover. Sexual prowess and performance were important elements in asserting masculinity for young early modern men and there was much concern during this period that love made men emotionally weak, soft, delicate and self-indulgent.[16] At the same time, a common cultural attitude that underpinned male sexual development was the idea that fornication was a pastime rather than a sin, as it encouraged the masculine attributes of conquest and possession.[17] Busks could symbolize ideas of sexually possessive masculinity as they were representative of the man's body; a phallic object which represented her lover in his most powerful and virile form which was then worn privately on the female body, expressing his sexual and loving desire.

John Donne also fetishized and begrudged the 'happy busk, which I envy, / That still can be, and still can stand so nigh', making a connection between the busk and his erection.[18] In his 'Elegy 19: To His Mistress Going to Bed' (1654), he also requested that his mistress 'Unpin that spangled breast-plate which you wear, / That th'eyes of busy fools may be stopped there. / Unlace your self, for that Harmonious chime, / Tells me from you, that now it is bed-time.'[19] In this elegy, Donne requested that the spangled stomacher pinned to the front of his lover's bodice be removed as it drew attention to her décolletage, and he described the 'harmonious chime' caused by metal aiglets hitting each other while being unlaced. This sound signalled 'bed-time' or, in other words, impending sexual activity in the bed chamber. Similarly, the Devonshire minister and poet Robert Herrick also fetishized the laces of bodies and bodices in his poem 'Delight in Disorder' (1648). In this poem, Herrick commented on the sexual delight of seeing the 'sweet disorder' in his mistress's dress. One such disorder was 'An erring lace, which here and there / Enthrals the crimson stomacher', referring to points that incorrectly or haphazardly laced the centre-front edges of a bodice over a stomacher, as was commonly seen in styles from the 1630s and 1640s.[20]

Men took delight in the sexual nature of foundation garments in both literature and reality; however, these sources do not account for female perspectives in early modern England. Certainly, the fetishized nature of garments could give women some degree of erotic agency in literature. During the interregnum, Nicholas Hookes published a series of poems titled *Amanda, a Sacrifice to an Unknown Goddess* (1653) in which he addressed a fictional goddess, possibly based on a real, but still unknown, muse. In the verse titled *To Amanda desirous to go to bed*, he wrote, 'Fairest, let me thy night-clothes air, / Come I le unlace thy stomacher; / Make me thy maiden-chamber-man.'[21] In this scene, Hookes fetishized both the process of unlacing and removing a stomacher and the daily rituals of female life, as he requested to become his mistress's 'maiden-chamber-man'. This verse also speaks to the erotic power that these fetishized garments had over the male mind: in his fantasies, Hookes wished to submit to his mistress, lowering himself from his mistress's master to her servant, giving her the sexual power in the bedchamber.

A woman's desire for a male suitor could also be declared through the gifting of a busk-point, ribbon that secured the busk into the bottom of bodies, as visible in Hollar's 1643 etching *Spring* (see Fig. 6.5). It was common for women to gift love-tokens to men, frequently in the form of embroidered

Welcom sweet Ladie you doe bring Spring
Rich presents of a hopefull Spring

That makes the Earth to looke so greene
As when shee first began to teeme.

Fig. 6.5 *Wenceslaus Hollar,* Spring, *1643, etching, Rijksmuseum, Amsterdam. The busk-point of ribbon is visible at the bottom of the centre-front of the bodies.*

handkerchiefs. Ribbon was another gift commonly given in both courtship and more generally as well. This tradition carried over into the milieu of sexuality where, as explained in Chapter 1, this small piece of ribbon was given much more sexual and social weighting due to its association with the female genitals. Busk-points appear often in seventeenth-century theatrical scripts, such as *The Shoemaker's Holiday* (1600). In this play the character Jane discovers that the husband she thought dead is still alive. When she abandons her new beau, he responds that 'he [her old husband] shall not have so much as a buske point from thee', alluding to women's habit of giving busk-points as signs of affection and promise.[22] The significance of receiving a busk-point is highlighted by Thomas Tomkin's *Lingua* (1607), when the character Phantastes exclaims, 'The Gordian knot which *Alexander* great, / Did whilom [in the past] cut with his all conquering sword: / Was nothing like thy Busk-point pretty Peate.'[23] This implies that sometimes convincing a woman to give up the busk-point that her admirer so desperately wanted could be very hard and often nearly impossible.[24]

Just as women wore busks that were given to them by male suitors, men were also recorded as wearing busk-points given to them by women. The gallant in Henry Fitzgeffry's *Certain Elegies, Done by Sundry Excellent Wits with Satires and Epigrams* (1618) is described as clogging his wrists 'With Busk-points, Ribbons or Rebato-Twists'.[25] While in Robert Burton's *The Anatomy of Melancholy* (1621) a male lover is described as wearing busk-points 'for a favour in his hat, or next to his heart'.[26] Finally, Marie Channing Linthicum has suggested that men who wore busk-points 'about their wrists or in other conspicuous places' often did so 'much to the envy of less fortunate suitors'.[27] Given the sexualized nature of busk-points, this public display of a romantic trophy clearly proclaimed the suitor's desirability and reinforced his masculine prowess. However, the rhetoric around foundation garments was not always so light-hearted and the display of female sexuality not always so celebrated.

Sexual temptation and feminine deception

Expressions of female sexual desire using busk-points may seem oddly out of place in a society where strict cultural and social practices policed women's agency. Indeed, discussions of foundation garments provoked a rich dialogue concerning female sexuality in early modern England. Of concern were the biblical ideas of temptation and deception, to which it was believed that women, as daughters of Eve, were most prone. As discussed in Chapter 2, many moralists – mainly male – criticized the idealized silhouette created by these foundation garments and implied that their use reflected the innate vanity of women and their desire to rebel by deforming God's perfect creation of the female body. Yet as sinful daughters of Eve, women's beauty was also threatening as it was closely tied to their sexuality. Women who were not beautiful enough were not seen as desirable by men, while women who were too beautiful were regarded as possessing the ability to lure and use men.[28] These debates about real or false beauty were intimately tied to discussions about real or false bodies. In turn, both were related to larger cultural concerns about deception and temptation that animated discourses of female sexuality.

Many contemporary sources about foundation garments demonstrate these anxieties. Although some authors delighted in the erotic appeal of these garments, others viewed them as infuriating obstructions. In France, Michel de Montaigne alluded to the connections between farthingales and deceitfulness:

> Why do women barricade those parts [of their bodies] that house our desires and their own? And what is the purpose of these huge bastions [farthingales] with which they armour their flanks, if it is not to trick us, to pull us to them even as they keep us away?[29]

To men like Montaigne, farthingales were strongholds that fortified women and closed them off to men. Busks were also couched in terms of warfare, envisioned as a sword that women used to protect themselves from male advances. Bodies were criticized for both concealing women's physical faults and also for shutting away their real desirable torsos, as when men went to embrace their wives they were 'nought but past-board, canvas, & whalebone'.[30] Such bodies of pasteboard and whalebone inhibited easy physical access to the real female body of flesh. This reality was used in the broadside ballad *The Hasty Bride-groom* (c. 1650–95) to emphasize the fervent desires of the wedding night, as the broadside describes the bride's bodies as being 'too straight laced', inhibiting the 'lusty' groom's ability to quickly reveal his new bride's naked body.[31]

Foundation garments positioned women as flirts, as their erotic appeal attracted men, yet their actual materiality denied them. This observation is visualized in a watercolour from the period of a young couple kissing in a somewhat awkward embrace – due to the woman's large French wheel farthingale that physically denies her lover the ability to sit against her body (see Fig. 6.6). William Averell's work *A Marvellous Combat of Contrarieties* (1588) also made this issue explicit:

> In a man three ounces of lust, in a woman nine; for what meaneth else their outward tricking and dainty trimming of their heads, the laying out of their hairs, the painting and washing of their faces, the opening of their breasts, & discovering them to their wastes, their bents of Whale bone to bear out their bums, their great sleeves and bombasted shoulders, squared in breadth to make their wastes small.[32]

Fig. 6.6 *Unknown Italian artist,* Royal, military and court costumes of the time of James I, c. *early seventeenth century, drawing and watercolour, Folger Shakespeare Library, Washington, DC.*

According to Averell, rolls of whalebone along with bodies, busks, wired sleeves, cosmetics and elaborate hairstyles were symbols of lust and lasciviousness, and women used these artificial means of dress to tempt men. While men were attracted to and frustrated by women who wore these foundation garments due to the paradoxical nature of their sexual allure, they were also disturbed by the possibility of what these garments concealed.

Women fooling men into marrying them by deceiving them with their outward appearance was a common trope in seventeenth-century literature.[33] Cosmetics were regularly targeted for their ability to conceal and display. Painted faces were alluring to men, but their artificiality always sowed seeds of doubt.[34] What were women hiding under all that *fucus* (lead-based foundation)? After all, why would a woman need to cover herself with face paint unless her intention was to deceive or defraud those around her? Like cosmetics, many literary sources positioned farthingales as both alluring and repelling to men. They drew the male attention to the possibilities of what could be underneath – hips, thighs and sexual organs – while simultaneously causing apprehension: what if a deformed, overweight or diseased body was also hidden underneath? This type of literature increased at the beginning of the seventeenth century as more women of the middling sorts, who were the main targets of such didactic literature, began to adopt farthingales and bum-rolls. Such ideas were made explicit in an early seventeenth-century epigram by Henry Fitzgeffry from his collection *Satires and Satirical Epigrams* (1617): 'Else (mincing Madam's) why do we (alas!) / Pine at your Pencil and conspiring Glass? / Your Curls, Pearls, Periwigs, your Whale bone wheels / That shelter all defects from head to heels.'[35] Just as women's periwigs and whale-bone wheels (French wheel farthingales) attracted men, they also hid physical defects that might otherwise deter men from pursuing such women. The previously mentioned French engraving *Entrée des Esperlucattes* also emphasized this point as it depicted the *esperlucattes*, or literally 'those who are difficult to deceive', as six male dancers who are dancing undressed from the waist down (exposing their farthingales) next to two fully clothed women mocking them for their deception (see Fig. 1.9).[36] Farthingales were therefore criticized as they allowed women to cover physical defects and trick men into finding them physically attractive when in reality they were not.

This idea is also present in the play *Ram-Alley: or Merry-Tricks* (1611) by the common-born dramatist Lording Barry. The play has the character Sir Oliver Small-Shanks deliver a monologue where he states that 'Women have tricks firks and farthinggales, / A generation are they full of subtilty, / And all most honest where they want the means. / To be otherwise.'[37] One of the tricks that women used to gain male attention was the farthingale, an emblem of deceptive femininity that made them seem more sexually attractive. This trope was common in other early modern writings. Musician Thomas Whythorne recorded in his autobiography that women's pride and lechery were damaging and the false beauty gained from their dress fooled unassuming men.[38] Another tract from the early seventeenth century, *The Arraignment of Lewd, Idle, Froward, and Unconstant Women* (1615), spoke specifically about women luring and trapping men with their looks. Though the tract was a mock treatise and brought together many different stereotypes of women, some contemporary female writers such as Rachel Speght and Ester Sowernam did read this work as a serious tirade against women masked as a raunchy lowbrow comedy and published damning responses.[39] Taken from the chapter titled, 'The Second Chapter showeth the manner of such women as live upon evil report: it also showeth that the beauty of women has been the bane of many a man, for it hath overcome valiant and strong men, eloquent and subtle men. And in a word it hath overcome all men, as by examples following shall appear', Joseph Swetnam wrote that women 'are sprung from the devil' and that they are 'called the hook of all evil, because men are taken by them as a fish is taken in with the hook'. The bait used to 'hook' men was beauty, 'for women have a thousand ways to entice thee, and ten thousand ways to deceive thee, and all such fools as are suitors unto them'.[40] Although Swetnam's work by no means represents the view of all men during this period, his opinions did stem from the commonly held belief that women were vain and used their looks to deceive men into marriage, money or other favours.

During the seventeenth century, foundation garments were explicitly linked to sexual promiscuity. In 1606, Barnabe Rich wrote that women must 'have a Mask, to cover an impudent face, a Periwig to hide a loathsome bush, a Buske to straighten a lascivious body'.[41] Women labelled as prostitutes or whores were often accused of using finery to hide bodies that were disfigured, diseased or frail – just as women who wore foundation garments were.[42] Sumptuous female clothing was believed to facilitate prostitution and women were commonly accused of coming across their finery via their sexual indiscretions. One common insult of the period was that a woman 'had got her fine apparel with her tail' as it was common for prostitutes to receive fine gifts of clothing from their clients.[43] Women were therefore warned about dressing too sumptuously outside the courts in case their reputations were brought into question.[44]

The idea that promiscuous women used rich attire to hide their physical flaws from men was even further conflated in relation to venereal disease. The character Sordido in Thomas Middleton's play *Women Beware Women* linked the farthingale with disease, stating that it concealed 'a diseased Wench in's Bed' which would cause 'rotten stuff in's Breeches'.[45] While Stephen Gosson in his *Pleasant Quips* stated that those 'hoopes that hips and haunch do hide' were not just invented for vanity and pride, but 'When whore in stews had gotten pox, / This French devise, kept coats from smocks'.[46] In effect, Gosson claimed that French prostitutes who had contracted syphilis (pox) in brothels had invented the farthingale to create a barrier between their gowns and diseased smocks. This voiced fears about the uncertain transmission of the disease and emphasized the common trope that blamed the French for syphilis.[47] However, during the sixteenth century 'coats' referred to a male garment similar to a jerkin that was worn over the doublet. So, another interpretation is that the farthingale created a protective barrier that separated diseased women from the rest of the population. Regardless of the exact interpretation, the point made by Gosson here is that women wore farthingales to conceal both diseased bodies and loose morals.

Pregnancy and concealment

Gosson's so-called pleasant quips touched on one of the most enduring fears that surrounded the development and continued use of the farthingale – that it concealed illegitimate pregnancy – as he rhymed that 'when paunch[s] of whore[s] grew out, / these hoops did help to hide their sin'.[48] Linking farthingales to the concealment of pregnancy had been a staple of slander since the fifteenth century. In 1468 a Spanish courtier named Alfonso de Palencia wrote that Juana of Portugal, queen of Castile, had adopted the fashion to conceal an illegitimate pregnancy, repeating contemporary gossip that linked the queen's extramarital affairs with criticism of aristocratic fashions. In reality, there were no references to hooped skirts of any kind in the queen's clothing inventory and it is likely that this rumour was the result of the political propaganda and factionalism that characterized politics in Castile at this time.[49] However, this rumour about Juana and the stereotype about farthingales that it cemented in popular thought would stay with this garment for centuries to come.

The Flemish engraving *The Vanity of Women: Masks and Bustles* (1600), which linked farthingales with vanity, as discussed in Chapter 2, also commented on the chastity of the women who wore the garment (see Fig. 1.8). The shop in which these women are being dressed is referred to as a 'shop of raging lovers' and next to the French farthingale roll hanging in the right side of the engraving is a sign that reads, 'I need to wear a *cachenfant* like the others: / Cost what it must: the madman wants to love the madwoman.'[50] This sign refers to women who bought French farthingale rolls to hide illegitimate pregnancies, as it calls these garment *cachenfants* or child-hiders. These were items of dress that fashion-crazed women used to hide pregnancies begot from their secret rendezvous with equally crazed men. Across the channel in England these views were also shared. In a 1603 sermon by M. Thomas Carew, he similarly preached that women 'wear monstrous vardugales [farthingales] which as is said, were invented by a strumpet to cover a great belly', linking these garments with the common tale of its scandalous origins once again.[51]

Plays performed regularly at both Blackfriars and the Globe theatres in London such as John Webster's *The Duchess of Malfy* (1612–13) also reiterated these ideas to the masses. Webster's play centres on a strong-willed Duchess, a widow who defies the wishes of her two powerful brothers and secretly marries below her station. In reaction to this betrayal, her brothers set about exacting their revenge. When the character Daniel de Bosola who has been sent to spy on the Duchess suspects that she is concealing a pregnancy he exclaims, 'A whirlwind strike off these bawd-farthingalls, / For, but for that, and the loose-bodied gown, / I should have discovered apparently / The young spring-hall cutting a caper in her belly.'[52] In this scene, farthingales are associated with illicit sexual activity as they are referred to as 'bawd-farthingalls' and this garment (alongside a loose-bodied gown) is accused of obscuring the character's ability to visually detect the Duchess's pregnancy, a deception which she later pays for with her life at the hands of her brothers.[53]

Obscuring pregnancy with a farthingale is also addressed in an epigram found in William Goddard's book *A Nest of Wasps* (1615):

> My ladies verdingall is wondrous wide
> But what a that? She wears it not so for pride
> Indeed she doth not sir. Yet if you'd know
> Why about her bum so huge a hoop doth go
> Ile tell it you. Pray sweet sir understand
> She for a maid doth goes, as yet un mand [unmarried]
> By virtue of her vardingall, she (well ye)
> Doth make poor men believe she hath no belly
> A rare trick tis: Great waists twill make seem Small
> And bellies barrel-big, seem naught at all.[54]

Not only did farthingales make women's waists seem small, alluding to the optical illusion created by these garments, but according to Goddard they were worn by women with 'bellies barrel-big' who wished to portray themselves as virginal maids. Rather than pride, these garments were instead indicative of illegitimate pregnancies hidden from unwitting male suitors.[55] Goddard was a common soldier turned poet and so his use of this trope indicates that these links between farthingales and concealment were widely understood.

Revisiting the discussion on the qualities of a potential wife between the characters Ward and Sordido in Thomas Middleton's play, *Women Beware Women*, Sordido claims that Ward should try to spy on his future bride Isabella when she is naked so that he can confirm that she has neither 'bump in back, nor belly', as 'these are the faults that will not make her pass'. When Ward refuses to do such a thing, Sordido replies:

> Then take her with all faults, with her clothes on!
> And they may hide a number with a bum-roll.
> Faith choosing of a Wench in a huge Farthingale,
> Is like the buying of ware under a great Pent-house,
> What with the deceit of one.[56]

After the marriage to Ward, Isabella continues her relationship with her lover Hippolito. When Ward discovers the affair, he exclaims, 'For he that marries a whore, looks like a fellow bound all his life time to a Meddler-tree . . . A pox on it, I thought there was some knavery a broach, for something stirred in her belly, the first night I lay with her.' Ward blames Sordido for not ensuring that Isabella was virtuous and virginal, to which Sordido replies, 'Alas, how would you have me see through a great farthingale sir? I cannot peep through a mill-stone, or in the going, to see what's down in the bottom.'[57] In comparing Isabella's farthingale to a millstone, which was used for grinding wheat and other grains, the character draws attention to the impenetrable properties of both. A farthingale was as solid as a millstone, and neither structure was visually or physically permeable when covering a woman's lower half.

Women were also accused of using bodies and busks to conceal pregnancies. A broadside ballad titled *The Peddler opening of his Pack, / To know of Maids what tis they Lack* (1620) stated that women needed 'A pair of Bodye, / to make you fine and slender: / A Buske as black as Jet, / to keep your bellies under / that are great.'[58] Later, a French text from 1655 detailing the history of 'Coqueterie' stated that the busk was used to 'hide the pregnancies of maids'.[59] The Restoration novel *The English Rogue* (1668) also described a woman whom the narrator had impregnated out of wedlock as 'lacing herself very straight, and keeping down her belly with three Busks'.[60] This scene was played out in reality over ninety years later in 1754, when the widow Sarah Jenkins was tried (and found not guilty) of infanticide. When her friend Thomas Wilks was interrogated, he claimed that Jenkins had been drinking with him and his wife at the alehouse and she had told them that 'she had got a bulk, that keeps down her belly so flat that no body can tell that she was with child, till she comes to the last month'. This bulk was in fact a busk that Jenkins went on to misplace while mending her stays at the Wilks's house.[61] In 1681 the servant Ann Wright was accused for the second time of concealing a pregnancy and birth. During the court's investigations, Thomas Suckett, a labourer working for the same household, testified that Ann's bodice had been 'close and hard tied' when she had brought him his dinner one night, and this had caused 'milk [to] come out of her breasts and come through her shift and down her bodice'.[62] Suckett's deposition reveals that Ann's attempts to hide her maternal body by lacing it tightly in cloth and whalebone had instead caused her lactating breasts to betray her secret.

Abby E. Zanger has suggested that the wearing of the *guardainfante* by pregnant court women in Spain may have allowed them to participate in court events for longer as it provided a visual buffer for pregnant bodies that were likely to be considered unappealing and disruptive.[63] The French wheel farthingale sat around the waist and so it could have concealed an early term pregnancy. However, this garment was almost always worn with stiffened bodies with center-fronts that could extend low onto the groin, making it difficult to conceal a full-term pregnancy. English portraits show that some women did discard these garments in late term pregnancy. A 1596 portrait of Anne Pope with her three children depicts her in the later stages of pregnancy (see Fig. 6.7). She wears a gown that was made to be worn with a fashionable French wheel farthingale, as the skirt contains flouncing that has been arranged and sewn into place. However, it is clear from the image that due to her pregnancy she

Fig. 6.7 *Marcus Gheeraerts the Younger,* Anne, Lady Pope with her children, c. *1596, oil on canvas, National Portrait Gallery, London.*

has forgone wearing any type of farthingale as there is no structure underneath the skirts. A more plausible assertion then is that these garments simply gave pregnant women extra time to make other arrangements for secret delivery, or they may have allowed women to stay on public display in the court for longer; but seldom, it seems, would they have been able to conceal a pregnancy to full term. We must also consider that the artificial silhouette created by certain styles of farthingales may have led to accusations of pregnancy. The appearance of French farthingale rolls underneath the outer clothing did give the illusion of a rounded stomach, as is visible in the Dutch engraving of a woman from 1620 (see Fig. 6.8) and my model (see Fig. 4.26). This combined with the layers of clothing worn over the top likely exacerbated already present fears about a woman's fidelity.

Bodies and busks also disturbed pamphleteers as they were linked to abortion as well as concealment. Again, it was pamphleteer Stephen Gosson who made this connection most explicit in his *Pleasant Quips* when he stated that 'the bawdy buske' keeps 'down flat / the bed wherein the babe should breed', meaning that it kept women's wombs empty. Gosson wondered whether busks prevented women from being pregnant because they acted as a weapon that guarded modesty and kept them

Fig. **6.8** *Adriaen Matham,* Clothing and Manners of Noblewomen and Countrywomen, c. *1619–23, engraving, Rijksmuseum, Amsterdam.*

chaste ('were buske to them [women], as stakes to gapes, / to barre the beasts from breaking in') or because they acted as objects that aborted pregnancy. Eventually he blamed their abortifacient qualities, stating that busks invited lasciviousness and marked women as whores who could give their bodies to many men without suffering the repercussions of pregnancy ('busks are but signs to tell, / Where Launderers for the camp do dwell').[64] In France, Ambroise Paré claimed that one cause of abortion was the 'powerful compression exercised by busks, which compress the belly'.[65] While in 1603, Tomison Johnson, the Puritan pastor's wife mentioned in Chapter 3, was chastised by her congregation because 'Whalebones in the bodies of petticoats' were 'against nature, being as the Physicians affirm hinderers of conceiving or procreating children'.[66] Finally, Jacob Rüff's medical handbook, the *Expert Midwife* (1637), also tells a tale of a woman who became pregnant out of wedlock and tried to 'extinguish and destroy' the foetus by tight-lacing her bodice 'straight and hard'.[67]

As discussed in Chapter 5, it was common for medical texts in the second half of the seventeenth century to blame mothers for the physical deformities in their children who they dressed in bodies and busks. However, the use of busks during pregnancy was also linked to deformities in children. A 1681 French treatise on pregnancy and post-natal care claimed in a section titled 'Abortion and its causes' that women cunningly tightened their bodies & used 'strong & rigid busks' to hide their pregnancies, reiterating long-held fears over busks and abortion.[68] This treatise also went on further to advise that women should not 'tighten themselves' using 'bodices with strong strips of whalebone' as it confined their bellies and impeded their 'children from taking their unrestricted growth', making them deformed.[69] Blaming the busk for spontaneous and sometimes planned abortions, as well as congenital deformity, was therefore common in both medical and popular literature. However, as we know, bodies were not always stiffened with things like baleen or busks, nor were they always tight-laced. A high-profile woman such as the queen was expected to bear multiple children and her pregnant body was both public and a state affair. The royal female body was therefore one that was closely monitored and looked after. Yet these garments were obviously not regarded as a danger to unborn royalty, as tailoring bills reveal that in May 1631 Queen Henrietta Maria continued to order new whalebone bodies at the

Fig. 6.9 *Maternity Bodies and stomacher owned by Mary Verney (nee Abell), c. 1665–75, English, Claydon House, Buckinghamshire. These bodies are made from one layer of patterned silk and one layer of herringbone linen, stitched with silk thread, boned with whalebone and bound with silk grosgrain ribbon.*

beginning of her fourth month of pregnancy with Princess Mary and in 1635 she paid her tailor for 'putting whalebone into all her Majesties stomachers when her Majesty was with child'.[70]

In fact, the earliest surviving pair of maternity bodies in England further suggests that these garments were commonly worn during pregnancy. The bodies reside at Claydon House in Buckinghamshire and date from the period 1665–75 (see Fig. 6.9). They are believed to have belonged to Mary Verney (née Abell), the wife of Edmund (Mun) Verney, who gave birth to their three children at the house during this decade.[71] These bodies are made from one layer of patterned silk and one layer of herringbone linen lining. They consist of nine panels that are stitched all over in pink and ivory silk thread, stiffened with whalebone and bound with pink silk grosgrain ribbon. The bodies do show signs of use and there is evidence of some strain on the eyelet holes around the waistline and abdomen, places where an expanding pregnancy would place the most tension on the garment.

Several allowances have been made in the design of this garment to accommodate pregnancy. Unlike normal V-shaped stomachers, the stomacher in the Verney bodies flares downwards into a bulbous shape that allowed the front lacing to be let out slowly over time as Mary's pregnancies progressed. My reconstruction of this garment, which was worn over a simulated pregnant form, showed this to be the case, as the stomacher curves around the top of the swelling abdomen (see Fig. 6.10). The original stomacher also has thinner pieces of baleen than the rest of the garment. This made it more flexible and able to mould comfortably around the pregnancy bump as it increased in size.[72] This was apparent in my own reconstruction as it did not use boning this thin and so bunched up underneath the lacing at times, especially when placed on a model with a bump that simulated pregnancy in the third trimester (see Fig. 6.11). Additionally, a thin piece of whalebone runs vertically across the narrowest part of the stomacher (see Fig. 6.12). It appears that this was used to reinforce this narrow boning and to stop it from bunching up, as this part of the stomacher is placed under the most pressure when laced.

Other adjustments to the design of this garment have also been made to accommodate pregnancy. These include shorter skirts or tabs on the front of the bodies that would comfortably sit over an expanding pregnancy bump, as shown in my reconstruction experiment (see Fig. 6.13). Shortening the tabs not only gives a softer silhouette under clothing, as it prevents long tabs from jutting outwards, but when the bodies were worn very little pressure was placed on the abdomen. Short-waisted bodies like that discussed in Chapter 5 would also have had the same effect, as pressure is placed more on the ribs than on the abdomen (see Fig. 5.17). Experimenting with this garment without its stomacher on a pregnant form also demonstrated that pregnant women could have left their bodies unlaced or only loosely laced around their bumps. Short-waisted garments or garments that were loosely laced around the bump would therefore have given support to the breasts without hindering a growing pregnancy, as depicted in the 1596 portrait of Lady Pope with her children (see Fig. 6.7).[73]

Finally, a thick and rigid piece of baleen has been placed in the centre-back of the garment. Such an addition may have helped to alleviate the lower back pain often experienced during late pregnancy.[74]

Fig. 6.10 *Author's reconstruction of the Verney maternity bodies, c. 1665–75. The bodies are mounted on a pregnant form. They are made from one layer of silk taffeta, one layer of linen, boned with plastic imitation baleen, bound with grosgrain ribbon and sewn with silk thread.*

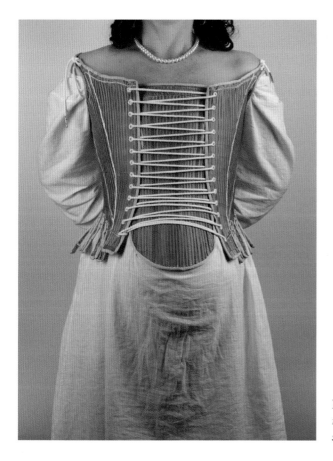

Fig. 6.11 *Author's reconstruction of the Verney maternity bodies worn by a model with a simulated third trimester pregnancy bump.*

Similar design allowances that accommodated pregnancy are visible in later eighteenth-century examples too.[75] Such garments are described in Denis Diderot's *L'Encyclopedie* (1751). The maternity stays shown in the top-left corner of the entry for 'Tailleur de Corps' contain side lacing that was let out to allow for an expanding belly (see Fig. 6.14). This adjustment also enabled this back-lacing eighteenth-century foundation garment to accommodate pregnancy without the arm holes needing to be altered and moved forward.[76]

The Verney bodies have not been heavily used and so it is unlikely that Mary wore this garment much when she was not pregnant. My reconstruction experiment did show though that this maternity garment could have been worn with a normal V-shaped stomacher on a non-pregnant body and still achieve the fashionable shape of the Restoration period (see Fig. 6.15). However, the shortened length of the centre-front was very apparent when the garment was worn like this. The centre-front panels on the Verney bodies are at least two inches (5 cm) shorter than other contemporary non-maternity garments, such as the pair of pink watered silk bodies from the Victoria and Albert Museum (see Fig. 1.24). While this was clearly done so that pressure was not placed on Mary's abdomen, to achieve the desirable non-maternal silhouette these centre-front panels would need to be longer, contain more

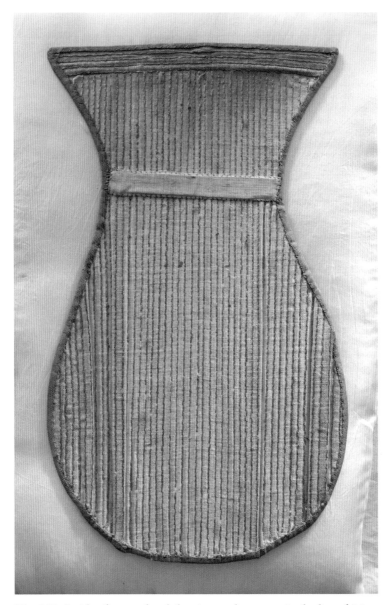

Fig. 6.12 *Inside of stomacher belonging to the maternity bodies of Mary Verney (nee Abell), c. 1665–75, English, Claydon House, Buckinghamshire. A horizontal piece of linen tape has been added to hold a wide piece of baleen.*

eyelets and be worn with a stomacher containing a busk that would exert pressure on and flatten the abdomen and create a smooth tapering line down to the groin.

On the other hand, these types of differences between maternity and non-maternity garments also indicate that a normal pair of bodies from this period could easily have been altered for pregnancy.

Fig. 6.13 *Author's reconstruction of the Verney maternity bodies worn by a model with a simulated pregnancy bump. The front panel and skirts of the garment have been shortened to comfortably sit over the expanding bump.*

Shortening the centre-front and skirts, adding a busk to the back and making up a new stomacher would have been quick alterations for any tailor or body-maker. Examining the material maternal record therefore shows us that the pregnant body was not always concealed by foundation garments. Rather, they accommodated the pregnant body in a way that did not hide the maternal form or restrict a growing foetus, but instead supported it.

Regulating sexual female bodies

By situating criticisms of foundation garments within a traditional framework of female sexual lasciviousness, temptation and deception the writings of early modern moralists demonstrate that these garments were disturbing because they threatened typical ways of regulating female sexuality. In early modern society the conception of an illegitimate child was associated with loose morals, and the sexual behaviour of both men and women, but more particularly women, was viewed as a public

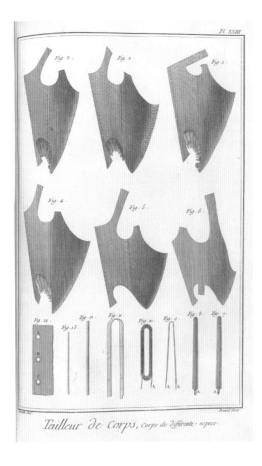

Fig. 6.14 *'Plate XXIII: Tailor of Bodies [stays], Bodices of Different Types', from Denis Diderot,* Encyclopédie, ou Dictionnaire raisonné des sciences, des arts et des métiers: Recueil de planches, sur les sciences, les arts libéraux, et les arts méchaniques avec leur explication, *Book 8, Vol. 9 (Paris, 1762–72), Metropolitan Museum of Art, New York. Maternity stays are depicted in fig. 3 of this plate.*

concern that needed to be regulated.[77] While a boy's adolescence focused on the idea of 'competitive manhood', which included drinking, fighting and sexual prowess, women as daughters of Eve were seen as possessing a powerful and destructive sexuality that needed to be controlled. Concepts of modesty and chastity were therefore instilled in girls from an early age through religious teachings or literature such as conduct manuals. The preoccupation with controlling women's sexual behaviour through these rigid gendered constructs influenced many aspects of daily life and women who fell afoul of these norms ran the risk of being labelled whores, witches or adulterers.[78] At the same time a woman's sexual desire for her husband was still deemed necessary for marriage and procreation. Popular but conflicting binaries such as these preached by didactic writers and from the pulpit often clashed with the realities of everyday life, and so the expression of female sexual desire occupied a precarious space in early modern society.

During this period the primary function of sexual behaviour remained the production of children. The distinction between what was sex and what was not, what was a licit or illicit activity, and even

Fig. 6.15 *Author's reconstruction of the Verney maternity bodies worn by a model with a normal V-shaped stomacher over a smock and with an outer petticoat. The front of the garment is shorter than other examples from the period and so does not create the deep V-shape of other contemporary bodies.*

what constituted a legal marriage, was based around whether or not the sexual practice could lead to the possibility of procreation.[79] In marriage, the pursuit of sex and sexual pleasure by a woman was seen as natural and normal as it led to procreation, and female pleasure was deemed necessary for conception to occur, as dominant medical thought maintained that women, like men, also had to release a seed through pleasure.[80] The possibility of reproduction therefore structured understandings of sexuality and the only approved sexuality for a woman was within the confines of marriage with her husband. Foundation garments were expected to maintain as well as reflect these social boundaries. While it was acceptable for women and men to exchange sexualized love tokens such as busks and busk-points within the confines of courtship and marriage, the use of foundation garments by prostitutes or female libertines was met with fear and anxiety as they aided unmarried women's forward expressions of sexual desire and the concealment of its repercussions.[81]

Although fornication was a punishable offence in England, pre-nuptial pregnancies amongst commoners were generally tolerated if the union was formalized. Indeed, in one Cumberland parish during the early seventeenth century, 60 per cent of brides were pregnant when they arrived at the altar.[82] Even though illegitimacy rates peaked in England between 1590 and 1610, overall illegitimacy during the seventeenth century remained quite low, between 2 and 5 per cent.[83] The point at which the foetus was animated with a soul was also debated and only a small number of English law cases classified abortion as murder.[84] It seems that early modern women also had regular access to birth control and abortifacients as remedies that dealt with how to induce menstruation, possibly a cure for infertility but also a method to terminate pregnancy, were widely available in cheap print.[85] Both socially and legally, contraception also held an ambivalent place during this period. Although religious doctrine taught that it was a woman's duty to bear children and fertility was emphasized as vital to the social, economic and political stability of society during this period, demographic studies have shown that some sort of regular family planning must have been attempted. In England, early modern families on average had only four to six children and in the second half of the seventeenth century the number of births declined for women over thirty, likely due to an increase in contraceptive methods such as abstinence or *coitus interruptus*.[86] Overall then, illegitimacy was not that common, attitudes towards abortion ambivalent and overall fertility rates were relatively stable.

Why then was criticism of foundation garments so preoccupied with women's sexuality and reproduction? In her examination of the marriage of Louis XIV to Maria Theresa of Spain in 1660, Abby E. Zanger highlighted the general unease felt at the French court in their first few days of contact with the king's new foreign bride. The *guardainfante* worn by the princess was not only a symbol of Spain, an enemy of the French for much of the century, but also inhibited the ability of the French to see her body. Not only did this make the princess appear 'misshapen or monstrous' to French tastes of bodily display but along with its connotations of concealing pregnancy, raised fears for the virginal princess's virtue (see Fig. 6.16).[87] The court's reaction to this hooped underskirt is a fascinating moment in French royal history, but was not, as this chapter has shown, unusual. Instead, foundation garments such as farthingales continued to draw on established tropes that highlighted both differences in cultural tastes of embodied display but also fears about deviant female sexuality. Just as Juana of Portugal supposedly hid her illegitimate pregnancies with a farthingale, this garment continued to obscure a woman's lower half during the seventeenth century, inhibiting the ability to visually read and regulate the sexual bodies of women, some of whom like Maria Theresa were the future mothers of dynastic heirs.

Towards the end of the Middle Ages the idea that women's bodies were full of secrets both fascinated and frustrated medical and non-medical communities alike. Katharine Park has argued that matters such as female virginity, fertility, generation and paternity were often referred to by male writers as 'the secrets of women'. Such a phrase had various meanings. One interpretation was medical, as those who dissected female bodies sought to understand conception and generation. Other meanings associated with the term were social and in this context such 'secrets of women' implied that they had knowledge

Fig. 6.16 *Jacques Laumosnier,* The meeting of Louis XIV and Felipe IV on the Island of Pheasants in 1659, *c. mid-seventeenth century, oil on canvas, Musée de Tessé, Le Mans.*

about the mysteries of procreation that was kept secret from men and used immorally.[88] As a result, women's bodies were continually scrutinized. During the late medieval period the size, shape and texture of breasts were believed to indicate whether a woman was virginal or not – large breasts that sagged signalled sexual experience, even if this was what we would understand to be a completely natural result of puberty.[89] During the seventeenth century, books with flap anatomy sheets enabled a type of voyeurism that continued to reinforce these ideas about the secrets of women as one had to lift the paper flaps to view into the generative female body.[90] These ideas extended into the eighteenth century as midwives, anatomists, physicians and others continued to ponder the wonders of generation.[91] The language of concealment and the mistrust of women's bodies was defined by this so-called secrecy during the medieval and early modern period.[92]

This discourse of mistrust and secrecy and the inability to visually read and to regulate the sexual bodies of women who wore foundation garments is reflective of wider cultural concerns about the organization of society: such as in the patriarchal household, where key ideas relating to femininity and masculinity were dictated, especially the belief that women should be chaste while men were to

Fig. 6.17 *Peter Lely,* Portrait of Louise de Keroualle, Duchess of Portsmouth, c. *1671–4, oil on canvas, The J. Paul Getty Museum, Los Angeles. The modes of undress common in Restoration portraits such as this example were conventions of art rather than reflective of everyday dressing practices.*

have authority. Although by the late seventeenth century a more casual attitude that encouraged female sexuality was celebrated in the court by Charles II, composed into verse by libertines such as John Wilmot and Sir Charles Sedley and portrayed visually in the *en déshabillé* portraiture of Sir Peter Lely (see Fig. 6.17), those outside these elite circles continued to paint the court as extravagant and immoral. Their critique of women's appearance no longer focused intensely on the artificial body as it had done earlier in the century, likely due to the increasing use of foundation garments at all levels of English society by the time of the Restoration. Instead, the sexual bodies of court women came into focus as satires once again began to connect the sexual vices of the king and his courtiers with national weakness.[93] Even Catherine of Braganza, who fashioned a place for herself in the minds of many as a virtuous, loyal wife and role model for respectable women, occasionally emulated the risqué styles of her husband's mistresses (see Fig. 6.18).[94] By 1663 the queen was noted to have done away with more modest styles first seen during her time in England, 'exposing her breast and shoulders without even the glaze of the lightest gauze, and her tucker, instead of standing upon her bosom was, with licentious boldness, turned down and lay upon her stays'.[95] Instead of having the lace collar that covered her

CATHARINA D.G. MAGNÆ. BRITANNIÆ. FRANCIÆ. ET HIBERNIÆ.
REGINA. FILIA IOANNIS IIII REG. PORTVG &c.

Fig. 6.18 *Abraham Bloteling after Peter Lely,* Portrait of Catherine of Braganza, Queen of England, *c. 1662–90, mezzotint and engraving, Rijksmuseum, Amsterdam.*

chest it was now tucked into the top of her stays (or bodies as they were called at the time), exposing her cleavage.

The Restoration court was perceived by many to disrupt traditional models of marriage, family and morality – models that were centred on patriarchal religious ideas of women and their place in a stable society.[96] The family unit tied by marriage and overseen by a male figure was understood as providing structure and stability to society, and those whose behaviour transgressed this social model were commonly perceived as disorderly. According to this model of social organization, female honour and chastity were defined as the greatest virtues of women and great efforts were made to secure this by policing women's bodies and reproductive organs – ideas reflected in descriptions of busk-points as sitting over the female honour.[97]

Maintaining the patrimonial character of the household and the chastity of wives also ensured the legality of family before the courts and established a legal recognition of paternity that safeguarded social stability by ensuring property and power was transmitted down paternal bloodlines.[98] Female adultery undermined the household, on which social morality and legality stood. Many men sought to avoid the stigma of becoming a cuckold, which undermined their ability to secure a stable, socially acceptable household and mocked their masculinity.[99] Female sexual indiscretion also left the question of paternity ambiguous. Was a child born into a marriage of an adulterous farthingale-wearing wife that of her husband or her lover? What did that mean for identity and the inheritance of property? Most importantly, what would that mean for social stability? Foundation garments became convenient scapegoats for these wider cultural concerns about female sexuality and deviance. Like the character Ward in *Women Beware Women*, who sought to establish that his future bride did not have a pregnancy bump hidden under her farthingale, the need to secure a virtuous body in a potential wife and to regulate chastity was even more important when it came to the nobility and the gentry. While a nobleman could bear dozens of illegitimate children to mistresses without stigma, as family inheritance and dynastic ties were passed down through the paternal bloodline, noblewomen were expected to bear only the children of their husbands. In this sense, there was much more at risk when dealing with the legitimacy of children of the elites, particularly the monarchy, and this made women's fertility and fidelity not just a social but a political concern as well.

The secrets of the female body did not just threaten to undermine masculine authority – it divided women too. The work of Laura Gowing has demonstrated that women were just as likely as men to use their proximity to each other, as well as their intimate access to other women's bodies in situations such as childbirth, in order to regulate sexuality. Women often shared intimate spaces such as beds where they were able to observe each other's bodies and it was also common for the mistress of the household to use her authority to check her female servant's bodies for signs of pregnancy if she suspected sexual indiscretions. Matrons with authority and knowledge were also employed by the courts and Bridewells (prisons) to examine women's bodies for signs of virginity and pregnancy.[100] Yet women could also be visual observers like men, and many women who were witnesses in infanticide trials testified that they suspected a woman of being pregnant or of giving birth due to a perceived change in her body shape. The case of Marie Riley is one example. In 1665 Marie, a 'single woman' from the village of Hetton in Yorkshire, was accused a second time of infanticide on account of the women of the village 'observing her body to be bigger than ordinary'.[101] Various court accounts such as this reveal that all women from elites to commoners therefore had, as Gowing has concluded, 'a sharp eye for each other's bodily transgressions'.[102]

It is not clear if women attempted to hide their pregnancies from prying community eyes with foundation garments any more than they did with other common items of female dress. Although the *guarainfante* ('*guardar el infante*', literally 'protect the infant') was regularly accused of hiding unwanted pregnancies in seventeenth-century Spain, there is little evidence to support the claim that women habitually used these garments to conceal pregnancies to full term, illegitimate or not.[103] In general, an early pregnancy would have been quite easy to conceal under the many layers of clothing made from yards of fabric that were commonly worn by *all* early modern women. In many cases, as my reconstruction experiments demonstrated, aprons may have been enough to conceal small to medium-sized pregnancy bumps. The various layers of garments would have made stomachs harder to visualize, especially as early modern women were less likely to gain as much weight as modern women during pregnancy.[104] What is clear, though, is that many women who had authority in the community, such as midwives, widows and married women, sought to maintain and reinforce the patriarchal organization of society by scrutinizing and demanding access to unmarried women's bodies in ways not permitted to men. More importantly, an understanding of the secrets of women's bodies and the patriarchal organization of early modern society reveals why foundation garments, which were so obviously intended to reshape the female silhouette, were continuously targeted for concealing female sexual indiscretions. These garments inhibited the ability of both men and women to regulate the chastity of the women around them, undermining not only ideas of chaste and submissive femininity, but also those of authoritative masculinity too, and thus the very organization of early modern society.

Conclusion

Examining foundation garments provides insights into a bawdy and often contradictory sexual culture in sixteenth- and seventeenth-century England. As the first part of this chapter demonstrated, sexual expression through these material objects was often fetishized and gave people a new vocabulary to communicate sexual desire and love. Importantly, these garments also opened a discursive space that afforded women a degree of flexibility at the same time that it reinforced their subordination to male authority and erotic desire. Foundation garments could give women sexual agency in the bedroom or, conversely, could produce anxiety and perpetuate common myths about female deviance and sexual sin. Examining the role of foundation garments also shows the ways that wider cultural concerns about female sexuality and deviances were regularly projected onto female dress. These garments provoked criticism not because they habitually did what was claimed, for there is little evidence to prove that foundation garments were used by women to conceal pregnancy any more than other items of dress during this period, but because they inhibited habitual ways of reading and regulating the female body.

At a time when modern understandings of anatomy did not exist and medical technology such as ultrasounds or blood tests were not available, sight and touch were the best ways to determine deformities, disease or pregnancy. These foundation garments made from solid materials such as whalebone, metal and wood that reshaped the female silhouette obscured these sensory habits of bodily regulation – thus leaving female bodies unreadable and potentially uncontrollable. Criticisms of these intimate garments therefore fed into larger cultural narratives about deviant female sexuality and about the generative mysteries of the female body, as well as the destructive forces of an unrestrained female sexuality on familial and social cohesion that was held together by male authority. Foundation garments were therefore an essential part of both celebrating and regulating female sexual bodies in sixteenth- and seventeenth-century England.

7

The respectable body

Rising consumption and the changing sensibilities of late seventeenth- and early eighteenth-century England

In 1631 the poet and moralist Richard Brathwaite wrote in his comedy *Whimsies* that the character of the jealous neighbour 'exclaims grievously against' his wife's 'Body-maker, and inverting his name, calls him directly Bawd-maker'.[1] Brathwaite's suggestion that body-makers were in fact bawd-makers not only implied that these garments and their makers made women lascivious, but echoed the many concerns about women's appearance, bodies and sexuality that had come to be associated with this garment during the seventeenth century. However, over a hundred years later the meanings attached to bodies, which were now called stays, were exactly the opposite. In 1740 the Reverend Wetenhall Wilkes wrote in his conduct manual, *A Letter of Genteel and Moral Advice to a Young Lady*, that women should 'Never appear in Company, without your Stays. Make it your general Rule, to lace in the Morning, before you leave your Chamber. The Neglect of this, is liable to the Censure of Indolence, Supineness of Thought, Sluttishness . . . The Negligence of loose Attire May oft' invite to loose Desire.'[2] In less than a century, bodies had gone from being superfluous garments that made women vain and sexually deviant to necessary items of female attire, so much so that when they were not worn, women were accused of being indolent and sluttish.

Unlike stays, the eighteenth-century equivalent of the farthingale, the hoop petticoat, was not accepted in such a way. Although some acknowledged that these devices 'served to keep men at a proper Distance', like their predecessors they also commented that it was well known that many Ladies who wore 'hoops of the greatest Circumference were not of the most impregnable Virtue'.[3] Why had attitudes that had been so fervently voiced during the seventeenth century in relation to foundation garments and women's morality changed so much in regard to bodies and stays, but so little in relation to farthingales and hoop petticoats by the early eighteenth century? The contrasting attitudes in these sources are not only indicative of changing cultural and social norms and expectations in the late seventeenth century, but also the part that foundation garments played in shaping these ideals of femininity.

This chapter will discuss how the increased consumption of foundation garments from 1650 to 1700 made bodies, busks and bum-rolls part of everyday attire for almost every woman in late seventeenth-century England. This development was linked to general trends of increased production and consumption during the second half of the century, trends that were largely driven by the consumption practices of the middling sorts. The increased buying power and influence of this social group, who championed pervasive notions of politeness, respectability and sensibility, radically transformed the meanings of foundation garments to suit their own social needs. After being imbued with these new understandings, foundation garments were used to continually reinforce these ideals of the middling sorts onto the female body, particularly that of modesty, shaping a new understanding of femininity that would characterize how women should appear and act in the late seventeenth and eighteenth centuries.

Changing consumption practices of the late seventeenth century

There have been at least five different 'consumer revolutions' proclaimed by historians, the most famous of which was identified as occurring during the late eighteenth century.[4] That period was, as Neil McKendrick influentially asserted, the moment when modern patterns of consumption first appeared, as 'a greater proportion of the population than in any previous society in human history' had the ability to 'enjoy the pleasures of buying consumer goods'.[5] However, recent studies have shown that increased consumption during the late eighteenth century was not so much a revolution but rather the next phase in a long evolution of European consumption practices.[6] Indeed, historians of Renaissance Italy have demonstrated that Italians of all social levels were very engaged with the market for luxury goods during the late fifteenth and sixteenth centuries.[7] Catherine Kovesi has even argued that economic changes during the late thirteenth century saw the northern Italian economies develop in ways that distinguished Renaissance Italy as one of the first consumer societies in the Western world.[8]

While the rise of modern consumption in Italy in the late thirteenth century is certainly an exception, it is indisputable that permanent changes to consumption practices did occur in north-west Europe in countries such as England and the Dutch Republic in the seventeenth century. This century saw the increased importation of raw products and consumer goods – many of which were sourced from overseas via global trade networks that were now well established – which were increasingly produced in large quantities aimed at the common and middling sorts of people.[9] Indeed, as Chapters 3 and 4 explored, the consumption of foundation garments by middling and common women began as early as the turn of the seventeenth century in England when whalebone became readily available. It was around this time that the production and retail of foundation garments by specialized industries also began. This indicates that access to innovative and new fashionable items of dress was well within the reach of some non-elite women much earlier than previously thought. However, it was not until the second half of the seventeenth century that a huge increase in the production and consumption of foundation garments made them not only relatively inexpensive and widely accessible, but also truly a part of everyday female attire for women of all social levels.

The probate accounts of Edward Harpur, a mercer and alderman from the town of Stockport in the North-West of England who died in 1650, demonstrate that by the mid-seventeenth century a notable shift had occurred in the wardrobes of middling women in England. Harpur was a prominent resident of Stockport, in both business and law, so his probate was large and listed various properties including 'burgages tenements' that he leased, as well as six shops in the market. At the time of their father's death, Edward's four daughters, Hannah, Sarah, Esther and Deborah, were aged approximately thirteen, twelve, ten and nine, and his probate provided a detailed account of their expenditure for a period of almost thirteen years.[10] During this time the three eldest daughters moved to London. Sarah went in 1653, Hannah in 1654 and Esther in 1657. As their uncle, Francis Harpur, continued to pay for their maintenance for some time, it is unlikely that they went into service in the capital. Instead it is possible that they went to boarding school or to arrange suitable marriages. The youngest sister, Deborah, is the only daughter who stayed in Stockport and she boarded with six different households until she was put into service in Bury in 1658.[11]

Although Deborah later launched a lawsuit over the handling of the probate executorship by her uncle, detailed court investigations show that the four sisters were relatively well looked after.[12] Certainly the expenditures listed by their uncle, also a mercer, in the maintenance accounts support such a conclusion, as the girls continued to wear the garments fit for the daughters of a mercer-cum-alderman. During this decade the sisters' wardrobes consisted mostly of petticoats and waistcoats, with only some gowns and hoods listed. All these garments were made from practical woollen fabrics such as kersey, broadcloth, serge and minikin, and occasionally silk. During the Interregnum, puritanical sentiments promoted simplicity in adornment; however, the republican government made no attempt to legally restrict dress.[13] Fashionable accessories and trims such as gloves, bands and neckerchiefs, coifs and aprons of various colours and hats therefore appear often in the Harpur probate. Although *A Discourse of Auxiliary beauty or Artificial handsomeness* (1656), by Bishop John Gauden, criticized the piety of women who wore 'a bombast or bolstered garment [bum-roll]' and bodies during this decade, foundation garments were also present in the wardrobes of the Harpur sisters.[14]

From the start of the account in 1650 there are entries detailing the consumption of bodies by each of the girls and they range in cost over the next decade from 1s. to 3s. 10d. Expenditure for the materials given to a tailor to make the bodies reveals that they were made from linen and whalebone, meaning that they were structural undergarments, not the bodices of gowns that would have been made from the same wool and silk as the rest of the garment.[15] Although the accounts show that the girls' bodies were routinely mended, Esther and Deborah, who were aged ten and nine at the start of accounts, purchased new pairs of bodies much more frequently than their older sisters, presumably due to adolescent growth (see Table 1). During the same decade, the diary of Thomas Larkham, a Puritan clergyman in Devon, records that in 1651 he 'Paid for a paire of bodies' for one of his female family members, and again in 1652 he paid for '2 paire of bodies for wife and daughter' at a cost of 8s. 4d.[16] The costs of the bodies in the Harpur and Larkham accounts, which range from 1s. to about 4s., are much less than the seven to eight shillings quoted in the late sixteenth-century Peckover accounts.[17] Considering that wages were also higher in the mid-seventeenth century than they had been fifty years earlier, these values mark a significant decrease in price, regardless of the materials used. What this suggests is that the consumption of bodies was becoming so widespread during the mid-seventeenth century, and raw materials such as baleen more readily available, that they were becoming cheaper to produce.

Busks were purchased by the Harpur sisters less often than bodies, with, on average, the girls consuming only one or two each during the ten-year period. This was probably due to the nature of the busk: as a long strong piece of wood or metal that could be taken out and used in multiple bodies, there was no need to replace it often. The nature of their production and how they were sourced might also account for their small presence in these records. As explained in Chapter 4, busks were routinely sourced from tailors, body-makers and farthingale-makers. Chapman traders who roamed the countryside selling ready-made clothing, haberdashery, accessories and courtship-gifts may also have sold busks.[18] It was also not unusual for busks to be given to young women, such as the Harpur girls, by potential suitors as a type of love token (discussed later in this chapter). Another consideration is that as the girls grew taller and needed new, longer busks, they may have simply passed their old ones down to each other and this would not be recorded in the accounts.

Bum-rolls, or 'A Roll for their waist', also appear in the records albeit much less than bodies do. The simple nature of these garments might account for this, as they are recorded as being made from inexpensive scotch cloth and would have been easily repaired by the sisters using the sewing supplies such as the needles and thread that appear often in the accounts. In 1650 all the sisters, except the

Table 1 Consumption of foundation garments by the Harpur sisters

	= Bodies purchased,	= Bodies mended,	= Bum-rolls purchased,	= Busks purchased
	Hannah (OLDEST)	Sarah	Esther	Deborah (YOUNGEST)
1650				
1651				
1652				
1653				
1654				
1655				
1656				
1657				
1658				
1659				
1660				

youngest, Deborah, received 'rolls', with the eldest, Hannah, receiving two. Deborah first received one in 1652 when she was about eleven years old, and it remained her only bum-roll in these bills until 1657 when she reached sixteen years of age. Assessing the costs of these rolls is difficult as multiple garments are often listed under the one expenditure in these accounts; however, 'a ball and 3 Rowles' were purchased in 1650 for 2s. 1d. in total.[19] An entry from nearly a decade earlier, in August 1641, in the account book of Joyce Jeffreys listed 'a bum roll' that cost 20d., meaning that these garments were quite inexpensive by the middle of the century.[20]

While Edward Harpur's estate looked after his daughters well, their clothing expenditure was trivial compared to that of the gentry. In 1659 a total of £3 14s. 3d. was spent on clothing for Deborah, which is substantially less than the approximately £12 that would have been spent on a daughter from the gentry during the same period.[21] Their uncle Francis was also under no obligation to provide them with items that he deemed unnecessary, so one may surmise that their consumption of these products is representative of what girls of this social status wore at the time. This is also supported by the household account books of Giles Moore, a rector in Horsted Keynes in Sussex, that date from the 1660s and 1670s. In these books, Moore recorded that he bought his ward and niece, the previously mentioned Martha Mayhew, several pairs of bodies during these decades in order to adequately habit her. Moore was himself quite humble in dress and opposed to lavish excess, and so it can be assumed that the applied this thrift to his niece's expenditure as well.[22] The probate account of husbandman Robert Parrat from Warboys in Huntingdonshire also reveals that bodies of various prices were purchased for his daughter in the mid-1670s.[23] By the middle of the seventeenth century in England it is apparent, then, that foundation garments were far from the luxury items that they had been at the start of the seventeenth century. Instead, they had become commonplace and a vital part of dress for the daughters of husbandmen and tradesmen, as well as the female relations of both Anglican and Puritan preachers (see Fig. 7.1).

The growth of the body-making trade and the increased availability of ready-made bodies in the last half of the century is also indicative of the growing acceptance of these garments as crucial items of middling and common women's dress. Unlike farthingale-makers, who appear to have been largely confined to London and had disappeared by the middle of the seventeenth century, the demand for bodies and body-making continued to grow outside the capital, challenging the monopoly of tailors who had previously made such items in these areas. By the 1630s there were body-makers in Norfolk and Lincolnshire. Robert Fewe of King's Lynn and William Townsend of Hilton are both listed as body-makers in 1632 and 1633 respectively.[24] In 1658 a 'Bodies Maker' from Swavesey in Cambridge called Richard Richman died and in 1677 Richard Fowlar, a 'BodisMaker' of Caversham in Oxfordshire, also made his will upon his death bed.[25] By the 1680s and 1690s, men who called themselves body-makers came from all around the country, from places such as Somerset, Gloucestershire, Dorset, Cambridgeshire and Huntingdonshire.[26] Provincial women no longer had to rely on tailors or specialist

Fig. 7.1 *Cornelis Pietersz Bega,* Two Maids Drinking and Smoking, *1663, oil on canvas, Städel Museum, Frankfurt am Main. The bodies worn by the Harpur sisters may have resembled those worn by these Dutch maids. The woman to the left wears a pair of brown bodies over a smock; the shoulder seam and the spot where the strap attaches to the front of the bodice is visible. The woman on the right wears a pair of bodies of a light brown or cream colour underneath a waistcoat that is open.*

artisans from London for their bodies; rather, they could acquire them locally from specialized body-makers.

By the middle of the seventeenth century, old patterns of production were also changing and ready-made apparel became an important part of the clothing market in England. Although ready-to-wear bodies had been available since at least the 1620s, and body-sellers had appeared not long after that, as discussed in Chapters 3 and 4, by the late seventeenth century, these garments were flooding the market in ready-made forms that were overwhelmingly aimed at the middling and common sorts. Upon his death in September 1665 the London Merchant Taylor John Dryer had in his shop '2 dozen [24] women's bodices made' and '2 dozen [bodices] unmade'.[27] Two years later, in 1667, the inventory of another London bodice maker, Thomas Beetham, listed not only all the raw materials needed by a bodice maker (such as parcels of whalebone) but also over a hundred finished bodies, and a parcel of nearly finished 'boddies unstitched'.[28] The following year, in 1668, the probate inventory of Sylvester Widmere the elder, a mercer from Marlow in Buckinghamshire, listed:

	£	s.	d.
27 pair of Bodice at 4s.	5	8	0
7 pair of Bodice at 3s.	1	1	0
3 pair of Bodice at 22d.	0	6	6
14 Stomachers at 11d.	0	12	10
8 pair of Bodice at 18d	0	12	0
5 pair of Bodice at 3s. 6d.	0	17	6
3 pair of Bodice at 2s. 4d.	0	7	0
2 pair of Bodice at 2s.	0	4	0[29]

The inventory of Samuel Bartlett, a milliner in Oxford, also reveals that at his death in 1675 he carried ready-made bodices in stock, possibly sourced from a local body-maker or a London supplier.[30] Not only did women have access to ready-made garments, but there was clearly a wide selection of bodies available at different price points.

The source that gives the clearest indication that by the late seventeenth century these garments had become common among all women in English society is Gregory King's *Annual Consumption of Apparel, 1688*.[31] According to this source, 1,000,000 'Bodyes and Stays' at approximately 8s. each were consumed in 1688, the same number as petticoats and waistcoats, while 200,000 'Masks, Fan and Busks' at approximately 1s. each were consumed in the same year as well.[32] No mention of bum-rolls

The merry Milk Maid
La Femme au-Lait.

Fig. 7.2 *Jacob Gole, after John Savage, after Marcellus Laroon II, 'The merry Milk Maid', from* The Cryes of the City of London Drawne after the Life 1688, *c. 1688–1724, print, Rijksmuseum, Amsterdam. This print series portrayed the hawkers of the streets of London, some of whom were well-known personalities in the city at the time. The milkmaid depicted here with tankards and silverware on her head wears a smock, petticoat, pair of bodies, apron and kerchief. The face of the milkmaid has been slightly altered from the original published in 1688; however, the dress is the same.*

is made, but this is likely due to their simple design, which meant that they could be made in the home. That same year the inventory of Edmund Fleare, a 'Bodys Maker' from Lincoln, also contained 207 pairs of pre-made bodies, for women, children and 'girls', some finished and others 'unstitch[ed]'.[33] The population of England is estimated to have been approximately 4.865 million in the mid-1680s.[34] If we assume that sex ratios were roughly even and therefore approximately half of this population were female (so, 2.433 million), and 92.55 per cent of this population were females over the age of four, then according to King's figures, in any given year up to half the female population of England was buying a new pair of bodies or stays.[35] Of course, some non-elite women may not have bought a new garment every year, while some elite women may have purchased many every year. However, these figures still demonstrate that women beyond the elite (who made up a small fraction of the population) were buying such items.

The increase in both production and consumption of foundation garments correlates with other observations that a wide range of fabrics and fashionable goods were available to towns and villages around England during this period, and this increased even more so in the final decades of the seventeenth century. Petty chapmen, whom Margaret Spufford described as reclothing the rural inhabitants of seventeenth-century England, were also recorded as having ready-made bodies in their inventories. The distribution networks of these salesmen, who went village to village selling consumer goods, reached even the most remote areas of the kingdom by 1700, meaning that provincial folk during this period increasingly had the means to access fashionable attire.[36] By the late seventeenth century then, foundation garments were part of everyday female dress for the women of England, as these once luxurious and elite garments were now seen as essential items of the female wardrobe along with shoes, smocks and hose (see Fig. 7.2).

From bodies to stays: changing terminology and female morality

Lynn Sorge-English has argued that 'it was around 1680 that stays became separate garments' due to the emergence of the loose-fitting mantua gown, as 'prior to that they were treated-as-one with the outer bodice. Their identity as a foundation garment in its own right can be seen to have begun in the closing decades of the seventeenth century.'[37] As this book has shown, foundation garments called bodies had been worn as both under- and outerwear throughout the seventeenth century and stays were not a new invention. The term 'stays' had been used before 1680, but it did not refer to an individual garment.[38] Instead, the word was almost always used in tailoring bills to refer to the stiffening in the garments being made. An early appearance of the term 'stays' is in the Verney papers of 1662 where it is used to describe the stiffened bodices of gowns: 'for stays and stiffenings'.[39] Additionally, this term often appeared in tailoring bills for menswear. 'Stay and buckram' are listed in an itemized account detailing the making of a men's coat in the records of the Clayton family of Surrey.[40] Even during the 1680s the term stays was still used to refer to the stiffening of bodies, as in 1685, after the death of Charles II, a pair of 'under boddeys' with 'packthread stays' were made for the Dowager Queen Catherine of Braganza.[41]

One of the first possible references to stays as a garment appears in a 1680 comedy by John Dryden, where the character Mrs Brainsick is described as going to the New Exchange to see her tailor 'to try her Stays for a new gown'.[42] This line refers to either the stiffening in the bodice of a gown or a separate pair of stays. By 1682, advertisements for lost goods included 'a pair of Hair-coloured Satin Stays, embroidered with Gold and Silver', and conduct books for women that mentioned 'a single pair of Stays' appeared.[43] The term 'stays' is first recorded in the Proceedings of the Old Bailey in September 1686, when Eleanor Jones of St. Botolph's without Aldersgate in London was found guilty and sentenced to death for theft. Included in her booty were garments of the latest fashion such as 'One Mantua Petticoat' and 'One pair of Silk Stays'.[44]

Tailoring bills, probate accounts and court records all show that during the closing decades of the seventeenth century both bodies and stays were similarly priced and made from the same materials. Both garments appear to have been made by tailors and possibly by body-makers too.[45] Narratives of seventeenth-century fashion tend to equate the emergence of stays with the appearance of the mantua gown, as both terms seem to have appeared at the same time.[46] However, bodies and stays were both worn with mantua gowns. Several court cases from the Old Bailey contain descriptions of whole outfits being stolen that include 'a serge Mantua, one Petticoat, one pair of Bodice'.[47] Like bodies, stays were also mentioned with sleeves, as the silk stays stolen by the previously mentioned Eleanor Jones were referred to alongside 'One pair of Silk Sleeves'. Indeed, a pair of yellow silk satin bodies or stays dating to the turn of the eighteenth century also contain matching sleeves that attached by laces or ribbon to the shoulder straps (see Fig. 7.3 and Fig. 7.4). The use of metallic trim on the front of the garment to create a V-shaped design also suggests that when these sleeves were removed this garment may also have been worn underneath a mantua, with this yellow front on show (see Fig. 7.5). This demonstrates that garments that have come to be known as stays technically fulfilled the same function as bodies in the closing decade of the seventeenth century, again confirming that they were not necessarily a new garment.

In 1688, Randle Holme used these terms interchangeably when he addressed the process of '*Lining the Bodies,* or *Stayes*', indicating that they were the same thing.[48] However, by 1700 there were clearly some physical differences, as in August of that year Thomas Harding and John Mahew of St Giles in the Fields in London were indicted for stealing 'a pair of Satin stayes' and 'a pair of Bodices'.[49] By the early eighteenth century, pairs of bodies are regularly mentioned in court records from the Old Bailey alongside stomachers, while stays are not.[50] Indeed, bodies/bodices and body-/bodice-makers were still regularly mentioned during the eighteenth century; however, these garments were referred to in a way that implied that were outdated and inexpensive.[51] It is possible that during the eighteenth-century, bodies still referred to earlier styles of foundation garments that laced over the front of a stomacher, while stays referred to new cutting-edge styles of a back-lacing garments that were usually associated with the mantua. It seems, then, that the 1680s was a decade of transition, not only in fashion with the widespread adoption of the mantua gown, but also in terminology. At the end of the seventeenth century there was little difference between bodies or stays, and they were used for the same purposes in women's dress.

Unlike France, where the earlier term *corps* (meaning body) continued to be used to refer to boned torso-shaping garments during the eighteenth century, by 1700 the terminology in England had irreversibly shifted.[52] Why then did the name for these garments change from bodies to stays in English but remain the same in French? The emergence of the term 'stays' can be attributed to new moral implications that were attached to bodies by the evolving genteel middling sorts of England who were now the largest consumers of these garments. As discussed in Chapter 2, during

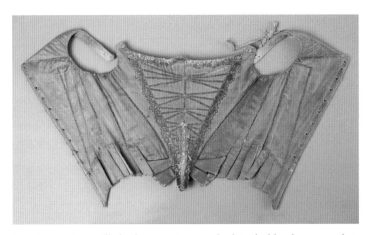

Fig. 7.3 *Yellow silk bodies or stays with detachable sleeves, c. late seventeenth century–early eighteenth century, French, Metropolitan Museum of Art, New York. The front of the garment is decorated with metallic trim and it is likely that this was made to be worn with a mantua gown.*

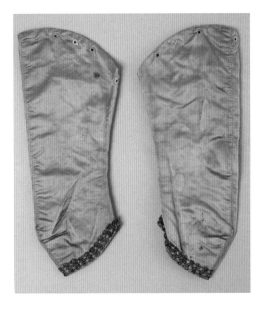

Fig. 7.4 *Detachable sleeves belonging to yellow silk bodies or stays, c. late seventeenth century–early eighteenth century, French, Metropolitan Museum of Art, New York.*

the late sixteenth and early seventeenth centuries the courtly concept of *sprezzatura* influenced elite ideals of femininity and encouraged the use of artificial court dress that included foundation garments. Unlike *sprezzatura*, which was the art of appearing, acting and speaking gracefully without revealing effort or thought, by the late seventeenth century a new culture of politeness emerged, particularly among the middling sorts in England who now represented more than half of the population.

Catherine de Neuville, Comtesse d'Armagnac.
fille du Mareschal Duc de Villeroy, Epouse en 1660 François de Lorraine Comte
d'Armagnac, Pair et grand Escuyer de France.

Fig. 7.5 *Nicolas Bonnart after Robert Bonnart,* Portrait of Catherine de Neuville, Countess of Armagnac *(French Fashion Print), c. 1685–95, etching and engraving, Rijksmuseum, Amsterdam. The green mantua is bustled over a lavender-coloured skirt embroidered with flowers; the front of a pair of yellow stays or a yellow stomacher is visible.*

Much of this culture of politeness was based on earlier concepts of courtesy, virtue and civility, which were key ideas that helped the elites to structure and interpret their social world.[53] By the end of the seventeenth century in England these terms had come to be associated with cultural ideas dictated by the middling sorts. This group desired to distinguish themselves from those they viewed as rough and savage – the common sorts and working poor – and also from those whom they deemed morally reprehensible, such as the aristocratic elites.[54] Rather than simply being courteous and civil, which had previously involved the associated ideas of virtue and gracefulness, one was now expected to show sentiment and sensibility in order to make oneself agreeable.[55]

Part of making oneself agreeable was self-presentation, and as Paul Goring has argued, the body 'served as an important (and problematic) textual space for the symbolic inscription of politeness and for the working out of what it meant to be polite.'[56] Although the culture of politeness was still concerned with the ways that actions were performed, it was less concerned with competing ostentatious displays of wealth, power and good-breeding through artificial means. Rather, politeness was more focused on the sensibilities of socialization, of which, for women, decorum and modesty were key components.[57] This is exemplified in a broadside ballad dating from the middle of the seventeenth century titled *News from Hide-Parke*, which told the tale of a 'North Country Gentleman, and a very Gaudy Gallant Lady of pleasure, whom he took up in the Park'. The ballad described the gentlemen's shock at discovering that his lady of the night was 'strait laced'.[58] Unlike popular commentary from the start of the century that had associated prostitutes with the fine and debauched clothing of the court, including bodies and farthingales, the country gentleman in the ballad was surprised to find a prostitute wearing straight-laced bodies due to the meanings of modesty that were increasingly associated with these garments

In fact, it is not just the term 'strait-laced', meaning strict or moral, that is derived from the changing morality of bodies. Rather than giving a woman a newer and better artificial *straight body*, as foundation garments had done at the start of the seventeenth century, by the end of the century these garments were now intended to help everything on the female torso *stay* in its proper place. This is alluded to in Nehemiah Grew's 1682 book *The Anatomy of Plants*, where he compared a 'Flower without its Impalement, would hang as uncouth and tawdry, as a Lady without her Bodies'.[59] Similar sentiments were voiced by the character Guillamour in Thomas D'Urfey's play *The Intrigues at Versailles* (1697): 'And the Night-gown there so loose and Negligent, looks just like the tawdry Countess of Jersey in a morning without her Stays.'[60] The breasts of women therefore required stays, or support, in order to keep women looking decent.[61] By this period, modesty was not only concerned with decency but also with the awareness of the sensibilities of others. In order to avoid causing offence or upsetting others, women could no longer let their bodies, or more importantly breasts, hang 'uncouth' and 'tawdry', so stays became a requirement of decent dress.

In fact, by the 1690s, torso-shaping foundation garments seem to have become so accepted as part of modest attire that they are not mentioned at all in criticisms of dress. Take for example the broadside ballad *The Young Mens Advise to Proud Ladies* (1692), which issued a 'friendly Caution against their Monstrous Dress, Exhorting them to modesty'. The broadside listed the fashions of the day, including Top Knots, paste-on beauty marks and commodes. It did not, however, refer to bodies, stays or bum-rolls, items that would most certainly have been included in the ballad's lists of 'Gawdy and Ranting Attire' if it been published only forty years earlier.[62] By the early eighteenth century, the association of stays with modesty was apparent. In a poem from 1724 titled *A Lover to His Fat Mistress with Stays*, the author writes:

Pray charming Silvia, do not think you raise
My modest Passion by your want of Stays;

I do not for your dangling Breasts adore ye,

That hang like new-milked Udders down before ye:

Or do I in those flabby Sides take pride,

That do your Apron-strings in Wallops hide.

You look like one from Virtues Bonds just freed,

Whose Dress declares you little Courtship need;

If so, at one Request, your Favours grant,

And please your self with what you seem to want.

But if you think my jealous Eyes to please,

And would be gently Conquered by degrees,

Raise my Esteem, and make me speak your praise,

Pray hide the Slit, and hasten your Stays.[63]

As Susan Vincent has noted in her analysis of this poem, it seems that by the eighteenth century a woman with 'upper body unconfined thus stepped beyond the whaleboned boundaries of propriety'.[64] Yet it also seems that without her stays, which kept everything in place, Silvia's attractiveness and sexual allure were lost as well.

Valerie Steele has also made this observation about attitudes to stays in the eighteenth century. She notes that many travellers to England frequently remarked that English women were always laced, often in comparison to French women who apparently were not, concluding that for the English unlaced equalled loose morals.[65] Indeed, prostitutes in brothels in early eighteenth-century art and literature were intentionally depicted without stays. In the foreground of plate 3 of William Hogarth's allegorical print series *A Rake's Progress*, one prostitute's stays are lying on the ground, seemingly, as Hogarth would like us to believe, along with her morals (see Fig. 7.6). This sentiment is confirmed in Samuel Richardson's 1748 novel *Clarissa, or, the History of a Young Lady*, as when the title character Clarissa Harlowe visits a brothel she exclaims that all the prostitutes were in 'shocking dishabille and without stays'.[66]

The changing consumer culture of late seventeenth-century England, which was driven by the spending power of the middling sorts, manipulated the meanings of bodies and stays, connecting them not with the debauched ostentation of the court but rather with modesty and morality. No longer did the older foundation garment known as bodies signify elite concepts of femininity. Rather, a straight-laced woman in stays was a decent and modest woman, one of good morals and one who represented the new pervasive ideal of polite femininity that was championed by the middling sorts of the late seventeenth century, and which would come to define the feminine ideal of the eighteenth century.

Fig. 7.6 *William Hogarth, 'The Orgy', plate 3 from* A Rake's Progress, *1735, etching and engraving, National Gallery of Art, Washington, DC.*

The busk and changing romantic sensibilities

The consumption of busks in the late seventeenth century is also reflective of the changing sensibilities of the middling sorts and of expected gender roles in courtship and marriage. Busks were often elaborately decorated with common love motifs, portraits and lovers' words, or poetry, making them highly emotional romantic accessories. Although busks had long been associated with desire, as discussed in Chapter 6, throughout the seventeenth century, busks with romantic inscriptions or initials provide material proof of their frequent use in courtship and marriage practices. Early modern English marriage mediated social and political order, and suitability for marriage was based on various criteria: age, wealth, social position and mutual affection. Courtships were generally long, taking anywhere from nine months to two years, and often involved parents, relatives, friends, neighbours and even employers. Due to the number of people involved, and the social significance of marriage, courtship often entailed performances or ritual acts that legitimized the seriousness of the engagement. The public exchange of gifts therefore served both a practical and symbolic function, as this act was an important signifier of the relationship between the two betrotheds.[67]

The types of gifts exchanged during the early modern period were extremely varied and could range from the mundane – household goods such as foodstuffs or animals – to very intricate and personalized love tokens such as love spoons or knitting sheaths. Items of dress, however, seem to have been the most popular gifts during courtship: gloves, handkerchiefs, shoes, girdles, watches, brooches and most frequently rings.[68] Love tokens, material objects imbued with significant ideas related to romantic love and given as gifts during courtship or marriage, were not just an outward sign of obligation and intent. These material objects also helped to negotiate and instantiate the process of falling in love for couples, as the act of gifting inherently intertwined material objects with emotions such as sadness and joy as these exchanges created attachments, and acknowledged or affirmed pre-existing bonds.[69] Objects and gifts, rather than words, were therefore crucial to mediating emotions, particularly romantic emotions, during the early modern period before the dominance of literacy.[70]

Although many historians have noted the immense significance that gifts carried during courtship, as the public display of giving and receiving linked the notion of mutual consent and public recognition to the union, the status of a gift as a token of a legal relationship remains in dispute.[71] Some historians argue that because valid marriages could be made in civil ceremonies before witnesses prior to the Hardwicke Marriage Act of 1753, gift giving was a physical manifestation of a wedded union or the strong intent to marry.[72] Meanwhile others have noted that there was no unanimous agreement over the status of marriage and courtship tokens, citing many court cases where gift giving took place but no formal attachment was considered by one of the participants.[73] For women, gifts received could be key pieces of evidence that both parties had consented to a union, particularly if sexual relations had taken place during the courtship and a woman's reputation was subsequently called into question.[74]

The overwhelming majority of references to busks in writings before 1650 were either related to sexual desire or sexual promiscuity, although some in relation to courtship do appear.[75] However, the sheer number of surviving busks that contain inscriptions associated with love and references to their gifting in literature indicate that busk giving during courtship must have been a normal and commonly practised act by the second half of the seventeenth century. A surviving seventeenth-century English wooden busk illustrates this practice. One side of the busk shows an engraved clover composed of four hearts, a cross, a three-pronged crown, chalice cup and two love birds. Also inscribed is the date of its gifting, 1675, and the Biblical reference 'Genesis XXIIII, Verse 67'. On the other side of the busk is an inscription referencing the biblical Isaac's love for his wife, which reads, 'ONCE A QUESTION I

Fig. 7.7 *Wooden busk (back), c. 1675, English, Victoria and Albert Museum, London.*

WAS ASKED WHICH MADE ME RETURN THESE ANSWERS THAT ISAAC LOVED RABEKAH HIS WIFE AND WHY MAY NOT I LOVE FRANSIS' (see Fig. 7.7). This busk was very much a marriage gift, as it refers specifically to a biblical passage on wedlock and must have been given at an advanced stage of courtship.

The poem *On a Juniper Tree, cut down to make Busks* (1684) by Aphra Behn expressed similar sentiments, as the tree reveals that for years it witnessed couples wooing and making love under its branches until it was eventually cut down and 'my body into busks was turned: Where I still guard the sacred store, And of Love's temple keep the door'.[76] It was only fitting that this tree was made into busks destined to be gifted to women and sit on their bodies next to their hearts. Similarly, the act of inscribing a busk often made an inanimate object speak on behalf of the giver, expressing their love and desire for the receiver. One French seventeenth-century ivory busk in the Metropolitan Museum of Art (see Fig. 7.8) contains three lines of script: 'Until Goodbye, / My Fire is Pure, / Love is United'.[77] Three engravings correspond with each line of script: a tear falling into a barren field, two hearts appearing in that field and finally a house with two hearts floating above it, presumably the home that the couple would share together in marriage.

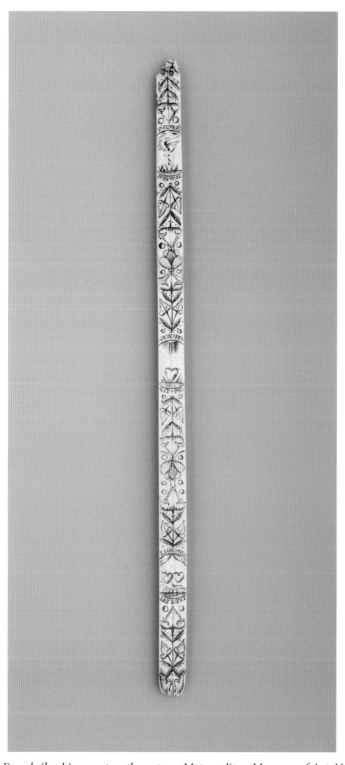

Fig. 7.8 *Ivory busk, French (back), seventeenth century, Metropolitan Museum of Art, New York.*

Like a wedding ring that that connected the binding word of marriage to a physical object which was then gifted, busks could symbolically and psychologically bind together a couple.[78] In some cases binding was evidently desired by busk giving. The inscription on another French seventeenth-century ivory busk exclaims, 'Love joins them, / it unites us, / To see you or else die' (see Fig. 7.9).[79] These lines are accompanied by engravings, the first a picture of two love hearts ('them'), the second these hearts being pierced by cupid's arrow ('us'), and the third a flower growing in the sun, the line implying that the lover, like the flower, cannot exist without the sustaining force of the other. The common motif of hearts being pierced and held together by cupid's arrow on many of these busks also points to love's binding qualities.

The use of busks to express the bonds of romantic love continued into the eighteenth century. One eighteenth-century busk held by the Victoria and Albert Museum contains prick decoration love hearts, diamonds and flowers and three pairs of insets. The top diamond-shaped pair of glass insets contains the red initials 'S' and 'D' with gilt love hearts below each letter. The round insets below contain the date 'July ye 20th 1796' and a flower, and another set of diamond-shaped insets also contain flowers

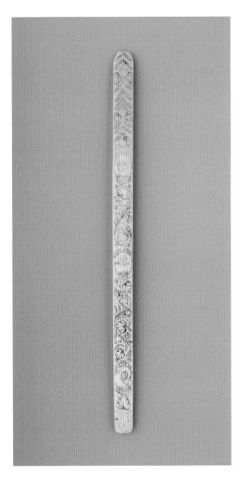

Fig. 7.9 *Ivory busk, French (back), seventeenth century, Metropolitan Museum of Art, New York.*

Fig. 7.10 *Stay busk, 1796, English, Victoria and Albert Museum, London.*

(see Fig. 7.10). Such initials may have been those of the wearer, but it is more likely that they were her lover's initials inscribed as a romantic token placed there to be worn against the heart.

Similarly, surviving eighteenth-century garters also contain embroidered sayings and verses. One eighteenth-century French pair proclaims, 'same hearts, same thoughts', whilst another states 'My motto is to love you, It will never change'.[80] Another English garter from the early eighteenth century also reads, 'AS KISSING WHEN TWO LOVERS MEET'.[81] Garters, like busks, could also be gifted to women by their lovers: Samuel Pepys noted in his diary in February 1661 that he sent his wife 'silk stockings and garters, for her Valentines'.[82] The addition of romantic words and images embroidered on these garters not only materially reaffirmed the affections of the giver, but reminded the wearer of those affections or the date of the gifting whenever she wore them. Like busks, garters also contained anthropomorphized verses acknowledging the intimate place on the female body where they sat. A pair of French embroidered silk garters from 1780 proclaims, 'United forever / I die where I cling' (see Fig. 7.11).[83] In the context of the garter, 'where I cling' refers to the lower thighs, which were only accessible to those most intimate with the wearer. The intimate position of both busks and garters on the female body, between breasts and on thighs, therefore marked them as suitable intimate objects for expressions of physical romantic love.

While some sort of mutual affection was deemed necessary for marriage, many scholars have convincingly argued that from the mid-seventeenth century onwards more emphasis was placed on securing romantic, love-based marriages. The cultural shift towards the idea that love should be the

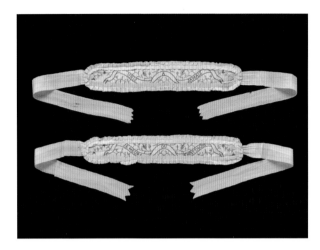

Fig. 7.11 *Pair of garters of embroidered silk, c. 1780, French, Victoria and Albert Museum, London.*

main reason for marriage, rather than economic or social stability, significantly influenced both mate selection and courtship practices during the late seventeenth century. This idea continued to spread rapidly during the Enlightenment of the eighteenth century until it became 'firmly rooted' in the nineteenth.[84] This surge in romantic love has been explored in relation to the consumerism of the eighteenth century by scholars such as Colin Campbell. As part of his interpretation of consumerism's origins, Campbell draws strong links between eighteenth-century consumerism by the 'middle-income market' and the century's turn towards romantic love, particularly in relation to the consumption of fiction books in the form of novels by women.[85] The eighteenth century also saw an explosion in literature that glamorized romance and female sensibility, as well as the proliferation of new mass-printed items such as Valentine's Day cards, with much of this market aimed at the middling sorts.[86] By identifying and correlating certain emotional and consumerist trends, scholars have convincingly argued that middling sorts consumerism, material culture and emotional change during the late seventeenth and early eighteenth centuries were closely related. It can be no coincidence, then, that the romanticization of busks in written sources, as well as the proliferation of busks bearing romantic inscriptions occurred around the same time in the seventeenth century, when new ideas of romantic love-based marriages began to take hold.

By the late seventeenth century the status of busks as love tokens had been firmly cemented in the consumer culture of the period. Four almost identical French busks from separate historical collections provide evidence that by the second half of the seventeenth century ready-made busks intended to be used specifically as love tokens were being mass produced in France. The first two busks are those previously mentioned ivory busks in the collection of the Metropolitan Museum of Art in New York (see Figs. 7.8 and 7.9), while two more are in the collection of the Louvre in Paris. All four busks are made from ivory, with one side consisting of a curved triangular cross-section with foliage details, and

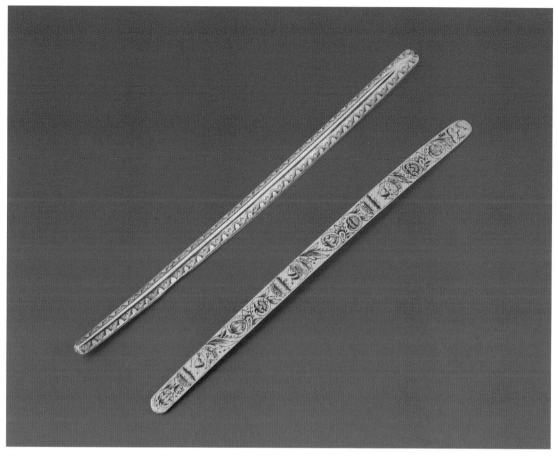

Fig. 7.12 *Two ivory busks (back), seventeenth century, Musée du Louvre, Paris. The intimate inscriptions are located on the back of the busks, and face inwards towards the body and the heart.*

the other flat and inscribed with images and sayings of love. The two busks in the collection of the Louvre begin with the same inscription, 'everywhere love', with arrows being fired at hearts, before going on to say 'united forever / only one hurts me' and 'passionate love / thinking of you', respectively (see Fig. 7.12).[87] By the eighteenth century in England the same was also true of ready-made wooden busks as three almost identical busks, including the carved wooden busk in Fig. 7.10, exist in separate historical collections.[88] The striking similarity in materials, design and style of the inscriptions on all of these objects suggests that they must have come from the same workshops in France and England, or that they were produced on a large scale and further customized at the point of sale.

Busks were an accessory to foundation garments that had previously been accused of causing abortion and miscarriage, as well as being linked to female lasciviousness. However, by the second half of the seventeenth century they had become love tokens that helped to materially instantiate romantic love and affirm bonds for courting couples during the early modern period and well into the nineteenth century. These material objects were not only important tokens of passionate and playful expressions of romantic love between individuals, but their changing materiality and increased consumption also reflects the changing sensibilities towards love in the late seventeenth century, particularly by the middling sorts. These changes in consumption practices and social and cultural attitudes made busks not only a popular love token that women could receive and wear, but also a truly acceptable object of feminine dress and femininity.

Rolls and hoops: skirting the boundaries of politeness and gentility

When Catherine of Braganza arrived in England in 1662 after her proxy marriage to Charles II in her homeland of Portugal, the writer John Evelyn noted in his diary:

> The Queen arrived, with a train of Portuguese Ladies in their monstrous fardingals or Guard-Infantas, their complexion olivader [dark olive] and sufficiently unagreeable. Her Majesty in the same habit, her foretop long and turned aside very strangely.[89]

The new queen and her ladies, it seems, did not make a particularly fashionable appearance in their new country. This was largely due to their unfamiliar Portuguese hairstyles and complexions, as well as their farthingales (*guardainfantes*), which were particularly unsightly to commentators such as Evelyn. By the 1660s, English fashions generally followed trends in France and the Dutch Republic, where large styles of hooped farthingales were no longer worn. Rather, English women chose to shape their hips and buttocks with small rolls that were more suited to ideals of late seventeenth-century English culture. During this century the middling sorts came to define their status in society through a set of ethics based on social judgement and personal achievement. The idea that social status was defined by one's morality as well one's birth or wealth became more common and respectability became an important platform on which people could show that they deserved esteem.[90] While some popular literature did make fun of fashionable rolls – such as the Scottish broadside ballad *An excellent New Play-house SONG, Called, The Bonny Milk-Maid* (c. 1684-95), which described a 'Miss of Courtly mould' who is 'Adorn'd with Pearl and Gold', make-up, a commode and with 'Cushions [that] plumps her tail' – for the most part, bodies, busks and modestly sized bum-rolls fit neatly into this respectable and genteel culture of the late seventeenth century.[91]

The acceptability of farthingales and their descendants, however, was much more precarious. Although large styles of farthingales had ceased to be fashionable in England by at least the 1630s, at the start of the eighteenth century a new skirt-shaping undergarment called the hoop petticoat

Fig. 7.13 *Antoine Hérisset,* Les Paniers [The Hoop Petticoats], c. *1730, etching, Rijksmuseum, Amsterdam.*

appeared, first in England in 1709 and then in France in 1718 (where it was called a *panier*).[92] Although its shape would change throughout the course of the century, becoming more oblong as the years progressed, at the start of the eighteenth century it consisted of a hooped bell-shaped underskirt that was round and large in circumference (see Fig. 7.13), much like the earlier Spanish farthingale had been. Within a few months of its appearance, debates over this garment erupted, particularly in the new periodicals and newspapers of the time. Many of these discussions revived concerns that had previously been voiced about farthingales, reframing them for eighteenth-century sensibilities.

Some commentators made comparisons between the farthingale and the hoop petticoat, stating that unlike the new hoop petticoat the 'ancient *Fardingale*' had been 'confined to a very moderate and decent Circumference', seemingly unaware or unwilling to concede that their own criticism of the hoop petticoat mirrored the opinions of their predecessors about farthingales in the sixteenth and seventeenth centuries.[93] Others recognized the benefits of this new garment to industry and commerce, as they jested that 'domestic producers of everything from woollens to cordage might profit from the amount of goods required' to make and cover the hoop petticoat.[94] Unlike stays, which were praised for protecting a woman's modesty in ways that complemented politeness, hoop petticoats regularly came under scrutiny for revealing rather than concealing the female body. On the 13 January 1710, less than a year after the hoop petticoat had first appeared, the satirical *Female Tatler* published a mock notice joking that men could invade a woman's private space without her knowledge by hiding under her skirts,

> Lost ... from under one of the Modish Petticoats of Twelve Yard circumference ... a Gem called Honour, supposed to be taken by some of Higgin's Scholars, who, while the Lady was descending from the Balcony to her Coach, very dexterously cast himself into one of the Folds of her Coat, and lay concealed, till Jehoe whipt forwards: She was ashamed to cry out, and the Darkness of the Night favoured his escape.[95]

A later satirical poem titled *On Hoops and High Heels*, submitted to *The Gentlemen's Magazine* in 1733, also mused that 'The Petticoat's of modest Use; / But should a Lady chance to fall, / The Hoop forbidden Secrets shows, / And lo! our Eyes discover all.'[96] Finally, a critic also wrote that 'I have been in a moderate large Room, where there have been but two Ladies, who had not enough space to move without lifting up their Petticoats higher than their Grandmothers would have thought decent.'[97]

Although many writers saw these garments as indecent, some women did in fact see them as essential to proper and modest dress. Such was the case in January 1727 when Elizabeth Burgis was accused of stealing a gold watch. When told that she should go before a Justice, she insisted that before she would she 'might send for a Cloak, and a Hoop-petticoat' to better attire herself.[98] Women also may have taken part in printed debates over this garment and defended their right to wear it. One broadside ballad from around 1720 titled *The Lady's Answer to the Several little Satires on the Hooped Petticoats* stated that women had 'contrived the Hoop to interpose' a 'sacred fence' between 'us and these confounded Creatures Beaux'; or in other words, women had started to wear the hoop petticoat to protect themselves from the unwelcome 'Encroachments of the Males'.[99] There were various interpretations of the hoop petticoat, many of which differed significantly between the genders. Overwhelmingly, however, as the nearly half a century of debates that took place in various eighteenth-century periodicals such as *The Tatler* and *The Gentleman's Magazine* attest, like the farthingale, the hoop petticoat was a controversial garment.

Placing arguments of female virtue aside, it seems that the main objection to old farthingales and new hoop petticoats in this culture of politeness and sensibility was the extravagant nature of these garments. During the eighteenth century the human body was viewed as an object whose elegance arose from the 'performance of an inscribed system of gestures and expressions', here mirroring sixteenth-century court notions of *sprezzatura*.[100] However, polite discourse increasingly rejected these older aristocratic expressions and they became less acceptable as the middling sorts began to dictate more of public life during this century.[101] Amanda Vickery has noted that as a result of this shift the possessions of those who claimed or wished to claim genteel status in the eighteenth century 'were contrived to have a genteel effect, rather than a dazzling elegance' or 'sumptuous magnificence' as they had done one hundred years earlier.[102]

This view was reflected in the earlier conduct book for women, *The Gentlewoman's Companion* (1673), which stated of the farthingale:

> I know not but that the fashion of wearing Farthingals of old, were politicly invented to hide the shame of great bellies unlawfully puffed up ... As in mode and fashion you are to avoid profusion, so you are to shun singularity: The one, as well as the other, will render you ridiculous... let the example of the most sober, moderate, and modest, be the pattern for your imitation.[103]

Not only were the scandalous origins of the farthingale invoked in this conduct book, but this 'old' fashion was contrasted with those politer codes of dress that had been established by the late seventeenth century. Farthingales had complemented earlier sixteenth- and seventeenth-century expressions of wealth, power and prestige, but their large size and extravagant nature did not fit the new polite agenda of the middling sorts who now shaped fashionable culture. Therefore, while *bums* or *rumps* signified modesty and restraint at the end of the century, the farthingale and its descendant the hoop petticoat did not fit 'within the Bounds of Decency and moderation', as the *Universal Spectator* proclaimed in 1741.[104] According to the new sensibilities of polite femininity and respectability of the middling sorts, these foundation garments were anything but sober, moderate, modest, and thus genteel, attire.

Conclusion

As historians such as Keith Wrightson and Woodruff D. Smith have argued, during the seventeenth century the meanings, uses and demand for certain commodities such as cotton, spices, sugar, coffee and tobacco was altered. This was largely due to the rising middling sorts who sought to 'establish a distinctive identity through their domestic consumption'.[105] Similarly, the shifting social landscapes, evolving cultural ideas and changing consumer practices of the middling sorts in England during the late seventeenth century also influenced the meanings associated with foundation garments. By the late seventeenth century, the rate of consumption of all manner of goods rapidly increased, with all types of dress becoming available at multiple price points. Foundation garments therefore became part of common attire for most women in England, from the aristocratic elites to Puritan preachers' daughters. While the exact design differences between bodies and stays is uncertain, the changing terminology that was used to refer to torso-shaping foundation garments during the latter part of the century was indicative of the stylistic and moral changes that these garments now signified.

Bodies, and later stays, were no longer connected to ideas of display, good breeding and the debauched ostentation of the court; rather, they came to show refinement through tasteful modesty, restraint and good morals, using clothing simply to cover the naked form, not to drastically alter it. The changing materiality and consumption habits relating to busks meant that they were also viewed as acceptable love tokens during courtship and marriage. Their role now reflected the changing sensibilities towards romantic love at the end of this century. While modestly sized bum-rolls fit neatly into the new culture of politeness, as they reflected ideas of gentility and restraint, farthingales and hoop skirts continued to receive criticism as the ostentatious nature of these large garments did not suit the new polite ideas of decency and moderation.

The changing political, economic and consumer landscape of late seventeenth-century England altered the meanings of foundation garments. No longer was it the elites, or those who aspired to elite ideas of femininity in their quest for upward social mobility, who dictated what these garments meant; rather, it was the growing middling sorts who imbued these garments with new meaning. This radically changed not only the perceptions of foundation garments, but also the perceptions of the women who wore them. These foundation garments, imbued with new meaning, were then used to reinforce notions of polite femininity onto the female body. It was this polite femininity, centred on polite discourse and its associated qualities of modesty, sensibility, respectability and gentility, which would come to visually define not only the feminine ideal of the late seventeenth century, but that of the later eighteenth and nineteenth centuries too.

Conclusion
Misconceptions and legacies

In an anonymous collection of 'jovial poems' published in 1661, a verse titled *The Concealment* listed all the desirable parts of the female body such as knees with garters, little feet and small fingers. However, when describing his lover's torso, the author of the poem noted that, 'Her hips did wear no Farthingal; / Her body straight, her belly round, / The whale-bone use there was not found.'[1] As demonstrated by the author of this poem, any discussion of the female body during the sixteenth and seventeenth centuries inevitably touched on the presence or absence of foundation garments of whalebone, wood, metal and cloth. This is because bodies and farthingales were inseparable from the parts of the female body that they covered and were often named after. A history of female foundation garments is a history of the female body. This book has shown that foundation garments affected perceptions of the female body during the early modern period through their influence on ideals of beauty and posture defined by good breeding and status, through medical discourses and common understandings of sexuality and modesty. By extension, the history of foundation garments is also a history of femininity, as the body was the primary site where gender differences were discussed, debated and policed during the early modern period.[2]

Even in the twenty-first century the body is arguably still the primary place where gender ideals are negotiated and inscribed for women and foundation garments are still regularly derided as they were in the past.[3] As such, this book has sought to reorient discussions about female foundation garments regarding class and gender relations, concepts of femininity and expressions of sexuality in Western European history. The raging debates about these sorts of garments during the eighteenth, nineteenth and twentieth centuries – and about the women who wear them now – have many of their origins in the sixteenth century. However, while these moralizing voices have often reiterated the same criticisms across the centuries, we should be careful of falling into the trap of thinking that all foundation garments – bodies and farthingales, stays and hoop petticoats (see Fig. 8.1), corsets and crinolines (see

Fig. 8.1 *Stays and Hoop Petticoat, c. 1750–80, English, Los Angeles County Museum of Art. The hoop petticoat is made from a plain weave linen and cane, and the stays are made from twill linen and baleen.*

Fig. 8.2) – were the same; they were not always used in the same way nor did they have the same meanings throughout history.

Valerie Steele has summarized that foundation garments, particularly corsets, were 'almost universally condemned as having been an instrument of women's oppression' by historians and feminist scholars from the 1960s to 1990s. This is because they were perceived as having 'functioned as a coercive apparatus through which patriarchal society controlled women and exploited their sexuality'.[4] According to these scholars, corsets, crinolines and bustles were garments designed to maintain and police middle-class Victorian femininity where ideal women were meek and submissive and confined to the bourgeois home in 'immobile submission'.[5] Such arguments not only patronize women of the past as victims without agency, but much of this scholarship, now an historical source in its own right, continues to colour our perceptions of these garments and their early modern predecessors to this day.[6] This is despite attempts in recent years by scholars to combat these arguments by pointing out that not all women corseted, that not all corsets were highly boned, that tightlacing

Fig. 8.2 *Bustle Cage Crinoline and Corset, c. 1862–75, English, Los Angeles County Museum of Art. The crinoline dates to 1862–70 and is made from a wool twill, plain weave cotton, cotton twill tape and steel. The corset dates to 1865–75 and is made from cotton (boning type unknown, likely baleen or steel).*

wasn't as common as critics from the era would have us believe and finally that these garments were worn by both sexes.[7]

As with many other ill-informed takes on history, there has also been a tendency to use the Victorian era as a lens through which to view the past. The projection of these ideas onto those foundation garments of the sixteenth and seventeenth centuries is not only anachronistic, it ignores the social and cultural nuances of this pre-modern period. A history of corsets and crinolines in the nineteenth century is not equivalent to a history of bodies and farthingales in the sixteenth and seventeenth centuries. Yet many scholars and much popular opinion continue to treat them as such. Like many other second wave feminists of the twentieth century, scholars such as Susan Brownmiller failed to understand the function of historical dress and the role that women played in shaping sartorial practices. She wondered why 'two powerful queens, Catherine Medici of France and Elizabeth of England, were among the first to wear the compressing cage', here echoing the sort of language used by contemporary male critics such as Montaigne and Bulwer to mock women and their dress.[8]

Not only was the Medici story a myth developed in the nineteenth century (there is no contemporary evidence that Catherine did any such thing), but Elizabeth spent most of her reign and life not wearing a corset – busks did not appear in her wardrobe until the 1580s and boned torso garments in the 1590s.[9] Although Brownmiller contended that men have never used items of dress that 'constrict[ed] or cause[d] pain', she conveniently, or unknowingly, failed to acknowledge that bodies and farthingales were originally a product of court culture that expected *both* men and women's bodies to conform to notions of beauty, restraint and control. Items of male dress like the bombast and whaleboned doublet existed during the early modern period and restricted male bodies too.[10]

Bodies and farthingales were not silly garments worn by silly women, although this is the impression that many enduring voices from the period, mainly male, as well as uninformed modern assessments that reiterate their criticism, would have us believe. The continual repetition of these ill-advised and often historically anachronistic sentiments not only undermines the agency of women but detracts from the real social and cultural value that these objects had in early modern society and the ways that they facilitated female expressions of agency – even if these expressions were constrained to varying degrees by the patriarchal system that governed everyday life. By falling into this trap of simplifying the female appearance in two ways – artificial bodies as bad and natural bodies as good – we are also guilty of perpetuating the same misogynistic rhetoric as moralists from the early modern period.

In the context of the sixteenth and seventeenth centuries it was overwhelmingly men who wondered why women would submit their bodies to foundation garments and who wanted to see them cast off. Yet women continued to wear them even in the face of all the criticisms of vanity, of sexual deviance and the scaremongering about the medical ills that have resonated over the centuries. Far from men forcing these garments onto women, the fashion for bodies and farthingales was much more influenced by practical clothing considerations, ideals of the aristocratic body for elites, aspirations for social status for the non-elites and, by the end of the century, ideas of modesty. This saw both materially literate female consumers and skilled makers work together to shape the appearances of early modern women. The differences between the reality of foundation garments and criticisms of them during the early modern period highlight contrasting ideals of femininity dictated by bodily performance, spectatorship and control, and demonstrate how these ideals were often publicly debated by those who wished to regulate how women should look.

As this book has demonstrated, contrary to the many voices that decried the use of these foundation garments by different sorts of women in early modern England, a variety of women had access to foundation garments and had much control over when, why and how they chose to wear them. Most surviving examples of bodies from this period are front lacing, making them easily adjustable, while busks were usually removable. Although farthingales shaped how women navigated sitting and walking, they were not as inconvenient or as wide as they have been portrayed. An investigation into the materiality and limitations of these garments through experimental historical dress reconstruction shows that many of the facts about them are not facts at all, but rather common tropes based on social anxieties that were employed by satirists and moralists throughout the early modern period and beyond in order to criticize women and their dress.

Most importantly, this book has demonstrated the ways that cultural and social expectations of women change over time, often dramatically. By the end of the seventeenth century the meanings attached to and the expected uses of foundation garments in the performance of femininity had changed from the previous century, and these changes set the expectations for later eighteenth-century notions of idealized femininity. Most strikingly, these *changes* show the way that the increased consumption of material goods by particular groups in society, in this case the middling sorts, altered the meanings of foundation garments. Women who wore bodies were no longer regarded as vain whores from a debauched court; they now came to be modest, polite and restrained as these garments came to be heavily imbued with the morality and sensibilities of the middling sorts who increasingly held cultural, social and sartorial power in early modern England.

In her book *Femininity*, first published in 1984, Brownmiller stated that 'no discussion of the feminine body in the western world can make real sense without getting a grip on the corset', for it has played a 'starring role in the body's history' for nearly five hundred years.[11] Brownmiller was not a supporter of corsets or foundation garments, viewing them as part of a history of female oppression, but she does raise an extremely important point. Female silhouette-shaping garments, such as bodies and farthingales, stays and hooped petticoats, corsets and crinolines have played an immensely important role in shaping Western perceptions of the female body and of femininity for over five centuries. Only by 'getting to grips' with foundation garments and understanding the nuances of these items of material culture in the context of their own times can we really understand how women not only experienced and displayed their own bodies in day to day life, but also the ways that their bodies and lives were understood and regulated as well.

Ultimately, the history of female foundation garments in sixteenth and seventeenth-century England is not an overarching narrative of female oppression. Rather, it is a history of feminine experience and of female agency where women chose to wear foundation garments that had not been widely used before. Women, men and objects of material culture such as bodies and farthingales all had an active role in shaping and defining notions of femininity in early modern England and these concepts continue to shape and influence Western perceptions of the female body and of femininity to this day.

Glossary

Aglets metal tags found on the end of laces (points) that enabled them to be easily threaded through the eyelet holes of clothing. Could be plain or ornamental.

Apprentice an apprentice was usually a young man or woman who entered into an indenture with an established craftsperson where they would live and work as part of their household for a period of time in exchange for training in a craft or trade.

Baize a woolen fabric of a plain weave with a long nap. Other spellings: bays.

Baleen keratinous plates in the mouth of baleen whales that form part of a filter-feeder system; *see also* **Whalebone.**

Band a type of neck collar that could be falling or standing. Usually made of linen or silk and decorated with lace; *see also* **Falling Band** and **Picadilly Collar**.

Basquine a Spanish-style kirtle or petticoat that was often worn with a Spanish farthingale; *see also* **Vasquine.**

Bents a type of dried reed or grass used to stiffen farthingales, bodies and sleeves.

Biliment the decorative border on a French hood, often made from precious metals with inset jewels.

Binding a narrow material, usually ribbon or leather, used to bind the raw edges of garments.

Bliaut a fitted or laced silk garment worn by men and women during the twelfth and thirteenth centuries.

Bobbin lace a type of lace made by twisting lengths of thread around pins that have been arranged in a pattern using bobbins (usually made from bone). Also known as Bone Lace.

Bodice the term derived from bodies and was often used interchangeably during the sixteenth and seventeenth centuries.

Bodies a garment that covered the torso, could be outer- or underwear and have detachable sleeves. Unstiffened or made from thick fabrics for most of the sixteenth century, it became more rigid and structured from the 1590s onwards with the addition of bents and whalebone. Predecessor of stays and corsets. Also known as pair of bodies and straight bodies.

Bodkin a small pointed tool usually made of metal or bone that was used to create holes between the fibres of fabrics for eyelets or used to lace garments together.

Body-maker a craftsperson who specialized in making bodies.

Body-seller a craftsperson who made and then sold bodies, or a retailer who sold ready-made bodies.

Bombast refers to the padding or stuffing used in clothing, usually made from wool.

Bone lace *see* **Bobbin Lace**.

Breeches garments that covered men's bodies from waist to knee.

Broadcloth one of the finest woollen cloths available during the early modern period, of a plain weave, highly fulled.

Brocade a fabric made from silk with a pattern made by introducing a supplementary weft. It had the appearance of being embroidered.

Buckram a heavy coarse fabric (usually of linen or hemp) that could be further stiffened with paste (paste buckram) or through starching. Other spellings: Buckeram, bonckaram.

Bum-roll the term referred to a roll that tied around the waist or hips and bolstered the skirts at the back. Usually stuffed with wool, cotton or horsehair, and sometimes stiffened with wire and whalebone. The colloquial name 'bum-roll' mostly appears in literature; *see also* **French farthingale roll**.

Busk a long, flat piece of wood, metal or bone that was placed down the front of early modern bodies, bodices and stays. It was often elaborately decorated and could contain inscriptions.

Busk-point a small piece of ribbon that was used to secure the busk into the bodies or stays. Usually threaded through a hole in the bottom of the busk and an eyelet in the garment and tied to secure.

Cabbage offcuts of fabric collected after cutting out the pieces of a garment.

Canvas a durable plain weave cloth made from linen or hemp and of various weights.

Carnation a light pink colour. Other spellings: carnacion.

Chamlet a lightweight fabric made from a mixture of silk, hair and linen. Other spellings: camlet, chamblett.

Chemise *see* **Smock**.

Cloth of gold an expensive fabric woven with threads of gold.

Cloth of silver an expensive fabric woven with threads of silver.

Clothworker a craftsperson who specialized in making woollen cloth.

Coat a sleeveless or short-sleeved male garment worn over the doublet, similar to a jerkin.

Codpiece a front flap or pouch that covered the male genitals and fastened to the front of the male hose. Popular from the late fifteenth to late sixteenth centuries.

Coif a decorative or plan linen close-fitting cap worn by women to cover their hair.

Collar linen trimmed with lace that sat around the neck. It could be propped upright with a Piccadil to frame the head or could lie flat; *see also* **Falling Band**.

Commode a wire frame used to hold up and support a top-knot or fontange headdress.

Corps piqué the French term for **Quilted Bodies**.

Corset a boned torso-shaping female undergarment of the nineteenth and twentieth centuries.

Cotte a sleeved garment that was laced at the front; the predecessor of kirtles.

Cotton could refer to either the cotton fibre, or before the mid-eighteenth century, a type of woollen cloth with a raised nap.

Cotton wool raw cotton fibres used as stuffing.

Crinoline a bell-shaped hooped underskirt made from cotton or linen, with whalebone or steel stiffening. Worn by women in the mid-nineteenth century.

Cypress a light and transparent fabric made of silk or linen. Other spellings: sipers.

Damask a monochrome fabric woven with a reversible floral or geometric pattern that was created by bringing the weft threads to the surface; commonly made using silk.

Doublet a sleeved upper-body garment that was worn over the shirt. Doublets were close fitting, bombast and sometimes even boned. It was originally a man's garment but female doublets became popular in the Elizabethan period.

Draper a dealer in cloth used in clothing, usually woollen cloth.

Ell a unit of measurement for fabric lengths. One English ell is equivalent to 1¼ yards (1.14 m).

Escoffion a medieval headdress made from padded or rolled fabrics that were stiffened with starch. The headdress resembled two horns over which was draped veils of fine silk or gauze.

Eyelet holes small holes with edges whipped stitched through which laces or points were threaded.

Falling band a collar that lay flat around the neck. Made from a rectuangular piece of linen or silk and often trimmed with bobbin lace.

Farthingale-maker a craftsperson who specialized in making farthingales.

Farthingale sleeves sleeve supports that were structured with whalebone and wire and made by both tailors and farthingale-makers.

Flouncing an ornamental gathering of fabric sewn or pinned in place on the garment. Flounced skirts were commonly created by gathering and ruching up the fabric before pinning it to the top of the French farthingale.

Forepart a decorative triangular-shaped piece of an underskirt, kirtle, petticoat or Spanish farthingale that was made from rich fabrics and was displayed through the front opening of an outer-skirt or gown.

Freemen upon completion of an apprenticeship an artisan could apply to become a full member of a company or guild, making them a freeman. Becoming a freeman allowed the craftsman to practice their trade as they wished and to take on apprentices. It also granted citizen status, allowing members to play a role in local government.

French bodies a sleeveless undergarment that was worn over the torso and stiffened with whalebone; also called whalebone bodies.

French farthingale roll style of farthingale that consisted of a large roll of fabric that was stiffened and resembled a modern lifebuoy which tied around the waist.

French gown a dress with a close-fitted bodice that featured a low neckline and full gathered skirts.

French hood a small stiffened bonnet worn by women towards the back of the head, covering the ears. It contained a decorative band called a biliment.

French wheel farthingale a style of farthingale that consisted of a several hoops made from cane or whalebone that radiated outwards from the level of the waistline.

Fontange *see* **Top Knot**.

Fustian a coarse mixed fibre fabric usually made from linen, wool and cotton.

Galloon a narrow lace, ribbon or band, made from silk, gold or silver thread, and used for trimming.

Garters bands of fabric or ribbon that were tied just above or below the knees to hold up the stockings.

Girdle a decorative cord, band or belt placed around the waist or hips.

Gorget ambiguous term used to describe a neck covering. Could refer to a partlet, small ruff, collar or falling band.

Gown this word had various meanings over the sixteenth and seventeenth centuries. It usually denoted a long outer garment with sleeves and worn by women and men. For much of this period, a gown for women referred to a skirt with a matching bodice, either attached or separate; *see also* **Loose Gown, Straight Gown** and **French Gown**.

Grosgrain ribbon a ribbon made from a type of silk taffeta that has a ribbed surface.

Guard a decorative band of fabric, often embroidered or embellished, that was applied to a garment as a border or along seams.

Guardainfante a seventeenth-century Spanish hooped skirt. Descended from the sixteenth-century Spanish farthingale, this garment was more structured around the hips and usually took on an oval rather than conical shape.

Guild a fraternity of craftspeople that oversaw the training and practice of their craft, acted as a representative body for their trade, and controlled what was made, bought and sold in their town or city; *see also* **Livery Company**.

Haberdasher a dealer or retailer who sold small items related to garment-making, usually trims like ribbon and lace and notions such as thread, buttons, needles, etc.

Hennin a headdress worn by women in the fifteenth century. It consisted of a cone with a veil that hung from the top. Also known as a steeple headdress.

Herringbone a weave with a distinctive V-shaped or broken zig-zag pattern. As a type of twill weave, it creates a durable, long-wearing fabric.

Hongreline a short waistcoat of French origin that was derived from the male *justacorps*. In seventeenth-century women's dress it was defined by its voluminous and flowing lower half.

Hoop petticoat an eighteenth-century hooped underskirt made with linen or cotton and stiffened with cane or whalebone. Its shape changed from round to oblong over the course of the century.

Hose could refer to stockings that extended to the hip, or, if described as 'upper', 'trunk' or 'Venetian', the term referred to what would later to be known as breeches.

Interlining the layers of fabric between the outside fabric and the inside lining.

Jerkin a sleeveless torso-covering V-shaped garment worn over the doublet by men for extra warmth.

Journeymen skilled wage labourers who were freemen but worked for others. Derived from the French term *journée*, meaning they were paid by the day. Their work was often insecure and many journeymen lived in the households of their employers.

Kerchief/kercher a covering for the head or neck; also called a neckerchief.

Kersey a coarse twill woven woollen cloth that was a yard wide.

Kirtle a sleeveless dress worn under a gown. By the mid- to late sixteenth century it could be worn over a petticoat, or as a substitute for a petticoat, by wealthy women. Kirtles could have a train (French kirtle) or could be trainless (round kirtle).

Kirtle bodies the fitted, sleeveless bodice of a kirtle, usually stiffened with canvas or buckram.

Lace a decorative trimming; *see also* **Bobbin Lace** and **Passement Lace**.

Lawn a very fine quality, expensive and often transparent type of linen.

Linen a fabric made from the fibres of the flax plant.

Lining the innermost layer of a fabric in a garment.

Livery company guilds or fraternities of craftspeople that developed in the medieval period in London. They oversaw the training and practice of their craft, acted as a representative body for their trade, and controlled what was made, bought and sold in the city. In London there were twelve great Livery Companies and they had considerable political power.

Liverymen an elected status within a London Livery Company that was a step above freeman status. It entitled the member to wear livery and gave him privileges such as voting rights in city and parliamentary elections. This group represented the City's most successful artisans and traders.

Loose gown a loose fitting gown, with or without sleeves, worn over the petticoat, kirtle, straight gown or suit.

Master a member of a Company or Guild who took on and trained apprentices. They were generally secure in their business and profited off the labour of others while in turn training the next generation of artisans. Alternatively, the master of a Company or Guild was the elected head of the organization.

Mantua a loose gown with an unboned bodice that was joined to an overskirt that could be bustled. In the late seventeenth century, it typically had cuffed sleeves and the overskirt was opened in the front to expose a decorative petticoat underneath. The bodice front could be left open, showing a decorative pair of bodies, stays or stomacher underneath.

Mercer a dealer in textile fabrics, especially silk and velvets. They could also dabble in haberdashery.

Minikin a plain weave worsted baize; *see also* **Baize**.

Nap the raised or fuzzy surface on fabric, especially woollen or velvet fabrics.

Neckerchief a square piece of cloth that was worn around the neck and covered the neck and chest area; *see also* **Kerchief / Kercher**.

Packthread a strong thread or cord.

Pad stitching a tailoring technique used to shape and stiffen garments. Stitches that look like this – \/\/\/ – are placed through several layers of fabric.

Paduasoy a type of ribbed or grosgrain silk fabric. Commonly spelled 'poudesway' in early modern records, the term is derived from the French 'peau de soie'.

Panel a section of a pair of bodies or stays that is joined by a seam.

Panier the French term for **Hoop Petticoat**.

Partlet a decorative or plain covering for the upper chest and neck, often used to cover a low neckline. Partlets could be made from silk, wool or linen, and be embroidered. They could be worn over the outer garment or tucked into the neckline.

Passement lace lace made from *passementerie*, or ornamental braids and trimmings made by twisting threads in the hands.

Pasteboard a type of cardboard made from multiple layers of paper glued together.

Pattens raised platforms designed to lift the wearer out of the mud and waste of the early modern street. They were usually made from wood or metal and slipped over the shoes on the wearer's feet.

Pattern a template of shapes which are then cut out in fabric and made into a garment.

Peak the bottom of the stomacher.

Peascod belly this term refers to the exaggerated stomach of certain styles of men's doublets during the late sixteenth and early seventeenth centuries. This exaggerated bulge that overhung the girdle was achieved through padding and boning.

Periwig a styled wig.

Petticoat from around 1550 to 1660, petticoat referred to a skirt that often, but not always, had an attached bodice (petticoat-bodies). Petticoats could be worn as outer garments with a waistcoat, or as undergarments under gowns. They were commonly red and worn by women of all social statuses. From 1660 onwards, petticoat referred to a skirt that was worn with a highly boned bodice to make a 'gown', or an underskirt (under-petticoat).

Petticoat bodies the sleeved or sleeveless bodice attached to a petticoat skirt that could be stiffened or unstiffened; also known as 'upper bodies'.

Picadilly collar a wide flat collar trimmed with lace and supported by an underproper. The term usually referred to the collar and the support. Other names: piccadill, rebato.

Piecing the technique of sewing small offcuts of fabric together to create a larger piece of fabric or a garment. Usually this was done when there was not enough fabric for a specific pattern piece.

Pile the raised surface or nap of a fabric.

Pinking the creation of ornamental cuts or edges in cloth or leather using a punch tool.

Points laces, usually of leather or ribbon tipped with aglets that threaded through eyelet holes in garments and tied to attach them together.

Poking stick a metal rod that was heated and used to mould the pleats of a starched ruff.

Quarterages membership fees paid quarterly by a freeman of a guild or company.

Quilted bodies a sleeveless garment that was worn over the torso and stiffened with whalebone. The term possibly comes from the French 'corps piqué', meaning 'stitched bodies', referring to the stitched bone casings on the bodies which created a quilted effect.

Ready-made a garment that was not made bespoke for a customer, sold finished and in standardized sizes. Most modern clothing is ready-made.

Rebato *see* **Picadilly Collar**.

Robe à la Française a style of gown derived from the mantua. It was characterized by fabric pleats at the back that fell loose from the shoulders. The front of the gown was open and pinned to a decorative stomacher. Also known as a sack-back gown.

Roll (rowle) *see* **Bum-roll** or **Wings**.

Rosette an ornamental trim made from ribbons shaped like a rose.

Ruff a gathered and starched frill worn around the neck. Derived from the decorative frills on cuffs and collars of shirts, they became a separate accessory during the final decades of the sixteenth century. Ruffs were made from white linen and often decorated by expensive and intricate bobbin lace.

Russett this term could refer to either a brown colour or to a coarse but lightweight undyed fabric made from wool.

Sackcloth a coarse fabric made of hemp.

Sarcenet a soft, sheer twilled silk fabric that originated in Italy, used for lining garments. Other spellings: sarsanet.

Satin a light-medium twill weave silk fabric with a dull back and shiny top surface.

Satin of bruges a cheaper imitation of silk satin, with a silk warp and wool or linen weft.

Saye a woollen twill cloth sometimes with a silk warp, manufactured in the South-West of England.

Scotch-cloth an inexpensive, poor quality linen, made in Scotland supposedly from nettle fibres.

Serge a lightweight twilled worsted fabric made from wool.

Shift *see* **Smock**.

Shop board a table or counter at which tailors, body-makers and farthingale-makers stood to cut cloth or sat on while sewing.

Silk a strong but luxurious feeling cloth made from the cocoon fibres of silkworms. There were many types of silk fabrics produced during the early modern period such as satin, taffeta, sarcenet, brocade and velvet.

Silkman a dealer in silk fabrics.

Skirts the tabs on a pair of bodies or stays; also a garment or the part of a garment that covered the body from the waist down. The skirt of a gown covered the body from waist to ankle and the skirt of a waistcoat was the part of the garment from waist to hip.

Slashing a technique where decorative cuts were made in fabric so that the undergarment or contrasting fabric underneath could be seen.

Smock a basic undergarment worn by both women and men of all levels of society during the early modern period. It resembled an oversized shirt that came to the knee and was usually made from linen or silk and could be elaborately decorated at the cuffs or neckline, with embroidery or frills. Other names: shift, shirt, chemise.

Spangles small round or oval pieces of flat metal, sewn onto a garment as embellishment; similar to modern sequins.

Spanish farthingale a style of farthingale that originated in fifteenth-century Spain. This style took the form of a cone consisting of graduated hoops that were sewn into the underskirt.

Starching the mixing of starch (extracted from grains) with water to form a paste that was applied to linen to stiffen it.

Stay-maker a craftsperson who specialized in making stays.

Stays the name given to stiffened torso-shaping female garments from the 1680s until the early nineteenth century.

Stomacher a V-shaped triangular panel, sometimes elaborately decorated, that filled in the front opening of a gown or bodice or under the front laces of bodies. Stomachers could be stiffened or unstiffened.

Straight bodies bodies stiffened with strong fabrics or bents and whalebone.

Straight gown a gown with a tight-fitted bodice.

Straight lacing a lacing style used for garments like bodies, bodices or doublets during the sixteenth and seventeenth centuries. This style involved threading one long lace through all the eyelet holes in a spiralled motion, unlike in later centuries where the lacings were criss-crossed over one another.

Suit an ensemble of matching garments or outfit. For women, petticoats and waistcoats made from the same fabric and worn together were called a suit during the seventeenth century.

Supportasse *see* **Underproper** and **Picadilly Collar**.

Surcoat a loose sleeveless outer garment worn by men and women during the Middle Ages.

Taffeta a plain woven silk with a stiff crispy texture.

Tailor a craftsperson who made, altered or repaired men and women's garments, usually outer garments.

Ticking a linen or cotton cloth that was tightly woven.

Tissue the finest version of cloth of gold or silver that was made from very fine metallic threads.

Top-knot a headdress common from the late 1680s until the early eighteenth century. It consisted of a linen cap trimmed with lace and ribbons with two long hanging lappets that was supported by a commode. Also known as a fontange.

Tucker a sheer collar similar to a kerchief in the eighteenth century. It was used to cover the chest and was tucked into the top of the bodice.

Tufted taffeta taffeta cloth woven with raised spots (tufts) that were cut to produce a velvet pile.

Tuke a heavier type of buckram.

Twill weave a weave characterized by its use of diagonal lines. It creates a durable, long-wearing fabric.

Underproper a stiffened support used to support a collar or ruff. It could be made from wire that was fashioned into decorative loops or pasteboard with bents, or whalebone that was covered in fabric; *see also* **Piccadilly Collar**.

Vasquine the sixteenth-century French term for a women's garment of Spanish origin, similar to a kirtle or petticoat; *see also* **Basquine**.

Velvet a fabric with a short pile, usually made of silk in the early modern period.

Venetian foot a unit of measurement. One Venetian foot is approximately 13 modern inches.

Vizard a mask worn by women, usually oval shaped and made from black fabric, worn to protect the skin from wind or sun burn.

Waistcoat a sleeved jacket-bodice that was usually worn over a petticoat. Waistcoats were worn by both elite and common women and could be stiffened or loose.

Warp the thread or yarn that is stretched over the loom during the production of cloth, which sits lengthwise in a fabric.

Watchet a light blue colour.

Weft the thread or yarn that is passed over and under the warp to create cloth.

Welts extra bands of fabric or trim applied to the edge or borders of a garment.

Whalebone the early modern term for baleen that had been cut down for use in clothing or decorative arts. Its unique flexibility and strength made it popular in clothing manufacturing until the twentieth century; *see also* **Baleen**.

Whale-fin the name given to raw baleen before being cut.

Wings decorative stiffened bands of fabric that sat over the shoulder seam of male doublets and jerkins, and female bodices, gowns and doublets. They were commonly used to hide where detachable sleeves tied onto the garment. They could be stiffened or padded.

Worsted fabric or yarn made from a long wool fleece that was combed out before spinning. It created a lightweight, cool fabric.

Yard a length of measurement. An Elizabethan/Stuart cloth-yard was an inch longer than an ordinary yard, or roughly 93.98 centimetres (37 inches).

Yeomanry the general body of freeman in a Livery Company who were not part of the ranks of the livery.

Notes

Introduction

1   George More, *A true Discourse Concerning the Certain Possession and Dispossession of Seven Persons in one Family in Lancashire* . . . (1600), 27–8. Emphasis added.

2   Rebecca Unsworth, 'Impossible Fashions? Making and Wearing Late Sixteenth-Century Clothing', MA diss. (Royal College of Art, London, 2013), 36; Evelyn Welch, 'Introduction', in *Fashioning the Early Modern: Dress, Textiles, and Innovation in Europe, 1500–1800*, ed. Evelyn Welch (Oxford: Oxford University Press, 2017), 6.

3   Janet Arnold, *Queen Elizabeth's Wardrobe Unlock'd: The Inventories of the Wardrobe of Robes prepared in July 1600, edited from Stowe MS 557 in the British Library, MS LR 2/121 in the Public Record Office, London, and MS V.b.72 in the Folger Shakespeare Library, Washington DC* (Leeds: Maney, 1988), 123; John Shearman, *Mannerism* (Harmondsworth: Penguin, 1967), 18; Unsworth, 'Impossible Fashions?', 55–6.

4   Jennifer Harris, '"Estroit Vestu Et Menu Cosu": Evidence for the Construction of Twelfth-Century Dress', in *Medieval Art: Recent Perspectives. A Memorial Tribute to C. R. Dodwell*, ed. Gale R. Owen-Crocker and Timothy Graham (Manchester: Manchester University Press, 1998), 89–103; Welch, 'Introduction', 6.

5   A pair of bodies could be referred to as 'bodyes' and this could alternatively be written as 'bodis' with the 'i' replacing the 'y'. This word may then have been written as 'bodice', with 'c' replacing 's'.

6   This transition in terminology is discussed in Chapter 7.

7   The twenty-first century has seen six major museum exhibitions on foundation garments: *Extreme Beauty: The Body Transformed* (2001) at the Metropolitan Museum of Art in New York; *La Mécanique des Dessous: Une Histoire indiscrète de la Silhouette* (2013) at Musée des Arts Décoratifs in Paris; *Undress – 350 Years of Underwear in Fashion* (2014) and *Undressed: A Brief History of Underwear* (2016) at the Victoria and Albert Museum in London; *Shaping the Body: 400 years of Fashion, Food and Life* (2016) at York Castle Museum; and *Structuring Fashion – Foundation Garments through History* (2018) at the Bayerisches Nationalmuseum Munich.

8   Technical studies of design have been more attentive to these garments: Norah Waugh, *Corsets and Crinolines* (1954; repr., Abingdon: Routledge, 1991); Ninya Mikhaila and Jane Malcolm-Davies, *The Tudor Tailor: Reconstructing Sixteenth-Century Dress* (London: Batsford, 2006); Susan North and Jenny Tiramani, eds., *Seventeenth-Century Women's Dress Patterns: Book One* (London: V&A Publishing, 2011); Susan North and Jenny Tiramani, eds., *Seventeenth-Century Women's Dress Patterns: Book Two* (London: V&A Publishing, 2012); Janet Arnold, Jenny Tiramani, Luca Costigliolo, Sébastien Passot, Armelle Lucas and Johanne Pietsch, *Patterns of Fashion 5: The Content, Cut, Construction and Context of Bodies, Stays, Hoops and Rumps c. 1595–1795* (London: School of Historical Dress, 2018).

9   David Kunzle, *Fashion and Fetishism: Corset, Tight Lacing and Other Forms of Body-Sculpture* (1982; reiss., Stroud: History Press, 2004); Valerie Steele, *The Corset: A Cultural History* (New Haven, CT: Yale University Press, 2001). A notable exception is Unsworth, 'Impossible Fashions?'.

10 Article-length studies of farthingales focus mostly on Spanish fashions. Amanda Wunder, 'Women's Fashions and Politics in Seventeenth-Century Spain: The Rise and Fall of the Guardainfante', *Renaissance Quarterly* 68, no. 1 (2015): 133–86; Mark D.

Johnston, 'Sex, Lies, and Verdugados: Juana of Portugal and the Invention of Hoopskirts', in *Medieval Clothing and Textiles 16*, ed. Monica L. Wright, Robin Netherton and Gale R. Owen-Crocker (Woodbridge: Boydell Press, 2020), 101–22.

11 Arnold, *Queen Elizabeth's Wardrobe Unlock'd*; Susan Vincent, *Dressing the Elite: Clothes in Early Modern England* (Oxford: Berg, 2003); Susan J. Vincent, *The Anatomy of Fashion: Dressing the Body from the Renaissance to Today* (Oxford: Berg, 2009).

12 Frank Matthias Kammel and Johannes Pietsch, eds., *Structuring Fashion: Foundation Garments through History* (Munich: Hirmer, 2019); Arnold, Tiramani, Costigliolo, Passot, Lucas and Pietsch, *Patterns of Fashion 5*; Lynn Sorge-English, *Stays and Body Image in London: The Staymaking Trade, 1680–1810* (Abingdon: Routledge, 2011). Other notable studies on the literary meanings of busks are: Ann Rosalind Jones and Peter Stallybrass, 'Of Busks and Bodies', in *The Forms of Renaissance Thought: New Essays in Literature and Culture*, ed. Leonard Barkan, Bradin Cormack and Sean Keilen (Basingstoke: Palgrave Macmillan, 2009); Ann Rosalind Jones and Peter Stallybrass, 'Busks, Bodices, Bodies', in *Ornamentalism: The Art of Renaissance Accessories*, ed. Bella Mirabella (Ann Arbor: University of Michigan Press, 2011).

13 Alexandra Shepard, *Accounting for Oneself: Worth, Status, and the Social Order in Early Modern England* (Oxford: Oxford University Press, 2015), 5.

14 Barry Reay, *Popular Culture in Seventeenth Century England* (London: Croom Helm, 1985), 1; Paul Goring, *Rhetoric of Sensibility in Eighteenth-Century Culture* (Cambridge: Cambridge University Press, 2005), 21.

15 Christopher Breward, *The Culture of Fashion: A New History of Fashionable Dress* (Manchester: Manchester University Press, 1995), 98.

16 Breward, *The Culture of Fashion*, 100.

17 Spufford and Mee discuss the difficulties of defining and ranking social sorts in terms of wealth and status during the early modern period. Margaret Spufford and Susan Mee, *The Clothing of the Common Sort: 1570–1700* (Oxford: Oxford University Press, 2017), 13–21.

18 K. Wrightson, 'The Social Order of Early-Modern England: Three Approaches', in *The World We Have Gained: Histories of Population and Social Structure*, ed. Lloyd Bonfield, Richard Michael Smith, Keith Wrightson and Peter Laslett (Oxford: Blackwell, 1986), 183; Shepard, *Accounting for Oneself*, 2, 94.

19 Norbert Elias, *The Civilising Process: The History of Manners and State Formation and Civilisation*, trans. E. Jephcott (Oxford: Blackwell, 1994), xii.

20 Stephen Mennell and John Goudsblom, 'Civilizing Processes – Myth or Reality? A Comment on Duerr's Critique of Elias', *Comparative Studies in Society and History* 39, no. 4 (1997): 730; Anna Bryson, *From Courtesy to Civility: Changing Codes of Conduct in Early Modern England* (Oxford: Clarendon Press, 1998), 11–12.

21 Georges Vigarello, *Concepts of Cleanliness: Changing Attitudes in France since the Middle Ages*, trans. Jean Birrell (1988; repr., Cambridge: Cambridge University Press, 2008), 58, 67; Georges Vigarello, 'The Skin and White Linen', in *Textiles: Critical and Primary Sources*, vol. 1, ed. Catherine Harper (London: Berg, 2012), 374.

22 Vigarello, *Concepts of Cleanliness*, 54, 60.

23 Will Fisher, *Materializing Gender in Early Modern English Literature and Culture* (Cambridge: Cambridge University Press, 2006), 64.

24 Fisher, *Materializing Gender*, 62.

25 Terrance S. Turner, 'The Social Skin', in *Reading the Social Body*, ed. C. B. Burroughs and J. Ehrenreich (Iowa City: University of Iowa Press, 1993), 15–39; Joanne Entwhistle, *The Fashioned Body: Fashion, Dress and Modern Social Theory* (Cambridge: Polity, 2000), 65; John Harvey, 'Showing and Hiding: Equivocation in the Relations of Body and Dress', *Fashion Theory* 11, no. 1 (2007): 66.

26 Catherine Richardson, 'Introduction', in *Clothing Culture, 1350–1650*, ed. Catherine Richardson (Aldershot: Ashgate, 2004), 8–9; Karen Newman, *Fashioning Femininity and English Renaissance Drama* (Chicago: University of Chicago Press, 1991), 4–5.

27 Jean Calvin, *The Sermons of M. John Calvin Upon the Fifth Book of Moses Called Deuteronomy*, trans. Arthur Golding (London: n.p., 1583), 773.

28 Phillip Stubbes, *The Anatomy of Abuses* (London: n.p., 1583), document image, 48. EEBO.

29 Joan W. Scott, 'Gender: A Useful Category of Historical Analysis', *American Historical Review* 91, no. 5 (1986): 1056–7; Kathleen Canning, *Gender History in Practice: Historical Perspectives on Bodies, Class, & Citizenship* (Ithaca, NY: Cornell University Press, 2006), 4.

30 Chris Mounsey, 'Introduction', in *Presenting Gender: Changing Sex in Early Modern Culture*, ed. Chris Mounsey (Lewisburg, PA: Bucknell University Press, 2001), 12.

31 Rachel Alsop, Annette Fitzsimons and Kathleen Lennon, *Theorizing Gender* (Oxford: Polity Press, 2002), 81; Laura Lee Downs, *Writing Gender History* (London: Hodder Arnold, 2004), 91.

32 For a discussion of men's clothing and changing notions of masculinity over the centuries, see Lydia Edwards, *How to Read a Suit: A Guide to Changing Men's Fashion from the 17th to the 20th Century* (London: Bloomsbury, 2020), 8–14.

33 Judith Butler, *Gender Trouble: Feminism and the Subversion of Identity* (New York: Routledge, 2006), 33, 185.

34 Barbara Burman and Ariane Fennetaux, *The Pocket: A Hidden History of Women's Lives, 1660–1900* (New Haven, CT: Yale University Press, 2019); Erin Griffey, ed., *Sartorial Politics in Early Modern Europe: Fashioning Women* (Amsterdam: Amsterdam University Press, 2019); Serena Dyer, *Material Lives: Women Makers and Consumer Culture in the 18th Century* (London: Bloomsbury, 2021).

35 See selected works: Evelyn Welch, *Shopping in the Renaissance: Consumer Cultures in Italy, 1400–1600* (New Haven, CT: Yale University Press, 2005); Ulinka Rublack, *Dressing Up: Cultural Identity in Renaissance Europe* (Oxford: Oxford University Press, 2010); Maria Hayward, *Rich Apparel: Clothing and the Law, Henry VIII's England* (Farnham: Ashgate, 2009); Aileen Ribeiro, *Fashion and Fiction: Dress in Art and Literature in Stuart England* (New Haven, CT: Yale University Press, 2005); John Styles, *The Dress of the People: Everyday Fashion in Eighteenth-century England* (New Haven, CT: Yale University Press, 2007).

36 Merry Wiesner-Hanks, 'Gender Theory and the Study of Early-Modern Europe', in *Practices of Gender in Late Medieval and Early Modern Europe*, ed. Megan Cassidy-Welch and Peter Sherlock (Turnhout: Brepols, 2008), 7.

37 Beverly Lemire, *Dress, Culture and Commerce: The English Clothing Trade before the Factory, 1660–1800* (New York: St. Martin's Press, 1997), 43.

38 Clare Haru Crowston, *Fabricating Women: The Seamstresses of Old Regime France, 1675–1791* (Durham, NC: Duke University Press, 2001), 4.

39 Karen Harvey, 'Introduction: Practical Matters', in *History and Material Culture: A Student's Guide to Approaching Alternative Sources*, ed. Karen Harvey (London: Routledge, 2009), 5. Similar sentiments are voiced in Burman and Fennetaux, *The Pocket*, 14–15.

40 Ian Hodder, 'Wheels of Time: Some Aspects of Entanglement Theory and the Secondary Products Revolution', *Journal of World Prehistory* 24, no. 2 (2011): 178.

41 My articulation here of how objects operate is influenced by many different material culture theories, particularly Hodder's entanglement theory and Keane's bundling theory. See Webb Keane, 'Semiotics and the Social Analysis of Material Things', *Language and Communication* 23, no. 3–4 (2003): 409–25; Hodder, 'Wheels of Time', 175–87; Lindsay Der and Francesca Fernandini, eds., *Archaeology of Entanglement* (Walnut Creek, CA: Left Coast Press, 2016); Robert Rotenberg, 'Material Agency in the Urban Material Culture Initiative', *Museum Anthropology* 37, no. 1 (2014): 36–7.

42 Leak R. Clark, *Collecting Art in the Italian Renaissance Court: Objects and Exchanges* (Cambridge: Cambridge University Press, 2018), 12.

43 Ulinka Rublack, 'Matter in the Material Renaissance', *Past & Present* 219, no. 1 (2013): 41–2.

44 Ulinka Rublack, 'Introduction I: The First Book of Fashion', in *The First Book of Fashion: The Book of Clothes of Matthaeus and Veit Konrad Schwarz of Augsburg*, ed. Ulinka Rublack and Maria Hayward (London: Bloomsbury, 2015), 19.

45 Butler, *Gender Trouble*, 33, 185; Scott, 'Gender', 1056–57; Canning, *Gender History in Practice*, 4.

46 Scholars of masculinity, such as R. W. Connell, Derek G. Neal and Alexandra Shepard, have explored how different codes of manhood (masculinities) function in relation to patriarchy and power relations. Feminist scholars such as Samantha Holland have also noted that we must 'avoid notions of essentialism' when studying femininity, as identity is not fixed but fluid and 'femininity should never be simply a singular descriptive term' but should refer to a collection of femininities. See Raewyn Connell, *Gender and Power: Society, the Person and Sexual Politics* (Sydney: Allen & Unwin, 1987); Derek G. Neal, *The Masculine Self in Late Medieval England* (Chicago: University of Chicago Press, 2008), 224; Karen Harvey and Alexandra Shepard, 'What Have Historians Done with Masculinity? Reflections on Five Centuries of British History, circa 1500–1950', *Journal of British Studies* 44, no. 2 (2005): 277–8; Samantha Holland, *Alternative Femininities: Body, Age and Identity* (Oxford: Berg, 2004), 9; David Glover and Cora Kaplan, *Genders* (London: Routledge, 2000), 4.

47 Neal, *The Masculine Self*, 224.

48 Vincent, *Dressing the Elite*, 6.

49 Chandra Mukerji, *From Graven Images: Patterns of Modern Materialism* (New York: Columbia University Press, 1983), 1–29.

50 Ribeiro, *Fashion and Fiction*, 1.

51 Aileen Ribeiro, *Gallery of Fashion* (London: National Portrait Gallery, 1999), 11; Ann Rosalind Jones and Peter Stallybrass, *Renaissance Clothing and the Materials of Memory* (Cambridge: Cambridge University Press, 2000), 35; Melanie Braun, Luca Costigliolo, Susan North, Claire Thornton and Jenny Tiramani, *17th-Century Men's Dress Patterns, 1600–1630* (London: Thames & Hudson in association with V&A Publishing, 2016), 48–9.

52 Ribeiro, *Fashion and Fiction*, 19.

53 Paula Findlen, 'Introduction: Early Modern Things – Setting Objects in Motion, 1500–1800', in *Early Modern Things: Objects and their Histories, 1500–1800*, ed. Paula Findlen (London: Routledge, 2013), 8.

54 Harold J. Cook, Pamela H. Smith and Amy R. W. Meyers, eds., *Ways of Making and Knowing: The Material Culture of Empirical Knowledge* (Ann Arbor: University of Michigan Press, 2014), 8.

55 Hilary Davidson, 'Reconstructing Jane Austen's Silk Pelisse, 1812–1814', *Costume* 49, no. 2 (2015): 208.

56 Jodi Reeves Flores and Roeland Paardekooper, eds., *Experiments Past: Histories of Experimental Archaeology* (Leiden: Sidestone Press, 2014), 7; Toni L. Carrell, 'Replication and Experimental Archaeology', *Historical Archaeology* 26, no. 4 (1992): 4.

57 See selected reading: Norah Waugh, *The Cut of Women's Clothes 1600–1930*, with diagrams by Margaret Woodward (London: Faber and Faber, 1968); Janet Arnold, *Patterns of Fashion 3: The Cut and Construction of Clothes for Men and Women, c. 1560–1620* (London: Macmillan, 1985); Arnold, Tiramani, Costigliolo, Passot, Lucas and Pietsch, *Patterns of Fashion 5*.

58 North and Tiramani, *Book One*; North and Tiramani, *Book Two*; Braun, Costigliolo, North, Thornton and Tiramani, *17th-Century Men's Dress Patterns*.

59 Hilary Davidson, 'The Embodied Turn: Making and Remaking Dress as an Academic Practice', *Fashion Theory*, Special Issue on 'The Making Turn', ed. Peter McNeil and Melissa Bellanta, 23, no. 3 (2019): 332.

60 Peter McNeil and Melissa Bellanta, 'Letter from the Editors: Fashion, Embodiment and the "Making Turn"', *Fashion Theory*, Special Issue on 'The Making Turn', ed. Peter McNeil and Melissa Bellanta, 23, no. 3 (2019): 325–8. Davidson also suggests that we should term this movement 'experimental history', as it borrows from experimental archaeology methodologies but digresses too. Davidson, 'Embodied Turn', 330, 338–9.

61 I chose not to reconstruct a Spanish farthingale as many other scholars have made and used this style in their research. Their findings are discussed alongside my own in this book.

62 Arnold, Tiramani, Costigliolo, Passot, Lucas and Pietsch, *Patterns of Fashion 5*, 34–5, 46–7, 68–9.

63 Jenny Tiramani, 'Reconstructing a Schwarz Outfit', in *The First Book of Fashion: The Book of Clothes of Matthaeus and Veit Konrad Schwarz of Augsburg*, ed. Ulinka Rublack and Maria Hayward (London: Bloomsbury, 2015), 374.

64 For a detailed outline of methodology, see Sarah A. Bendall, 'The Case of the "french vardingale": A Methodological Approach to Reconstructing and Understanding Ephemeral Garments', *Fashion Theory*, Special Issue on 'The Making Turn', ed. Peter McNeil and Melissa Bellanta, 23, no. 3 (2019): 363–99.

65 Davidson has outlined the main ways that dress historians approach experimental history and reconstruction, as well as the challenges historians face when trying to articulate this historical methodology, including terminology. Davidson, 'Embodied Turn', 336–8, 340–5.

66 The boning channels of the Verney Maternity bodies were machine sewn.

67 Kate Gill, 'Replica-Making and Informed Compromise: The Case of a Seventeenth Century Man's Coat', poster presented at the University of Glasgow: Research Network for Textile Conservation, Dress & Textile History & Technical Art History, 2012, https://www.gla.ac.uk/media/media_276748_en.pdf.

68 Davidson, 'Reconstructing Jane Austen's Silk Pelisse', 215.

69 Laura Gowing, *Common Bodies: Women, Touch, and Power in Seventeenth-Century England* (New Haven, CT: Yale University Press, 2003), 2.

Chapter 1

1 Desiderius Erasmus, *The Erasmus Reader*, ed. Erika Rummel (Toronto: University of Toronto Press, 1990), 108.

2 Vincent, *Dressing the Elite*, 8.

3 Gowing, *Common Bodies*, 6.

4 Gowing, *Common Bodies*, 2; Patricia Simons, *The Sex of Men in Premodern Europe* (Cambridge: Cambridge University Press, 2011), 18, 293.

5 Hilary Davidson, 'Medieval Romance and Trade', in *Fashion: The Ultimate Book of Costume and Style* (London: Dorling Kindersley, 2012), 43–113; Katherine L. French, 'Genders and Material Culture', in *The Oxford Handbook of Women and Gender in Medieval Europe*, ed. Judith M. Bennet and Ruth Mazo Karras (Oxford: Oxford University Press, 2013), 199.

6 Breward, *Culture of Fashion*, 13–14; Monica L. Wright, 'The Bliaut: An Examination of the Evidence in French Literary Sources', in *Medieval Clothing and Textiles*, vol. 14, ed. Robin Netherton and Gale R. Owen-Crocker (Woodbridge: The Boydell Press, 2018), 68.

7 The possibility of any sort of medieval corset has been refuted by Kay Staniland. 'Corsettus' during this period referred to a loose tunic-like garment worn by men and women. Kay Staniland, 'The Medieval "Corset"', *Costume* 3 (1969): 10–13.

8 Beatrix Nutz, 'Bras in the 15th Century? A Preliminary Report', in *The North European Symposium for Archaeological Textiles XI*, ed. Johanna Banck-Burgess and Carla Nübold (Rahden: Westf, 2013), 223–4.

9 A corselet is a modern shaping device. It usually consists of a modern brassiere, stretchy or stiffened material that extends to the waist or thighs, and sometimes laces in the back.

10 Beatrix Nutz, 'From Soft to Hard: Deliberately Concealed Body Shaping Garments from Tyrol', in *Structuring Fashion: Foundation Garments through History*, ed. Frank Matthias Kammel and Johannes Pietsch (Munich: Hirmer, 2019), 20–1.

11 Janetta Rebold Benton, *Materials, Methods, and Masterpieces of Medieval Art* (Westport, CT: ABC-CLIO, 2009), 226; Hilary Davidson, 'Renaissance Splendour', in *Fashion: The Ultimate Book of Costume and Style* (London: Dorling Kindersley, 2012), 113–67.

12 Katherine Morris Lester, Bess Viola Oerke and Helen Westermann, *Accessories of Dress: An Illustrated Encyclopedia* (New York: Dover Publications, 2004), 16–18.

13 Eleri Lynn, *Tudor Fashion* (New Haven, CT: Yale University Press, 2017), 36.

14 Lynn, *Tudor Fashion*, 36.

15 Vincent, *Dressing the Elite*, 6.

16 Quoted in Maria Hayward, *The Great Wardrobe Accounts of Henry VII and Henry VIII* (London: London Record Society, 2012), 88–9.

17 Lynn, *Tudor Fashion*, 36; Thessy Schoenholzer Nichols, 'It does not need to be hard to hold', in *Structuring Fashion: Foundation Garments through History*, ed. Frank Matthias Kammel and Johannes Pietsch (Munich: Hirmer, 2019), 31.

18 *Vertugado* is derived from the Spanish word *verdugo*, which described wicker or cane branches that were freshly cut and green and used to make the hoops for this skirt. Johnston, 'Sex, Lies, and Verdugados', 102.

19 Quoted in Gordon Kipling, ed., *The Receipt of the Lady Katherine* (Oxford: Published for the Early English Text Society by the Oxford University Press, 1990), 43.

20 Maria Hayward, 'Spanish Princess or Queen of England? The Image, Identity and Influence of Catherine of Aragon at the Courts of Henry VII and Henry VIII', in *Spanish Fashion at the Courts of Early Modern Europe*, vol. 2, ed. José Luis Colomer and Amalia Descalzo (Madrid: Centro de Estudios Europa Hispánica, 2014), 19–20, 25.

21 'Satten de bruges crimsen pro una verdingale', quoted in Arnold, *Queen Elizabeth's Wardrobe Unlock'd*, 124.

22 Quoted in Maria Hayward, *Dress at the Court of King Henry VIII* (London: Routledge, 2007), 162.

23 Randle Cotgrave, *A Dictionary of the French and English Tongues* (London: n.p., 1611), BAS-BAS.

24 See Chapter 4 for a detailed description of what Elizabeth I's farthingales were made from.

25 Arnold, *Queen Elizabeth's Wardrobe Unlock'd*, 123; Amalia Descalzo, 'Spanish Male Costume in the Habsburg Period', in *Spanish Fashion at the Courts of Early Modern Europe*, vol. 1, ed. José Luis Colomer and Amalia Descalzo (Madrid: Centro de Estudios Europa Hispánica, 2014), 15; Carmen Bernis and Amalia Descalzo, 'Spanish Female Dress in the Habsburg Period', in *Spanish Fashion at the Courts of Early Modern Europe*, vol. 1, ed. José Luis Colomer and Amalia Descalzo (Madrid: Centro de Estudios Europa Hispánica, 2014), 39–40.

26 Glenn Richardson, *Renaissance Monarchy: The Reigns of Henry VIII, Francis I and Charles V* (London and New York: Arnold, 2002), 1; Hugh Trevor-Roper, *The Crisis of the Seventeenth Century: Religion, the Reformation, and Social Change* (Indianapolis: Liberty Fund, 2002), 52.

27 The terms 'bodies' and 'pairs of bodies' were interchangeable during the early modern period and referred to the same garment. This terminology is equivalent to the use of trousers and pair of trousers in modern English.

28 Quoted in Hilary Doda, 'Of Crymsen Tissue: The Construction of A Queen – Identity, Legitimacy and the Wardrobe of Mary Tudor', MA Diss. (Nova Scotia, Canada: Dalhousie University, 2011), 56.

29 María José Redondo Cantera, 'The Inventories of Empress Isabella of Portugal', in *Los inventories de Carlos V y la familia imperial/The Inventories of Charles V and the Imperial Family*, vol. 2, ed. Fernando Checa Cremades (Madrid: fernando villaverde ediciones, 2010), 1258, 1311–33.

30 Roberta Orsi Landini and Bruna Niccoli, *Moda a Firenze 1540–1580: Lo stile di Eleonora di Toledo e la sua influenza* (Florence: Pagliai Polistampa, 2007), 132.

31 Other Spanish styles often cited as being early corsets are the *basquine* (Spanish) or *vasquine* (French). However, these garments appear to have been more like petticoats and kirtles than a separate boned underbodice.

32 Naming certain garments after their country of origin was common during this period and is telling of the different ways in which fashion was disseminated. The English were influenced by French fashions and so attributed the rolls to the French, while the Spanish had control of the Low Countries, and so it passed to the Spanish from there. Bernis and Descalzo, 'Spanish Female Dress in the Habsburg Period', 60–1.

33 TNA: SP 70/144, fol. 63.

34 Arnold, *Queen Elizabeth's Wardrobe Unlock'd*, 122.

35 Transcribed in Elizabeth Stern, 'Peckover and Gallyard: Two Sixteenth-century Norfolk Tailors', *Costume* 15 (1981): 16–20.

36 Around this time, the wardrobe accounts of the queen also mention 'half farthingales' with these rolls. It is unclear what these were, but they may have been another variation of this new style. BL: MS Egerton 2806, fol 166r.

37 It is likely that other styles also existed. A 'Scotch' or Scottish farthingale is mentioned amongst women's belongings in the play *Eastward Hoe* (1605), and the wardrobe accounts of Elizabeth I mention both 'half' farthingales and 'great' farthingales. Lack of evidence means that it is hard to say for certain what stylistic differences existed. TNA: LC 5/32, fol. 103; George Chapman, Ben Jonson and John Marston, *Eastward Hoe* (London: n.p., 1605), A4r.

38 More, *A true Discourse Concerning the Certain Possession and Dispossession*, 27.

39 Henrietta Maria wears what could be a similar farthingale in an engraving of her marriage to Charles I in 1625, so it is possible that these styles of farthingales were still popular in England at this time. See Erin Griffey, *On Display: Henrietta Maria and the Materials of Magnificence at the Stuart Court* (New Haven, CT: Yale University Press, 2015), 56.

40 Anne Hollander, *Seeing through Clothes* (Berkeley: University of California Press, 1993), 104.

41 Robert Crowley, *One and Thirty Epigrams wherein are briefly Touched so many Abuses, that May and Ought to be Put Away* (London: n.p., 1550), document image 32. EEBO.

42 Thomas Middleton, *The Works of Thomas Middleton: In Five Volumes*, vol. 5, ed. Alexander Dyce (London: n.p., 1840), 491.

43 Cotgrave, *Dictionary of the French and English Tongues*, HAV-HAV.

44 During the 1570s, references to bodies were often made in relation to kirtles and petticoats, as both garments contained fitted bodices attached to skirts.

45 TNA: LC 5/33.

46 Samantha Bullat, who is a tailor for the Jamestown–Yorktown Foundation in Williamsburg, Virginia, has made several bodies stiffened with linen and rabbit hide glue. She notes that while they give a smooth silhouette, movement does eventually crease the paste buckram. Samantha Bullat, private correspondence via email, 20 June 2020.

47 BL: Egerton MS 2806, fol. 179r.

48 BL: Egerton MS 2806, fols. 166v, 173v.

49 Randle Holme, *The Academy of Armory* (Chester: n.p., 1688), 94.

50 BL: Egerton MS 2806, fol. 189r.

51 Johannes Pietsch, 'Establishing Identity: Stays from Southern Germany in the Collection of the Bayerisches Nationalmuseum', in *Structuring Fashion: Foundation Garments through History*, ed. Frank Matthias Kammel and Johannes Pietsch (Munich: Hirmer, 2019), 74–5.

52 Hollander, *Seeing Through Clothes*, 104.

53 'cette busquée si mignonne' quoted in Kunzle, *Fashion and Fetishism*, 154.

54 Holme, *The Academy of Armory*, 94.

55 A codpiece is visible on the red hose of the man in Fig. 1.2. For more on codpieces, see Rublack, *Dressing Up*, 17–18; Hayward, *Dress at the Court of King Henry VIII*, 100–3; Simons, *The Sex of Men*, 98–105; Fisher, *Materializing Gender*, 59–82.

56 John Marston, *The Malcontent* (1603), ed. M. L. Wine (Lincoln: University of Nebraska Press, 1964), 75.

57 Barnabe Rich, *Faults, Faults, and Nothing Else but Faults* (London: n.p., 1606), 21v.

58 Anon, *The Maids Metamorphosis* (London: n.p., 1600), c3r.

59 Arnold has suggested that bents were used in bodies with sleeves periodically during the 1580s, although it is unclear what purpose this material served in the garment. Arnold, *Queen Elizabeth's Wardrobe Unlock'd*, 147.

60 TNA: LC 5/36, fol. 133.

61 TNA: LC 5/36, fol. 251.

62 During the 1590s, 'ballen boddis' (baleen bodies) are also present in the wardrobe accounts of Anne of Denmark, who was then Queen of Scotland. NRS: E35/14, fol. 5r.

63 TNA: STAC 8/94/17, fol. 12.

64 Randle Cotgrave's 1611 French–English dictionary confirmed that *French bodies* were those that were stiffened with whalebone, as he translated 'balenes' to mean 'whall bones; Whall-bone bodies; French bodies.' Cotgrave, *Dictionary of the French and English Tongues*, BAL-BAL.

65 John Marston, *Jack Drums Entertainment: or The Comedy of Pasquill and Katherine* (London: n.p., 1601), F3v.

66 Quoted in Janet Arnold, 'The "pair of straight bodies" and "a pair of drawers" dating from 1603 which Clothe the Effigy of Queen Elizabeth I in Westminster Abbey', *Costume* 41 (2007): 9.

67 Robert I. Lublin, *Costuming the Shakespearean Stage: Visual Codes of Representation in Early Modern Theatre and Culture* (Farnham: Ashgate, 2011), 5.

68 Spufford and Mee, *Clothing of the Common Sort*, 77.

69 Diary entry from 2 November 1617. Anne Clifford, 'The Knole Diary, 1603–1619', in *The Diaries of Lady Anne Clifford*, ed. D. J. H. Clifford (Wolfeboro Falls, NH: Alan Sutton, 1991), 64.

70 George Mason, *Grammaire Angloise pour Facilement et Promptement apprendre la langue Angloise* (Paris: n.p., 1625), 185–6.

71 John Ager Bills: TNA: LR 5-64, January to March 1631; TNA: LR 5/65, January to March 1632; TNA: LR 5/65, April to June 1632; TNA. LR 5/64, Christmas Quarter.

72 Suzanne Lussier, '"Habillement de la Dite Dame Reine": An Analysis of the Gowns and Accessories in Queen Henrietta Maria's Trousseau', *Costume* 52, no. 1 (2018): 44, n. 15.

73 TNA: LR 5/66, John Ager bill for October 1638 to March 1639.

74 John Bulwer, *Anthropometamorphosis: Man Transformed* (London: n.p., 1653), 547.

75 Probate Will of Dame Honor Proctor, 1624–5, transcribed in John Richard Walbran, James Raine and J. T. Fowler, *Memorials of the Abbey of St. Mary of Fountains*, vol. II, part I (Ripon: n.p., 1863), 352.

76 TNA: LR 5/64. George Gelin bill for April, May and June 1631, entry is for 25 April.

77 TNA: LR 5/64, George Gelin bill for April, May and June 1631. Entry for 12 May. Bodies with visible stitching were also referred to as 'quilted'. References to 'stitched bodies' in bills from Henrietta Maria's French tailor seem to follow the French convention of designating when boning was visible, as the French referred to these types of bodies as 'corps piqué [stitched bodies]'. Ben Jonson, *The Works of Ben Jonson*, ed. William Gifford (Boston: Phillips, Sampson, and Co., 1853), 829–83; Arnold, *Queen Elizabeth's Wardrobe Unlock'd*, 147.

78 TNA: LR 5/64, George Gelin bill for April, May and June 1631. Entries are for 26 and 27 April, 8, 11, 12 May.

79 These bodies are attributed to Dame Elizabeth Filmer, wife of Sir Edward Filmer, who died in 1638. However, stylistically they date to a later period, between 1640 and 1660. It is more likely they belonged to her daughter, also named Elizabeth.

80 Kunzle, *Fashion to Fetishism*, 90; Sandy Feinstein, 'Donne's "Elegy 19": The Busk between a pair of Bodies', *Studies in English Literature, 1500–1900* 34 (1994): 70–2; Jones and Stallybrass, 'Of Busks and Bodies', 262–7.

81 Quoted in Ruth Gilbert, *Early Modern Hermaphrodites: Sex and Other Stories* (Basingstoke: Palgrave, 2002), 2.

82 H. F. Lippincott, ed., *'Merry Passages and Jests': A manuscript Jestbook of Sir Nicholas Le Strange (1603–1655)* (Salzburg, n.p., 1974), 101.

83 Gowing, *Common Bodies*, 20.

84 Chapman, Jonson and Marston, *Eastward Hoe*, A4v-Br.

85 See Chapter 7 for a discussion of the wardrobe of the Harpur sisters of Stockport during the 1650s.

86 Holme, *The Academy of Armory*, 95.

87 Burman and Fennetaux, *The Pocket*, 40–2.

88 Bodice is a variant spelling of "bodys" (bodys = bodis = bodice).

89 Kathleen M. Brown, *Foul Bodies: Cleanliness in Early America* (New Haven, CT: Yale University Press, 2009), 26.

90 Vigarello, *Concepts of Cleanliness*, 58, 67.

91 Vigarello, 'The Skin and White Linen', 374.

92 Embroidered bodies that resemble those in the portrait by Voet (Fig. 1.27) exist in English collections. Examples include a pair of bodies with sleeves removed in the Victoria and Albert Museum and a sleeved-pair owned by the Middleton family of Wollaton Hall in Nottingham. Embroidered pair of bodies (bodice), *c.* 1670–90, Victoria and Albert Museum, London, 20-1899; Court bodies of embroidered black silk with sleeves, Middleton Collection, Nottingham City Museum and Galleries, CT Loan 3.25. See Arnold, Tiramani, Costigliolo, Passot, Lucas and Pietsch, *Patterns of Fashion 5*, 74.

93 Janet Arnold, 'A Mantua c. 1708–9 Clive House Museum, College Hill, Shrewsbury', *Costume* 4, no. 1 (1970): 26–7; Avril Hart, 'The Mantua: Its Evolution and Fashionable Significance in the Seventeenth and Eighteenth Centuries', in *Defining Dress: Dress as Object, Meaning, and Identity*, ed. Amy Le Haye (Manchester: Manchester University Press, 1999), 99–100.

94 I disagree with the interpretation that 'the spread of the new dress demanded a new type of underwear to preserve women's stiff silhouette' and that stays became separate garments after the widespread adoption of the mantua between 1680 and 1700. Indeed, the terminology changed from bodies to stays, but bodies were used as undergarments long before this, worn under waistcoats and the like. This is discussed in more detail in Chapter 7. Crowston, *Fabricating Women*, 37; Sorge-English, *Stays and Body Image*, 25–6.

95 TNA: LR 5/76, William Gostlin bill for Christmas Quarter 1584; TNA: LR 5/76, Mary Mandoue bill for Christmas Quarter 1584; TNA: LR 5/76, Peter Lombard bill for Christmas Quarter 1684; TNA: LR 5/79, Peter Lombard bill for Christmas Quarter 1685; TNA: LR 5/80, Nicholas Charlton bill for Christmas Quarter 1686.

96 TNA: LR 5/76, Peter Lombard bill for Christmas Quarter 1684; TNA: LR 5/76, Peter Lombard bill for Midsummer Quarter 1685; TNA: LR 5/78, Peter Lombard bill for Midsummer Quarter 1686.

97 Holme, *The Academy of Armory*, 94.

Chapter 2

1 For more on this, see Catherine Kovesi, ed., *Luxury and the Ethics of Greed in Early Modern Italy* (Turnhout: Brepols, 2019); Evelyn Welch, ed., *Fashioning the Early Modern: Dress, Textiles, and Innovation in Europe, 1500–1800* (Oxford: Oxford University Press, 2017); Griffey, *Sartorial Politics*.

2 Peter Laslett, *The World we have Lost: Further Explored*, 3rd edn (London: Routledge, 2005), 27.

3 Shepard, *Accounting for Oneself*, 2, 94.

4 R. Malcolm Smuts, 'Art and Material Culture of Majesty', in *The Stuart Court and Europe: Essays in Politics and Political Culture*, ed. R. Malcolm Smuts (Cambridge: Cambridge University Press, 1996), 88–9.

5 Peter Burke, *The Fortunes of the Courtier: The European Reception of Castiglione's Cortegiano* (Oxford: Polity Press, 1995), 27.

6 Frank Whigham, 'Interpretation at Court: Courtesy and the Performer–Audience Dialectic', *New Literary History* 14, no. 3 (1983): 629.

7 For definitions of these measurements – yards and ells – and how they differ to modern measurements, see the Glossary.

8   Anne Buck, 'The Clothes of Thomasine Petre, 1555–1559', *Costume* 24 (1990): 25.

9   Buck, 'The Clothes of Thomasine Petre', 18.

10 Mikhaila and Malcolm-Davies, *Tudor Tailor*, 35.

11 Eugenia Paulicelli, *Writing Fashion in Early Modern Italy: From Sprezzatura to Satire* (Farnham: Ashgate, 2014), 32.

12 FSL: X.d.486, fol. 9r.

13 Arnold, *Queen Elizabeth's Wardrobe Unlock'd*, 124; BL: MS 5751a, fol. 79.

14 CUL: Dd 1.26, fol. 28r.

15 TNA: LR 5/64-7.

16 Bulwer, *Anthropometamorphosis,* 541.

17 William Warner, *Albions England* (London: n.p., 1602), 218.

18 Abby E. Zanger, *Scenes from the Marriage of Louis XIV: Nuptial Fictions and the Making of Absolutist Power* (Stanford, CA: Stanford University Press, 1997), 53.

19 Quoted in Martin A. S. Hume, ed., *Calendar of State Papers, Spain (Simancas)*, vol. 2, 1568–79 (London: Her Majesty's Stationery Office, 1894), 626–42. British History Online, http://www.british-history.ac.uk/cal-state-papers/simancas/vol2/pp626-642.

20 Vincent, *Dressing the Elite*, 5.

21 Magdalena de Pazzis Pi Corrales, 'From Friendship to Confrontation: Philip II, Elizabeth I, and Spanish–English Relations in the Sixteenth Century', in *The Image of Elizabeth I in Early Modern Spain*, ed. Guerrero Eduardo Olid and Fernandez Esther (Lincoln: University of Nebraska Press, 2019), 66–9.

22 BL: MS Egerton 2806, fol 77v; MS Egerton 2806, fol. 150v.

23 Neither author explains why they believe this to be the case. Vincent, *Dressing the Elite*, 35; Anna Reynolds, *In Fine Style: The Art of Tudor and Stuart Fashion* (London: Royal Collection, 2013), 42.

24 The use of farthingales to stress the continuity of reigns has been suggested by Michael S Dobson and Nicola J. Watson, *England's Elizabeth: An Afterlife in Fame and Fantasy* (Oxford: Oxford University Press, 2002), 50. 57; Jemma Field, 'The Wardrobe Goods of Anna of Denmark, Queen Consort of Scotland and England (1574–1619)', *Costume* 51, no. 1 (2017): 17.

25 E. Jane Burns, 'Speculum of the Courtly Lady: Women, Love, and Clothes', *Journal of Medieval and Early Modern Studies* 29, no. 2 (1999): 259.

26 Burke, *The Fortunes of the Courtier*, 31.

27 Clare McManus, *Women on the Renaissance Stage: Anna of Denmark and Female Masquing in the Stuart Court, 1590–1619* (Manchester: Manchester University Press, 2002), 29.

28 Pauline M. Smith, *The Anti-Courtier Trend in Sixteenth-Century French Literature* (Geneva: Droz, 1966), 26.

29 Georges Vigarello, 'The Upward Training of the Body from the Age of Chivalry to Courtly Civility', in *Fragments for a History of the Human Body, Part Two*, ed. Michel Feher, Ramona Naddaff and Nadia Tazi (New York: Zone, 1989), 151.

30 Giovanni Della Casa, *Galatée ou la Manière dont un Gentilhomme se doit Gouverner en Toute Compagne* (Paris: n.p., 1562), 510–12, translated and quoted in Vigarello, 'Upward Training of the Body', 153.

31 Philippe Perrot, *Le corps Féminin: Le Travail des Apparences, XVIIIe – XIX siècle* (Paris: Éditions du Seuil, 1984), 72.

32 Étienne Tabourot, *Les Bigarrures et Touches du Seigneur des Accords* (Paris: n.p., 1603), 23v.

33 Vincent, *Anatomy of Fashion*, 50.

34 Ruth M. Green, *The Wearing of Costume: The Changing Techniques of Wearing Clothes and How to Move in Them from Roman Britain to the Second World War* (London: Sir Isaac Pitman and Sons, 1966), 17.

35 John Hayward, *Annals of the First Four Years of the Reign of Queen Elizabeth*, vol. 7, ed. John Bruce (London: Camden Society, 1840), 7.

36 Mason, *Grammaire Angloise*, 194.

37 Thomas Middleton, 'Women Beware Women', in *Two new Plays* (London: n.p., 1657), 119.

38 Margaret Cavendish, *CCXI Sociable Letters Written by the Thrice Noble, Illustrious, and Excellent Princess, the Lady Marchioness of Newcastle* (London: n.p., 1664), 261.

39 Vigarello, 'Upward Training of the Body', 151–2.

40 Braun, Costigliolo, North, Thornton and Tiramani, *17th-Century Men's Dress Patterns*, 16–17.

41 Henry Fitzgeffry, *Satires: and Satirical Epigrams* (London: n.p., 1617), F5v.

42 CUL: Dd 1.26, fol. 2v.

43 TNA: LR 5/76, Peter Lombard bill, Midsummer Quarter 1685.

44 Stern, 'Peckover and Gallyard', 16.

45 By the time of her death, Lady Jane Stanhope was twice widowed: first to Sir Roger Townsend and then Henry Berkeley, 7th Baron Berkeley.

46 FSL: X.d.258, fols. 1v-2r.

47 Many literary examples from the period praised women for their narrow or small waists. Devendra Singh, Peter Renn and Adrian Singh, 'Did the perils of abdominal obesity affect depiction of feminine beauty in the sixteenth to eighteenth-century British literature? Exploring the health and beauty link', *Proceedings of the Royal Society* 274 (2007): 892–3.

48 This is discussed further in Chapter 5.

49 'Les Françaises ont des tailles fort minces: elles se plaisent à enfler leurs robes de la ceinture en bas par des paniers [faldiglie] et des vertugadins et autre artifices, ce qui rend leur tournure encore plus élégante . . . Par-dessus la chemise, elles ont un corset ou camisole qu'elles appellent corps piqué, qui rend la tournure plus légère et plus svelte.' Niccolò Tommaseo, *Relations des ambassadeurs vénitiens sur les affaires de France au XVIe siècle*, vol. 2 (Paris: n.p., 1838), 557–9.

50 Chapman, Jonson and Marston, *Eastward Hoe*, A4r.

51 Kim M. Phillips, 'The Breasts of Virgins: Sexual Reputation and Young Women's Bodies in Medieval Culture and Society', *Cultural and Social History* 15, no. 1 (2018): 1–19.

52 Nutz, 'Bras in the 15th Century?', 223–4.

53 Phillips, 'Breasts of Virgins', 14.

54 Nichols, 'It does not need to be hard to hold', 30–1.

55 Jane Malcolm-Davies, Caroline Johnson and Ninya Mikhaila, '"And her black satin gown must be new-bodied": The Twenty-First-Century Body in Pursuit of the Holbein Look', *Costume* 42, no. 1 (2008): 22.

56 Malcolm-Davies, Johnson and Mikhaila, '"And her black satin gown must be new-bodied"', 25–8.

57 Clare Backhouse, *Fashion and Popular Print in Early Modern England: Depicting Dress in Black-Letter Ballads* (London: I.B. Tauris, 2017), 164.

58 Emily F. Winerock, 'Reformation and Revelry: The Practices and Politics of Dancing in Early Modern England, c. 1550– c.1640', PhD diss. (Toronto: University of Toronto, 2012), 154–5.

59 Winerock, 'Reformation and Revelry', 71–2.

60 'Quand vouldrez torner, laissés libre la main gaulche de la damoiselle, & gettés vostre bras gaulche sur son dos, en la prenant & serrát de vostre main gaulche par le faulx du corps au dessus de sa hanche droicte, & en mesme instant getterez vostre main

droicte au dessoubz de son busq pour l'ayder à saulter quand la pousserez devant vous avec vostre cuisse gaulche.' Thoinot Arbeau, *Orchésographie et Traicte en Forme de Dialogue par lequel Toutes Personnes Peuvent Facilement Apprendre & Practiquer L'honneste Exercice des Dances* (Langres: n.p., 1589), 64v.

61 'Nonsuch perform La Volta', Nonsuch History and Dance, Youtube, 12 September 2010, 1:36, https://www.youtube.com/watch?v=3TTe473IERE.

62 Richard Brathwaite, *The English Gentlewoman* (London: n.p., 1631), *v.

63 Garments often targeted in moralist literature were elaborate headwear, large ruffs, masks, low necked gowns, busks, bodies and farthingales, as well as expensive cloth and cosmetics.

64 The term 'Puritan' is difficult to define but in England it referred to Presbyterians and Calvinists, as well as Anglicans who had more radical views. See Kenneth L. Campbell, *Windows into Men's Souls: Religious Nonconformity in Tudor and Early Stuart England* (Plymouth, MA: Lexington Books, 2012), 13.

65 *The Lamentation of a New Married Man Briefly Declaring the Sorrow and Grief that Comes by Marrying a Young Wanton Wife* (London: n.p., 1629).

66 J. Dod and R. Cleaver, *A Godly Form of Household Government* (London: n.p., 1612), 167–8.

67 Stephen Gosson, *Pleasant Quips for Upstart Newfangled Gentlewomen* (London: n.p., 1596), title page.

68 Gosson, *Pleasant Quips*, B1v.

69 'Venez belles filles auecq fesses maigres: / Bien tost les ferayie rondes & alaigres.'

70 'Orne moy auecq la masque laide ordre et sale: / Car laideur est en moy la beaute principale.'

71 Stubbes, *Anatomy of Abuses*, document image 52. EEBO.

72 Michel de Montaigne, *Essays Written in French by Michael Lord of Montaigne, Knight of the Order of S. Michael, gentleman of the French Kings chamber: done into English, according to the last French edition*, trans. John Florio (London: n.p., 1613), 133.

73 Montaigne, *Essays Written in French*. References to iron and whalebone do not appear in the original French editions (published 1580, 1588, 1595) by Montaigne.

74 Reed Benhamou, 'The Restraint of Excessive Apparel: England 1337–1604', *Dress* 15, no. 1 (1989): 33; Danae Tankard, *Clothing in 17th-Century Provincial England* (London: Bloomsbury, 2019), 30–1.

75 Ribeiro, *Fashion and Fiction*, 182; Vincent, *Dressing the Elite*, 128–9; Tankard, *Clothing in 17th-Century Provincial England*, 30–1.

76 Diane Owen Hughes, 'Regulating Women's Fashions', in *A History of Women in the West: Silences of the Middle Ages*, ed. Georges Duby and Michelle Perrot (Cambridge, MA: Belknap Press of Harvard University Press, 1992), 119, 144; Hayward, *Rich Apparel*, 119.

77 Hugh Latimer, *Fruitful Sermons Preached by the Right Reverend Father, and Constant Martyr of Jesus Christ M. Hugh Latimer* (London: n.p., 1584), 280v–1.

78 Thomas Carew, *Certain Godly and Necessary Sermons* (London: : n.p., 1603), S7.

79 More, *A true Discourse Concerning the Certain Possession and Dispossession*, 26–7.

80 *A True Relation of the birth of three Monsters in the City of Namen in Flanders* (London, n.p., 1609), A4–A4r; Julie Crawford, *Marvelous Protestantism: Monstrous Births in Post-Reformation England* (Baltimore, MD: Johns Hopkins University Press, 2005), 56–61.

81 Leonard Wright, *A Summons for Sleepers* (London: n.p., 1589), 31.

82 Vincent has also commented on this link between elite fashions and deformity. Vincent, *Dressing the Elite*, 128–9.

83 Bulwer, *Anthropometamorphosis*, 338–9.

84 Bulwer, *Anthropometamorphosis*, 338–9.

85 Bulwer, *Anthropometamorphosis*, 327, 338–9.

86 Frances E. Dolan, 'Taking the Pencil out of God's Hand: Art, Nature, and the Face-Painting Debate in Early Modern England', *PMLA* 108, no. 2 (1993): 224–39.

87 'D'ont plusieurs qui parent la chair puante, / S'en vont auecq les diables en la gehenne ardante.'

88 Latimer, *Fruitful Sermons*, 280v–1.

89 Thomas Middleton, *A Mad World, my Masters* (London: n.p., 1608), F5.

90 Ben Jonson, *The Works of Benjamin Jonson: The Second Volume* (London: n.p., 1640), 96.

91 Edith Snook, *Women, Beauty and Power in Early Modern England: A Feminist Literary History* (Basingstoke: Palgrave Macmillan, 2011), 98; Vincent, *Dressing the Elite*, 29–41, 129.

92 Unsworth, 'Impossible Fashions?', 32.

93 *Jone is as good as my Lady* (London: A.M., *c.* 1620). EBBA, 20108.

94 *The Fantastic Age: OR, The Anatomy of Englands Vanity, In Wearing the Fashions Of several Nations, With good Exhortations, Against Transmutations* (London, n.p., *c.* 1633–69). EBBA, 30318.

95 James Knowles, '"Can ye not tell a man from a marmoset?": Apes and others on the Early Modern Stage', in *Renaissance Beasts: Of Animals, Humans, and Other Wonderful Creatures*, ed. Erica Fudge (Urbana: University of Illinois Press, 2004), 142.

96 Kenneth Gouwens, 'Human Exceptionalism', in *The Renaissance World*, ed. John Jeffrie Matin (London: Routledge, 2009), 428.

97 Ann Rosalind Jones, 'Nets and Bridles: Early Modern Conduct Books and Sixteenth-century Women's Lyrics', in *The Ideology of Conduct: Essays in Literature and the History of Sexuality*, ed. N. Armstrong and L. Tennenhouse (London: Methuen, 1987), 52; Brathwaite, *The English Gentlewoman*, ¶¶r.

98 Stubbes, *Anatomy of Abuses*, document image 49. EEBO.

99 Breward, *Culture of Fashion*, 87; Ribeiro, *Fashion and Fiction*, 159.

100 Robert Zaller, 'The Figure of the Tyrant in English Revolutionary Thought', *Journal of the History of Ideas* 54, no. 4 (1993): 586–7.

101 Civility during this period is generally defined as behaving in an orderly way and 'accommodating manners'. For women it often meant possessing decency, gracefulness, decent affability, sweet behaviour and politeness. See Jennifer Richards, 'Introduction', in *Early Modern Civil Discourses*, ed. Jennifer Richards (Basingstoke: Palgrave MacMillan, 2003), 7; Bryson, *From Courtesy to Civility*, 49.

102 Andrew Borde, *The First Book of the Introduction of Knowledge*, ed. F. Furnivall (London: English Text Society, 1870), 116.

103 William Harrison, *Description of England, Book II* (n.p.p.: n.p., 1587), 168–9.

104 *The Fantastic Age.*

105 Griffey, *On Display*, 41.

106 Griffey, *On Display*, 81, 146.

107 Anne of Austria's household accounts from the 1630s note that her '*vertugadier[s]*' (farthingale-makers) Francois Carre and Pierre Dore made '*bourletz*' (rolls) for the Queen and her ladies. AN: KK//203, Reine Anne d'Autriche: Trésorerie générale de ses Maison et finances, 1632; TNA: LR 5/64.

108 For discussions of this court–society divide in England, see Perez Zagorin, 'The Court and the Country: A Note on Political Terminology in the Earlier Seventeenth Century', *English Historical Review* 77, no. 303 (1962): 309; Lawrence Stone, *The Causes of the English Revolution, 1529–1642* (London: Routledge and Kegan Paul, 1972), 91–117; Claus Uhlig, *Hofkritik im England*

des Mittelalters und der Renaissance (Berlin, n.p., 1973); P. W. Thomas, 'Two Cultures: Court and Country under Charles I', in *Origins of the English Civil War*, ed. Conrad Russell (London: Macmillan, 1973), 168–9; Kevin Sharpe and Peter Lake, eds., *Culture and Politics in Early Stuart England* (Stanford, CA: Stanford University Press, 1993); R. Malcolm Smuts, *Culture and Power in England, 1585–1685*, Social History in Perspective (London: Red Globe Press, 1999), 79.

109   Jones, 'Nets and Bridles', 55; Brathwaite, *The English Gentlewoman*, 4¶r.

Chapter 3

1   Thomas Heywood, *The Second Part Of, If you Know Not Me, You Know Nobody* (London: n.p., 1606), B.

2   Country women, particularly gentlewomen, were regularly depicted as obsessed with the latest fashions. Tankard, *Clothing in 17th-Century Provincial England*, 138.

3   Steele, *The Corset*, 1–33; Vincent, *Dressing the Elite*, 6; Kimberly Chrisman, 'Unhoop the Fair Sex: The Campaign Against the Hoop Petticoat in Eighteenth-Century England', *Eighteenth-Century Studies* 30, no. 1 (1996): 8.

4   Tankard, *Clothing in 17th-Century Provincial England*; Paula Hohti, 'Cheap Magnificence? Imitation and Low-Cost Luxuries in Renaissance Italy', in *Luxury and the Ethics of Greed in Early Modern Italy*, ed. Catherine Kovesi (Turnhout: Brepols, 2019), 277–94; Rosa Salzburg, 'Disseminating Luxury on the Streets of Italian Renaissance Cities', in *Luxury and the Ethics of Greed in Early Modern Italy*, ed. Catherine Kovesi (Turnhout: Brepols, 2019), 169–88; Spufford and Mee, *Clothing of the Common Sort*; Paula Hohti, 'Dress, dissemination and innovation: Artisan "Fashions" in Renaissance Italy', in *Fashioning the Early Modern: Dress, Textiles, and Innovation in Europe, 1500–1800*, ed. Evelyn Welch (Oxford: Oxford University Press, 2017), 152; Rublack, *Dressing Up*.

5   Hohti, 'Dress, dissemination,and innovation', 152; Ulinka Rublack, 'The First Book of Fashion', Cambridge University on Vimeo video, 15 May 2015, 8:00, https://vimeo.com/66225880.

6   Tankard, *Clothing in 17th-Century Provincial England*, 177–9; Spufford and Mee, *Clothing of the Common Sort*, 255–61.

7   Barry Coward, *The Stuart Age: England, 1603–1714,* 2nd edn (London: Longman, 1994), 58.

8   Wrightson, 'The Social Order of Early-Modern England', 191; Hayward, *Rich Apparel*, 52.

9   Coward, *The Stuart Age*, 44; Tankard, *Clothing in 17th-Century Provincial England*, 1.

10   Shepard, *Accounting for Oneself,* 7.

11   Joan Paget and Toney Sale, eds., *Charlton Kings Probate Records, 1600–1800* (Charlton Kings, UK: Charlton Kings Local History Society, 2003), v.

12   Spufford and Mee, *Clothing of the Common Sort*, 5.

13   Mary Hodges, 'Widows of the "Middling Sort" and their Assets in Two Seventeenth-Century Towns', in *When Death Do Us Part: Understanding and Interpreting the Probate Records of Early Modern England*, ed. Tom Arkell, Nesta Evans and Nigel Goose (Oxford: Leopard's Head Press, 2000), 309.

14   Paget and Sale, *Charlton Kings Probate Records*, v; D. G. Vaisey, ed., *Probate Inventories of Lichfield and District, 1568–1680* (n.p.p.: C.H. Vyse Ltd for the Staffordshire Record Society, 1969), 35.

15   'Inventory 59, Margaret Pyd, widow, 1559', transcribed in Edward Roberts and Karen Parker, eds., *Southampton Probate Inventories, 1447–1575*, vol. 1 (Southampton: Southampton University Press, 1992), 150–3.

16   Santina M. Levey, 'References to Dress in the Earliest Account Book of Bess of Hardwick', *Costume* 34, no. 1 (2000): 15.

17   'Inventory 59, Margaret Pyd, widow, 1559', 150–3.

18   TNA: CP40/1157.

19 LMA: DW/PA/05/1559/007.

20 Transcribed in John Webb, ed., *Poor Relief in Elizabethan Ipswich* (Ipswich: Suffolk Records Society, 1966), 72.

21 Mikhaila and Malcolm-Davies, *The Tudor Tailor,* 23.

22 Samantha Bullat, private correspondence via email, 20 June 2020.

23 From the Dutch word 'burgher' meaning middle class/bourgeois. Thomas Platter, *Thomas Platter's Travels in England, 1599,* ed. and trans. Clare Williams (London: Jonathan Cape, 1937), 182.

24 Bernis and Descalzo, 'Spanish Female Dress in the Habsburg Period', 50; Nichols, 'It does not need to be hard to hold', 31.

25 George Johnson, *A discourse of some troubles and excommunications in the banished English Church at Amsterdam* (Amsterdam: n.p., 1603), 135–6.

26 Quoted in Eleanor Hubbard, *City Women: Money, Sex, and the Social Order in Early Modern London* (Oxford: Oxford University Press, 2012), 59–60.

27 'Inventory 146, Anne Lloyd, widow, 1617', transcribed in Jeanne Jones, ed., *Stratford-Upon-Avon Inventories, 1538–1699*, vol. 1 (Bristol: Dugdale Society in association with the Shakespeare Birthplace Trust, 2002), 297–8.

28 'Inventory 231', transcribed in E. R. C. Brinkworth and J. S. W. Gibson, eds., *Banbury Wills and Inventories: Part 2, 1621–1650* (Banbury: Banbury Historical Society, 1976), 2–3.

29 'Inventory 44, Katherine Ware. Single woman. St Ewen, 1625', transcribed in Edwin George, Stella George and Peter Fleming, eds., *Bristol Probate Inventories, Part 1: 1542–1650* (Bristol: Bristol Record Society, 2002), 60.

30 'Inventory 112Q', transcribed in C. B. Phillips and J. H. Smith, eds., *Stockport Probate Records, 1620–1650* (Stroud: Alan Sutton Publishing/Records Society of Lancashire and Cheshire, 1992), 318–19.

31 'Will 44, Jane Gooden of Timperley county Chester, widow, 23 August 1611', transcribed in Frank Farnsworth Starr and James Junius Goodwin, eds., *English Goodwin Family Papers: Being Material Collected in the Search for the Ancestry of William and Ozias Goodwin, Immigrants of 1632 and Residents of Hartford, Connecticut,* vol. 1 (Hartford, CT: n.p., 1921), 399.

32 Spufford and Mee, *Clothing of the Common Sort*, 97.

33 Quoted in Spufford and Mee, *Clothing of the Common Sort*, 142.

34 Margaret Spufford, *The Great Reclothing of Rural England: Petty Chapmen and their Wares in the Seventeenth Century* (London: Hambledon Press, 1984), 1–2.

35 Mikhaila and Malcolm-Davies, *The Tudor Tailor*, 22.

36 Unsworth, 'Impossible Fashions?', 66.

37 The bum-rolls of the Harpur sisters of Stockport were made from the cheap fabric known as Scotch-cloth. See Chapter 7.

38 Dinah Eastop, 'Outside In: Making Sense of the Deliberate Concealment of Garments within Buildings', *Textile* 4, no. 3 (2006): 240.

39 Eastop, 'Outside In', 241.

40 The Sittingbourne bodies are extremely similar in cut to the Filmer bodies, which date to roughly the same period.

41 OHC: Pec.33/1/1.

42 The reasons for this are still not completely understood. N. B. Harte notes that it was for political and constitutional reasons, while Maria Hayward claims that James felt pressure not only from gentlemen in his court but also the emerging lower born professional classes from which some of his favourites came. N. B. Harte, 'State Control of Dress and Social Change in Pre-Industrial England', in *Trade, Government and Economy in Pre-Industrial England*, ed. D. C. Coleman and A. H. John (London: Weidenfeld & Nicolson, 1976), 148; Hayward, *Rich Apparel*, 25.

43 Benhamou, 'The Restraint of Excessive Apparel', 33.

44 'Enforcing Statutes of Apparel, Greenwich, June 15, 1574, 16 Elizabeth I', transcribed in Paul L. Hughes and James F. Larkin, eds., *Tudor Royal Proclamations,* vol. 2, *The Later Tudors (1553–1587)* (New Haven, CT: Yale University Press, 1969), 385–6.

45 Quoted in Wilfrid Hooper, 'The Tudor Sumptuary Laws', *English Historical Review* 30, no. 119 (1915): 447.

46 Stubbes, *Anatomy of Abuses*, document image 21. EEBO.

47 Breward, *Culture of Fashion*, 54–5; Mikhaila and Malcolm-Davies, *The Tudor Tailor*, 35.

48 Tim Reinke-Williams, 'Women's clothes and female honour in early modern London', *Continuity and Change* 26, no. 1 (2011): 76–8.

49 Nicholas Udall, *Ralph Roister Doister* (1567), ed. Clarence Griffin Child (New York: Octagon Books, 1979), 89.

50 Tankard, *Clothing in 17th-Century Provincial England*, 39.

51 Dolly MacKinnon, '"Charity is worth it when it looks that good": Rural Women and Bequests of Clothing in Early Modern England', in *Women, Identities and Communities in Early Modern Europe*, ed. Stephanie Tarbin and Susan Broomhall (Aldershot: Ashgate, 2008), 79–93.

52 BL: Egerton MS 3054, fol. 37r.

53 'Probate of Elizabeth Dixon, spinster, 1622, Deddington Oxfordshire, Inventory, 296/4/43', Oxford Wills Index, 1516–1857, British Record Society & Findmypast, https://www.findmypast.co.uk/transcript?id=GBOR/OR/OXFORDWILLS/01009778/1&fulfillmentTypeKey=6827.

54 J. Davis, 'Marketing Secondhand Goods in Late Medieval England', *Journal of Historical Research in Marketing* 2, no. 3 (2010): 270–86; Kate Kelsey Staples, 'Fripperers and the Used Clothing Trade in Late Medieval London', *Medieval Clothing and Textiles* 6 (2010): 151–71; Tankard, *Clothing in 17th-Century Provincial England*, 65–71.

55 Susan Vincent, 'Production and Distribution', in *A Cultural History of Dress and Fashion: In the Renaissance*, vol. 3, ed. Elizabeth Currie (London: Bloomsbury, 2018), 53.

56 This trickle-down theory was first proposed by Georg Simmel. See Georg Simmel, *Simmel on Culture: Selected Writings*, ed. David Frisby and Mike Featherstone (London: Sage Publications, 1997), 187–219.

57 Vincent, 'Production and Distribution', 53.

58 Jones and Stallybrass, *Materials of Memory*, 187–9.

59 Quoted in Andrew Gurr, *Playgoing in Shakespeare's London* (Cambridge: Cambridge University Press, 1987), 234.

60 Quoted in Jones and Stallybrass, *Materials of Memory*, 191.

61 Hubbard, *City Women*, 22, 34.

62 BL: Egerton MS 3054, fols. 34v, 37r.

63 T. S. Willian, *The Early History of the Russia Company, 1553–1603* (Manchester: Manchester University Press, 1956), 7, 133–4; Gordon Jackson, *The British Whaling Trade* (Liverpool: Liverpool University Press, 2005), 3–4.

64 Transcribed in W. H. Overall and H. C. Overall, eds., *Analytical index to the series of records known as the Remembrancia. Preserved among the Archives of the City of London, A.D. 1579–1664. Prepared by the authority of the Corporation of London, under the superintendence of the Library Committee* (London: n.p., 1878), 409.

65 Jackson, *British Whaling Trade*, 5.

66 James I, *By the King. A Proclamation concerning the bringing in of Whale-fins into his Majesties Dominions, &c.* (London: n.p., 1614).

67 James I, *By the King. A Proclamation inhibiting the Importation of Whale fins into his Majesties Dominions by any, but the Muscovy Company* (London: n.p., 1619).

68 Charles I, *By the King, A proclamation inhibiting the Importation of Whale Fins, or Whale Oil, into his Majesties Dominions by any, but the Muscovia Company* (London: n.p., 1636).

69 Starr and Goodwin, *English Goodwin Family Papers*, 399.

70 Lemire, *Dress, Culture and Commerce*, 44–50, 220; Nigel Sleigh-Johnson, 'Aspects of the Tailoring Trade in the City of London in the Late Sixteenth and Earlier Seventeenth Centuries', *Costume* 37 (2003): 28.

71 Spufford and Mee, *Clothing of the Common Sort*, 39.

72 'Probate inventory of John Utting of Great Yarmouth in the Country of Norfolk, Linen Draper', transcribed in Spufford, *The Great Reclothing of Rural England*, 184–5.

73 Lemire, *Dress, Culture and Commerce*, 127, 257.

74 J. A. Sharpe, *Crime in Seventeenth-Century England: A County Study* (Cambridge: Cambridge University Press, 1983), 91–114; J. M. Beattie, *Crime and the Courts in England, 1660–1800* (Oxford: Clarendon, 1986), 187.

75 ERO: T/A 418/69/18, indictment of Thomas Dixon of Mousham in Chelmsford, 23 July 1601; ERO: T/A 418/113/38, indictment of Richard Read of Colchester in Witham, 13 July 1635.

76 ERO: T/A 418/82/32, indictment of Martha Bowers of Birch in Chelmsford, 1 July 1611.

77 'Mary Biglin, Elenor Bayly. Theft: other. 1st July 1687', t16870701-43, OBP, https://www.oldbaileyonline.org/browse.jsp?div=t16870701-43.

78 'Hannah Mayle. Theft: grand larceny. 29th June 1692', t16920629-44, OBP, https://www.oldbaileyonline.org/browse.jsp?div=t16920629-44.

79 Henry Peacham, *The Truth of our Times Revealed out of one Mans Experience* (London: n.p., 1638), 63–4.

80 Hayward, *Rich Apparel*, 44.

81 Shepard, *Accounting for Oneself*, 1–2.

82 Shepard, *Accounting for Oneself*, 303.

83 Platter, *Thomas Platter's Travels in England*, 179.

84 Spufford and Mee, *Clothing of the Common Sort*, 257.

85 Bills on dress were brought before the House of Commons in 1610, 1614, 1621, 1636 and 1628. Harte, 'State Control of Dress and Social Change', 149.

86 LMA: COL/CC/17/01/008.

87 John Evelyn, *A Character of England as it was Lately Presented in a Letter to a Noble Man of France* (London: n.p., 1659), 47.

88 Hubbard, *City Women*, 112.

89 Reinke-Williams, 'Women's clothes and female honour', 77–8.

90 Reinke-Williams, 'Women's clothes and female honour', 72.

91 Hubbard, *City Women*, 49–51.

92 Michael Mascuch, 'Social Mobility and Middling Identity: The Ethos of British Autobiographies, 1600–1750', *Social History* 20 (1995): 45–61.

93 Hubbard, *City Women*, 175.

94 Ben Jonson, *Poetaster* (London: n.p., 1602), C1.

95 Cotgrave, *Dictionary of the French and English Tongues*, HAV-HAV.

96   Samuel Pepys, *Diary and Correspondence of Samuel Pepys, Esq., F.R.S. from his Ms. Cypher in the Pepysian Library*, vol. 7, ed. Richard Griffin Braybrooke and Mynors Bright (New York: Dodd, Mead and Company, 1885), 115.

97   Shepard, *Accounting for Oneself*, 2.

98   Thomas Dekker, *The Shoemakers Holiday* (London: n.p., 1600), C3v.

99   Michael Mangan, *A Preface to Shakespeare's Tragedies* (Abingdon: Routledge, 2014), 85.

100 TNA: SP 46/49, fol. 55.

101 'Les femmes des bourgeois portent un vertugadin seigneurial qui dépasse leur état, prodiguant la soie et la fourrure comme les femmes de qualité.' Antoine Jacmon, *Mémoires d'Antoine Jacmon, bourgeois du Puy*, ed. Augustin Chassaing (Saint-Laurent Le Puy-en-Velay : Marchessou fils, 1885), xii.

102 'Le grand vertugadin est commun aux Françoises / Dont usent maintenant librement les bourgeoises / Tout de mesme que font les dames si ce n'est / Qu avec un plus petit la bourgeoise paroist.' Eusèbe Castaigne, *Discours nouveau sur la mode* (Paris: n.p., 1613), 16.

103 Woodruff D. Smith, *Consumption and the Making of Respectability, 1600–1800* (New York: Routledge, 2002), 44; Tankard, *Clothing in 17th-Century Provincial England*, 39–41

104 Jonathan Gil Harris, 'Introduction', in *Thomas Dekker: The Shoemaker's Holiday*, ed. Johnathan Gil Harris (London and New York: Bloomsbury, 2008), vii.

105 Dekker, *Shoemakers Holiday*, D4r.

106 Ann C. Christensen, 'Being Mistress Eyre in Dekker's The Shoemaker's Holiday and Deloney's The Gentle Craft', *Comparative Drama* 42, no. 4 (2008): 462–3.

Chapter 4

1   John Taylor, *All the Works of John Taylor the Water-Poet* (London: n.p., 1630), 254.

2   Samuel Butler, 'A Huffing Courtier, 1667–9', in *Characters and Passages from Note-books*, ed. A. Waller (Cambridge: n.p., 1908), 36.

3   Elizabeth Currie, *Fashion and Masculinity in Renaissance Florence* (London: Bloomsbury Academic, 2016), 70.

4   Sleigh-Johnson, 'Aspects of the Tailoring Trade', 28; Lemire, *Dress, Culture and Commerce*, 44–50.

5   Sophie Jane Pitman, 'The Making of Clothing and the Making of London, 1560–1660', PhD diss. (Cambridge: University of Cambridge, 2017), 35.

6   Sleigh-Johnson, 'Aspects of the Tailoring Trade', 25; Pitman, 'The Making of Clothing', 87.

7   Arnold discussed Elizabeth's tailors and farthingale-makers in detail. Arnold, *Queen Elizabeth's Wardrobe Unlock'd*, 177–80, 196.

8   TNA: LR 6/154/9; TNA: SC6/JAS1/1646; Jemma Field, *Anna of Denmark: The Material and Visual Culture of the Stuart Courts, 1589–1619* (Manchester: Manchester University Press, 2020), 128.

9   '1593, Robert Hewes, Drapers' Company', ROLLCO, http://londonroll.org.

10   TNA: LR 5/63.

11   '1608, John Ager, Draper's Company', ROLLCO, http://londonroll.org.

12   One of the earliest references to a body-maker comes from 1599 when Robert Norman was made a freeman after serving an apprenticeship under Anthony Norman, 'a body maker' in Cree Church, London. '1599, Robert Norman, Drapers' Company', ROLLCO, http://londonroll.org.

13 Barnabe Rich, *The Honestie of This Age* (London: n.p., 1614), 36–7.

14 J. R. Kellett, 'The Breakdown of Gild and Corporation Control over the Handicraft and Retail Trade in London', *Economic History Review* 10 (1957): 94.

15 The data used in this chapter to investigate apprenticeships, size and location of the body-making and farthingale-making trades in London's Drapers and Clothworkers' companies between the years 1590 and 1700 is compiled from apprenticeship and freeman records, quarterage books and Poll Tax Records. See *Records of London's Livery Companies Online* (ROLLCO), londonroll.org; DCA: Q.B.1., Q.B.2., Q.B.3., Q.B.4, Q.B.5.; DCA: Boyd's Roll Register of Apprentices and Freeman; '1641 Poll Tax records', transcribed in A. H. Johnson, *The history of the Worshipful Company of the Drapers of London, preceded by an introduction on London and her Gilds up to the close of the XVth century*, vol. 4 (Oxford: Clarendon Press, 1922), 130–60, 365; D. J. Keene and Vanessa Harding, *Historical Gazetteer of London Before the Great Fire Cheapside; Parishes of All Hallows Honey Lane, St Martin Pomary, St Mary Le Bow, St Mary Colechurch and St Pancras Soper Lane* (London: Centre for Metropolitan History, 1987), British History Online, http://www.british-history.ac.uk/no-series/london-gazetteer-pre-fire/.

16 Body-makers such as John Bishopp bound many apprentices in the Merchant Taylors' Company during the 1660s, as did Richard Turrett. Sarah Birt has also found references to 'bodice-makers' in binding books from the Merchant Taylors' Company between the years 1658 and 1688. PROB 11/396/371; Guildhall Library: MS 34038/15, fols. 309, 408; Sarah Birt, 'Women, Guilds and the Tailoring Trades: The Occupational Training of Merchant Taylors' Company Apprentices in Early Modern London', *London Journal* (2020): 8–9, DOI: 10.1080/03058034.2020.1810881; Sleigh-Johnson, 'Aspects of the Tailoring Trade', 27.

17 Paul Griffiths, 'Politics made visible: order, residence and uniformity in Cheapside, 1600–45', in *Londinopolis: Essays in the Cultural and Social history of Early Modern London*, ed. Paul Griffiths and Mark S. R. Jenner (Manchester: Manchester University Press, 2000), 176–81.

18 Vanessa Harding, 'Shops, Markets and Retailers in London's Cheapside, c. 1500–1700', in *Buyers and Sellers: Retail Circuits and Practices in Medieval and Early Modern Europe*, ed. Bruno Blondé, Peter Stabel, Jon Stobart and Ilja Van Damme (Turnhout: Brepols, 2006), 156; Griffiths, 'Politics made visible', 176.

19 Harding, 'Shops, Markets and Retailers', 156; Hazel Forsyth, *London's Lost Jewels: The Cheapside Hoard* (London: Philip Wilson Publishers Ltd, 2013), 22–4.

20 When both Francis and his son John died, the property was left first to his widow Elizabeth Ager and then to his nephews, Francis Ager (son of the farthingale-maker John) and John Prichard, both body-makers.

21 'St. Mary le Bow 104/21-2', in Keene and Harding, *Historical Gazetteer of London Before the Great Fire*, 294–8.

22 Arnold, *Queen Elizabeth's Wardrobe Unlock'd*, 181; Sleigh-Johnson, 'Aspects of the Tailoring Trade', 25.

23 Sleigh-Johnson, 'Aspects of the Tailoring Trade', 25.

24 Arnold, *Patterns of Fashion 3*, 3.

25 'Chock, John, Bodice-maker, St. Thomas, 1668', in Edwin and Stella George, eds., *Bristol Probate Inventories, 1657–1689*, vol. 57 (Bristol: Bristol Record Society, 2005), 38–39.

26 J. A. Johnston, ed., *Probate Inventories of Lincoln Citizens 1661–1714*, vol. 8 (Lincoln: Lincoln Record Society, 1991), 96–7.

27 Marloes Rijkelijkhuizen, 'Whales, Walruses, and Elephants: Artisans in Ivory, Baleen, and Other Skeletal Materials in Seventeenth- and Eighteenth-Century Amsterdam', *International Journal of Historical Archaeology* 13, no. 4 (2009): 413.

28 TNA: LR 5/66, John Ager bill for October to March 1638–9; '1618, 1628, John Ager', Drapers' Company', ROLLCO, http://londonroll.org.

29 I have found no record of farthingale-makers in common records such as marriage, burial, court, tax or probate records after 1615.

30 Bruno Blondé, Peter Stabel, Jon Stobart and Ilja Van Damme, eds., *Buyers and Sellers: Retail Circuits and Practices in Medieval and Early Modern Europe* (Turnhout: Brepols, 2006); Vincent, 'Production and Distribution'; Lemire, *Dress, Culture and Commerce*; Serena Dyer, 'Shopping and the Senses: Retail, Browsing and Consumption in 18th-Century England', *History*

Compass 12, no. 9 (2014): 694–703; Nancy C. Cox and Karin Dannehl, *Perceptions of Retailing in Early Modern England* (London: Routledge, 2017); Welch, *Shopping in the Renaissance*; Kovesi, *Luxury and the Ethics of Greed*.

31 Tankard, *Clothing in 17th-Century Provincial England*, 76; Vincent, 'Production and Distribution', 45.

32 Kate Smith, 'Sensing Design and Workmanship: The Haptic Skills of Shoppers in Eighteenth-Century London', *Journal of Design History* 25 (2012): 1–10; Dyer, *Material Lives*, 9–14.

33 Rublack, 'Matter in the Material Renaissance', 45–6, 52.

34 Ulinka Rublack and Maria Hayward, eds., *The First Book of Fashion: The Book of Clothes of Matthaeus and Veit Konrad Schwarz of Augsburg* (London: Bloomsbury, 2015); Sophie Pitman, 'Prodigal Years? Negotiating Luxury and Fashioning Identity in a Seventeenth-century Account Book', *Luxury* 3, no. 1–2 (2016): 7–31; Tankard, *Clothing in 17th-Century Provincial England*, 51– 4.

35 For a detailed investigation of the Queen's artificers in the Great Wardrobe, see Arnold, *Queen Elizabeth's Wardrobe Unlock'd*, 163–240

36 Arnold, *Queen Elizabeth's Wardrobe Unlock'd*, 170–2.

37 Arnold, *Queen Elizabeth's Wardrobe Unlock'd*, 179.

38 '1593, Robert Hewes, Drapers' Company'; DCA: Q.B.2., fol. 122.

39 Griffey, *On Display*, 80–2.

40 BL: Egerton MS 2806, fol. 166v.

41 BL: Egerton MS 2806, fol. 185v.

42 TNA: LR 5/67, John Ager bill for April to September 1639.

43 TNA: LR 5/79, Peter Lombard bill for Lady Day 1686.

44 The gifting of homemade busks is discussed in Chapter 7.

45 Sleigh-Johnson, 'Aspects of the Tailoring Trade', 25; Currie, *Fashion and Masculinity*, 70.

46 FSL: X.d.486, Folio 15v.

47 FSL: X.d.428 (131).

48 Tankard, *Clothing in 17th-Century Provincial England*, 81.

49 Tankard, *Clothing in 17th-Century Provincial England*, 147–8.

50 Harding, 'Shops, Markets and Retailers', 160.

51 DCA: A IV, 148.

52 'St. Mary le Bow 104/7', in Keene and Harding, *Historical Gazetteer of London Before the Great Fire*, 237–9.

53 DCA: Q.B.2., fol. 226; DCA: Q.B.3., fol. 198; '1632, Theophilus Rylie, Drapers' Company', ROLLCO, http://londonroll.org.

54 BL: Egerton MS 3054, fol. 34v.

55 Currie, *Fashion and Masculinity*, 71.

56 See Sorge-English for a discussion of the erotic nature of stay-fitting in the eighteenth century. Sorge-English, *Stays and Body Image*, 199–210.

57 Hubbard, *City Women*, 197–8.

58 '1671, Anne Simpkins, Drapers' Company', ROLLCO, http://londonroll.org; '1694, Eliz Cooke, Clothworkers' Company', ROLLCO, http://londonroll.org.

59 BLO: MS Morrell 6, fol. 110r.

60 Birt, 'Women, Guilds and the Tailoring Trades', 8–9.

61 TNA: PROB 11/432/51.

62 Vincent, 'Production and Distribution', 47; Tankard, *Clothing in 17th-Century Provincial England*, 89.

63 SHC: LM/COR/7/52.

64 Judith Morley and her son James Gresham were from the middling gentry. Judith's income came from estates inherited from her first husband, Thomas Gresham. Tankard, *Clothing in 17th-Century Provincial England*, 90–3, 129.

65 Surviving petticoat skirts from this period are longer at the back than the front, as the padding of the farthingale or roll lifts the skirts at the back. My own reconstruction experiments found that when a medium-sized bum roll was worn, skirts required approximately 3 inches (7.5 cm) of additional length at the back so that the hem sat evenly around the feet.

66 Pink Silk Waistcoat, *c.* 1610–20, English, Victoria and Albert Museum, London, 179-1900. Discussed in North and Tiramani, *Book One*, 34.

67 Philip Gawdy, *Letters of Philip Gawdy of West Harling, Norfolk, and of London to various members of his family, 1579–1616*, ed. Isaac Herbert Jeayes (London: n.p., 1906), 77.

68 Tankard, *Clothing in 17th -Century Provincial England*, 98, 138.

69 BLO: MS Morrell 6, fol. 174r.

70 Margaret A. Pappano and Nicole R. Rice, 'Medieval and Early Modern Artisan Culture', *Journal of Medieval and Early Modern Studies* 43, no. 3 (2013): 477–8.

71 Patrick Wallis, 'Apprenticeship and Training in Premodern England', *Journal of Economic History* 68, no. 3 (2008): 847.

72 This is based on measurements in eighteenth-century stay-making manuals and reconstructors' observations. M. de Garsault, *Art du tailleur: contenant le tailleur d'habits d'hommes, les culottes de peau, le tailleur de corps de femmes & enfants, la couturière & la marchande de modes* (Paris: n.p., 1769), 40; Arnold, Tiramani, Costigliolo, Passot, Lucas and Pietsch, *Patterns of Fashion 5*, 154.

73 Maria Hayward, 'A Shadow of a Former Self: Analysis of an Early Seventeenth-Century Boy's Doublet from Abingdon', in *Everyday Objects: Medieval and Early Modern Material Culture and its Meanings*, ed. Tara Hamling and Catherine Richardson (Abingdon and New York: Taylor & Francis, 2016), 114; Arnold, Tiramani, Costigliolo, Passot, Lucas and Pietsch, *Patterns of Fashion 5*, 10.

74 The theft of such innovative stay patterns during this century was not uncommon. Sorge-English, *Stays and Body-Image*, 85–6; Arnold, Tiramani, Costigliolo, Passot, Lucas and Pietsch, *Patterns of Fashion 5*, 10.

75 Arnold, *Queen Elizabeth's Wardrobe Unlock'd*, 183.

76 Holme, *The Academy of Armory*, 94.

77 For this reason, the boning channels in my reconstruction of the Verney Maternity bodies were machine sewn.

78 Quoted in Hubbard, *City Women*, 198

79 Sorge-English, *Stays and Body Image*, 21.

80 Luca Costigliolo, 'The Bodyes Maker', in *Seventeenth-Century Women's Dress Patterns: Book Two*, ed. Susan North and Jenny Tiramani (London: V&A Publishing, 2012), 9.

81 Stern, 'Peckover and Gallyard', 16; TNA: LR 5/76, Peter Lombard bill for Midsummer Quarter 1685.

82 Holme, *The Academy of Armory*, 94.

83　Thomas D'Urfey, *The Campaigners, or, The Pleasant Adventures at Brussels* (London: n.p., 1698), 33.

84　FSL: X.d.492 (21).

85　BLO: MS. Top. Lines. c. 5., fol. 214.

86　In shape and construction this garment resembles the watered pink silk bodies at the Victoria and Albert Museum (see Fig. 4.14) and the Verney maternity bodies (see Fig 6.9). Holme, *The Academy of Armory*, 94.

87　Arnold, 'The "pair of straight bodies"', 1–3; Luca Costigliolo, 'From Straight bodies to Stays', in *Seventeenth-Century Women's Dress Patterns: Book Two*, ed. Susan North and Jenny Tiramani (London: V&A Publishing, 2012), 10.

88　The boning channels of the original effigy bodies were constructed using a running stitch, as opposed to a backstitch, and were only bound with one strip of leather. This reinforces what we know of these 1603 bodies: that they were made in haste for the queen's effigy and were not intended to be worn daily.

89　Although these are believed to be of Dutch origin, they also reflect the styles of bodies worn in England during this period.

90　Costigliolo, 'From Straight Bodies to Stays', 10.

91　Ivory Satin Bodice, English, *c.* 1660–9, Victorian and Albert Museum, London, 429-1889; North and Tiramani, *Book Two*, 66–9.

92　Holme, *The Academy of Armory*, 94.

93　BLO: MS. Top. Lines. c. 5., fol. 248.

94　Taken from curatorial entry provided by the Curator at Pilgrim Hall Museum.

95　Arnold, *Queen Elizabeth's Wardrobe Unlock'd*, 196; Arnold, *Patterns of Fashion* 3, 7.

96　Arnold, Tiramani, Costigliolo, Passot, Lucas and Pietsch, *Patterns of Fashion* 5, 120, 157.

97　BL: MS Egerton 2806, fol. 97v.

98　BL: MS Egerton 2806, fol. 23r.

99　Arnold, *Queen Elizabeth's Wardrobe Unlock'd*, 195; TNA: LC 5/33, fol. 40.

100　Joseph Robertson, *Inventaires de la Royne Descosse, Douairiere de France: Catalogues of the Jewels, Dresses, Furniture, Books, and Paintings of Mary Queen of Scots 1556–1569* (Edinburgh: n.p., 1863), xxviii, n. 3, 60–74.

101　Jacqueline Boucher, *Deux Épouses et Reines à la fin du XVIe siècle: Louise de Lorraine et Marguerite de France* (Saint-Etienne : Université de Saint-Etienne, 1995), 101.

102　For a full step-by-step description of the reconstruction process, see Bendall, 'The Case of the "french vardinggale"'.

103　Janet Arnold supplied a pattern for a French wheel farthingale based on her interpretation of the sources available. Her version of this style of farthingale consisted of two pieces of rectangular-shaped fabric pleated into a waistband. This created a wheel shape that is supported by two hooped boning channels, and measures under 1 m in width. Ninya Mikhaila and Jane Malcolm-Davies have also drafted a pattern for a wheel-style farthingale measuring under 1 m in width. Their pattern is oval-shaped with a centre-back opening and made to be worn on top of a large roll for support and stability. See Arnold, *Patterns of Fashion* 3, 126; Mikhaila and Malcolm-Davies, *Tudor Tailor*, 122–4.

104　Stern, 'Peckover and Gallyard', 16.

105　Mikhaila and Malcolm-Davies, *Tudor Tailor*, 122–4

106　DCA: Q.B.2., fol. 12; '1618, 1628, John Ager, Draper's Company', ROLLCO, http://londonroll.org; '1610, 1626, Francis Ager, Draper's Company', ROLLCO, http://londonroll.org.

107　Embroidered Bodice, *c.* 1600, English, Kyoto Costume Institute, AC6328 89-16.

Chapter 5

1   Ronnie Mirkin, 'Performing Selfhood: The Costumed Body as a Site of Mediation Between Life, Art and Theatre in the English Renaissance', in *Body Dressing*, ed. Joanne Entwistle and Elizabeth Wilson (Oxford: Berg, 2001), 156.

2   Clifford, 'The Knole Diary, 1603–1619', 55.

3   Thomas Larkham, *The diary of Thomas Larkham 1647–1669*, ed. Susan Hardman Moore (Woodbridge: Boydell Press, 2011), 259.

4   Linda Baumgarten, *What Clothes Reveal: The Language of Clothing in Colonial and Federal America* (New Haven, CT: Yale University Press in Associations with The Colonial Williamsburg Foundation, 2002), 166; Rublack, *Dressing Up*, 19; Vincent, *Dressing the Elite*, 59.

5   Vincent, *Dressing the Elite*, 57–9.

6   Francis Glisson, *A Treatise of the Rickets being a Disease Common to Children* (London: n.p., 1651), 321.

7   'un peitit corps un peu dur qui lui tienne la taille'. Marie de Rabutin-Chantal, Marquise de Sévigné, *Lettres de Madame Sévigné*, ed. Bernard Raffali (Paris: Garnier-Flammarion, 1976), 194.

8   Newtown explains that as 'infants grew older, their temperatures rose, and this had a drying and strengthening effect'. Hannah Newton, *The Sick Child in Early Modern England, 1580–1720* (Oxford: Oxford University Press, 2012), 38–9.

9   Frans de le Boë, *Dr. Franciscus de le Boe Sylvius Of childrens Diseases Given in a Familiar Style for Weaker Capacities* (London: n.p., 1682), 147.

10   Denis Bruna and Sophie Vesin, 'L'énigme des corsets de fer', in *La Mécanique des Dessous: Une Histoire indiscrète de la Silhouette*, ed. Denis Bruna (Paris: Les Arts Décoratifs, 2013), 67–8.

11   Ambroise Paré, *The works of that Famous Surgeon Ambrose Parey*, trans. Thomas Johnson (London: n.p., 1649), 581–2.

12   Landini and Niccoli, *Moda a Firenze*, 131.

13   Bulwer, *Anthropometamorphosis*, 340–1.

14   Paré, *The works of that Famous Surgeon*, 581.

15   Kunzle notes that this paragraph was added in the 1579 edition and the English translation of 1634 placed much more emphasis on this than Paré did in his original. Kunzle, *Fashion and Fetishism*, 155.

16   Alison Sim, *The Tudor Housewife* (1996; reiss., Montreal: McGill-Queen's University Press, 2000), 22; Susan Broomhall, 'Health and Science', in *A Cultural History of Childhood and Family in the Early Modern Age*, ed. Sandra Cavallo and Silvia Evangelisti (Oxford: Berg, 2010), https://search-credoreference-com.ezproxy2.acu.edu.au/content/entry/bergcfema/health_and_science/0.

17   John Locke, *Some Thoughts Concerning Education* (London: n.p., 1693), 10–11.

18   Attributed to Hannah Woolley, *The Gentlewomans Companion; or, A guide to the female sex containing directions of behaviour, in all places, companies, relations, and conditions, from their childhood down to old age* (London: n.p., 1673), 80–1. Emphasis added to draw attention to the language that the author has taken from earlier authors.

19   Elaine Hobby, *Virtue of Necessity: English Women's Writing, 1646–1688* (London: Virago Press, 1988), 173–4.

20   Rebecca Gibson, 'Effects of Long Term Corseting on the Female Skeleton: A Preliminary Morphological Examination', *Nexus: The Canadian Student Journal of Anthropology* 23, no. 2 (2015): 51–5.

21   Katherine Marie Klingerman, 'Binding Femininity: An Examination of the effects of Tightlacing on the Female Pelvis', MA diss. (Baton Rouge: Louisiana State University and Agricultural and Mechanical College, 2006), 53.

22   Steele, *The Corset*, 71.

23   Gibson, 'Effects of Long Term Corseting', 45.

24 Kevin Stagg, 'Representing physical difference: the materiality of the monstrous', in *Social Histories of Disability and Deformity*, ed. David M. Turner and Kevin Stagg (New York: Routledge, 2006), 20–1.

25 Crawford, *Marvelous Protestantism*, 46–9.

26 Lynn Botelho, 'Old age and Menopause in Rural Women of early modern Suffolk', in *Women and Ageing in British Society since 1500*, ed. Lynn Botelho and Pat Thane (London: Routledge, 2001), 46.

27 Botelho, 'Old age and Menopause', 51.

28 Tankard, *Clothing in 17th-Century Provincial England*, 30.

29 Joyce Jeffreys, *The Business and Household Accounts of Joyce Jeffreys, Spinster of Hereford, 1638–1648*, ed. Judith M. Spicksley (London: British Academy, 2015), 76.

30 Jeffreys bought two busks in 1641 and one busk in 1647. BL: Egerton MS 3054, fols. 43v, 45v, 68r.

31 Mikhaila and Malcolm-Davies, *Tudor Tailor*, 10.

32 John Marston, *The Malcontent* (London: n.p., 1604), E3v.

33 Costigliolo, 'From Straight bodies to Stays', 10; Arnold, 'The "pair of straight bodies"', 5.

34 Valerie Steele, 'A Museum of Fashion Is More Than a Clothes-Bag', *Fashion Theory* 2, no. 4 (1998): 329.

35 Vincent, *Dressing the Elite*, 47.

36 Hilary Davidson and Anna Hodson, 'Joining Forces: the intersection of two replica garments', in *Textiles and Text: Re-establishing the Links Between Archival and Object-Based Research: Postprints*, ed. Maria Hayward and Elizabeth Kramer (London: Archetype, 2007), 206 – 8.

37 Davidson and Hodson, 'Joining Forces', 206 – 8.

38 'Fit' here refers to the gap between the front lacing of the effigy bodies. The smaller the gap between the front lacings, the better the fit.

39 Colleen Gau, 'Physiologic Effects of Wearing Corsets: Studies with Reenactors', *Dress* 26, no. 1 (1999): 69.

40 Steele, *The Corset*, 70.

41 Jackie Marshall-Ward, 'Mode and Movement', *Costume* 34 (2000): 125.

42 There was a 3-inch (7.5 cm) difference in torso length between my shortest and tallest model. Short model (pictured) body measurements: shoulders to waist, 13 in. / 33 cm; bust, 29½ in. / 74.93 cm; waist, 23½ in. / 59.7 cm; hips, 32½ in. / 83 cm. Tall model (not pictured) body measurements: shoulders to waist, 16 in. / 40.6 cm; bust, 29 in. / 73.5 cm; waist, 26 in. / 66 cm; hips, 36 in. / 91.5 cm.

43 'Report of England made by Giovanni Michiel to the Venetian Senate (13 May 1557)', transcribed in Rawdon Brown, ed., *Calendar of State Papers Relating To English Affairs in the Archives of Venice, vol. 6, pt. 2, 1555–1558* (London: n.p., 1877), 1058; Francis Bacon, *The Felicity of Queen Elizabeth: and her times, with other things* (London: n.p., 1651), 18.

44 Green, *Wearing of Costume*, 21.

45 North and Tiramani, *Book Two*, 99.

46 Front-lacing garments with stomachers that have been altered for size, such as the Leeds bodies (see Fig. 4.9), must have been for substantial bodily change, or for a new owner.

47 Davidson and Hodson, 'Joining Forces', 207–8.

48 Breastfeeding and stays in the eighteenth century are discussed in detail in Catriona Fisk, 'Confined by History: Dress and the Maternal Body 1750–1900', PhD Diss. (Sydney: University of Technology Sydney, 2020), 309– 67.

49   Just over half of the eighteenth-century skeletons in Christ Church cemetery in Spitalfields examined by Klingerman showed deformities of the ribs. Klingerman attributes the normality of ribs in many of the skeletons to the fact that some of them belonged to domestic servants and labourers who would have corseted less, if at all. However, during the eighteenth century most women owned and wore stays. Klingerman, 'Binding Femininity', 40, 46; Arnold, Tiramani, Costigliolo, Passot, Lucas and Pietsch, *Patterns of Fashion 5*, 28.

50   Quoted in Spufford and Mee, *Clothing of the Common Sorts*, 96.

51   Smaller sized clothing tends to survive as few others can wear it and it cannot be easily made into something else. The Pfalz-Neuburg bodies have a waist measurement of 20 inches (51 cm) and the effigy bodies 21½ inches (54.5 cm). When laced over a stomacher, the waist of the Filmer bodies can vary from 20 to 23 inches (51–58.4 cm), whilst the 1660s Green Silk women's court bodice from the Museum of London has a 19-inch (48 cm) waist. The natural waistline of the women who wore these would have been slightly larger when not laced into these garments. See Arnold, *Patterns of Fashion 3*, 127.

52   Women's Stays, c. late 18th century, American, Philadelphia Museum of Art, 1998-162-51 a,b.

53   Lauren Marks (@markslauren), 'Today it's all about the luscious 17th Century!. TLDR: Swipe to see how stays shape my body', Instagram photos, 22 August 2020, https://www.instagram.com/p/CEMYahOAXMh/?igshid=xstoqfe5kz9x.

54   The bodies have been scaled-up and altered from a pattern in *Patterns of Fashion 5*. Marks's uncorseted measurements are 47 –35–47 inches (119.4–90–119.4 cm). Her measurements wearing these seventeenth-century bodies are 46–36–47 (116.84–91.44–119.4 cm). Marks, 'Today it's all about the luscious 17th Century!'; Lauren Marks, private correspondence via email, 24 and 25 August 2020.

55   Marshall-Ward, 'Mode and Movement', 125.

56   Chapman, Jonson and Marston, *Eastward Hoe*, A4r.

57   William Goddard, *A Nest of Wasps Lately Found out and Discovered in the Low-countries, Yielding as Sweet Honey as Some of our English Bees* (Low Countries: n.p., 1615), G ijv.

58   Chapman, Jonson and Marston, *Eastward Hoe*, B.

59   William Shakespeare, *The Merry Wives of Windsor* (London: n.p., 1630), F.

60   Carol Chillington Rutter, 'Unpinning Desdemona – the Movie', created 2007 / updated 5 August 2011, The Capital Centre hosted by the University of Warwick, UK, http://www2.warwick.ac.uk/fac/cross_fac/capital/teaching_and_learning/projects/unpinning/.

61   Marshall-Ward, 'Mode and Movement', 125–6.

62   Translated and quoted in Owen Hughes, 'Regulating Women's Fashions', 149.

63   Madame D'Aulnoy, *The lady's travels into Spain; or, a genuine relation of the religion, laws, commerce, customs, and manners of that country* (London: n.p., 1774), 182–3.

64   Arnold, Tiramani, Costigliolo, Passot, Lucas and Pietsch, *Patterns of Fashion 5*, 69.

65   Jacqueline Viaux, *Le Meuble en France au XVIIIe siècle* (Paris: Presses universitaires de France, 1962), 67.

66   John Heywood, *The Life and Works of John Heywood*, ed. Robert George, Whitney Bolwell and Robert W. Bolwell (New York: Columbia University Press, 1921), 7, n. 20.

67   'No. 70, Il Schifanoya to the Castellan of Mantua (30 May 1559)', transcribed in Rawdon Brown and G. Cavendish Bentinck, eds., *Calendar of State Papers Relating to English Affairs in the Archives of Venice, vol. 7, 1558–1580* (London: n.p., 1890), 92.

68   Isabelle Paresys, 'Paraitre et se vetir au XVIe siecle: Morales Vestimentaires', in *Paraître et se vêtir au XVIe siècle: actes du XIIIe Colloque du Puy-en-Velay*, ed. Marie F. Viallon (Saint-Etienne: Publications de l'université de Saint-Etienne, 2006), 18.

69   John Chamberlain, *The Letters of John Chamberlain*, vol. 1, ed. Norman Egbert McClure (Philadelphia: n.p., 1939), 426.

70   One Venetian foot is approximately 13 modern inches. Rudolf Wittkower, 'S. Maria della Salute: Scenographic Architecture and the Venetian Baroque', in *Modern Perspectives in Western Art History: An Anthology of Twentieth-century Writings on the Visual Arts*, ed. W. Eugene Kleinbauer (Toronto: University of Toronto Press in association with the Medieval Academy of America, 1989), 188, n. 20.

71   'No. 131: Horatio Busino to the Signori Giorgio, Francesco and Zaccaria Contarini (22 December 1617)', transcribed in Allen B. Hinds, ed., *Calendar of State Papers Relating to English Affairs in the Archives of Venice, vol. 15, 1617–1619* (London: n.p., 1909), 80.

72   One Castilian bara was 33 inches or 83.82 cm, and Arnold estimates a hand span to be about 22.8 cm. Arnold, *Queen Elizabeth's Wardrobe Unlock'd*, 196.

73   Arnold, *Queen Elizabeth's Wardrobe Unlock'd*, 196.

74   Buck, 'The Clothes of Thomasine Petre', 25.

75   Chapman, Jonson and Marston, *Eastward Hoe*, A4r.

76   Mikhaila and Malcolm-Davies, *The Tudor Tailor*, 9.

77   Raphael Holinshed, *The First Volume of the Chronicles of England, Scotland, and Ireland* (London: n.p., 1577), 97.

78   Stubbes, *Anatomy of Abuses*, C3.

79   'Enforcing Statutes of Apparel, Westminster, 6 May, 1562, 4 Elizabeth I', transcribed in Hughes and Larkin, *Tudor Royal Proclamations*, 189.

80   'Enforcing Statutes of Apparel, Westminster, 6 May, 1562, 4 Elizabeth I', 187.

81   Vincent, *Dressing the Elite*, 130–1.

82   Merry E. Wiesner-Hanks, 'Introduction', in *Mapping Gendered Routes and Spaces in the Early Modern World*, ed. Merry E. Wiesner-Hanks (Abingdon: Routledge, 2016), 11.

83   Doreen Massey, *Space, Place, and Gender* (Cambridge: Polity Press, 1994), 2; Laura Gowing, '"The freedom of the streets": Women and Social Space, 1560–1640', in *Londinopolis: Essays in the Cultural and Social History of Early Modern London*, ed. Paul Griffiths and Mark S. R. Jenner (Manchester: Manchester University Press, 2000), 131.

84   Gowing, '"The freedom of the streets"', 131.

85   Women who did frequent the streets often fell into one of three main categories: prostitutes, gossips or scolds. Gowing, '"The freedom of the streets"', 131.

86   Wunder, 'Women's Fashions', 148.

87   Translated and quoted in Zanger, *Scenes from the Marriage of Louis XIV*, 49.

88   Chrisman, 'Unhoop the Fair Sex', 12–13; Reed Benhamou, 'Who Controls This Private Space? The Offense and Defense of the Hoop in Early Eighteenth-Century France and England', *Dress* 28, no. 1 (2001): 13–22.

89   Carew, *Certain Godly and Necessary Sermons*, R6v–R7.

Chapter 6

1   Kunzle, *Fashion and Fetishism*; Valerie Steele, *Fetish: Fashion, Sex, and Power* (New York: Oxford University Press, 1996); Leigh Summers, *Bound to Please: A History of the Victorian Corset* (London: Berg, 2001); Larry Utley, *Fetish Fashion: Undressing the Corset* (San Francisco: Green Candy Press, 2002).

2   Thomas Nash, *Christs Tears over Jerusalem Whereunto is Annexed a Comparative Admonition to London* (London: n.p., 1613), 145.

3 Thomas Hall, *Divers Reasons and Arguments Against Painting, Spots, naked Backs, Breasts, Arms &c* (London: n.p., 1654), 107–9.

4 Angela McShane, 'Revealing Mary', *History Today* 54 (2004): 40–6; Backhouse, *Fashion and Popular Print*, 164–8.

5 John Dunton, *The Ladies Dictionary* (London: n.p., 1694), 185.

6 Dunton, *The Ladies Dictionary*, 401.

7 Patricia Simons has discussed this theme of concealing and veiling in early modern culture. Patricia Simons, 'The Visual Dynamics of (Un)Veiling in Early Modern Culture', in *Visual Cultures of Secrecy in Early Modern Europe*, ed. Timothy McCall, Sean Roberts and Giancarlo Fiorenza (Kirksville, MO: Truman State University Press, 2013), 42.

8 John Fletcher, *Fathers own Son* (London: n.p., 1660), G2.

9 Steele, *Fetish,* 5.

10 Edward Phillips, *The mysteries of love & eloquence* (London: n.p., 1685), 14–15.

11 Alexander Pope, *The Rape of the Lock* (London: n.p., 1714), 12.

12 'Doux Jouis Sopirer Vn à mant / & Qui Voudroict bien tenir ma plase'.

13 John Marston, *The Scourge of Villainy: Three Books of Satires* (London: I. R., 1598), F6r–v. The term 'busk envy' is borrowed from Sandy Feinstein. Feinstein, 'Donne's "Elegy 19"', 17.

14 Diana O'Hara, *Courtship and Constraint: Rethinking the Making of Marriage in Tudor England* (Manchester: Manchester University Press, 2000), 71.

15 Translation by Jones and Stallybrass, 'Of Busks and Bodies', 266.

16 Anthony Fletcher, 'Manhood, the Male Body, Courtship and the Household in Early Modern English', *Historical Association* 84, no. 275 (1999): 421.

17 Anthony Fletcher, *Gender, Sex, and Subordination in England, 1500–1800* (New Haven, CT: Yale University Press, 1995), 93; Mark Breitenberg, *Anxious Masculinity in Early Modern England* (Cambridge: Cambridge University Press, 1996), 128.

18 John Donne, *The Harmony of the museum*, ed. R. C. (London: n.p., 1654), 2.

19 Donne, *The Harmony of the museum*, 2.

20 Robert Herrick, *Hesperides* (London: 1648), 29.

21 Nicholas Hookes, *Amanda, a Sacrifice to an Unknown Goddess* (London: 1653), 30.

22 Dekker, *Shoemakers Holiday*, Iv.

23 Thomas Tomkis, *Lingua: or The Combat of the Tongue, and the Five senses for Superiority* (London: n.p., 1607), D2.

24 The Gordian knot is a phrase that alludes to a tale of Alexander the Great who attempted to unfasten the mythical Gordian Knot in order to rule over Asia, only to become frustrated and cut through it with his sword. In the early modern context it implies that one must think outside the box to solve a problem.

25 Fitzgeffry, *Satires,* B5v–B6.

26 Robert Burton, *The Anatomy of Melancholy* (Oxford: n.p., 1621), 613–14.

27 Marie Channing Linthicum, *Costume in the Drama of Shakespeare and his Contemporaries* (Oxford: Hacker Art Books, 1936), 178.

28 Anu Korhonen, 'To See and To Be Seen: Beauty in the Early Modern London Street', *Journal of Early Modern History* 12 (2008): 336–40.

29 Translated and quoted in Benhamou, 'Who Controls This Private Space?', 13.

30 Richard Brathwaite, *Ar't Asleepe Husband?* (London: n.p., 1640), 314.

31 *The Hasty Bridegroom. OR, The Rarest Sport that hath been Tried, Between a Lusty Bride-groom and his Bride* (London: n.p., *c.* 1693–5). EBBA, 33310.

32 William Averell, *A Marvellous Combat of Contrarieties* (London: n.p., 1588), B2.

33 Ribeiro, *Fashion and Fiction*, 171.

34 Farah Karim-Cooper, *Cosmetics in Shakespearean and Renaissance Drama* (Edinburgh: Edinburgh University Press, 2006), 35, 111.

35 Fitzgeffry, *Satires,* B5v.

36 Arnold, *Patterns of Fashion 3*, 10.

37 Lording Barry, *Ram-Alley: or Merry-Tricks* (London: n.p., 1611), H4.

38 Korhonen, 'To See and Be Seen', 343.

39 Rachel Speght, *A Mouzell for Melastomus, the cynical baiter of, and fouled mouthed barker against Evahs sex* (London: n.p., 1617).

40 Joseph Swetnam, *The Arraignment of Lewd, Idle, Frorward, and Unconstant Women* (London: n.p., 1615), 14–16.

41 Rich, *Faults, Faults, and Nothing Else but Faults*, 21.

42 Laura Gowing, *Domestic Dangers: Women, Words, and Sex in Early Modern London* (Oxford: Oxford University Press, 1996), 80; Reinke-Williams, 'Women's clothes and female honour', 70.

43 Quoted in Bernard Capp, *When Gossips meet: Women, Family, and Neighbourhood in Early Modern England* (Oxford: Oxford University Press, 2003), 230.

44 Hubbard, *City Women*, 225; Reinke-Williams, 'Women's clothes and female honour', 70.

45 Middleton, 'Women Beware Women', 120.

46 Gosson, *Pleasant Quips*, B1v.

47 It was common in England for French materials to be associated with syphilis and ostentation, and Spanish and Italian fabrics with popery and lasciviousness. Roze Hentschell, 'Treasonous Textiles: Foreign Cloth and the Construction of Englishness', *Journal of Medieval and Early Modern Studies* 32, no. 3 (2002): 545–6.

48 Gosson, *Pleasant Quips*, B1v.

49 Arnold, *Queen Elizabeth's Wardrobe Unlock'd*, 194; Johnston, 'Sex, Lies, and Verdugados', 101–6, 110–12.

50 'Vn cachenfant come les autres me fault porter: / Coufte qu'il coufte: le fol la folle veult aymer.'

51 Carew, *Certain Godly and Necessary Sermons*, R6v–R7.

52 John Webster, *The Tragedy of the Duchess of Malfy* (London: n.p., 1623), D3v.

53 Amanda Wunder discusses a later Spanish play called *El Disfrazado* (1649) with a very similar plot line involving a character, Doña Clara, who hides her illegitimate pregnancy from her brother with a *guardainfante*. Wunder, 'Women's Fashions', 145.

54 Goddard, *Nest of Wasps*, G ijr.

55 Terms such as big-bellied or great-bellied were commonly used to refer to pregnancy in seventeenth-century England. Antonia Fraser, *The Weaker Vessel: Woman's Lot in Seventeenth-Century England* (London: Weidenfeld and Nicolson, 1984), 60.

56 Middleton, 'Women Beware Women', 119–20.

57 Middleton, 'Women Beware Women', 180.

58 *The Peddler opening of his Pack, To know of Maids what tis they Lack* (London: n.p., 1620). EBBA, 20109.

59 'Le Busc de Sophonisbe, pour cacher la grossesse des filles', in François Hédelin Aubignac, *Nouvelle Histoire du Temps, ou La Relation Véritable du Royaume de la Coqueterie* (Paris: n.p., 1655), 104.

60 Richard Head, *The English Rogue Described* (London: n.p., 1668), 84–5.

61 'Elizabeth Maddox, Sarah Jenkins. Killing: infanticide. 4th December 1754', t17541204-33, OBP, https://www.oldbaileyonline.org/browse.jsp?div=t17541204-33.

62 Quoted in Laura Gowing, 'Secret Births and Infanticide in Seventeenth-Century England', *Past & Present* 156 (1997): 93.

63 Zanger, *Scenes from the Marriage of Louis XIV*, 54.

64 Gosson, *Pleasant Quips*, Br.

65 Quoted in Kunzle, *Fashion and Fetishism*, 155.

66 Johnson, *A discourse of some troubles*, 135.

67 Jacob Rüff, *The Expert Midwife* (London: n.p., 1637), 60.

68 'De l'avortement, & de ses causes ... ce qui peut encore arriver, si la femme se serre trop le corps, & presse son ventre avec des buscs forts & roides, pour se rendre la taille plus dégagée, ou pour celer par cette ruse sa grossesse', in François Mauriceau, *Traité des Maladies des Femmes Grosses* (Paris: n.p., 1681), 182.

69 'D'abord que les femmes se sentent grosses, ou qu'elles s'en doutent, elles ne doivent point se serrer, comme elles font ordinairement , avec ces corps-de-robes garnis de fortes branches de baleine, dont elles se servent pour paroistre de belle taille; ce qui leur blesse assez souvent le sein: & enfermant ainsi leur ventre dans un moule si estroit , elles empêchent que leurs enfans ne puissent prendre leur libre accroissement dans la matrices souvent elles les font venir avant terme, & quelquefois mesme contrefaits.' Mauriceau, *Traité des Maladies*, 119.

70 TNA: LR 5/64, George Gelin's Bill for April, May and June 1631; TNA: LR 5/66, George Gelin's Bill for Midsummer quarter 1635. Erin Griffey also discusses wardrobe purchases that the queen made at the time of her pregnancies. Griffey, *On Display*, 109–15.

71 Edmund Verney was the son of the royalist Sir Ralph Verney who was made the Baronet of Middle Claydon by Charles II in 1662.

72 The boning channels in the original stomacher are approximately ⅛-inch (4 mm) wide, while my reconstruction contains ¼-inch-wide (6 mm) channels. See Arnold, Tiramani, Costigliolo, Passot, Lucas and Pietsch, *Patterns of Fashion 5*, 69.

73 Harriet Waterhouse, 'A Fashionable Confinement: Whaleboned Stays and the Pregnant Woman', *Costume* 41, no. 1 (2007): 58.

74 Arnold, Tiramani, Costigliolo, Passot, Lucas and Pietsch, *Patterns of Fashion 5*, 69.

75 Sorge-English, *Stays and Body Image*, 101; Fisk, 'Confined by History', 309–67.

76 Waterhouse, 'Fashionable Confinement', 60.

77 Bernard Capp, 'The Double Standard Revisited: Plebeian Women and Male Sexual Reputation in Early Modern England', *Past & Present* 162 (1999): 72–7.

78 Fletcher, *Gender, Sex and Subordination*, 5–6, 76, 85–94.

79 Ian Frederick Moulton, 'Erotic Representations, 1500–1750', in *The Routledge History of Sex and the Body, 1500 to the Present*, ed. Sarah Toulalan and Kate Fisher (Abingdon: Routledge, 2013), 215; Sarah Toulalan, *Imagining Sex: Pornography and Bodies in Seventeenth-Century England* (Oxford: Oxford University Press, 2007), 32.

80 Lauren Kassell, 'Medical Understandings of the Body, c. 1500–1750', in *The Routledge History of Sex and the Body, 1500 to the Present*, ed. Sarah Toulalan and Kate Fisher (Abingdon: Routledge, 2013), 65; Gowing, *Common Bodies*, 82–3.

81 The receiving of busks in courtship and marriage will be discussed in more detail in Chapter 7.

82 Richard Adair, *Courtship, Illegitimacy and Marriage in Early Modern England* (Manchester: Manchester University Press, 1996), 92–3.

83 Susan Dwyer Amussen, *An Ordered Society: Gender and Class in Early Modern England* (Oxford: Blackwell, 1988), 111; Gowing, *Common Bodies*, 8.

84 Carla Spivack, 'To "bring down the flowers": the cultural context of abortion law in early modern England', *William & Mary Journal of Women and the Law* 14, no. 1 (2007): 109–10; Lianne McTavish, 'Reproduction, c. 1500–1750', in *The Routledge History of Sex and the Body, 1500 to the Present*, ed. Sarah Toulalan and Kate Fisher (Abingdon: Routledge, 2013), 356.

85 McTavish, 'Reproduction, c. 1500–1750', 358; Laura Gowing, *Gender Relations in Early Modern England* (Abingdon: Routledge, 2012), 105.

86 Sarah Toulalan, '"To[o] much eating stifles the child": Fat bodies and reproduction in early modern England', *Historical Research* 87, no. 235 (2014): 65; Fraser, *The Weaker Vessel*, 60–8; McTavish, 'Reproduction, c. 1500–1750', 354.

87 Zanger, *Scenes from the Marriage of Louis XIV*, 53–6.

88 Katharine Park, *Secrets of Women: Gender, Generation, and the Origins of Human Dissection* (New York: Zone, 2006), 23–6.

89 Phillips, 'The Breasts of Virgins', 9–12.

90 Timothy McCall and Sean Roberts, 'Introduction', in *Visual Cultures of Secrecy in Early Modern Europe*, ed. Timothy McCall, Sean Roberts and Giancarlo Fiorenza (Kirksville, MO: Truman State University Press, 2013), 15.

91 Raymond Stephanson and Darren N. Wagner, 'Introduction', in *The Secrets of Generation: Reproduction in the London Eighteenth Century*, ed. Raymond Stephanson and Darren N. Wagner (Toronto: University of Toronto Press, 2015), 4–5.

92 Monica H. Green, 'From "Diseases of Women" to "Secrets of Women": The Transformation of Gynaecological Literature in the Later Middle Ages', *Journal of Medieval and Early Modern Studies* 30 (2000): 14; Park, *Secrets of Women*, 93.

93 Tim Harris, '"There is none that love him but Drunk Whores and Whoremongers": Popular Criticisms of the Restoration Court', in *Politics, Transgression, and Representation at the Court of Charles II*, ed. Julia Marciari Alexander and Catharine MacLeod (New Haven, CT: Yale University Press, 2007), 42–3.

94 Maria Hayward, '"The best of Queens, the most obedient wife": Fashioning a Place for Catherine of Braganza as Consort to Charles II', in *Sartorial Politics in Early Modern Europe: Fashioning Women*, ed. Erin Griffey (Amsterdam: Amsterdam University Press, 2019), 228–9, 234.

95 Quoted in Hayward, '"The best of Queens"', 234.

96 Kevin Sharpe, '"Thy Longing Country's Darling and Desire": Aesthetics, Sex, and Politics in the England of Charles II', in *Politics, Transgression, and Representation at the Court of Charles II*, ed. Julia Marciari Alexander and Catharine MacLeod (New Haven, CT: Yale University Press, 2007), 2, 14.

97 Gowing, *Common Bodies*, 52; Patricia M. Crawford, *Blood, Bodies and Families in Early Modern England* (Harlow: Pearson, 2004), 67.

98 Matthew Gerber, *Bastards: Politics, Family and Law in Early Modern France* (New York: Oxford University Press, 2012), 7.

99 Sheila O'Connell, 'Love Pleasant, Love Unfortunate: Women in Seventeenth-Century Popular Prints', in *Politics, Transgression, and Representation at the Court of Charles II*, ed. Julia Marciari Alexander and Catharine MacLeod (New Haven, CT: Yale University Press, 2007), 63–7.

100 Gowing, *Common Bodies*, 71

101 TNA: ASSI 45/7/2/119, Deposition of Marie Franckland of Hetton, Yorkshire, February 13, 1665.

102 Gowing, *Common Bodies*, 65.

103 Wunder, 'Women's Fashions', 179.

104 Gowing, 'Secret Births and Infanticide', 91, n. 7.

Chapter 7

1 Richard Brathwaite, *Whimsies: or, a New Cast of Characters* (London: n.p., 1631), 189.

2 Wetenhall Wilkes, *A Letter of Genteel and Moral Advice to a Young Lady* (London: n.p., 1740), 188.

3 Sophronius, 'Universal Spectator, January 31. No. 643: Of the Modern HOOP PETTICOATS', in *The London Magazine and Monthly Chronologer* (London: n.p., 1741), 75.

4 For a discussion of these five consumer revolutions, see Jan De Vries, *The Industrious Revolution: Consumer Behaviour and the Household Economy, 1650 to the Present* (Cambridge: Cambridge University Press, 2008), 4–5, 37–9.

5 Neil McKendrick, John Brewer and J. H. Plumb, eds., *The Birth of a Consumer Society: The Commercialization of Eighteenth-Century England* (Bloomington: Indiana University Press, 1982), 9.

6 Linda Levy Peck, *Consuming Splendor: Society and Culture in Seventeenth-Century England* (Cambridge: Cambridge University Press, 2005); Cox and Dannehl, *Perceptions of Retailing*, 161–2.

7 Paula Hohti Erichsen, *Artisans, Objects and Everyday Life in Renaissance Italy: The Material Culture of the Middling Class* (Amsterdam: Amsterdam University Press, 2020); Welch, *Shopping in the Renaissance*;

8 Catherine Kovesi, '*Luxus*: How Luxury Acquired its Lustre', in *Luxury and the Ethics of Greed in Early Modern Italy*, ed. Catherine Kovesi (Turnhout: Brepols, 2019), 7.

9 De Vries, *The Industrious Revolution*, 52–8, 122–3; Smith, *Consumption*, 41; Lorna Weatherill, 'The meaning of consumer behaviour in late seventeenth- and early eighteenth-century England', in *Consumption and the World of Goods*, ed. John Brewer and Roy Porter (London: Routledge, 1994), 206–27; Joan Thirsk, *Economic Policy and Projects: The Development of a Consumer Society in Early Modern England* (Oxford: Oxford University Press, 1978), 158.

10 The following discussion of the sisters' clothing is based on the expenditure accounts detailed in the probate record of Edward Harpur. This probate is 'Inventory 99', transcribed in Phillips and Smith, *Stockport Probate Records*, 249–98.

11 C. C. Phillips, 'Orphan and Family: Bringing up Edward Harpur's Orphan Daughters, 1650–66', *Historical Research* 68, no. 167 (2007), 293–7.

12 Phillips, 'Orphan and Family', 291.

13 Ribeiro, *Fashion and Fiction*, 200.

14 John Gauden, *A Discourse of Auxiliary Beauty* (London: n.p., 1656), 44.

15 Entry for 17 March 1650, 'for linen cloth for Sarahs bodyes thread and whale bone', transcribed in Phillips and Smith, *Stockport Probate Records*, 272.

16 Larkham, *Diary*, 36, 48.

17 Stern, 'Peckover and Gallyard', 16–21.

18 Spufford, *The Great Reclothing of Rural England*, 89.

19 Phillips and Smith, *Stockport Probate Records*, 270.

20 BL: Egerton MS 3054, fol. 45r.

21 Phillips, 'Orphan and Family', 298.

22 Tankard, *Clothing in 17th-Century Provincial England*, 144–9.

23 Spufford and Mee, *Clothing of the Common Sort*, 97.

24 NRO: KL/C50/288; '1633, William Townsend, Drapers' Company', ROLLCO, http://londonroll.org.

25 TNA: PROB 11/280/187; TNA: PROB 11/353/433.

26 TNA: PROB 11/449/420; TNA: PROB 11/407/207; TNA: PROB 11/398/240; TNA: PROB 11/379/444; TNA: PROB 11/367/188.

27 LMA: CLC/313/K/C/009/MS19504/007/077.

28 Quoted by Lemire, *Dress, Culture and Commerce*, 63.

29 'Inventory 15', transcribed in Michael Reed, ed., *Buckinghamshire probate inventories, 1661–1714* (Aylesbury: Buckinghamshire Record Society, 1988), 40.

30 Lemire, *Dress, Culture and Commerce*, 60.

31 Spufford and Mee have analysed King's annual consumption of apparel. They concluded that King's estimates are a reasonably accurate reflection of consumption trends by 1688. Spufford and Mee, *Clothing of the Common Sort*, 25–42.

32 N. B. Harte, 'The Economics of Clothing in the Late Seventeenth Century', *Textile History* 22, no.2 (1991): 293.

33 Costigliolo, 'The Bodyes Maker', 8–9.

34 E. A. Wrigley and R. S. Schofield, *The Population History of England 1541–1871: A Reconstruction* (Cambridge: Cambridge University Press, 1989), 210.

35 Gregory King estimated the age structure of the English population in 1695, stating that 14.9 per cent of the population consisted of children 0–4 years. If we assume evenly divided sex ratios, then female children in this age group made up 7.45 per cent of the total population. Wrigley and Schofield, *The Population History of England*, 218.

36 Spufford, *The Great Reclothing of Rural England*, 21.

37 Sorge-English, *Stays and Body Image*, 5.

38 'Stays', 'her stays' and 'pair of stays' were searched in several large databases containing digitized early modern sources such as EEBO, OBP and ECCO. The earliest possible reference to this garment in these databases dates to 1680.

39 Quoted in North and Tiramani, *Book Two*, 58.

40 FSL: X.d.492 (50).

41 TNA: LR 5/76, Peter Lombard bill for Midsummer Quarter 1685.

42 John Dryden, *The Kind Keeper, or, Mr. Limberham a Comedy* (London: n.p., 1680), 5.

43 'Advertisements', *The Loyal Protestant, and True Domestic Intelligence*, Issue 218, 10 October 1682, 2. Seventeenth and Eighteenth Century Nichols Newspapers Collection; Anon., *Fifteen Real Comforts of Matrimony being in Requital of the Late Fifteen Sham Comforts* (London: n.p., 1683), 9.

44 'Trial of Eleanor Jones, September 1686', t16860901-30, OBP, https://www.oldbaileyonline.org/browse.jsp?div=t16860901-30.

45 A Mr Browne of Tooley Street in Southwark was later named a 'Boddice & Stay maker' in a 1715 court deposition. Certainly, a tailor or body-maker would have possessed the skills to make stays, as they were constructed using the same sorts of specialized techniques and materials used to make bodies such as whalebone. 'City of London Sessions, Sessions Papers – Justices' Working Documents, 8th February 1715–25th November 1715', LMSLPS150260007, London Lives, 1690-1800, https://www.londonlives.org/browse.jsp?div=LMSLPS150260007.

46 Sorge-English, *Stays and Body Image*, 5; Crowston has also argued that 'the spread of the new dress [mantua] demanded a new type of underwear to preserve women's stiff silhouette'. Crowston, *Fabricating Women*, 37.

47 'Mary Biglin, Elenor Bayly'; 'Hannah Mayle'. Hannah Mayle was also indicted for stealing 'Two Serge Mantua Gowns, value 17 s. a Baize petticoat, a pair of Bodice' in 1692.

48 Holme, *The Academy of Armory*, 94.

49 'Thomas Harding, John Mahew. Theft: burglary. 28th August 1700', OBP, t17000828-46, https://www.oldbaileyonline.org/browse.jsp?div=t17000828-46.

50 Select examples include 'Letitia. Theft: grand larceny. 4th December 1723', t17231204-1, OBP, https://www.oldbaileyonline.org/browse.jsp?div=t17231204-1; 'James Bird, John Hemp. Violent Theft: highway robbery. 8th December 1725', OBP, t17251208-35, https://www.oldbaileyonline.org/browse.jsp?div=t17251208-35; 'Elizabeth Cartwright. Theft: grand larceny. 6th September 1739', t17390906-24, OBP, https://www.oldbaileyonline.org/browse.jsp?div=t17390906-24.

51 Sorge-English, *Stays and Body Image*, 24–7.

52 Sébastien Passot, '"Are You Sure This Is What He Means?" Considerations on Dress Terminology in French Sources and Their Subsequent Translation', in *Structuring Fashion: Foundation Garments through History*, ed. Frank Matthias Kammel and Johannes Pietsch (Munich: Hirmer, 2019), 63–8.

53 Bryson, *From Courtesy to Civility*, 47–50.

54 Shepard, *Accounting for Oneself*, 7; Keith Thomas, *In Pursuit of Civility: Manners and Civilisation in Early Modern England* (Waltham, MA: Brandeis University Press, 2018), 55–6.

55 Bryson, *From Courtesy to Civility*, 49; Goring, *Rhetoric of Sensibility,* 22; Smith, *Consumption*, 41.

56 Goring, *Rhetoric of Sensibility,* 6.

57 Lawrence E. Klein, 'Politeness and the Interpretation of the British Eighteenth Century', *Historical Journal* 45, no. 4 (2002): 874; Philip Carter, *Men and the Emergence of Polite Society: Britain 1660–1800* (Harlow: Longman, 2001), 63.

58 *News from Hide-Parke* (London, *c.* 1647–65). EBBA, 33597.

59 Nehemiah Grew, *The Anatomy of Plants with an Idea of a Philosophical History of Plants* (London: n.p., 1682), 35.

60 Thomas D'Urfey, *The Intrigues at Versailles* (London: n.p., 1697), 21.

61 The term stays could have been taken from the nautical term used to describe ropes, wire or rods on sailing vessels that stabilize the mast. Bodies and later stays acted in much the same way, as they were used to stabilize farthingales and to anchor clothing such as the mantua gown to the torso.

62 *THE Young Mens ADVICE TO Proud Ladies* (1692). EBBA, 33415.

63 Anon., *Laugh and be Fat: Or, an Antidote against Melancholy*, 9th edn (London: n.p., 1724), 122.

64 Vincent, *Anatomy of Fashion*, 46.

65 C. L. von Pöllnitz stated in 1733 that 'They are always laced, and 'tis as rare to see a Woman here [in England] without her Stays on, as it is to see one at Paris in full Dress.' When Madame du Bocage visited England in 1750 she too noted that 'The women use no paint and are always laced.' Quoted in Steele, *The Corset*, 26.

66 Quoted in Steele, *The Corset*, 26.

67 O'Hara, *Courtship and Constraint*, 1–31; Fletcher, 'Manhood, the Male Body, Courtship', 427.

68 Peter Rushton, 'The Testament of Gifts: Marriage Tokens and Disputed Contracts in North-East England, 1560–1630', *Folk Life* 24 (1985): 26; Diana O'Hara, 'The Language of Tokens and the Making of Marriage', *Rural History* 3, no. 1 (1992): 15; Zita Thornton, 'The Romance of Welsh Lovespoons', *Antiques & Collecting Magazine* 105 (2001): 44–8; Knitting Sheath *c.* 1679, English, Victoria and Albert Museum, London, 774–1907.

69 Louise Purbrick, '"I love giving presents": The Emotion of Material Culture', in *Love Objects: Emotion, Design and Material Culture*, ed. Anna Moran and Sorcha O'Brien (London: Bloomsbury, 2014), 34.

70 Stephanie Downes, Sally Holloway and Sarah Randles, 'Introduction', in *Feeling Things: Objects and Emotions through History*, ed. Stephanie Downes, Sally Holloway and Sarah Randles (Oxford: Oxford University Press, 2018), 1–7.

71 Jennifer McNabb, 'Ceremony versus Consent: Courtship, Illegitimacy, and Reputation in Northwest England, 1560–1610', *Sixteenth Century Journal* 37, no. 1 (2006): 73.

72 Rushton, 'The Testament of Gifts', 25.

73 O'Hara, *Courtship and Constraint*, 62; McNabb, 'Ceremony versus Consent', 73.

74 Ilona Bell, *Elizabethan Women and the Poetry of Courtship* (Cambridge: Cambridge University Press, 1998), 9; Gowing, *Gender Relations*, 35.

75 The only references made to gift giving and busks before 1650 all relate to women giving their busk-points to men as gifts, as discussed in Chapter 6. All surviving English and French busks containing romantic inscriptions that were surveyed in this study date from the second half of the seventeenth century.

76 Aphra Behn, *Poems Upon Several Occasions with, a Voyage to the Island of Love* (London: n.p., 1684), 19–24.

77 'IVS QVES AV REVOIR / MON FEV EST PVR / LAMOVR LES IOINT'.

78 Lauren Fried, 'Binding Bodies and Transforming Texts: The Wooden Engraved Stay Busk as a Seventeenth Century Love Token' MA Research Paper (London: Royal College of Art, 2012), 13.

79 'LAMOVR LES IOINT / ELLE NOVS VNIT / [. . .] VOIR OV MOVRIR'. The inscription on the last line is hard to decipher due to the age of the busk. The translation is either 'Vo[us] voir ou mourir' or 'Ou voir ou mourir'.

80 'MEMES COEVRS, MEMES PENSEES', Garter (one of a pair), 18th century, French, Museum of Fine Arts, Boston, 43.2339; 'MA DEVISE EST DE VOUS AIME, ES DE ME JAMAIS CHANGER', Garter, 18th Century, French, Museum of Fine Arts, Boston, 38.1390a.

81 Garter, *c.* 1700–29, English, Victoria and Albert Museum, London, T.42-1955.

82 Samuel Pepys, *Diary and Correspondence of Samuel Pepys, ESQ., F.R.S., from his Ms. Cypher in the Pepysian Library*, vol. 1, ed. Richard Griffin Braybrooke and Mynors Bright (New York: Dodd, Mead and Company, 1885), 338.

83 'UNIS A JAMAIS / JE MEURS OU JE M'ATTACHE'. In this context, 'I die' could also mean to orgasm, as this was common double entendre at the time.

84 Stephanie Coontz, *Marriage, A History: From Obedience to Intimacy or How Love Conquered Marriage* (New York: Viking, 2005), 5, 123, 146; Peter N. Stearns, 'Modern Patterns in Emotions History', in *Doing Emotions History*, ed. Susan J. Matt and Peter N. Stearn (Champaign: University of Illinois Press, 2014), 25.

85 Colin Campbell, *The Romantic Ethic and the Spirit of Modern Consumerism*, new extended edn (London: Palgrave Macmillan: 2018), Springer Ebooks, 59–62.

86 Amanda Vickery, *The Gentleman's Daughter: Women's Lives in Georgian England* (New Haven, CT: Yale University Press, 1998), 41; Sally Holloway, 'Love, Custom & Consumption: Valentine's Day in England c. 1660–1830', *Cultural and Social History* 17, no. 3 (2020): 295–314.

87 The inscriptions on these busks are: 'PARTOVT AMOVR / VNIS A JAMAIS / VN SVEL ME BLESE', accompanied by engravings of arrows being fired at a love heart, two hearts being pierced by an arrow and one heart pierced with an arrow. 'PARTOVT AMOVR / ARDANTE AMOVR / PENSE A VOUS', followed by engravings of two upside down hears next to arrows, two hearts together under the sun and a flower.

88 A wooden busk sold by Christies Auction House in 2005 is dated 'Feb ye 11th 1796' and contains two sets of diamond and round glass insets. It also has a triangular cross-section and prick decoration of similar designs. The top glass insets also contain a pair of red initials, 'A' and 'B', with gilt gold love hearts below; the style and font of these insets are almost identical to those on the busk in the Victoria and Albert collection. The earliest dated busk of the three, dated 'NOV ye 3d 1795', was also sold by Christies Auction House in 1998 and is described as a stay busk with a 'triangular section' and a 'chip-carved ornament, inset with painted paper panels' that are set below glass.
'Lot 88: A Chip-Carved Sycamore Stay-Busk', Christie's, London, http://www.christies.com/LotFinder/lot_details. aspx?intObjectID=4538985; 'A treen stay busk, late 18th century', Christie's, London, http://www.christies.com/lotfinder/ lot/a-treen-stay-busk-late-18th-century-1336638-details.aspx?from=searchresults&intObjectID=1336638&sid=61407991-5fb1- 4bcf-851e-ca5352bb7613.

89 John Evelyn, *Memoirs, Illustrative of the Life and Writings of John Evelyn*, vol. 1, 2nd edn., ed. William Bray (London: n.p., 1819), 348.

90 Craig Muldrew, 'Class and Credit: Social Identity, Wealth and the Life Course in Early Modern England', in *Identity and Agency in England, 1500–1800*, ed. Henry French and Jonathan Barry (New York: Palgrave, 2004), 148–9; Smith, *Consumption*, 62.

91 *An excellent New Play-house SONG, Called, The Bonny Milk-Maid* (*c*. 1684–95). EBBA, 33829.

92 Chrisman, 'Unhoop the Fair Sex', 8; Benhamou, 'Who Controls This Private Space?', 14.

93 Sophronius, 'Of the Modern HOOP PETTICOATS', 75.

94 Quoted in Benhamou, 'Who Controls This Private Space?', 13.

95 No. 82, 13 January 1710, quoted in Reed Benhamou, 'Clothing in the Age of Watteau', in *Antoine Watteau: Perspectives on the Artist and the Culture of his Time*, ed. Mary D. Sheriff (Newark: University of Delaware Press, 2006), 142.

96 Sylvanus Urban, *The Gentleman's Magazine: OR, Monthly Intelligencer. For the YEAR 1733*, vol. 3 (London: n.p., 1733), 131.

97 Sophronius, 'Of the Modern HOOP PETTICOATS', 76.

98 'Elizabeth Burgis. Theft: theft from a specified place. 13th January 1727', t17270113-18), OBP, https://www.oldbaileyonline.org/browse.jsp?div=t17270113-18.

99 *The Lady's Answer to the Several little Satires on the Hooped Petticoats*, *c*. 1720. National Library Scotland, Ry.III.c.36 (139).

100 Goring, *The Rhetoric of Sensibility*, 5–6.

101 Goring, *The Rhetoric of Sensibility*, 60.

102 Vickery, *The Gentleman's Daughter*, 13.

103 Woolley, *The Gentlewomans Companion*, 58–60.

104 Sophronius, 'Of the Modern HOOP PETTICOATS', 76.

105 Smith, *Consumption*, 3, 224–6; Keith Wrightson, *Earthly Necessities: Economic Lives in Early Modern Britain, 1470–1750* (London: Penguin, 2002), 300.

Conclusion

1 W. N., *The Second Part of Merry Drollery* (London: n.p., 1661), 151.

2 Newman, *Fashioning Femininity*, 4–5.

3 For overviews of twenty-first-century corset criticisms, see Alanna McKnight, 'The Kurious Kase of Kim Kardashian's Korset', *Fashion Studies* 3, no. 1 (2020): 1–20; Rebecca Gibson, *The Corseted Skeleton: A Bioarchaeology of Binding* (New York: Springer International Publishing, 2020), 204–15.

4 Steele, *The Corset*, 1

5 Helene E. Roberts, '"The Exquisite Slave": The Role of Clothes in the Making of the Victorian Woman', *Signs: Journal of Women in Culture and Society* 2 (1977): 557–8; Elizabeth Wilson, *Adorned in Dreams: Fashion and Modernity* (London: Virago, 1985), 30; Summers, *Bound to Please*, 2–9.

6 Many modern news articles on corsets reveal how ideas from the nineteenth century and second wave feminist scholarship continue to colour how modern women view corsetry, including early modern bodies and stays: Alexander Fury, 'Can a Corset Be Feminist?', *New York Times Style Magazine*, 25 November 2016, https://www.nytimes.com/2016/11/25/t-magazine/fashion/corset-history-feminism.html; Emine Saner, 'What a waist: why the corset has made a regrettable return', *Guardian*, 27 June 2019, https://www.theguardian.com/lifeandstyle/2019/jun/27/corset-regrettable-return-mothercare-waist-training.

7 Steele, *The Corset*, 35–176; Alanna McKnight, 'Damsels in This Dress: Female Agency and the Demise of the Corset', in *Fashion: Tyranny and Revelation*, ed. Damayanthie Eluwawalage (Leiden: Brill, 2016), 221–9.

8   Susan Brownmiller, *Femininity* (1984; reiss., New York: Open Road Integrated Media, 2013), 46–8.

9   The earliest reference I have found to the myth of Catherine de' Medici introducing the corset to France dates from 1778. During the nineteenth century, further details – that they were metal corsets and that the queen forced her court ladies to wear them to achieve 13-inch waists (33 cm) – were added. Germain-François Poullain de Saint-Foix, *Oeuvres complettes de M. de Saint-Foix, historiographe des ordres du roi*, vol. 4 (Paris: n.p., 1778), 277; William Barry Lord, *The Corset and the Crinoline* (London: n.p., 1868), 72.

10   Brownmiller, *Femininity*, 46–8.

11   Brownmiller, *Femininity*, 47.

Bibliography

Manuscript sources

Archives Nationals (AN)

AN, KK//203, Reine Anne d'Autriche: Trésorerie générale de ses Maison et finances, 1632.

Bodleian Libraries, University of Oxford (BLO)

MS Morrell 6: Oxford Tailors' Guild Election and Order book, 1570–1710.
MS. Top. Lines. c. 5.: Household bills and receipts of the Hussey Family of Honington and Doddington, late 17th–early 18th cent.

British Library, London (BL)

Add MS 5751a: Miscellaneous Wardrobe Warrants.
Egerton MS 2806: Register of Warrants to the Great Wardrobe, 1568–1589.
Egerton MS 3054: Accounts of Joyce Jeffries, 1638–1648.

Cambridge University Library, Cambridge (CUL)

Dd 1.26: Inventory of Queen Anne of Denmark's wardrobe, 1607–1611.

Drapers' Company Archive, London (DCA)

A IV, 148: Drapers Company Deed, 1652.
Boyd's Roll Register of Apprentices and Freeman.
Q.B.1.: Quarterage book for 1605–18.
Q.B.2.: Quarterage book for 1617–27.
Q.B.3.: Quarterage book for 1628–42.
Q.B.4.: Quarterage book for 1642–52.
Q.B.5: Quarterage book for 1653–64.

Essex Record Office, Chelmsford (ERO)

T/A 418/69/18: Calendar of Essex Assizes held at Chelmsford.
T/A 418/82/32: Calendar of Essex Assizes held at Chelmsford.

T/A 418/113/38: Calendar of Essex Assizes held at Witham.

Folger Shakespeare Library, Washington, DC (FSL)

X.d.258: Inventories of Jane Berkeley, 1605, 1611 and 1618. Bacon-Townshend Collection, 1550–1640.
X.d.428 (131): Letter from Elizabeth Wingfield, St. Johns London, to Elizabeth Hardwick Talbot, Countess of Shrewsbury. 8
    December, 1585.
X.d.486: Account book of Sir William and Lady Cavendish of Chatsworth, Michaelmas 1548–1550.
X.d.492: Bills and receipts of the Clayton family of Marden and Bletchingley, Surrey, 1616–1778.

Guildhall Library, London

MS 34038/15: Merchant Taylors' Company apprentice bindings.

London Metropolitan Archives (LMA)

CLC/313/K/C/009/MS19504/007/077: Inventory of John Dryver, Citizen and Merchant Taylor, St Giles Cripplegate, Middlesex.
    25 September, 1665.
COL/CC/17/01: Corporation of London, Court of Common Council Byelaws.
DW/PA/05/1559/007: Probate will of Widow Cicely Bolton from Thames Ditton Claygate, dated 16 March, 1559.

National Records of Scotland, Edinburgh (NRS)

E35/14: Volume of accounts of apparel furnished to the queen and her gentlewomen and servants. 28 August 1591 to
    1 February 1595/6.

Norfolk Record Office, Norwich (NRO)

KL/C50/288: Title deeds, King's Lynn. 20 August, 1632.

Oxford Historical Centre, Oxford (OHC)

Pec.33/1/1: Will of Ellen Bicke, Spinster, Cropredy Oxfordshire, 1627.

Surrey History Centre, Woking (SHC)

LM/COR/7: Letters of the Gresham Family.

The National Archives, Kew (TNA)

ASSI 45/7/2/119: Depositions and Case papers relating to Mary Ryley, 1665. Northern Assizes Depositions, 1559–1971.
CP40/1157: Court of Common Pleas: Plea Rolls. Chief Justice's roll, 1 Mary, Hilary term 1554.
LC 5/32: Lord Chamberlain's Department – Great Wardrobe, 1554–1569.
LC 5/33: Lord Chamberlain's Department – Great Wardrobe, 1562–1567, 1585.
LC 5/36: Lord Chamberlain's Department – Great Wardrobe, 1585–1593.
LR 5/64: Queen Henrietta Maria Household, 1627–1633.
LR 5/65: Queen Henrietta Maria Household, 1632–1633.

LR 5/66: Queen Henrietta Maria Household, 1634–1638.

LR 5/67: Queen Henrietta Maria Household, 1639–1640 and 1660–1667.

LR 5/76: Queen Catherine Household, 1672–1685.

LR 5/78: Queen Catherine Household, 1686.

LR 5/79: Queen Catherine Household, 1685–1687.

LR 6/154/9: Queen Anne's Jointure, declaration of account of Sir George Carew, Vice-Chamberlain and Receiver General.

PROB 11/353/433: Will of Richard Fowlar, Bodice Maker of Caversham, Oxfordshire. 14 April, 1677.

PROB 11/367/188: Will of Robert Whitehead, Bodice Maker of Branton, Huntingdonshire. 15 July, 1681.

PROB 11/379/444: Will of Darrington Hall, Bodice Maker of Swasey, Cambridgeshire. 2 April, 1685.

PROB 11/396/371: Will of John Bishop, Body Maker of Saint Olave Southwark, Surrey. 24 September, 1689.

PROB 11/398/240: Will of John Haudleigh, Bodice Maker of Melbury Bubb, Dorset. 8 February, 1690.

PROB 11/407/207: Will of Edward Mitchell, Bodice Maker of Wotton under Edge, Gloucestershire. 2 December, 1691

PROB 11/432/51: Will of Richard Hall, Bodice Maker of Saint Mary Le Savoy, Middlesex, 9 June, 1696.

PROB 11/449/420: Will of John King, Bodice Maker of Yeovil, Somerset. 13 March, 1699.

SC6/JAS1/1646: Possessions of queen Anne. Declaration of receiver-general's account.

SP 46/49: State Papers Domestic, Williamson papers 1586–1594.

SP 70: Secretaries of State: State Papers Foreign, Elizabeth I.

STAC 8/94/17: Court of Star Chamber Proceedings, James I. Exhibits attached to the Bill of Complaint in Condytt et al. v. Chubbe et al.

Museum and gallery collections

Bayerisches Nationalmuseum, Munich.

Biblioteca Nacional de España, Madrid.

Bilbao Fine Arts Museum.

Boughton House, Northamptonshire: Buccleuch Collection.

British Museum, London.

Clark Art Institute, Williamstown, Massachusetts.

Claydon House, Buckinghamshire: Verney Collection.

Gemäldegalerie, Berlin.

Kunsthistorisches Museum, Vienna.

Kunstmuseum Basel.

Kyoto Costume Institute.

Leeds Museums and Galleries, Leeds.

Los Angeles County Museum of Art.

Manchester City Galleries: Gallery of Costume, Platt Hall.

Metropolitan Museum of Art, New York.

Musée de Tessé, Le Mans.

Musée des Beaux-Arts de la Ville de Paris.

Musée des beaux arts de Rennes.

Musée du Louvre, Paris.

Museo Etnográfico de Castilla y León – FUNDOS.

Museo Nacional D'Art De Catalunya, Barcelona.

Museum of Fine Arts, Boston.

Museum of London.National Gallery of Art, Washington, DC.

National Gallery of Victoria.

National Portrait Gallery, London.

Nottingham City Museum and Galleries: Middleton Collection.

Philadelphia Museum of Art.

Pilgrim Hall Museum, Plymouth, Massachusetts.

Rijksmuseum, Amsterdam.
Sittingbourne Heritage Museum: Plough Finds Collection.
Städel Museum, Frankfurt am Main.
Tate Gallery, London.
Victoria and Albert Museum, London.
Wallace Collection, London.
Westminster Abbey, London.
Woburn Abbey, Bedforshire.

Digital repositories of manuscript and printed sources

British History Online, http://www.british-history.ac.uk/.
Early English Books Online (EEBO), https://search.proquest.com/eebo.
Eighteenth Century Collections Online (ECCO), https://www.gale.com/intl/primary-sources/eighteenth-century-collections-online
London Lives, 1690–1800, https://www.londonlives.org/.
The Proceedings of the Old Bailey (OBP), https://www.oldbaileyonline.org.
Records of London's Livery Companies Online (ROLLCO), http://londonroll.org.
Seventeenth and Eighteenth Century Nichols Newspapers Collection, https://www.gale.com/c/seventeenth-and-eighteenth-century-nichols-newspapers-collection.
UCSB English Broadside Ballad Archive (EBBA), http://ebba.english.ucsb.edu/.
Wellcome Library, https://wellcomelibrary.org/collections/digital-collections/.

Printed primary sources

Anon. *Fifteen Real Comforts of Matrimony being in Requital of the Late Fifteen Sham Comforts*. London: n.p., 1683.
Anon. *Laugh and be Fat: Or, an Antidote against Melancholy*. 9th edition. London: n.p., 1724.
Arbeau, Thoinot. *Orchésographie et Traicte en Forme de Dialogue par lequel Toutes Personnes Peuvent Facilement Apprendre & Practiquer L'honneste Exercice des Dances*. Langres: n.p., 1589.
Aubignac, François Hédelin. *Nouvelle Histoire du Temps, ou La Relation Véritable du Royaume de la Coqueterie*. Paris: n.p., 1655.
Averell, William. *A Marvellous Combat of Contrarieties*. London: n.p., 1588.
Bacon, Francis. *The Felicity of Queen Elizabeth: and her times, with other things*. London: n.p., 1651.
Barry, Lording. *Ram-Alley: or Merry-*Tricks. London: n.p., 1611.
Behn, Aphra. *Poems Upon Several Occasions with, a Voyage to the Island of Love*. London: n.p., 1684.
Boë, Frans de le. *Dr. Franciscus de le Boe Sylvius Of childrens Diseases Given in a Familiar Style for Weaker Capacities*. London: n.p., 1682.
Borde, Andrew. *The First Book of the Introduction of Knowledge*. Edited by F. Furnivall. London: English Text Society, 1870.
Brathwaite, Richard. *The English Gentlewoman*. London: n.p., 1631.
Brathwaite, Richard. *Whimsies: or, a New Cast of Characters*. London: n.p., 1631.
Brathwaite, Richard. *Ar't Asleepe Husband?*. London: n.p., 1640.
Brinkworth, E. R. C. and J. S. W. Gibson, eds. *Banbury Wills and Inventories: Part 2, 1621–1650*. Banbury: Banbury Historical Society, 1976.
Brown, Rawdon, ed. *Calendar of State Papers Relating To English Affairs in the Archives of Venice*, vol. 6, pt. 2, 1555–1558. London: n.p., , 1877.
Brown, Rawdon and G. Cavendish Bentinck, eds. *Calendar of State Papers Relating to English Affairs in the Archives of Venice*, vol. 7, 1558–1580. London: n.p., 1890.
Bulwer, John. *Anthropometamorphosis: Man Transformed*. London: n.p., 1653.
Burton, Robert. *The Anatomy of Melancholy*. Oxford: n.p., 1621.

Butler, Samuel. *Characters and Passages from Note-books*. Edited by A. Waller. Cambridge: n.p., 1908.

Calvin, Jean. *The Sermons of M. John Calvin Upon the Fifth Book of Moses Called Deuteronomy*. Translated by Arthur Golding. London: n.p., 1583.

Carew, Thomas. *Certain Godly and Necessary Sermons.* London: n.p., 1603.

Castaigne, Eusèbe. *Discours nouveau sur la mode*. Paris: n.p., 1613.

Cavendish, Margaret. *CCXI Sociable Letters Written by the Thrice Noble, Illustrious, and Excellent Princess, the Lady Marchioness of Newcastle*. London: n.p., 1664.

Chamberlain, John. *The Letters of John Chamberlain*, vol. 1. Edited by Norman Egbert McClure. Philadelphia: n.p., 1939.

Chapman, George, Ben Jonson and John Marston, *Eastward Hoe*. London: n.p., 1605.

Charles I. *By the King, A proclamation inhibiting the Importation of Whale Fins, or Whale Oil, into his Majesties Dominions by any, but the Muscovia Company*. London: n.p., 1636.

Clifford, Anne. *The Diaries of Lady Anne Clifford*. Edited by D. J. H. Clifford. Wolfeboro Falls, NH: Alan Sutton, 1991.

Cotgrave, Randle. *A Dictionary of the French and English Tongues*. London: n.p., 1611.

Crowley, Robert. *One and Thirty Epigrams wherein are briefly Touched so many Abuses, that May and Ought to be Put Away*. London: n.p., 1550.

D'Aulnoy, Madame. *The lady's travels into Spain; or, a genuine relation of the religion, laws, commerce, customs, and manners of that country*. London: n.p., 1774.

Dekker, Thomas. *The Shoemakers Holiday*. London: n.p., 1600.

Della Casa, Giovanni. *Galatée ou la Manière dont un Gentilhomme se doit Gouverner en Toute Compagne*. Paris: n.p., 1562.

Dod, J. and R. Cleaver. *A Godly Forme of Household Government*. London: n.p., 1612.

Donne, John. *The Harmony of the museum*. Edited by R. C. London: n.p., 1654.

Dryden, John. *The Kind Keeper, or, Mr. Limberham a Comedy*. London: n.p., 1680.

Dunton, John. *The Ladies Dictionary*. London: n.p., 1694.

D'Urfey, Thomas, *The Intrigues at Versailles*. London: n.p., 1697.

D'Urfey, Thomas, *The Campaigners, or, The Pleasant Adventures at Brussels.* London: n.p., 1698.

Erasmus, Desiderius. *The Erasmus Reader*. Edited by Erika Rummel. Toronto: University of Toronto Press, 1990.

Evelyn, John. *A Character of England as it was Lately Presented in a Letter to a Noble Man of France*. London: n.p., 1659.

Evelyn, John. *Memoirs, Illustrative of the Life and Writings of John Evelyn*, vol. , 2nd edition. Edited by William Bray. London: n.p., 1819.

Fitzgeffry, Henry. *Satires: and Satirical Epigrams*. London: n.p., 1617.

Fletcher, John. *Fathers own Son.* London: n.p., 1660.

Garsault, M. de. *Art du tailleur: contenant le tailleur d'habits d'hommes, les culottes de peau, le tailleur de corps de femmes & enfants, la couturière & la marchande de modes*. Paris: n.p., 1769.

Gauden, John. *A Discourse of Auxiliary Beauty.* London: n.p., 1656.

Gawdy, Philip. *Letters of Philip Gawdy of West Harling, Norfolk, and of London to various members of his family, 1579–1616*. Edited by Isaac Herbert Jeayes. London: n.p., 1906.

George, Edwin and Stella George, eds. *Bristol Probate Inventories, 1657–1689*, vol. 57. Bristol: Bristol Record Society, 2005.

George, Edwin, Stella George and Peter Fleming, eds. *Bristol Probate Inventories, Part 1: 1542–1650*. Bristol: Bristol Record Society, 2002.

Glisson, Francis. *A Treatise of the Rickets being a Disease Common to Children.* London: n.p., 1651.

Goddard, William. *A Nest of Wasps Lately Found out and Discovered in the Low-countries, Yielding as Sweet Honey as Some of our English Bees*. n.p.p.: n.p., 1615.

Gosson, Stephen. *Pleasant Quips for Upstart Newfangled Gentlewomen*. London: n.p., 1596.

Grew, Nehemiah. *The Anatomy of Plants with an Idea of a Philosophical History of Plants.* London: n.p., 1682.

Hall, Thomas. *Divers Reasons and Arguments Against Painting, Spots, naked Backs, Breasts, Arms &c*. London: n.p., 1654.

Harrison, William. *Description of England, Book II*. n.p.p.: n.p., 1587.

Hayward, John. *Annals of the First Four Years of the Reign of Queen Elizabeth*, vol. 7. Edited by John Bruce. London: Camden Society, 1840.

Head, Richard. *The English Rogue Described*. London: n.p., 1668.

Herrick, Robert. *Hesperides.* London: n.p., 1648.

Heywood, John. *The Life and Works of John Heywood.* Edited by Robert George, Whitney Bolwell and Robert W. Bolwell. New York: Columbia University Press, 1921.

Heywood, Thomas. *The Second Part Of, If you Know Not Me, You Know Nobody*. London: n.p., 1606.

Hinds, Allen B., ed. *Calendar of State Papers Relating to English Affairs in the Archives of Venice*, vol. 15, 1617–1619. London: n.p., 1909.

Holinshed, Raphael. *The First Volume of the Chronicles of England, Scotland, and Ireland*. London: n.p., 1577.

Holme, Randle. *The Academy of Armory, or, A Storehouse of Armory and Blazon*. Chester: n.p., 1688.

Hookes, Nicholas. *Amanda, a Sacrifice to an Unknown Goddess*. London: n.p., 1653.

Hughes, Paul L. and James F. Larkin, eds. *Tudor Royal Proclamations*, vol. 2, The Later Tudors (1553–1587). New Haven, CT: Yale University Press, 1969.

Hume, Martin A. S. *Calendar of State Papers, Spain (Simancas)*, vol. 2, 1568–1579. London: Her Majesty's Stationery Office, 1894.

Jacmon, Antoine. *Mémoires d'Antoine Jacmon, bourgeois du Puy*. Edited by Augustin Chassaing. Saint-Laurent Le Puy-en-Velay: Marchessou fils, 1885.

James I. *By the King. A Proclamation concerning the bringing in of Whale-fins into his Majesties Dominions, &c.* London: n.p., 1614.

James I. *By the King. A Proclamation inhibiting the Importation of Whale fins into his Majesties Dominions by any, but the Muscovy Company*. London: n.p., 1619.

Jeffreys, Joyce. *The Business and Household Accounts of Joyce Jeffreys, Spinster of Hereford, 1638–1648*. Edited by Judith M. Spicksley. London: British Academy, 2015.

Johnson, George. *A discourse of some troubles and excommunications in the banished English Church at Amsterdam*. Amsterdam: n.p., 1603.

Johnston, J. A., ed. *Probate Inventories of Lincoln Citizens 1661–1714*, vol. 8. Lincoln: Lincoln Record Society: 1991.

Jones, Jeanne, ed. *Stratford-Upon-Avon Inventories, 1538–1699*, vol. 1. Bristol: Dugdale Society in association with the Shakespeare Birthplace Trust, 2002.

Jonson, Ben. *Poetaster*. London: n.p., 1602.

Jonson, Ben. *The Works of Benjamin Jonson: The Second Volume*. London: n.p., 1640.

Jonson, Ben. *The Works of Ben Jonson*. Edited by William Gifford. Boston: Phillips, Sampson, and Co., 1853.

Kipling, Gordon, ed. *The Receipt of the Lady Katherine*. Oxford: Published for the Early English Text Society by the Oxford University Press, 1990.

Larkham, Thomas. *The Diary of Thomas Larkham 1647–1669*. Edited by Susan Hardman Moore. Woodbridge: Boydell Press, 2011.

Latimer, Hugh. *Fruitful Sermons Preached by the Right Reverend Father, and Constant Martyr of Jesus Christ M. Hugh Latimer*. London: n.p., 1584.

Lippincott, H. F., ed. *'Merry Passages and Jests': A manuscript Jestbook of Sir Nicholas Le Strange (1603–1655)*. Salzburg: n.p., 1974.

Locke, John. *Some Thoughts Concerning Education*. London: n.p., 1693.

Lord, William Barry. *The Corset and the Crinoline*. London: n.p., 1868.

Marston, John. *The Scourge of Villainy: Three Books of Satires*. London: I. R., 1598.

Marston, John. *Jack Drums Entertainment: or The Comedy of Pasquill and Katherine*. London: n.p., 1601.

Marston, John. *The Malcontent*. London: n.p., 1604.

Marston, John. *The Malcontent (1603)*. Edited by M. L. Wine. Lincoln: University of Nebraska Press, 1964.

Mason, George. *Grammaire Angloise pour Facilement et Promptement apprendre la langue Angloise*. Paris: n.p., 1625.

Mauriceau, François. *Traité des Maladies des Femmes Grosses*. Paris: n.p., 1681.

Middleton, Thomas. *A Mad World, my Masters*. London: n.p., 1608.

Middleton, Thomas. *Two new Plays*. London: n.p., 1657.

Middleton, Thomas. *The Works of Thomas Middleton: In Five Volumes*, vol. 5. Edited by Alexander Dyce. London: n.p., 1840.

Montaigne, Michel de. *Essays Written in French by Michael Lord of Montaigne, Knight of the Order of S. Michael, gentleman of the French Kings chamber: done into English, according to the last French edition*. Translated by John Florio. London: n.p., 1613.

More, George. *A true Discourse Concerning the Certain Possession and Dispossession of Seven Persons in one Family in Lancashire*. n.p.p.: n.p., 1600.

N., W. *The Second Part of Merry Drollery*. London: n.p., 1661.

Nash, Thomas. *Christs Tears over Jerusalem Whereunto is Annexed a Comparative Admonition to London*. London: n.p., 1613.

Overall, W. H. and H. C. Overall, eds. *Analytical index to the series of records known as the Remembrancia. Preserved among the Archives of the City of London, A.D. 1579–1664. Prepared by the authority of the Corporation of London, under the superintendence of the Library Committee*. London: n.p., 1878.

Paget, Joan and Toney Sale, eds. *Charlton Kings Probate Records, 1600–1800*. n.p.p.: Charles Kings Local History Society, 2003.

Paré, Ambroise. *The works of that Famous Surgeon Ambrose Parey*. Translated by Thomas Johnson. London: n.p., 1649.

Peacham, Henry. *The Truth of our Times Revealed out of one Mans Experience*. London: n.p., 1638.

Pepys, Samuel. *Diary and Correspondence of Samuel Pepys, ESQ., F.R.S., from his Ms. Cypher in the Pepysian Library*, vol. 1. Edited by Richard Griffin Braybrooke and Mynors Bright. New York: Dodd, Mead and Company, 1885.

Pepys, Samuel. *Diary and Correspondence of Samuel Pepys, Esq., F.R.S. from his Ms. Cypher in the Pepysian Library*, vol. 7. Edited by Richard Griffin Braybrooke and Mynors Bright. New York: Dodd, Mead and Company, 1885.

Phillips, C. B. and J. H. Smith, eds. *Stockport Probate Records, 1620–1650*. Stroud: Alan Sutton/Records Society of Lancashire and Cheshire, 1992.

Phillips, Edward. *The mysteries of love & eloquence*. London: n.p., 1685.

Platter, Thomas. *Thomas Platter's Travels in England, 1599*. Edited and translated by Clare Williams. London: Jonathan Cape, 1937.

Pope, Alexander. *The Rape of the Lock*. London: n.p., 1714.

Rabutin-Chantal, Marie de, Marquise de Sévigné, *Lettres de Madame Sévigné*. Edited by Bernard Raffali. Paris: Garnier-Flammarion, 1976.

Reed, Michael, ed. *Buckinghamshire Probate Inventories, 1661–1714*. Aylesbury: Buckinghamshire Record Society, 1988.

Rich, Barnabe. *Faults, Faults, and Nothing Else but Faults*. London: n.p., 1606.

Rich, Barnabe. *The Honestie of This Age*. London: n.p., 1614.

Roberts, Edward and Karen Parker, eds. *Southampton Probate Inventories, 1447–1575*, vol. 1. Southampton: Southampton University Press, 1992.

Robertson, Joseph. *Inventaires de la Royne Descosse, Douairiere de France: Catalogues of the Jewels, Dresses, Furniture, Books, and Paintings of Mary Queen of Scots 1556–1569*. Edinburgh: n.p., 1863.

Rüff, Jacob. *The Expert Midwife*. London: n.p., 1637.

Saint-Foix, Germain-François Poullain de. *Oeuvres complettes de M. de Saint-Foix, historiographe des ordres du roi*, vol. 4. Paris: n.p., 1778.

Shakespeare, William. *The Merry Wives of Windsor*. London: n.p., 1630.

Speght, Rachel. *A Mouzell for Melastomus, the cynical baiter of, and fouled mouthed barker against Evahs sex*. London: n.p., 1617.

Starr, Frank Farnsworth and James Junius Goodwin, eds. *English Goodwin Family Papers: Being Material Collected in the Search for the Ancestry of William and Ozias Goodwin, Immigrants of 1632 and Residents of Hartford, Connecticut*, vol. 1. Hartford, CT: n.p., 1921.

Stubbes, Phillip. *The Anatomy of Abuses*. London: n.p., 1583.

Swetnam, Joseph. *The Arraignment of Lewd, Idle, Frorward, and Unconstant Women*. London: n.p., 1615.

Tabourot, Étienne. *Les Bigarrures et Touches du Seigneur des Accords*. Paris: n.p., 1603.

Taylor, John. *All the Works of John Taylor the Water-Poet*. London: n.p., 1630.

Tomkis, Thomas. *Lingua: or The Combat of the Tongue, and the Five senses for Superiority*. London: n.p., 1607.

Tommaseo, Niccolò. *Relations des ambassadeurs vénitiens sur les affaires de France au XVIe siècle*, vol. 2. Paris: n.p., 1838.

Udall, Nicholas. *Ralph Roister Doister*, 1567. Edited by Clarence Griffin Child. New York: Octagon Books, 1979.

Vaisey, D. G., ed. *Probate Inventories of Lichfield and District, 1568–1680*. n.p.p.: C. H. Vyse Ltd for the Staffordshire Record Society, 1969.

Walbran, John Richard, James Raine and J. T. Fowler, *Memorials of the Abbey of St. Mary of Fountains*, vol. 2, part 1. Ripon: n.p., 1863.

Warner, William. *Albions England*. London: n.p., 1602.

Webb, John ed. *Poor Relief in Elizabethan Ipswich*. Ipswich: Suffolk Records Society, 1966.

Webster, John. *The Tragedy of the Duchess of Malfy*. London: n.p., 1623.

Wilkes, Wetenhall. *A Letter of Genteel and Moral Advice to a Young Lady*. London: n.p., 1740.

Woolley, Hannah (attributed). *The Gentlewomans Companion; or, A guide to the female sex containing directions of behaviour, in all places, companies, relations, and conditions, from their childhood down to old age*. London: n.p., 1673.

Wright, Leonard. *A Summons for Sleepers*. London: n.p., 1589.

Ballads, pamphlets and newspapers

'Advertisements'. *The Loyal Protestant, and True Domestic Intelligence*. Issue 218, 10 October 1682.

Anon. *The Maids Metamorphosis*. London: n.p., 1600.

Anon. *A True Relation of the birth of three Monsters in the City of Namen in Flanders*. London, n.p., 1609.

Anon. *Jone is as good as my Lady*. London: A.M., *c.* 1620.

Anon. *The Peddler opening of his Pack, To know of Maids what tis they Lack*. London: n.p., 1620.

Anon. *The Lamentation of a New Married Man Briefly Declaring the Sorrow and Grief that Comes by Marrying a Young Wanton Wife*. London: n.p., 1629.

Anon. *The Fantastic Age: OR, The Anatomy of Englands Vanity, In Wearing the Fashions Of several Nations, With good Exhortations, Against Transmutations*. London: n.p., *c.* 1633–69.

Anon. *News from Hide-Parke*. London: n.p., *c.* 1647–65.

Anon. *An excellent New Play-house SONG, Called, The Bonny Milk-Maid*. n.p.p.: n.p., *c.* 1684–95.

Anon. *THE Young Mens ADVICE TO Proud Ladies*. n.p.p.: n.p., 1692.

Anon. *The Hasty Bridegroom. OR, The Rarest Sport that hath been Tried, Between a Lusty Bride-groom and his Bride*. London: n.p., *c.* 1693–5.

Anon. *The Lady's Answer to the Several little Satires on the Hooped Petticoats*. n.p.p.: n.p., *c.* 1720.

Sophronius. 'Universal Spectator, January 31. No. 643: Of the Modern HOOP PETTICOATS', in *The London Magazine and Monthly Chronologer*. London: n.p., 1741.

Sylvanus, Urban. *The Gentleman's Magazine: OR, Monthly Intelligencer. For the YEAR 1733*, vol. 3. London: n.p., 1733.

Secondary works

Adair, Richard. *Courtship, Illegitimacy and Marriage in Early Modern England*. Manchester: Manchester University Press, 1996.

Alsop, Rachel, Annette Fitzsimons and Kathleen Lennon, *Theorizing Gender*. Oxford: Polity Press, 2002.

Amussen, Susan Dwyer. *An Ordered Society: Gender and Class in Early Modern England*. Oxford: Blackwell, 1988.

Arnold, Janet. 'A Mantua c. 1708–9 Clive House Museum, College Hill, Shrewsbury'. *Costume* 4, no. 1 (1970): 26–31.

Arnold, Janet. *Patterns of Fashion 3: The Cut and Construction of Clothes for Men and Women, c. 1560–1620*. London: Macmillan, 1985.

Arnold, Janet. *Queen Elizabeth's Wardrobe Unlock'd: The Inventories of the Wardrobe of Robes Prepared in July 1600, Edited from Stowe MS 557 in the British Library, MS LR 2/121 in the Public Record Office, London, and MS V.b.72 in the Folger Shakespeare Library, Washington DC*. Leeds: Maney, 1988.

Arnold, Janet, Jenny Tiramani, Luca Costigliolo, Sébastien Passot, Armelle Lucas and Johanne Pietsch. *Patterns of Fashion 5: The Content, Cut, Construction and Context of Bodies, Stays, Hoops and Rumps c. 1595–1795*. London: School of Historical Dress, 2018.

Backhouse, Clare. *Fashion and Popular Print in Early Modern England: Depicting Dress in Black-Letter Ballads*. London: I.B. Tauris, 2017.

Baumgarten, Linda. *What Clothes Reveal: The Language of Clothing in Colonial and Federal America*. New Haven, CT: Yale University Press in Associations with The Colonial Williamsburg Foundation, 2002.

Beattie, J. M. *Crime and the Courts in England, 1660–1800*. Oxford: Clarendon, 1986.

Bell, Ilona. *Elizabethan Women and the Poetry of Courtship*. Cambridge: Cambridge University Press, 1998.

Bendall, Sarah A. 'The case of the "french vardinggale": A Methodological Approach to Reconstructing and Understanding Ephemeral Garments'. *Fashion Theory*, Special Issue on 'The Making Turn', edited by Peter McNeil and Melissa Bellanta, 23, no. 3 (2019): 363–99.

Benhamou, Reed. 'The Restraint of Excessive Apparel: England 1337–1604'. *Dress* 15, no. 1 (1989): 27–38.

Benhamou, Reed. 'Who Controls This Private Space? The Offense and Defense of the Hoop in Early Eighteenth-Century France and England'. *Dress* 28, no. 1 (2001): 13–22.

Benhamou, Reed. 'Clothing in the Age of Watteau'. In *Antoine Watteau: Perspectives on the Artist and the Culture of his Time*, edited by Mary D. Sheriff, 133–49. Newark: University of Delaware Press, 2006.

Benton, Janetta Rebold. *Materials, Methods, and Masterpieces of Medieval Art*. Westport, CT: ABC-CLIO, 2009.

Bernis, Carmen and Amalia Descalzo. 'Spanish Female Dress in the Habsburg Period'. In *Spanish Fashion at the Courts of Early Modern Europe*, vol. 1, edited by José Luis Colomer and Amalia Descalzo, 39–75. Madrid: Centro de Estudios Europa Hispánica, 2014.

Birt, Sarah. 'Women, Guilds and the Tailoring Trades: The Occupational Training of Merchant Taylors' Company Apprentices in Early Modern London'. *London Journal* (2020): 8–9, DOI: 10.1080/03058034.2020.1810881.

Botelho, Lynn. 'Old Age and Menopause in Rural Women of Early Modern Suffolk'. In *Women and Ageing in British Society since 1500*, edited by Lynn Botelho and Pat Thane, 43–65. London: Routledge, 2001.

Boucher, Jacqueline. *Deux Épouses et Reines à la fin du XVIe siècle: Louise de Lorraine et Marguerite de France*. Saint-Etienne: Université de Saint-Etienne, 1995.

Brammall, Kathryn M. 'Monstrous Metamorphosis: Nature, Morality, and the Rhetoric of Monstrosity in Tudor England'. *Sixteenth Century Journal* 27, no. 1 (1996): 3–21.

Braun, Melanie, Luca Costigliolo, Susan North, Claire Thornton and Jenny Tiramani, *17th-Century Men's Dress Patterns, 1600–1630*. London: Thames & Hudson in association with V&A Publishing, 2016.

Breitenberg, Mark. *Anxious Masculinity in Early Modern England*. Cambridge: Cambridge University Press, 1996.

Breward, Christopher. *The Culture of Fashion: A New history of Fashionable Dress*. Manchester: Manchester University Press, 1995.

Broomhall, Susan. 'Health and Science'. In *A Cultural History of Childhood and Family in the Early Modern Age*, edited by Sandra Cavallo and Silvia Evangelisti. Oxford: Berg Publishers, 2010, https://search-credoreference-com.ezproxy2.acu.edu.au/content/entry/bergcfema/health_and_science/0.

Brown, Kathleen M. *Foul Bodies: Cleanliness in Early America*. New Haven, CT: Yale University Press, 2009.

Brownmiller, Susan. *Femininity*. New York: Open Road Integrated Media, 2014. First published 1984 by Linden Press/Simon & Schuster.

Bruna, Denis and Sophie Vesin. 'L'énigme des corsets de fer'. In *La Mécanique des Dessous: Une Histoire indiscrète de la Silhouette*, edited by Denis Bruna, 67–9. Paris: Les Arts Décoratifs, 2013.

Bryson, Anna. *From Courtesy to Civility: Changing Codes of Conduct in Early Modern England*. Oxford: Clarendon Press, 1998.

Buck, Anne. 'The Clothes of Thomasine Petre, 1555–1559'. *Costume* 24 (1990): 15–33.

Burke, Peter. *The Fortunes of the Courtier: The European Reception of Castiglione's Cortegiano*. Oxford: Polity Press, 1995.

Burman, Barbara and Ariane Fennetaux. *The Pocket: A Hidden History of Women's Lives, 1660–1900*. New Haven, CT: Yale University Press, 2019.

Burns, E. Jane. 'Speculum of the Courtly Lady: Women, Love, and Clothes'. *Journal of Medieval and Early Modern Studies* 29, no. 2 (1999): 253–92.

Butler, Judith. *Gender Trouble: Feminism and the Subversion of Identity*. New York: Routledge, 2006.

Campbell, Colin. *The Romantic Ethic and the Spirit of Modern Consumerism*. New extended edition. London: Palgrave Macmillan: 2018.

Campbell, Kenneth L. *Windows into Men's Souls: Religious Nonconformity in Tudor and Early Stuart England*. Plymouth, MA: Lexington Books, 2012.

Canning, Kathleen. *Gender History in Practice: Historical Perspectives on Bodies, Class, & Citizenship*. Ithaca, NY: Cornell University Press, 2006.

Cantera, María José Redondo. 'The Inventories of Empress Isabella of Portugal'. In *Los inventories de Carlos V y la familia imperial/ The Inventories of Charles V and the Imperial Family*, vol. 2, edited by Fernando Checa Cremades, 1245–78. Madrid: fernando villaverde ediciones, 2010.

Capp, Bernard. 'The Double Standard Revisited: Plebeian Women and Male Sexual Reputation in Early Modern England'. *Past & Present* 162 (1999): 70–100.

Capp, Bernard. *When Gossips Meet: Women, Family, and Neighbourhood in Early Modern* England. Oxford: Oxford University Press, 2003.

Carrell, Toni L. 'Replication and Experimental Archaeology'. *Historical Archaeology* 26, no. 4 (1992): 4–13.

Carter, Philip. *Men and the Emergence of Polite Society: Britain 1660–1800*. Harlow: Longman, 2001.

Chrisman, Kimberly. 'Unhoop the Fair Sex: The Campaign Against the Hoop Petticoat in Eighteenth-Century England'. *Eighteenth-Century Studies* 30, no. 1 (1996): 5–23.

Christensen, Ann C. 'Being Mistress Eyre in Dekker's The Shoemaker's Holiday and Deloney's The Gentle Craft'. *Comparative Drama* 42, no. 4 (2008): 451–80.

Clark, Leak R. *Collecting Art in the Italian Renaissance Court: Objects and Exchanges*. Cambridge: Cambridge University Press, 2018.

Connell, Raewyn. *Gender and Power: Society, the Person and Sexual Politics*. Sydney: Allen & Unwin, 1987.

Cook, Harold J., Pamela H. Smith and Amy R. W. Meyers, eds. *Ways of Making and Knowing: The Material Culture of Empirical Knowledge*. Ann Arbor: University of Michigan Press, 2014.

Coontz, Stephanie. *Marriage, A History: From Obedience to Intimacy or How Love Conquered Marriage*. New York: Viking, 2005.

Corrales, Magdalena de Pazzis Pi. 'From Friendship to Confrontation: Philip II, Elizabeth I, and Spanish–English Relations in the Sixteenth Century'. In *The Image of Elizabeth I in Early Modern Spain*, edited by Guerrero Eduardo Olid and Fernandez Esther, 51–80. Lincoln: University of Nebraska Press, 2019.

Costigliolo, Luca. 'The Bodyes Maker'. In *Seventeenth-Century Women's Dress Patterns: Book Two*, edited by Susan North and Jenny Tiramani, 8–9. London: V&A Publishing, 2012.

Costigliolo, Luca. 'From Straight Bodies to Stays'. In *Seventeenth-Century Women's Dress Patterns: Book Two*, edited by Susan North and Jenny Tiramani, 10–11. London: V&A Publishing, 2012.

Coward, Barry. *The Stuart Age: England, 1603–1714*. 2nd edition. London: Longman, 1994.

Cox, Nancy C. and Karin Dannehl, *Perceptions of Retailing in Early Modern England*. London: Routledge, 2017.

Crawford, Julie. *Marvelous Protestantism: Monstrous Births in Post-Reformation England*. Baltimore, MD: Johns Hopkins University Press, 2005.

Crawford, Patricia M. *Blood, Bodies and Families in Early Modern England*. Harlow: Pearson, 2004.

Crowston, Clare Haru. *Fabricating Women: The Seamstresses of Old Regime France, 1675–1791*. Durham, NC: Duke University Press, 2001.

Currie, Elizabeth. *Fashion and Masculinity in Renaissance Florence*. London: Bloomsbury Academic, 2016.

Davidson, Hilary. 'Medieval Romance and Trade'. In *Fashion: The Ultimate Book of Costume and Style*, 43–113. London: Dorling Kindersley, 2012.

Davidson, Hilary. 'Renaissance Splendour'. In *Fashion: The Ultimate Book of Costume and Style*, 113–67. London: Dorling Kindersley, 2012.

Davidson, Hilary. 'Reconstructing Jane Austen's Silk Pelisse, 1812–1814'. *Costume* 49, no. 2 (2015): 198–223.

Davidson, Hilary. 'The Embodied Turn: Making and Remaking Dress as an Academic Practice'. *Fashion Theory*, Special Issue on 'The Making Turn', edited by Peter McNeil and Melissa Bellanta, 23, no. 3 (2019): 329–62.

Davidson, Hilary and Anna Hodson. 'Joining Forces: the intersection of two replica garments'. In *Textiles and Text: Re-Establishing the Links Between Archival and Object-Based Research: Postprints*, edited by Maria Hayward and Elizabeth Kramer, 204–10. London: Archetype, 2007.

Davis, J. 'Marketing Secondhand Goods in Late Medieval England'. *Journal of Historical Research in Marketing* 2, no. 3 (2010): 270–86.

Der, Lindsay and Francesca Fernandini, eds., *Archaeology of Entanglement*. Walnut Creek, CA: Left Coast Press, 2016.

Descalzo, Amalia. 'Spanish Male Costume in the Habsburg Period'. In *Spanish Fashion at the Courts of Early Modern Europe*, vol. 1, edited by José Luis Colomer and Amalia Descalzo, 15–38. Madrid: Centro de Estudios Europa Hispánica, 2014.

De Vries, Jan. *The Industrious Revolution: Consumer Behaviour and the Household Economy, 1650 to the Present*. Cambridge: Cambridge University Press, 2008.

Dobson, Michael S. and Nicola J. Watson, *England's Elizabeth: An Afterlife in Fame and Fantasy*. Oxford: Oxford University Press, 2002.

Dolan, Frances E. 'Taking the Pencil out of God's Hand: Art, Nature, and the Face-Painting Debate in Early Modern England'. *PMLA* 108, no. 2 (1993): 224–39.

Downes, Stephanie, Sally Holloway and Sarah Randles. 'Introduction'. In *Feeling Things: Objects and Emotions through History*, edited by Stephanie Downes, Sally Holloway and Sarah Randles, 1–7. Oxford: Oxford University Press, 2018.

Downs, Laura Lee. *Writing Gender History*. London: Hodder Arnold, 2004.

Dyer, Serena. *Material Lives: Women Makers and Consumer Culture in the 18th Century*. London: Bloomsbury, 2021.

Eastop, Dinah. 'Outside In: Making Sense of the Deliberate Concealment of Garments within Buildings'. *Textile* 4, no. 3 (2006): 238–55.

Edwards, Lydia. *How to Read a Suit: A Guide to Changing Men's Fashion from the 17th to the 20th Century*. London: Bloomsbury 2020.

Elias, Norbert. *The Civilising Process: The History of Manners and State Formation and Civilisation*. Translated by E. Jephcott. Oxford: Blackwell Publishers, 1994.

Entwistle, Joanne. *The Fashioned Body: Fashion, Dress and Modern Social Theory*. Cambridge: Polity, 2000.

Feinstein, Sandy. 'Donne's "Elegy 19": The Busk between a Pair of Bodies'. *Studies in English Literature, 1500–1900* 34 (1994): 61–77.

Field, Jemma. 'The Wardrobe Goods of Anna of Denmark, Queen Consort of Scotland and England (1574–1619)'. *Costume* 51, no. 1 (2017): 3–27.

Field, Jemma. *Anna of Denmark: The Material and Visual Culture of the Stuart Courts, 1589–1619*. Manchester: Manchester University Press, 2020.

Findlen, Paula. 'Introduction: Early Modern Things: Setting Objects in Motion, 1500–1800'. In *Early Modern Things: Objects and their Histories, 1500–1800*, edited by Paula Findlen, 3–27. London: Routledge, 2013.

Fisher, Will. *Materializing Gender in Early Modern English Literature and Culture*. Cambridge: Cambridge University Press, 2006.

Fletcher, Anthony. *Gender, Sex, and Subordination in England, 1500–1800*. New Haven, CT: Yale University Press, 1995.

Fletcher, Anthony. 'Manhood, the Male Body, Courtship and the Household in Early Modern English'. *Historical Association* 84, no. 275 (1999): 419–36.

Flores, Jodi Reeves and Roeland Paardekooper, eds. *Experiments Past: Histories of Experimental Archaeology*. Leiden: Sidestone Press, 2014.

Forsyth, Hazel. *London's Lost Jewels: The Cheapside Hoard*. London: Philip Wilson Publishers Ltd, 2013.

Fraser, Antonia. *The Weaker Vessel: Woman's Lot in Seventeenth-Century England*. London: Weidenfeld and Nicolson, 1984.

French, Katherine L. 'Genders and Material Culture'. In *The Oxford Handbook of Women and Gender in Medieval Europe*, edited by Judith M. Bennet and Ruth Mazo Karras, 197–209. Oxford: Oxford University Press, 2013.

Gau, Colleen. 'Physiologic Effects of Wearing Corsets: Studies with Reenactors'. *Dress* 26, no. 1 (1999): 63–70.

Gerber, Matthew. *Bastards: Politics, Family and Law in Early Modern France*. New York: Oxford University Press, 2012.

Gibson, Rebecca. 'Effects of Long Term Corseting on the Female Skeleton: A Preliminary Morphological Examination'. *Nexus: The Canadian Student Journal of Anthropology* 23, no. 2 (2015): 45–60.

Gibson, Rebecca. *The Corseted Skeleton: A Bioarchaeology of Binding*. New York: Springer International Publishing, 2020.

Gilbert, Ruth. *Early Modern Hermaphrodites: Sex and Other Stories*. Basingstoke: Palgrave, 2002.

Glover, David and Cora Kaplan. *Genders*. London: Routledge, 2000.

Goring, Paul. *Rhetoric of Sensibility in Eighteenth-Century Culture*. Cambridge: Cambridge University Press, 2005.

Gouwens, Kenneth. 'Human Exceptionalism'. In *The Renaissance World*, edited by John Jeffrie Matin, 415–34. London: Routledge, 2009.

Gowing, Laura. *Domestic Dangers: Women, Words, and Sex in Early Modern London*. Oxford: Oxford University Press, 1996.

Gowing, Laura. 'Secret Births and Infanticide in Seventeenth-Century England'. *Past & Present* 156 (1997): 87–115.

Gowing, Laura. '"The freedom of the streets": Women and Social Space, 1560–1640'. In *Londinopolis: Essays in the Cultural and Social history of Early Modern London*, edited by Paul Griffiths and Mark S. R. Jenner, 130–51. Manchester: Manchester University Press, 2000.

Gowing, Laura. *Common Bodies: Women, Touch, and Power in Seventeenth-Century England*. New Haven, CT: Yale University Press, 2003.

Gowing, Laura. *Gender Relations in Early Modern England*. Abingdon: Routledge, 2012.

Green, Monica H. 'From "Diseases of Women" to "Secrets of Women": The Transformation of Gynaecological Literature in the Later Middle Ages'. *Journal of Medieval and Early Modern Studies* 30 (2000): 5–40.

Green, Ruth M. *The Wearing of Costume: The Changing Techniques of Wearing Clothes and How to Move in Them from Roman Britain to the Second World War*. London: Sir Isaac Pitman and Sons, 1966.

Griffey, Erin. *On Display: Henrietta Maria and the Materials of Magnificence at the Stuart Court*. New Haven, CT: Yale University Press, 2015.

Griffey, Erin., ed., *Sartorial Politics in Early Modern Europe: Fashioning Women*. Amsterdam: Amsterdam University Press, 2019.

Griffiths, Paul. 'Politics made visible: order, residence and uniformity in Cheapside, 1600–45'. In *Londinopolis: Essays in the Cultural and Social history of Early Modern London*, edited by Paul Griffiths and Mark S. R. Jenner, 176–96. Manchester: Manchester University Press, 2000.

Gurr, Andrew. *Playgoing in Shakespeare's London*. Cambridge: Cambridge University Press, 1987.

Harding, Vanessa. 'Shops, Markets and Retailers in London's Cheapside, c. 1500–1700'. In *Buyers and Sellers: Retail Circuits and Practices in Medieval and Early Modern Europe*, edited by Bruno Blondé, Peter Stabel, Jon Stobart and Ilja Van Damme, 155–70. Turnhout: Brepols, 2006.

Harris, Jennifer. '"Estroit Vestu Et Menu Cosu": Evidence for the Construction of Twelfth-Century Dress'. In *Medieval Art: Recent Perspectives. A Memorial Tribute to C. R. Dodwell*, edited by Gale R. Owen-Crocker and Timothy Graham, 89–103. Manchester: Manchester University Press, 1998.

Harris, Jonathan Gil. 'Introduction'. In *Thomas Dekker: The Shoemaker's Holiday*, edited by Johnathan Gil Harris, vii–xxix. London and New York: Bloomsbury, 2008.

Harris, Tim. '"There is none that love him but Drunk Whores and Whoremongers": Popular Criticisms of the Restoration Court'. In *Politics, Transgression, and Representation at the Court of Charles II*, edited by Julia Marciari Alexander and Catharine MacLeod, 35–58. New Haven, CT: Yale University Press, 2007.

Hart, Avril. 'The Mantua: Its Evolution and Fashionable Significance in the Seventeenth and Eighteenth Centuries'. In *Defining Dress: Dress as Object, Meaning, and Identity*, edited by Amy Le Haye, 93–103. Manchester: Manchester University Press, 1999.

Harte, N. B. 'State Control of Dress and Social Change in Pre-Industrial England'. In *Trade, Government and Economy in Pre-Industrial England*, edited by D. C. Coleman and A. H. John, 132–65. London, Weidenfeld & Nicolson: 1976.

Harte, N. B. 'The Economics of Clothing in the Late Seventeenth Century'. *Textile History* 22, no.2 (1991): 277–96.

Harvey, John. 'Showing and Hiding: Equivocation in the Relations of Body and Dress'. *Fashion Theory* 11, no. 1 (2007): 665–94.

Harvey, Karen. 'Introduction: Practical Matters'. In *History and Material Culture: A Student's Guide to Approaching Alternative Sources*, edited by Karen Harvey, 1–23. London: Routledge, 2009.

Harvey, Karen and Alexandra Shepard. 'What Have Historians Done with Masculinity? Reflections on Five Centuries of British History, circa 1500–1950'. *Journal of British Studies* 44, no. 2 (2005): 274–80.

Hayward, Maria. *Dress at the Court of King Henry VIII*. London: Routledge, 2007.

Hayward, Maria. *Rich Apparel: Clothing and the Law in Henry VIII's England*. Farnham: Ashgate, 2009.

Hayward, Maria. *The Great Wardrobe Accounts of Henry VII and Henry VIII*. London: London Record Society, 2012.

Hayward, Maria. 'Spanish Princess or Queen of England? The Image, Identity and Influence of Catherine of Aragon at the Courts of Henry VII and Henry VIII'. In *Spanish Fashion at the Courts of Early Modern Europe*, vol. 2, edited by José Luis Colomer and Amalia Descalzo, 11–36. Madrid: Centro de Estudios Europa Hispánica, 2014.

Hayward, Maria. 'A Shadow of a Former Self: Analysis of an Early Seventeenth-Century Boy's Doublet from Abingdon'. In *Everyday Objects: Medieval and Early Modern Material Culture and its Meanings*, edited by Tara Hamling and Catherine Richardson, 107–18. Abingdon and New York: Taylor & Francis, 2016.

Hayward, Maria. '"The best of Queens, the most obedient wife": Fashioning a Place for Catherine of Braganza as Consort to Charles II'. In *Sartorial Politics in Early Modern Europe: Fashioning Women*, edited by Erin Griffey, 227–52. Amsterdam: Amsterdam University Press, 2019.

Hentschell, Roze. 'Treasonous Textiles: Foreign Cloth and the Construction of Englishness'. *Journal of Medieval and Early Modern Studies* 32, no. 3 (2002): 543–70.

Hobby, Elaine. *Virtue of Necessity: English Women's Writing, 1646–1688*. London: Virago Press, 1988.

Hodder, Ian. 'Wheels of Time: Some Aspects of Entanglement Theory and the Secondary Products Revolution'. *Journal of World Prehistory* 24, no. 2 (2011): 175–87.

Hodges, Mary. 'Widows of the "Middling Sort" and their Assets in Two Seventeenth-Century Towns'. In *When Death Do Us Part: Understanding and Interpreting the Probate Records of Early Modern England*, edited by Tom Arkell, Nesta Evans and Nigel Goose, 306–24. Oxford: Leopard's Head Press, 2000.

Hohti, Paula. 'Dress, Dissemination and Innovation: Artisan "Fashions" in Renaissance Italy'. In *Fashioning the Early Modern: Dress, Textiles, and Innovation in Europe, 1500–1800*, edited by Evelyn Welch, 143–65. Oxford: Oxford University Press, 2017.

Hohti, Paula. 'Cheap Magnificence? Imitation and Low-Cost Luxuries in Renaissance Italy'. In *Luxury and the Ethics of Greed in Early Modern Italy*, edited by Catherine Kovesi, 277–94. Turnhout: Brepols, 2019.

Hohti Erichsen, Paula. *Artisans, Objects and Everyday Life in Renaissance Italy: The Material Culture of the Middling Class*. Amsterdam: Amsterdam University Press, 2020.

Holland, Samantha. *Alternative Femininities: Body, Age and Identity*. Oxford: Berg, 2004.

Hollander, Anne. *Seeing Through Clothes*. Berkeley: University of California Press, 1993.

Holloway, Sally. 'Love, Custom & Consumption: Valentine's Day in England c. 1660–1830'. *Cultural and Social History* 17, no. 3 (2020): 295–314.

Hooper, Wilfrid. 'The Tudor Sumptuary Laws'. *English Historical Review* 30, no. 119 (1915): 433–49.

Hubbard, Eleanor. *City Women: Money, Sex, and the Social Order in Early Modern London*. Oxford: Oxford University Press, 2012.

Hughes, Diane Owen. 'Regulating Women's Fashions'. In *A History of Women in the West: Silences of the Middle Ages*, edited by Georges Duby and Michelle Perrot, 136–158. Cambridge, MA: Belknap Press of Harvard University Press, 1992.

Jackson, Gordon. *The British Whaling Trade*. Liverpool: Liverpool University Press, 2005.

Johnson, A. H. *The history of the Worshipful Company of the Drapers of London, preceded by an introduction on London and her Gilds up to the close of the XVth century*, vol. 4. Oxford: Claredon Press, 1922.

Johnston, Mark D. 'Sex, Lies, and Verdugados: Juana of Portugal and the Invention of Hoopskirts'. In *Medieval Clothing and Textiles 16*, edited by Monica L. Wright, Robin Netherton and Gale R. Owen-Crocker, 101–22. Woodbridge: Boydell Press, 2020.

Jones, Ann Rosalind. 'Nets and Bridles: Early Modern Conduct Books and Sixteenth-century Women's Lyrics'. In *The Ideology of Conduct: Essays in Literature and the History of Sexuality*, edited by N. Armstrong and L. Tennenhouse, 39–72. London: Methuen, 1987.

Jones, Ann Rosalind and Peter Stallybrass, *Renaissance Clothing and the Materials of Memory*. Cambridge: Cambridge University Press, 2000.

Jones, Ann Rosalind and Peter Stallybrass. 'Of Busks and Bodies'. In *The Forms of Renaissance Thought: New Essays in Literature and Culture*, edited by Leonard Barkan, Bradin Cormack and Sean Keilen, 261–76. Basingstoke: Palgrave Macmillan, 2009.

Jones, Ann Rosalind and Peter Stallybrass. 'Busks, Bodices, Bodies'. In *Ornamentalism: The Art of Renaissance Accessories*, edited by Bella Mirabella, 85–101. Ann Arbor: University of Michigan Press, 2011.

Karim-Cooper, Farah. *Cosmetics in Shakespearean and Renaissance Drama*. Edinburgh: Edinburgh University Press, 2006.

Kassell, Lauren. 'Medical Understandings of the Body, c. 1500–1750'. In *The Routledge History of Sex and the Body, 1500 to the Present*, edited by Sarah Toulalan and Kate Fisher, 57–74. Abingdon: Routledge, 2013.

Keane, Webb. 'Semiotics and the Social Analysis of Material Things'. *Language and Communication*, 23, no. 3–4 (2003): 409–25.

Keene, D. J. and Vanessa Harding, *Historical Gazetteer of London Before the Great Fire Cheapside; Parishes of All Hallows Honey Lane, St Martin Pomary, St Mary Le Bow, St Mary Colechurch and St Pancras Soper Lane*. London: Centre for Metropolitan History, 1987.

Kellett, J. R. 'The Breakdown of Gild and Corporation Control over the Handicraft and Retail Trade in London'. *Economic History Review* 10 (1957): 381–94.

Klein, Lawrence E. 'Politeness and the Interpretation of the British Eighteenth Century'. *Historical Journal* 45, no. 4 (2002): 869–98.

Knowles, James. '"Can ye not tell a man from a marmoset?": Apes and Others on the Early Modern Stage'. In *Renaissance Beasts: Of Animals, Humans, and Other Wonderful Creatures*, edited by Erica Fudge, 138–63. Urbana: University of Illinois Press, 2004.

Korhonen, Anu. 'To See and To Be Seen: Beauty in the Early Modern London Street'. *Journal of Early Modern History* 12 (2008): 335–60.

Kovesi, Catherine. '*Luxus*: How Luxury Acquired its Lustre'. In *Luxury and the Ethics of Greed in Early Modern Italy*, edited by Catherine Kovesi, 3–20. Turnhout: Brepols, 2019.

Kovesi, Catherine, ed., *Luxury and the Ethics of Greed in Early Modern Italy*. Turnhout: Brepols, 2019.

Kunzle, David. *Fashion and Fetishism: Corset, Tight Lacing and Other Forms of Body-Sculpture*. Stroud: History Press, 2004. First published 1982 by Rowman and Littlefield.

Landini, Roberta Orsi and Bruna Niccoli, *Moda a Firenze 1540–1580: Lo stile di Eleonora di Toledo e la sua influenza*. Florence: Pagliai Polistampa, 2007.

Laslett, Peter. *The World We Have Lost: Further Explored*. 3rd edition. London: Routledge, 2005.

Lemire, Beverly. *Dress, Culture and Commerce: The English Clothing Trade before the Factory, 1660–1800*. New York: St. Martin's Press, 1997.

Lester, Katherine Morris, Bess Viola Oerke and Helen Westermann, *Accessories of Dress: An Illustrated Encyclopedia*. New York: Dover Publications, 2004.

Levey, Santina M. 'References to Dress in the Earliest Account Book of Bess of Hardwick'. *Costume* 34, no. 1 (2000): 13–24.

Linthicum, Marie Channing. *Costume in the Drama of Shakespeare and his Contemporaries*. Oxford: Hacker Art Books, 1936.

Lublin, Robert I. *Costuming the Shakespearean Stage: Visual Codes of Representation in Early Modern Theatre and Culture*. Farnham: Ashgate, 2011.

Lussier, Suzanne. '"Habillement de la Dite Dame Reine": An Analysis of the Gowns and Accessories in Queen Henrietta Maria's Trousseau'. *Costume* 52, no. 1 (2018): 26–47.

Lynn, Eleri. *Tudor Fashion*. New Haven, CT: Yale University Press, 2017.

MacKinnon, Dolly. '"Charity is worth it when it looks that good": Rural Women and Bequests of Clothing in Early Modern England'. In *Women, Identities and Communities in Early Modern Europe*, edited by Stephanie Tarbin and Susan Broomhall, 79–93. Aldershot: Ashgate, 2008.

Malcolm-Davies, Jane, Caroline Johnson and Ninya Mikhaila. '"And her black satin gown must be new-bodied": The Twenty-First-Century Body in Pursuit of the Holbein Look'. *Costume* 42, no. 1 (2008): 21–9.

Mangan, Michael. *A Preface to Shakespeare's Tragedies*. Abingdon: Routledge, 2014.

Marshall-Ward, Jackie. 'Mode and Movement'. *Costume* 34 (2000): 123–8.

Mascuch, Michael. 'Social Mobility and Middling Identity: The Ethos of British Autobiographies, 1600–1750'. *Social History* 20 (1995): 45–61.

Massey, Doreen. *Space, Place, and Gender*. Cambridge: Polity Press, 1994.

McCall, Timothy and Sean Roberts. 'Introduction'. In *Visual Cultures of Secrecy in Early Modern Europe*, edited by Timothy McCall, Sean Roberts and Giancarlo Fiorenza, 1–23. Kirksville, MO: Truman State University Press, 2013.

McKendrick, Neil, John Brewer and J. H. Plumb, eds. *The Birth of a Consumer Society: The Commercialization of Eighteenth-Century England*. Bloomington: Indiana University Press, 1982.

McKnight, Alanna. 'Damsels in This Dress: Female Agency and the Demise of the Corset'. In *Fashion: Tyranny and Revelation*, edited by Damayanthie Eluwawalage, 221–9. Leiden: Brill, 2016.

McKnight, Alanna. 'The Kurious Kase of Kim Kardashian's Korset'. *Fashion Studies* 3, no. 1 (2020): 1–20.

McManus, Clare. *Women on the Renaissance Stage: Anna of Denmark and Female Masquing in the Stuart Court, 1590–1619*. Manchester: Manchester University Press, 2002.

McNabb, Jennifer. 'Ceremony versus Consent: Courtship, Illegitimacy, and Reputation in Northwest England, 1560–1610'. *Sixteenth Century Journal* 37, no. 1 (2006): 59–81.

McNeil, Peter and Melissa Bellanta. 'Letter from the Editors: Fashion, Embodiment and the "Making Turn"'. *Fashion Theory*, Special Issue on 'The Making Turn', edited by Peter McNeil and Melissa Bellanta, 23, no. 3 (2019): 325–8.

McShane, Angela. 'Revealing Mary'. *History Today* 54 (2004): 40–6.

McTavish, Lianne. 'Reproduction, c. 1500–1750'. In *The Routledge History of Sex and the Body, 1500 to the Present*, edited by Sarah Toulalan and Kate Fisher, 351–71. Abingdon: Routledge, 2013.

Mennell, Stephen and John Goudsblom. 'Civilizing Processes – Myth or Reality? A Comment on Duerr's Critique of Elias'. *Comparative Studies in Society and History* 39, no. 4 (1997): 729–33.

Mikhaila, Ninya and Jane Malcolm-Davies, *The Tudor Tailor: Reconstructing Sixteenth-Century Dress*. London: Batsford, 2006.

Mirkin, Ronnie. 'Performing Selfhood: The Costumed Body as a Site of Mediation Between Life, Art and Theatre in the English Renaissance'. In *Body Dressing*, edited by Joanne Entwistle and Elizabeth Wilson, 143–64. Oxford: Berg, 2001.

Moulton, Ian Frederick. 'Erotic Representations, 1500–1750'. In *The Routledge History of Sex and the Body, 1500 to the Present*, edited by Sarah Toulalan and Kate Fisher, 207–22. Abingdon: Routledge, 2013.

Mounsey, Chris. 'Introduction'. In *Presenting Gender: Changing Sex in Early Modern Culture*, edited by Chris Mounsey, 11–23. Lewisburg, PA: Bucknell University Press, 2001.

Mukerji, Chandra. *From Graven Images: Patterns of Modern Materialism*. New York: Columbia University Press, 1983.

Muldrew, Craig. 'Class and Credit: Social Identity, Wealth and the Life Course in Early Modern England'. In *Identity and Agency in England, 1500–1800*, edited by Henry French and Jonathan Barry, 147–77. New York: Palgrave, 2004.

Neal, Derek G. *The Masculine Self in Late Medieval England*. Chicago: University of Chicago Press, 2008.

Newman, Karen. *Fashioning Femininity and English Renaissance Drama*. Chicago: University of Chicago Press, 1991.

Newton, Hannah. *The Sick Child in Early Modern England, 1580–1720*. Oxford: Oxford University Press, 2012.

Nichols, Thessy Schoenholzer. 'It does not need to be hard to hold'. In *Structuring Fashion: Foundation Garments through History*, edited by Frank Matthias Kammel and Johannes Pietsch, 29–37. Munich: Hirmer, 2019.

North, Susan and Jenny Tiramani, eds. *Seventeenth-Century Women's Dress Patterns: Book One*. London: V&A Publishing, 2011.

North, Susan and Jenny Tiramani, eds. *Seventeenth-Century Women's Dress Patterns: Book Two*. London: V&A Publishing, 2012.

Nutz, Beatrix. 'Bras in the 15th Century? A Preliminary Report'. In *The North European Symposium for Archaeological Textiles XI*, edited by Johanna Banck-Burgess and Carla Nübold, 221–5. Rahden/Westf: n.p., 2013.

Nutz, Beatrix. 'From Soft to Hard: Deliberately Concealed Body Shaping Garments from Tyrol'. In *Structuring Fashion: Foundation Garments Through History*, edited by Frank Matthias Kammel and Johannes Pietsch, 19–27. Munich: Hirmer, 2019.

O'Connell, Sheila. 'Love Pleasant, Love Unfortunate: Women in Seventeenth-Century Popular Prints'. In *Politics, Transgression, and Representation at the Court of Charles II*, edited by Julia Marciari Alexander and Catharine MacLeod, 61–78. New Haven, CT, and London: Yale University Press, 2007.

O'Hara, Diana. 'The Language of Tokens and the Making of Marriage'. *Rural History* 3, no. 1 (1992): 1–40.

O'Hara, Diana. *Courtship and Constraint: Rethinking the Making of Marriage in Tudor England*. Manchester: Manchester University Press, 2000.

Pappano, Margaret A. and Nicole R. Rice. 'Medieval and Early Modern Artisan Culture'. *Journal of Medieval and Early Modern Studies* 43, no. 3 (2013): 473–85.

Paresys, Isabelle. 'Paraitre et se vetir au XVIe siecle: Morales Vestimentaires'. In *Paraître et se vêtir au XVIe siècle: actes du XIIIe Colloque du Puy-en-Velay*, edited by Marie F. Viallon, 11–36. Saint-Etienne: Publications de l'université de Saint-Etienne, 2006.

Park, Katharine. *Secrets of Women: Gender, Generation, and the Origins of Human Dissection*. New York: Zone, 2006.

Passot, Sébastien. '"Are You Sure This Is What He Means?" Considerations on Dress Terminology in French Sources and Their Subsequent Translation'. In *Structuring Fashion: Foundation Garments through History*, edited by Frank Matthias Kammel and Johannes Pietsch, 63–71. Munich: Hirmer, 2019.

Paulicelli, Eugenia. *Writing Fashion in Early Modern Italy: From Sprezzatura to Satire*. Farnham: Ashgate, 2014.

Peck, Linda Levy. *Consuming Splendor: Society and Culture in Seventeenth-Century England*. Cambridge: Cambridge University Press, 2005.

Perrot, Philippe. *Le corps Féminin: Le Travail des Apparences, XVIIIe–XIX siècle*. Paris: Éditions du Seuil, 1984.

Phillips, C. C. 'Orphan and Family: Bringing up Edward Harpur's Orphan Daughters, 1650–66'. *Historical Research* 68, no. 167 (2007), 286–301.

Phillips, Kim M. 'The Breasts of Virgins: Sexual Reputation and Young Women's Bodies in Medieval Culture and Society'. *Cultural and Social History* 15, no. 1 (2018): 1–19.

Pietsch, Johannes. 'Establishing Identity: Stays from Southern Germany in the Collection of the Bayerisches Nationalmuseum'. In *Structuring Fashion: Foundation Garments Through History*, edited by Frank Matthias Kammel and Johannes Pietsch, 73–83. Munich: Hirmer, 2019.

Purbrick, Louise. '"I love giving presents": The Emotion of Material Culture'. In *Love Objects: Emotion, Design and Material Culture*, edited by Anna Moran and Sorcha O'Brien, 23–35. London: Bloomsbury, 2014.

Reay, Barry. *Popular Culture in Seventeenth Century England*. London: Croom Helm, 1985.

Reinke-Williams, Tim. 'Women's clothes and female honour in early modern London'. *Continuity and Change* 26, no. 1 (2011): 69–88.

Reynolds, Anna. *In Fine Style: The Art of Tudor and Stuart Fashion*. London: Royal Collection, 2013.

Ribeiro, Aileen. *Gallery of Fashion*. London: National Portrait Gallery, 1999.

Ribeiro, Aileen. *Fashion and Fiction: Dress in Art and Literature in Stuart England*. New Haven, CT: Yale University Press, 2005.

Richards, Jennifer. 'Introduction'. In *Early Modern Civil Discourses*, edited by Jennifer Richards, 1–18. Basingstoke: Palgrave MacMillan, 2003.

Richardson, Catherine. 'Introduction'. In *Clothing Culture, 1350–1650*, edited by Catherine Richardson, 1–25. Aldershot: Ashgate, 2004.

Richardson, Glenn. *Renaissance Monarchy: The Reigns of Henry VIII, Francis I and Charles V*. London and New York: Arnold, 2002.

Rijkelijkhuizen, Marloes. 'Whales, Walruses, and Elephants: Artisans in Ivory, Baleen, and Other Skeletal Materials in Seventeenth- and Eighteenth-Century Amsterdam'. *International Journal of Historical Archaeology* 13, no. 4 (2009): 409–29.

Roberts, Helene E. '"The Exquisite Slave": The Role of Clothes in the Making of the Victorian Woman'. *Signs: Journal of Women in Culture and Society* 2 (1977): 554–69.

Rotenberg, Robert. 'Material Agency in the Urban Material Culture Initiative'. *Museum Anthropology* 37, no. 1 (2014): 36–45.

Rublack, Ulinka. *Dressing Up: Cultural Identity in Renaissance Europe*. Oxford: Oxford University Press, 2010.

Rublack, Ulinka. 'Matter in the Material Renaissance'. *Past & Present* 219, no. 1 (2013): 41–85.

Rublack, Ulinka. 'Introduction I: The First Book of Fashion'. In *The First Book of Fashion: The Book of Clothes of Matthaeus and Veit Konrad Schwarz of Augsburg*, edited by Ulinka Rublack and Maria Hayward, 1–26. London: Bloomsbury, 2015.

Rushton, Peter. 'The Testament of Gifts: Marriage Tokens and Disputed Contracts in North-East England, 1560–1630'. *Folk Life* 24 (1985): 25–31.

Salzburg, Rosa. 'Disseminating Luxury on the Streets of Italian Renaissance Cities'. In *Luxury and the Ethics of Greed in Early Modern Italy*, edited by Catherine Kovesi, 169–88. Turnhout: Brepols, 2019.

Scott, Joan W. 'Gender: A Useful Category of Historical Analysis'. *American Historical Review* 91, no. 5 (1986): 1053–75.

Sharpe, J. A. *Crime in Seventeenth-Century England: A County Study*. Cambridge: Cambridge University Press, 1983.

Sharpe, Kevin. '"Thy Longing Country's Darling and Desire": Aesthetics, Sex, and Politics in the England of Charles II'. In *Politics, Transgression, and Representation at the Court of Charles II*, edited by Julia Marciari Alexander and Catharine MacLeod, 1–32. New Haven, CT: Yale University Press, 2007.

Shearman, John. *Mannerism*. Harmondsworth: Penguin, 1967.

Shepard, Alexandra. *Accounting for Oneself: Worth, Status, and the Social Order in Early Modern England*. Oxford: Oxford University Press, 2015.

Sim, Alison. *The Tudor Housewife*. Montreal: McGill-Queen's University Press, 2000. First published 1996 by Sutton Publishing Limited.

Simmel, Georg. *Simmel on Culture: Selected Writings*, edited by David Frisby and Mike Featherstone. London: Sage Publications, 1997.

Simons, Patricia. *The Sex of Men in Premodern Europe*. Cambridge: Cambridge University Press, 2011.

Simons, Patricia. 'The Visual Dynamics of (Un)Veiling in Early Modern Culture'. In *Visual Cultures of Secrecy in Early Modern Europe*, edited by Timothy McCall, Sean Roberts and Giancarlo Fiorenza, 24–53. Kirksville, MO: Truman State University Press, 2013.

Singh, Devendra, Peter Renn and Adrian Singh. 'Did the perils of abdominal obesity affect depiction of feminine beauty in the sixteenth to eighteenth-century British literature? Exploring the health and beauty link'. *Proceedings of the Royal Society* 274 (2007): 891–4.

Sleigh-Johnson, Nigel. 'Aspects of the Tailoring Trade in the City of London in the Late Sixteenth and Earlier Seventeenth Centuries'. *Costume* 37 (2003): 24–32.

Smith, Kate. 'Sensing Design and Workmanship: The Haptic Skills of Shoppers in Eighteenth-Century London'. *Journal of Design History* 25 (2012): 1–10.

Smith, Pauline M. *The Anti-Courtier Trend in Sixteenth-Century French Literature*. Geneva: Droz, 1966.

Smith, Woodruff D. *Consumption and the Making of Respectability, 1600–1800*. New York: Routledge, 2002.

Smuts, R. Malcolm. 'Art and Material Culture of Majesty'. In *The Stuart Court and Europe: Essays in Politics and Political Culture*, edited by R. Malcolm Smuts, 86–112. Cambridge: Cambridge University Press, 1996.

Smuts, R. Malcolm. *Culture and Power in England, 1585–1685*, Social History in Perspective. London: Red Globe Press, 1999.

Snook, Edith. *Women, Beauty and Power in Early Modern England: A Feminist Literary History*. Basingstoke: Palgrave Macmillan, 2011.

Sorge-English, Lynn. *Stays and Body Image in London: The Staymaking Trade, 1680–1810*. Abingdon: Routledge, 2011.

Spivack, Carla. 'To "bring down the flowers": the cultural context of abortion law in early modern England'. *William & Mary Journal of Women and the Law* 14, no. 1 (2007): 107–51.

Spufford, Margaret. *The Great Reclothing of Rural England: Petty Chapmen and their Wares in the Seventeenth Century*. London: Hambledon Press, 1984.

Spufford, Margaret and Susan Mee, *The Clothing of the Common Sort: 1570–1700*. Oxford: Oxford University Press, 2017.

Stagg, Kevin. 'Representing physical difference: the materiality of the monstrous'. In *Social Histories of Disability and Deformity*, edited by David M. Turner and Kevin Stagg, 19–38. New York: Routledge, 2006.

Staniland, Kay. 'The Medieval "Corset"'. *Costume* 3 (1969): 10–13.

Staples, Kate Kelsey. 'Fripperers and the Used Clothing Trade in Late Medieval London'. *Medieval Clothing and Textiles* 6 (2010): 151–71.

Stearns, Peter N. 'Modern Patterns in Emotions History'. In *Doing Emotions History*, edited by Susan J. Matt and Peter N. Stearn, 14–40. Champaign: University of Illinois Press, 2014.

Steele, Valerie. *Fetish: Fashion, Sex, and Power*. New York: Oxford University Press, 1996.

Steele, Valerie. 'A Museum of Fashion is More Than a Clothes-Bag'. *Fashion Theory* 2, no. 4 (1998): 327–35.

Steele, Valerie. *The Corset: A Cultural History*. New Haven, CT: Yale University Press, 2001.

Stephanson, Raymond and Darren N. Wagner. 'Introduction'. In *The Secrets of Generation: Reproduction in the Long Eighteenth Century*, edited by Raymond Stephanson and Darren N. Wagner, 3–36. Toronto: University of Toronto Press, 2015.

Stern, Elizabeth. 'Peckover and Gallyard: Two Sixteenth-century Norfolk Tailors'. *Costume* 15 (1981): 13–23.

Stone, Lawrence. *The Causes of the English Revolution, 1529–1642*. London: Routledge and Kegan Paul, 1972.

Summers, Leigh. *Bound to Please: A History of the Victorian Corset*. London: Berg, 2001.

Tankard, Danae. *Clothing in 17th-Century Provincial England*. London: Bloomsbury, 2019.

Thirsk, Joan. *Economic Policy and Projects: The Development of a Consumer Society in Early Modern England*. Oxford: Oxford University Press, 1978.

Thomas, Keith. *In Pursuit of Civility: Manners and Civilisation in Early Modern England*. Waltham, MA: Brandeis University Press, 2018.

Thornton, Zita. 'The Romance of Welsh Lovespoons'. *Antiques & Collecting Magazine* 105 (2001): 44–8.

Tiramani, Jenny. 'Reconstructing a Schwarz Outfit'. In *The First Book of Fashion: The Book of Clothes of Matthaeus and Veit Konrad Schwarz of Augsburg*, edited by Ulinka Rublack and Maria Hayward, 373–96. London: Bloomsbury, 2015.

Toulalan, Sarah. *Imagining Sex: Pornography and Bodies in Seventeenth-Century England*. Oxford: Oxford University Press, 2007.

Toulalan, Sarah. '"To[o] much eating stifles the child": Fat bodies and reproduction in early modern England'. *Historical Research* 87, no. 235 (2014): 65–93.

Trevor-Roper, Hugh. *The Crisis of the Seventeenth Century Religion, the Reformation, and Social Change*. Indianapolis: Liberty Fund, 2002.

Turner, Terrance S. 'The Social Skin'. In *Reading the Social Body*, edited by C. B. Burroughs and J. Ehrenreich, 15–39. Iowa City: University of Iowa Press, 1993.

Utley, Larry. *Fetish Fashion: Undressing the Corset*. San Francisco: Green Candy Press, 2002.

Viaux, Jacqueline. *Le Meuble en France au XVIIIe siècle*. Paris: Presses universitaires de France, 1962.

Vickery, Amanda. *The Gentleman's Daughter: Women's Lives in Georgian England*. New Haven, CT: Yale University Press, 1998.

Vigarello, Georges. *Concepts of Cleanliness: Changing Attitudes in France since the Middle Ages*. Translated by Jean Birrell, 1988. Cambridge: Cambridge University Press, 2009.

Vigarello, Georges. 'The Skin and White Linen'. In *Textiles: Critical and Primary Sources*, vol. 1, edited by Catherine Harper, 374–89. London: Berg, 2012.

Vincent, Susan. *Dressing the Elite: Clothes in Early Modern England*. Oxford: Berg, 2003.

Vincent, Susan. *The Anatomy of Fashion: Dressing the Body from the Renaissance to Today*. Oxford: Berg, 2009.

Vincent, Susan. 'Production and Distribution'. In *A Cultural History of Dress and Fashion in the Renaissance*, vol. 3, edited by Elizabeth Currie, 37–55. London: Bloomsbury, 2018.

Wallis, Patrick. 'Apprenticeship and Training in Premodern England'. *Journal of Economic History* 68, no. 3 (2008): 832–61.

Waterhouse, Harriet. 'A Fashionable Confinement: Whaleboned Stays and the Pregnant Woman'. *Costume* 41, no. 1 (2007): 53–65.

Waugh, Norah *The Cut of Women's Clothes 1600–1930*, with diagrams by Margaret Woodward. London: Faber, 1968.

Waugh, Norah. *Corsets and Crinolines*. Abingdon: Routledge, 1991 (1954).

Weatherill, Lorna. *Consumer Behaviour and Material Culture in Britain, 1660–1760*. London and New York: Routledge, 1988.

Weatherill, Lorna. 'The meaning of consumer behaviour in late seventeenth- and early eighteenth-century England'. In *Consumption and the World of Goods*, edited by John Brewer and Roy Porter, 206–27. London: Routledge, 1994.

Welch, Evelyn. *Shopping in the Renaissance: Consumer Cultures in Italy, 1400–1600*. New Haven, CT: Yale University Press, 2005.

Welch, Evelyn. 'Introduction'. In *Fashioning the Early Modern: Dress, Textiles, and Innovation in Europe, 1500–1800*, edited by Evelyn Welch, 1–32. Oxford: Oxford University Press, 2017.

Whigham, Frank. 'Interpretation at Court: Courtesy and the Performer–Audience Dialectic'. *New Literary History* 14, no. 3 (1983): 623–39.

Wiesner-Hanks, Merry. 'Gender Theory and the Study of Early-Modern Europe'. In *Practices of Gender in Late Medieval and Early Modern Europe*, edited by Megan Cassidy-Welch and Peter Sherlock, 7–23. Turnhout: Brepols, 2008.

Wiesner-Hanks, Merry E. 'Introduction'. In *Mapping Gendered Routes and Spaces in the Early Modern World*, edited by Merry E. Wiesner-Hanks, 1–11. Abingdon: Routledge, 2016.

Willian, T. S. *The Early History of the Russia Company, 1553–1603*. Manchester: Manchester University Press, 1956.

Wilson, Elizabeth. *Adorned in Dreams: Fashion and Modernity*. London: Virago, 1985.

Wittkower, Rudolf. 'S. Maria della Salute: Scenographic Architecture and the Venetian Baroque'. In *Modern Perspectives in Western Art History: An Anthology of Twentieth-Century Writings on the Visual Arts*, edited by W. Eugene Kleinbauer, 165–92. Toronto: University of Toronto Press in association with the Medieval Academy of America, 1989.

Wright, Monica L. 'The Bliaut: An Examination of the Evidence in French Literary Sources'. In *Medieval Clothing and Textiles*, vol. 14, edited by Robin Netherton and Gale R. Owen-Crocker, 61–79. Woodbridge: Boydell Press, 2018.

Wrightson, K. 'The Social Order of Early-Modern England: Three Approaches'. In *The World We Have Gained: Histories of Population and Social Structure*, edited by Lloyd Bonfield, Richard Michael Smith, Keith Wrightson and Peter Laslett, 177–202. Oxford: Blackwell, 1986.

Wrightson, Keith. *Earthly Necessities: Economic Lives in Early Modern Britain, 1470–1750*. London: Penguin, 2002.

Wrigley, E. A., and R. S. Schofield, *The Population History of England 1541–1871: A Reconstruction*. Cambridge: Cambridge University Press, 1989.

Wunder, Amanda. 'Women's Fashions and Politics in Seventeenth-Century Spain: The Rise and Fall of the Guardainfante'. *Renaissance Quarterly* 68, no. 1 (2015): 133–86.

Zagorin, Perez. 'The Court and the Country: A Note on Political Terminology in the Earlier Seventeenth Century'. *English Historical Review* 77, no. 303 (1962): 306–11.

Zaller, Robert. 'The Figure of the Tyrant in English Revolutionary Thought'. *Journal of the History of Ideas* 54, no. 4 (1993): 585–610.

Zanger, Abby E. *Scenes from the Marriage of Louis XIV: Nuptial Fictions and the Making of Absolutist Power*. Stanford, CA: Stanford University Press, 1997.

Unpublished MA and PhD theses

Doda, Hilary. 'Of Crymsen Tissue: The Construction of A Queen: Identity, Legitimacy and the Wardrobe of Mary Tudor'. MA diss. Halifax, Nova Scotia: Dalhousie University, 2011.

Fisk, Catriona. 'Confined by History: Dress and the Maternal Body 1750–1900'. PhD diss. Sydney: University of Technology Sydney, 2020.

Fried, Lauren. 'Binding Bodies and Transforming Texts: The Wooden Engraved Stay Busk as a Seventeenth Century Love Token'. MA research paper. London: Royal College of Art, 2012.

Klingerman, Katherine Marie. 'Binding Femininity: An Examination of the Effects of Tightlacing on the Female Pelvis'. MA diss. Baton Rouge: Louisiana State University and Agricultural and Mechanical College, 2006.

Pitman, Sophie Jane. 'The Making of Clothing and the Making of London, 1560–1660'. PhD diss. Cambridge: University of Cambridge, 2017.

Unsworth, Rebecca. 'Impossible Fashions? Making and Wearing Late Sixteenth-Century Clothing'. MA diss. London: Royal College of Art, 2013.

Winerock, Emily F. 'Reformation and Revelry: The Practices and Politics of Dancing in Early Modern England, c. 1550– c.1640'. PhD diss. Toronto: University of Toronto, 2012.

Other online sources

Christies Auction House, http://www.christies.com/.

Guardian, https://www.theguardian.com/.

Instagram, https://www.instagram.com/.

New York Times, https://www.nytimes.com/.

University of Glasgow, https://www.gla.ac.uk/.

University of Warwick, http://www2.warwick.ac.uk/.

Vimeo, https://vimeo.com/.

YouTube, https://www.youtube.com/.

Illustrations

Introduction

Chapter 1

Chapter 2

Chapter 3

Chapter 4

Chapter 5

Chapter 6

Chapter 7

Conclusion

Index

Numbers in *italics* indicate an image.